Photoshop® Elements
Basics & Beyond

D1358661

Photo Editing-Organizing
Digital Scrapbooking

Patty Debowski
The Digital Scrapbook Teacher

For updates to this book, or to sign up for our
free Photoshop® Elements Tips Newsletter, go to
www.TheDigitalScrapbookTeacher.com

Photoshop® Elements-Basics & Beyond
Photo Editing-Organizing-Digital Scrapbooking
By Patty Debowski

Editor-In-Chief – Nancy Carter
Assistant Editor – Michael Adam

Trademarks
Products and trademark names are used for information purposes only with no intention of infringement upon those trademarks.

Adobe®, the Adobe® logo, Photoshop®, and Photoshop® Elements are either registered trademarks or trademarks of Adobe Systems Incorporated in the United States and/or other countries. All screen shots are from Adobe® Photoshop Elements® unless otherwise specified. Adobe® product screenshots reprinted with permission from Adobe® Systems Incorporated. THIS PRODUCT IS NOT ENDORSED OR SPONSORED BY ADOBE® SYSTEMS INCORPORATED, PUBLISHER OF ADOBE® PHOTOSHOP ELEMENTS.

Microsoft®, Windows®, Windows Vista®, Windows® 7, and the Windows logo are either registered trademarks or trademarks of Microsoft Corporation in the United States and/or other countries. Screen shots used with permission by Microsoft.

Mac®, the Mac® logo, and Macintosh® are trademarks of Apple Inc., registered in the United States and/or other countries.

Warning and Disclaimer
This book is designed to give information about photo editing, organizing, and digital scrapbooking with Photoshop Elements and expresses the author's views and opinions only. All information is as accurate as possible and no warranty is implied. Patty Debowski and The Digital Scrapbook Teacher shall have no liability or responsibility to any person who suffers damage from the disc included with this book or information from this book. It is imperative that you always duplicate a photo before editing it, back up your files frequently, and run virus protection on a regular basis.

All website addresses published were correct at the time of printing but may have changed due to reasons beyond our control.

Printing History:
March 2011 First Edition
Printed in China

ISBN-13: 978-0-9796959-9-5
Library of Congress Catalog Card Number: 2010937468

Published by:
The Digital Scrapbook Teacher
18837 Brookhurst Street Suite 201
Fountain Valley, CA 92708
www.TheDigitalScrapbookTeacher.com

Table of Contents

Acknowledgements

This book and The Digital Scrapbook Teacher in its entirety would not be possible without the help and support of my husband, Mike. Why he puts up with me some days (O.K....every day) I don't know. While I don't say it enough, thank you for your support always, I love you.

Robbi Sanders, thank you for jumping in head first. Your help, support, and guidance means so much to me. If you're looking for a Boot Camp in your area, it's Robbi you need to charm, not me! To Robbi's husband Joe, thanks for putting up with us! We apologize for all of those lonely nights you spend at home!

Without my editor Nancy Carter, this book would have never come to be. Nancy's push was what I needed to get started, and her continual nudges and encouragement got me through the last few pages. You were my hero on my first book and you are definitely my hero after this one!

Thank you to my children, Kristin, Ryan, and Chris for continually scheduling your lives around me and pitching in to help. Kristin and Gary thank you for sharing my beautiful grandchildren with me and my students, who love to watch them grow up. To my grandchildren Logan, Kirra, Gannon (and Cooper the dog) thank you for giving me a reason to take so many photos.

To my friends Dee Steger, Stephanie Blay, and Robbi Sanders thank you for your patience, support and advice now, and always. Dee thank you for helping to settle me down and for making me put my big girl panties on more than once.

Thank you to my good friends Andrea Bunnell and Sherrie Lodge for filling in my Grama duties when I'm unavailable, which has been way too much lately!

Dash Cotter, Nami Aoyagi, Shirley Lewerenz, and Sharon Love thank you for dropping everything and helping me with only a moment's notice, I really appreciate it!

Thank you to Bob Gager and his team at Adobe for their patience and help.

Pam Park and your team at Wacom, thank you for your help and patience.

Cindy Wyckoff of Scrapbook Dimensions Magazine and Ashley Smith of PolkaDotPotato.com, thank you for your friendship, experience, and kind words of advice.

James Neal, thank you for pulling it all together and making it look good, all the time!

Thank you to the designers who contributed their great products for the DVD included in the back of this book. Please be sure visit their blogs and say thank you yourself. While you're there, check out their new products.

The members of my November 2010, Intermediate/Advanced Digital Scrapbooking Workshop inspired me to take this book and my classes in a new direction, thank you for your inspiration.

Thank you to all of my students, particularly a woman in King of Prussia, PA, who when she learned that she could exactly match her text to a color in her photo loudly screamed "OMG!" in the middle of class. Your excitement is contagious, you are the reason I love what I do.

Come to Boot Camp!
Earn Your Digi-Degree

For information about our Boot Camps and other classes see *www.TheDigitalScrapbookTeacher.com*

Introduction

While surrounded by piles of photos and scrapbook supplies in what was once my living room, my oldest son Ryan popped his head in the door. Trying to be helpful he said "You know…they make these really nice photo albums that you can slide your regular photos in so that people can look at them". What a concept…photos in an album where you can actually see them.

Sure, he enjoyed seeing his scrapbook pages, but to be honest, they were few and far between. His high school football album came out of the bookcase when his football buddies came over, but the rest of the photos documenting his life were still in plastic tubs waiting.

What are they waiting for? To be lightened up so that you could see who was actually in the photo. The perfect piece of scrapbook paper or embellishment to make the perfect page of course! And most of all, for the perfect day when I had hours of free time to scrapbook and eat bonbons. My life isn't perfect and it never will be! I needed to simplify my life. Besides that, my local grocery store doesn't carry bonbons anymore.

Several years after this conversation, I began my journey in digital scrapbooking. In 2007 I wrote my first book *Digital & Hybrid Scrapbooking & Card-Making with Photoshop Elements,* often called the Bible of Digital Scrapbooking. If you bought it, thank you! If you didn't buy it don't worry, this book will cover the basics of that book and beyond.

What I've discovered since I started teaching people how to scrapbook digitally, is that I wasn't alone with some of my feelings. Scrapbooking is supposed to be fun, and yet there is a tremendous amount of guilt in the scrapbooking community because our scrapbooks are not completed and up to date and our photos aren't great. Over the last few years I've conducted an informal poll in my classes and you know what, hardly anybody has all of their scrapbooks up to date, so you're not alone.

My goal is for you to have fun with your photos. Yes, computers can be frustrating but take a tip that's helped my students: when you sit down at your computer, pretend you're a four year old child. Press all the buttons and try all the bells and whistles (unless you're in my class and I'm trying to teach you something), you'll have fun and won't be frustrated. As long as you're working on a copy of your photo, everything will be fine.

I've tried to set this book up so that you can use the mega index to find whatever you need quickly. Even though I know a lot of people did read my first book cover to cover, I don't expect you to read every page in this book. Be sure to read the *First Things First* chapter first to get you on your way. If you're brand new to photo editing and digi-scrapping, and want to make a scrapbook page or other project, read the *Hot to Use* chapter second.

If you're frustrated with a tool you're using, open up the *Tools and Tips* chapter and you'll quickly figure out what the problem is. Enhance your photos with some of the techniques shown in the *Cool Stuff with Photos* chapter. And, when you make one of those classical ID 10 T errors (read between the lines); like I still do, the expanded *What Did I Do Wrong* chapter will be there to help you out. Most importantly, keep the book where you can grab it to look up something quickly, because I still do!

One more thing…in my tutorials I'll use the term scrapbook page. Please understand that this can be any kind of project that you're working on, whether it's a card, brochure for work, etc. Most of all have fun! For even more fun, bring a friend and come to one of our classes, workshops, crops, or Boot Camps.

Grab some photos, open up your computer, pick a tutorial and get started NOW!

All templates and digital supplies shown on this page are available at *www.TheDigitalScrapbookTeacher.com*. Photo credit: We Got the Bell-Ray Lopez, Rays Photography, Oh Brother and Almost 2-Madeline Arenas Cubrix Photography.

How to Install Photoshop Elements

These instructions show how to install Photoshop Elements from a disc using Windows XP. Other Windows Operating Systems will be similar. I prefer to buy my software on a disc so that just in case I need it I always have it available after a new version of the program is released. If you have downloaded the program via a direct purchase from Adobe, the installation instructions will be similar. Both Mac and PC versions now come in one box.

If you have used the Photoshop Elements Organizer in earlier versions, take a few minutes to make a back up prior to installing a new version. You should be doing this regularly anyway.

To install Photoshop Elements, put the DVD into the disc drive of your computer. A dialog box similar to the one below will probably appear automatically. I have the Photoshop Elements/Premier Elements bundle, but I'll only install the Photoshop Elements program in this example. Adobe Premiere Elements is a video editing program that works in conjunction with the Photoshop Elements Editor and Organizer.

If the dialog box does not automatically appear, open the disc drive and double click on the Set Up file.

Choose the language for the installation from the drop down list and click OK.

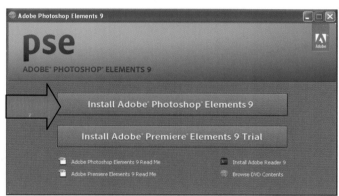

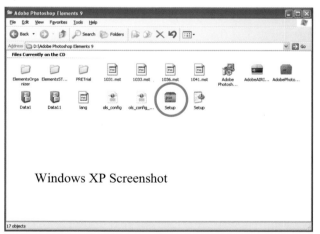

Windows XP Screenshot

The installation Wizard will appear, click Next.

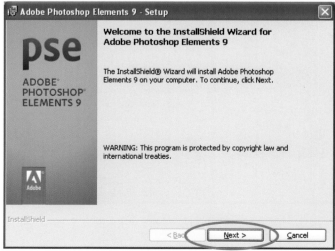

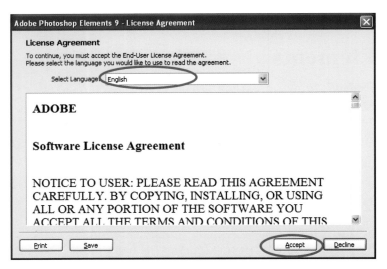

Read the Software License Agreement and click the Accept button.

Choose a Country/Region from the drop down list.

If you are using a 30 day trial version, click that button. If not, click the button that says I have a serial number to install the licensed version.

Enter the serial number from the back of the DVD case. I entered my serial number without the hyphens and it was rejected. Be smarter than I am and enter the hyphens to begin with!

If you purchased the program via a download, enter the serial number provided to you and keep it in a safe place.

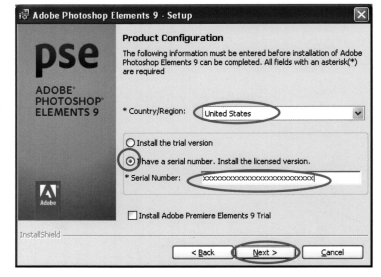

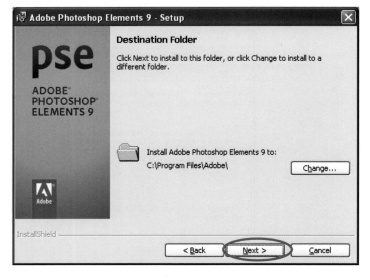

Adobe will tell you where it's putting the program on your computer. If you would like it installed somewhere else, click the Change button, otherwise click the Next button.

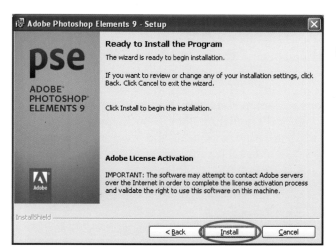

Click the Install button.

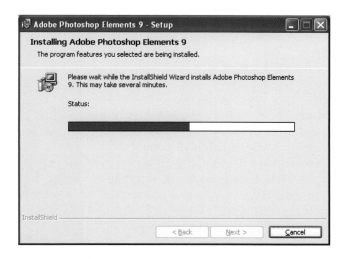

Wait "several" minutes.

Once the installation is complete, click the Finish button.

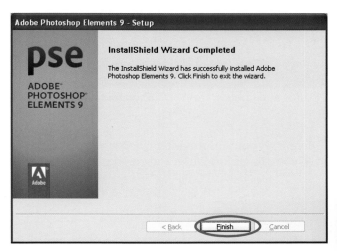

If you installed a trial version of Photoshop Elements, you will be reminded of how many days you have left on your 30 day trial version.

Once the trial has expired, you will need to purchase the program. When you purchase the program, you do not need to reinstall it, just start the program and enter the serial numbers in the boxes circled below (no hyphens required).

If you have earlier versions of Photoshop Elements on your computer, you do not need to uninstall them, but you can only open one version of Photoshop Elements at a time. I can open files that were created in earlier versions of Photoshop Elements

The computer must be able to connect to the internet and check in with Adobe, or it will behave like a 30 day trial version until you allow it internet access.

Deactivating Photoshop Elements

Adobe allows you to install Photoshop Elements 9 on two of your computers. The problem comes if you get a new computer or the hard drive crashes.

Let's say you have Photoshop Elements installed on your desktop and laptop computer. You get a new laptop and send the old laptop to college with one of your kids. Even if your kid's not using Photoshop Elements on the old laptop you won't be able to install it on your new laptop. Basically, if you try to install the program on more than two computers with the same serial number, it will only allow you to use it on a 30 day trial until the other computer is deactivated.

This issue hung me up on Photoshop Elements 8. For some reason, when I tried to reinstall the program on my computer it said it was already installed on two computers. We never could figure out what the problem was or what other computer it was installed on. By then, Photoshop Elements 9 had been introduced, so I didn't take the time to call Adobe and investigate the problem. Because I own several copies of Photoshop Elements, I've had to get smarter. Now, so there's no confusion in the future I write on the program box, near the serial number what computer I've installed it on.

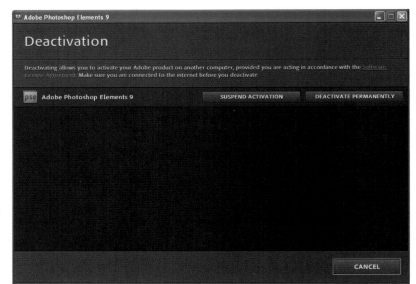

To deactivate the program, connect to the internet and open the Editor and choose Help>Deactivate. Choose to Suspend Activation or Deactivate Permanently.

In the event you are having a problem with the program, and need your System Information, choose Help>System Info. There is a Copy button in the event you need to copy the information and email it to someone.

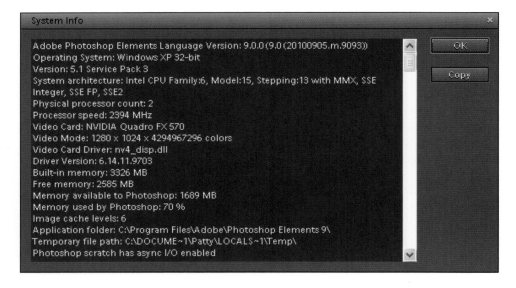

The Basics

Program Basics

Before you can do anything, you need to know how to open, close, and save a file in Photoshop Elements. We have also thrown in a few other basics that will help you along the way.

Open

There are several ways to open an image into the Editor.

If there are no images open, double clicking in the center of the screen will launch the Open dialog box.

If you are using the Editor, from the Menu bar, choose File>Open (Ctrl>O, Mac: Cmd>O). Select the images you want to open and click the Open button as shown below.

If you are using the Organizer (good for you), select the images you want to open. From the Menu bar, choose Edit>Edit with Photoshop Elements (Ctrl>I, Mac: Cmd>I). You can also select the images, click on the Fix tab, and choose Full Photo Edit.

I prefer to use the Ctrl>I shortcut.

Selecting Multiple Images

Did you know you can select more than one image at a time? I can't count the number of times I've watched my students open one image at a time because they didn't know these two tricks.

To select several images in a row, click on the first one, hold the Shift key and click on the last one, all images in between will be selected.

To select several images not in a row, click on the first one, hold the Ctrl key (Mac: Cmd key) and click on other images.

File View

Did you know you can choose how your files are displayed? Each operating system has a View Menu (circled on the right). Two of my favorite views are Icons or Thumbnails so I can see what the image looks like and Details so I can see the file type, size, dimensions, and the date the file was last modified.

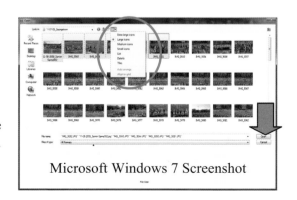

Microsoft Windows 7 Screenshot

Open Recently Edited

Did you just use an image and want to open it again? Photoshop Elements keeps track of the last ten images you opened. Choose File>Open Recently Edited and quickly reopen the image.

To display up to 30 recently opened images on the list, choose Edit>Preferences> Saving Files (Mac: Photoshop Elements >Preferences>Saving Files) from the Menu bar, and enter a new number in the box that says: Recent file list contains 10 files.

Open As

If I want to open a jpeg image into the Camera Raw editor, I can choose File>Open As. Specify in the Open As box (red arrow) that you want to Open As a Camera Raw image and click the Open button. The image will open in the Camera Raw Editor as shown below.

Microsoft Windows 7 Screenshot

Place

From the Menu bar, choose File>Place and it will look pretty much like you are opening a single image. Instead of clicking on the Open button, you will click on the Place button. This is where the similarity ends.

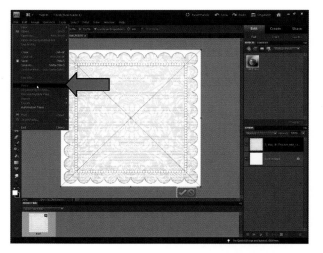

The image is placed on the active image as a new Smart Object layer (symbol shown circled below). The image is centered and resized to fit, keeping its aspect ratio. The new image is **not** added to the Project bin.

Note: If you choose to place a multi-layer PSD file it will be flattened into a single layer.

In my example the mat is 12" x 12" but the Background layer is 8" x 8". To confirm the transformation (resizing), check the green checkmark ✓.

If I were to place this square mat onto an 8.5" x 11" scrapbook page the mat would be resized but would still remain square.

Why would you want to use this? If you were using an 8" x 8" template and all of your papers were 12" x 12" using Place might save you some time resizing your papers.

If you have a small photo from a camera phone, placing the photo on the page (File>Place), and resizing it while the X is still visible **may** improve the print quality, but then again, it **may not**. Try it and see.

Importing a Frame from a Video

Have you ever had your camera on video mode when you thought you were taking a still photo? Or maybe you took a video and want to use one of the frames as a photo. It's easy to do with Photoshop Elements, although depending on your camera, the image may be very small.

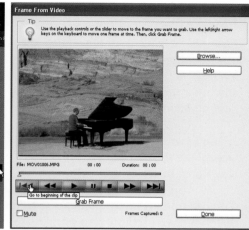

From the Menu bar, just as you would when opening an image, choose File>Import>Frame from Video. Click on the Browse button to locate the video file.

Now the fun begins! Instead of using the arrow buttons below the video, use the Arrow keys on your keyboard to move the video one frame at a time. Once you have the frame you want, click on the Grab Frame bar and the frame will become the active image. If you want to you may open several frames. Click the Done button when you're finished.

Switching Between Open Images

You've opened several images, but how do you switch between them? Double click on the image thumbnail in the Project bin to change the active image.

The highlighted thumbnail (circled) is the active (big) image.

Duplicating an Image

Never, never, never, edit an original photo! I can tell you this from personal experience!

There are several ways to make a duplicate of an image. The one way I use most often is to open the original image in Photoshop Elements and choose File>Duplicate.

A dialog box will appear with the file name with the word copy added to the end of it. Click OK, or type in a new file name and then click OK. So you don't forget, close the original file now.

You can also right click (Mac: Ctrl>Click) on the thumbnail in the Project bin and choose Duplicate.

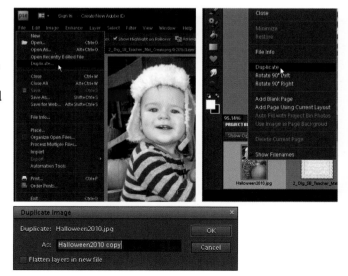

File Info

From the Menu bar, choose File>Info to
display information about the image.
You can add copyright information, or
any other information you want to add
here yourself.

If you have added tags with the
Organizer, they will appear in the
Keywords box.

You can add information about supplies
that you have used on your projects so
you don't forget what you used. Some
digital scrapbooking galleries will pick
up this information and display it in the
gallery.

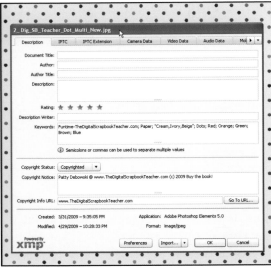

The example shows a paper from the Funtime paper kit available at *www.TheDigitalScrapbookTeacher.com.*To
save you time all of the JPEG and PSD files sold by *www.TheDigitalScrapbookTeacher.com* have tags pre-
applied to them

Undo/Redo Buttons

Make a mistake? Tap the Undo button and your mistake is gone.
Decide you really didn't make a mistake? Tap the Redo button.

The shortcut for Undo is Ctrl>Z (Mac: Cmd>Z)
The shortcut for Redo is Ctrl>Y (Mac: Cmd>Y)

Undo History

From the Menu bar, choose Window>Undo History to display the
Undo History panel. This panel displays the last 50 steps that
have been done to this image. To increase the number of steps
saved, choose Edit>Preferences>Performance (Mac: Photoshop
Elements>Preferences>Performance) from the Menu bar and
increase the History States number. Be aware this will probably
slow down Photoshop Elements.

Want to go back to when you cropped the image? Click on the
Crop line (arrow) and make another change. All of the previous
history will be erased, which may be easier than tapping the Undo
button several times.

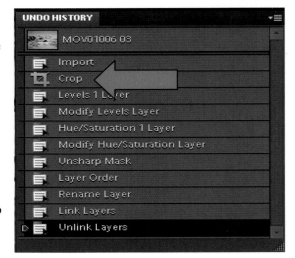

All Undo history is lost when the file is closed.

To remove the Undo History panel from the Panel bin, click on the Reset Panels button located to the left of the
Undo button.

Revert

Every once in awhile, I start editing an image and want to Undo all of my changes. An easy way to do this if you haven't saved yet is to choose Edit>Revert (Shift>Ctrl>A, Mac: Shift>Cmd>A). If you have already saved the image, open the Undo History and click on the first step.

Rulers

To display the rulers, choose View>Rulers (Shift>Ctrl>R, Mac: Shift>Cmd>R). Rulers are only visible at the top and left sides of the Image Window. Rulers are not visible in Quick or Guided Edit.

By default, the rulers begin at zero at the top left corner of the image. To change the zero point, click where the two dotted lines intersect (circled) and drag to a new point.

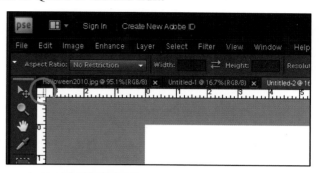

As I have done in the example on the right.
You may want to change the zero point to mark the center of a project.

To return the zero point to the default setting, double click on the intersection of the dotted lines again.

Double click on one of the rulers, or choose Edit>Preferences>Units & Rulers (Mac: Photoshop Elements>Preferences>Units & Rulers) to change the method of measurement.

Grids

From the Menu bar, choose View>Grids (Ctrl>'(apostrophe), Mac: Cmd>'(apostrophe). Grids are visible in Full, Quick and Guided Edit. Grids are not printed when you print your project. The default setting for Grids is one gridline every one inch with 4 subdivisions. It's easy to change them.

To change the Grid, choose Edit>Preferences>Guides & Grid (Mac: Photoshop Elements>Preferences>Guides & Grid). I will often change the Gridline from every one inch to 50 or 33.33 **percent** to divide my page evenly in half or in thirds.

50 percent works great to mark the fold line of a card, or the middle of a 24" x 12" inch scrapbook page.

33.33 percent works well to work with the Rule of Thirds, which says that the most interesting parts of the image should be where the lines intersect.

By default, the Grid lines are gray but you can click inside the box circled and choose your own color. The style can be changed from Lines to Dashed Lines or Dots.

Changing the zero point for your Ruler will display the grids differently.

Guides

Guides are lines that you can add to your file at any position you choose. Guides do not print.

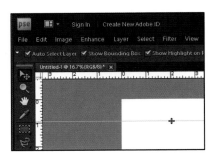

To add a horizontal Guide line, click and drag down from the top ruler. To add a vertical Guide line, click and drag from the side ruler. If you ever want to drag a horizontal Guide line from the side ruler, hold the Alt key (Mac: Opt key). The same goes for dragging vertical Guide line from the top ruler.

To move a Guide, select the Move tool (V), hover over the Guide and the cursor will change as shown on the example on the right. Click and drag the Guide to a new position.

To hide Guides, choose View>Guides (Ctrl>; (semi-colon), Mac: Cmd>; (semi-colon). To remove a Guide, drag it back to the Ruler or choose View>Clear Guides.

To lock the guides, choose View>Lock Guides (Ctrl>Alt>; (semi-colon), Mac: Cmd>Opt>; (semi-colon).

Holding the Shift key as you drag out a new Guide will make the Guide snap to the ruler marks. To add a new Guide to an exact location, choose View>New Guide. Choose the Orientation and the position. For the position, you can use any form of measurement. I could have used 6 inches to mark the center of a 12" x 12" inch page or I can enter 50%.

From the Menu bar, choose Edit>Preferences>Guides and Grid to change the color or style (lines or dashed lines) of the guides.

Snap to Guides & Snap to Grid

From the Menu bar, choose View>Snap to Guides or Snap to Grid to turn these features on or off. When adding a Guide to a file, it will snap to Grids. The Move tool and Crop tool will also snap to Guides or Grids which can be annoying at times. If you're having trouble with your cursor jumping around, this may be the reason.

I used Guides in several tutorials in this book when making selections with the Rectangular Marquee tool (M) because the selection border easily snaps to the Guides allowing me to make a perfect selection.

Saving Files

I can't stress enough how important it is to save often. New to Photoshop Elements 9 is a tiny icon that appears at the top right corner of the file thumbnail in the Project bin (shown circled on the right) to indicate unsaved changes. This little icon...as small as it is has helped me remember to save more often.

There are two basic formats we will save in, whether the file is a photo or project: Photoshop Documents (PSD files) to save all of our layers and JPEG files that can be sent to a photo processor. We'll save first as a PSD.

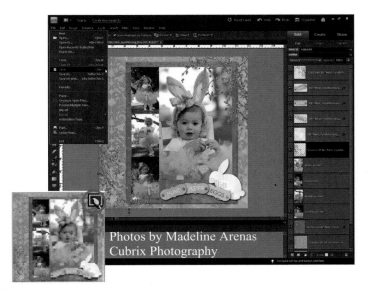

Photos by Madeline Arenas
Cubrix Photography

From the Menu bar, choose File>Save (Ctrl>S, Mac: Cmd>S) to save this cute page made by my friend Shirley Lewerenz. Shirley made this page with the Peppermint Creative April Morning Kit by Miss Mint which is included on the *Photoshop Elements – Basics & Beyond* DVD.

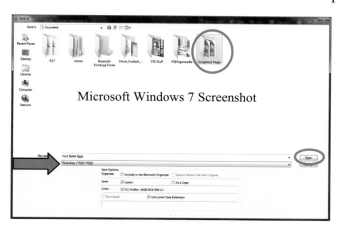

Microsoft Windows 7 Screenshot

The Save As dialog box will open. Choose a location to save the page. I save all of my scrapbook pages in a Scrapbook Pages folder, so I'll always know where to find them. Double click to open the Scrapbook Pages folder.

Type a File Name if you haven't already named the page and choose a format which will be Photoshop PSD. We are saving in this format to retain all of our layers. Click the Save button. As you are building your project, choose File>Save often. Mac Users have a floppy disc icon at the top of their screen that they can click on. Note: I do not save my scrapbook pages in the Organizer because I have had problems in the past, so I uncheck the Include in the Organizer box.

If you are printing at home, you can print directly from the PSD file. If you will be printing your page with a photo processor, you will need to save the page as a JPEG file. Saving as a JPEG file flattens **all** the layers into one.

From the Menu bar, choose File>Save As (Shift>Ctrl>S, Mac: Shift>Cmd>S). The Save as dialog box will appear. Choose a location to save your page. In my example below, it is being saved in my Scrapbook Pages folder. Type a File Name if needed. Choose the format, which is JPEG. Click Save.

The JPEG options dialog box will open. Choose the following options: Matte: None, Quality: 10, Format Options: Baseline ("Standard"). Click OK. Saving as a Quality #10 is a digital scrapbooking industry standard. If you are saving a special photo you may want to save as a Quality #12. Save the photo both ways and print them to see if you notice a difference. The only difference I notice is the file size, which is a lot bigger when saving as #12.

Microsoft Windows 7 Screenshot

Saving a File with Transparency

If you make your own digital scrapbooking elements, or you want to save an image with transparency, you will need to save it as a PSD file which creates a larger file, or you can save it as a PNG file. Maybe you completed my Pet Eye tutorial in the Cool Stuff with Photos – Cosmetic Surgery chapter and wanted to save the dog's eye to use on other problem photos. Sure, you could save the entire photo as a PSD file, but it would be a lot faster to have just the dog eye as a single transparent PNG file. While saving the eye as a JPEG file will produce a smaller file, but will fill the transparent areas with white.

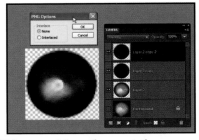

Before saving as a PNG file, to reduce the file size, crop the image to remove any excess transparent areas.

To save as a PNG file, choose File>Save As. Choose a location to save the file and type a file name. If you will use it in the future, you may want to include this file in the Organizer. From the format drop down list, choose PNG and click the Save button.

When the PNG Options dialog box appears, choose Interlace: None and click the OK button. Now the next time you open the file, it will be a single layer file with transparency.

Saving for the Web

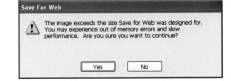

The number one reason digital scrapbookers save files for the web is to upload their pages to online galleries to share with others. I haven't had much luck using File>Save for Web because my file sizes are so big, and because some galleries don't accept GIF images.

What I normally do is choose Image>Resize>Image Size from the Menu bar and resize the image manually.

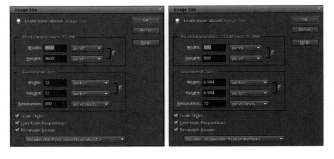

The example on the left is the original page, and the example on the right is the resized page for an online gallery.

Notice I have reduced the Resolution from 300 to 72 ppi. I have also reduced the width and height from 3600 pixels to 500 pixels.

I have also selected Bicubic Sharper because it is supposed to be best for reduction. Click OK, and save as a JPEG file.

Printing

If you are going to print at your local printer or at a photo processor like *www.PersnicketyPrints.com*, *www.PolkaDotPotato.com*, or *www.Costco.com*, you will need to save the file as a JPEG first as explained earlier in this chapter and upload it to their website. To print at home you don't even need to save the file first, but I recommend that you do.

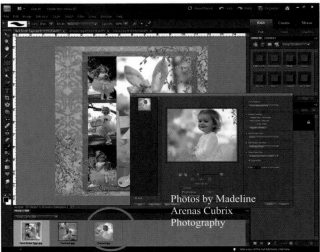

Photoshop Elements is rather quirky when it comes to printing on your own. When I first tried to print something at home I thought maybe I was too tired because the program wasn't working the way it used to. In my example I have three pages open that my friend Shirley Lewerenz made with the April Morning kit by Miss Mint at Peppermint Creative available on the *Photoshop Elements - Basics & Beyond* DVD. To print, from the Menu bar choose File>Print (Ctrl>P, Mac: Cmd>P). As you can see, my active image is not the image showing in the Print dialog box. Check out the Project bin where you can see that the thumbnail surrounded by blue is the image that will be printed. If you have also experienced this issue, you're not alone, and you're not crazy!

Select the thumbnails in the Project bin that you want to print by clicking on one, and then Ctrl clicking (Mac: Cmd clicking) on the others before choosing File>Print.

Follow the Print dialog box prompts:

1. Click on the dropdown list and choose a printer.

2. Click on the Change Settings button and from the Paper Type drop down list choose the type of paper you are using. It's important to choose the kind of paper you're using so that the printer knows how to apply the ink. Click on the Print Quality button (shown below) to verify that you have the correct settings. I am using an Epson R1900 printer and have chosen the Best Photo setting and the Double-Sided Matte Paper option in the 12 x 12 in size. I have also checked the Borderless button to print my page without borders. This dialog box will look different if you have a different printer than I do. Click the OK button.

Photos by Madeline Arenas Cubrix Photography

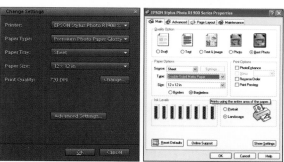

3. Select the Paper Size; you may have to set up custom paper sizes for cards, envelopes, etc. for your specific printer. Each printer is a little bit different.

4. Choose Individual Prints as the type of print.

5. Select the print size, for me it is the actual 12" x 12" size.

6. I have unchecked Crop to Fit. You may want to check this when printing a photo so you don't get white edges around the photo.

7. Choose the number of copies for every image displayed in the Print dialog box. You can't adjust this so that you print two copies of one image and four copies of another. If you want to print a different number of prints for each image, open them into the Print dialog box separately.

The Rotate buttons below the thumbnail work only if you rotate a square image. Rotate a photo and parts of it will be cropped off. To see the other images that are ready to print, click on the arrow button circled above.

When you have double checked everything, tap the Print button. Always let your prints breathe for a couple of days before you put them in a page protector or frame, because it may leave a fog or film residue.

Other Printing Options

To create a picture package or contact sheet select the images and follow the same prompts above from the Organizer. As shown in the example, there are some issues with the Picture Package option, especially if you have not cropped your photos to the specific sizes listed on the drop down list. You can easily make your own picture package for photos or scrapbook pages.

If you use 13" x 19" photo paper to print your scrapbook pages or print your pages at Costco, you can save money by essentially creating your own picture package. To do this, create a new blank file (File>New>Blank File). For the size enter the size of your paper (13" x 19", Costco members enter 12" x 18"). The Resolution must be 300 ppi, Color Mode is RGB, and choose a white background.

Open the scrapbook page(s) you want to print. Double click on the plain white page so that it is the active image. From the Menu bar, choose View>New Guide, click the Vertical button and type 12 inches in the Position box. Create another guide, this time click on the Horizontal button and type 6 inches in the position box. From the Menu bar, choose View>Snap to>Guides to help you line up the images.

Drag a page that you want printed as a 12" x 12" page UP from the Project bin onto the plain white page. By dragging it UP to the blank page any layers on the scrapbook pages will be flattened which is OK. The scrapbook page will land in the exact center of the page, select the Move tool (V) and move it to the left edge where it will snap to the Guide.

Photos by Madeline Arenas Cubrix Photography

There are several ways to resize the other two 12" x 12" pages so that they are 6" x 6". The problem that I've encountered is that if I resize the page I forgot that I did that and then I save it in the small size. If you think you might do this from the Menu bar, choose File>Duplicate and make a copy of it.

To resize the page from the Menu bar choose Image>Resize>Image Size. Check all three boxes: Scale Styles, Constrain Proportions, and Resample Image. From the drop down list choose: Bicubic Sharper (best for reduction). Enter 6" x 6" in the Document Size boxes and the Pixel Dimensions should automatically change to 1800 Width and 1800 Height. Click OK. Double click in the Project bin to display the picture package image. Drag the 6" x 6" page UP to the picture package page and drag it to the top right corner. Repeat with the next page. You can also use the same scrapbook page and create two 6" x 6" pages to be used as gifts. Three 4" x 6" photos will also fit in the left over area and since at the time this book was printed Costco charges the same for a 12" x 12" page as they do a 12" x 18" page they're basically free.

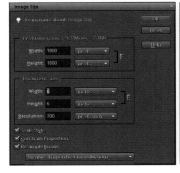

If you are going to do this with photos be sure to crop them first into standard sizes with the Crop tool (C). Remember to enter 300 ppi on the Crop tool Option bar to make sure that when you drag them onto your new blank file that they truly are the size you cropped them into.

Photos by Madeline Arenas Cubrix Photography

Closing Files

To close a file, choose File>Close (Ctrl>W, Mac: Cmd>W). If you made changes to the file and did not save them, you will receive a warning asking you if you want to save the changes.

You may also right click on a thumbnail in the Project bin, or click on the X on the tab to close an image. Mac users click on the red button.

If you have several files open, choose File>Close All (Alt>Ctrl>W, Mac: Opt>Cmd>W).

If you would like to close all open files and Photoshop Elements, choose File>Exit (Ctrl>Q, Mac: Cmd>Q). In addition Mac users click on the red dot on the top right area of their screen or Windows users can click on the X on the top right corner of their screen.

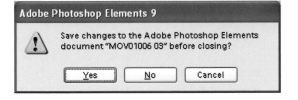

Shopping, Downloading, & Unzipping

While the 3200+ pieces of digital scrapbooking art on the *Photoshop Elements Basics & Beyond DVD* will keep you busy for a while, you will soon venture out on the web to purchase new supplies. Some designers like *www.TheDigitalScrapbookTeacher.com* sell their art on discs and also by downloads. Purchasing on a disc saves you the time of downloading and unzipping and creates a backup copy for you. Purchasing by download is instant gratification!

To purchase art, you will need to create an account and pay for it. Most stores accept PayPal because it's so easy to use and they don't want the responsibility of your credit card information. After you make a purchase, you will be supplied with download links. Click on the download link and choose the Save option. Choose a location where you want your computer to save the zip (compressed) file. I can't stress enough how important this step is. In my classes I see a lot of my students who don't understand this concept and download in random places all over their computer, and can never find anything. What I recommend is to make a folder for each store where you shop and download any purchases you make from that store into that folder. This way, if you have problems with the download later, you know which shop to contact. If you download into a folder for a specific designer and they change shops, the new shop probably won't take care of your problem because they didn't sell it to you in the first place. Use the Organizer to tag your supplies by designer so that you can always find your favorite designer's art.

In this example I am downloading into a folder named The Digital Scrapbook Teacher which is a subfolder of my Scrapbooking Supplies folder. After I click on The Digital Scrapbook Teacher and click the Open button, I will see a status bar showing the download progress.

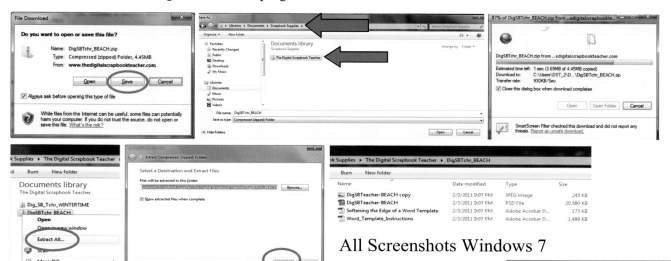

All Screenshots Windows 7

To unzip the files, right click on the file and choose Extract All. When the Extract Compressed Zipped Folders dialog box opens, click on the Extract button. Try to unzip your files as soon as you download them so that you know if there are any problems. If a zip file from a digital scrapbooking store asks you for a password, the file is corrupt. Delete the corrupt file and download it to a different location on your computer to see if that helps. If not, email the store where you purchased it.

Downloading can be very time consuming, I know, I just downloaded and unzipped over 3200 pieces of scrapbook supplies for this book. I use a free unzipping program that I love called ExtractNow that unzips multiple files at one time. Drag the zip files to the program icon and click on the Extract button. You can change the settings so that it automatically extracts archives, deletes or recycles the archives, and lots of other options. Check it out at *www.ExtractNow.com*.

Scraplifting, Galleries, TOU, & Piracy

Scraplifting can be a pretty controversial subject depending on who you talk to. Basically, Scraplifting involves copying a layout or design idea. Is it wrong for your own personal use (not for design contests or publishing in magazines)? Maybe, maybe not, there are some online stores that actually have Scraplift Challenges. They show you a page made by a designer and you post your rendition in their gallery. The designers I've asked about this subject don't mind if their sample pages are copied as long as you buy their kit, which is probably why the sample page was created in the first place. The right thing to do is to give credit where credit is due. If you used someone's idea, fess up. In a gallery you can list this information. If you share it online or with a friend, just say something like special thanks to…..for helping me conquer scrapper's block or something like that.

Uploading your pages to a gallery to share with others is fun and easy. Most galleries have rules that say most of art used on the page must be purchased in their store, so be sure to read their rules. Be sure to check the file size requirements, which for this gallery is 150 kb. This example shows how to upload pages to the *PeppermintCreative.com* gallery after you have created a free account.

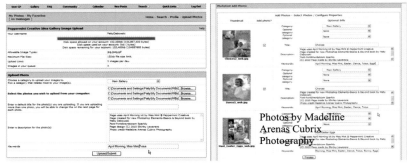

Photos by Madeline Arenas Cubrix Photography

Be sure to list the products and fonts that were used to create the page. Adding keywords helps other people find a page so that when they have scrapper's block, they can get some ideas. I also added Shirley Lewerenz as the page designer and Madeline Arenas as the photographer. Some galleries have a tab for viewing camera or EXIF data. If you have added kit information to the scrapbook page file by typing it into the File Info box from the File Menu, this information will automatically display and you don't need to type it in again.

It's important that you use the digital files you purchase or receive for free in the manner they are meant to be used. Even forwarding a newsletter with a freebie in it may be viewed as piracy, because the freebie in the newsletter is meant for subscribers only. There are three basic designations of digital scrapbooking art: Personal Use, Scrap for Hire/Others, and Commercial Use. All digital art will come with a TOU (Terms of Use) file. This file may be in JPEG, PDF, text or other file format. The example on the right is Angel Hartline's TOU which is very explicit about what you can and cannot do with her art; you can see this in her folder on the *Photoshop Elements – Basics & Beyond* DVD.

If you are creating digital scrapbooking supplies for sale, you must use commercial use products. Do not try to use another designer's products and call them your own. Some commercial use products require that you list them in your credits and others do not, so also check this.

There are stiff penalties for copyright infringement, so if someone asks you for a copy of a kit you just downloaded or asks you to share the download link, just nicely tell them no. Digital designers work very hard to create great products at low prices. My friend Ashley Smith once explained it this way "Many digital designers are young mothers who pursue their line of work so they can stay home with their children. When you share their art, you are taking away their diaper money". On the left are file sharing reminders from Miss Mint at Peppermint Creative and Anita Richards.

If you are unsure about how you can use art, be sure to read the TOU file included in the folder or on the website where you purchased it. Jen Strange has taken a lot of time to put information about digital piracy on this blog: *http://jenjen.typepad.com/stoppiracy/piracy_101/*
This is an excerpt from the blog: "A quick definition of piracy: Piracy is the theft, reproduction, or redistribution of a copyrighted work without the permission or knowledge of the creator/copyright holder. YES, redistributing something you got for free is still piracy. If you didn't create it, DON'T redistribute it!

First Things First

Turn on your computer! Many new users of Photoshop Elements are concerned about the very basics, this step is about as basic as you can get.

Double click on the Photoshop Elements icon on your desktop to start the program and the Welcome screen will open as shown.

You do not have to sign in with your Adobe ID to use Photoshop Elements unless you are registering the program.

To save a step in the future, click on the drop down list (red arrow) and change it so that Photoshop Elements opens with either the Editor or Organizer open behind the Welcome screen.

I normally have Photoshop Elements open in the Organizer, but this is a personal preference and can be easily changed in the future. Choose an option and click OK. Now click on the Editor button to open the Editor.

I know you're chomping at the bit to get started, but I've found that by changing a few settings on the program you can make it much easier to use. This applies to both beginning and advanced users of Photoshop Elements. These are changes that we make in our hands on classes and Boot Camps.

Have no fear, changing these settings is easy!

If you find as you follow tutorials in the book, that your screen does not look the same as my examples, check this chapter to see if you have made all of my recommended changes.

Document Dimensions

I like to have the size of the document I'm working on displayed at the bottom of my screen. Click on the ▶ Shown (circled above) and choose Document Dimensions.

Change Preferences

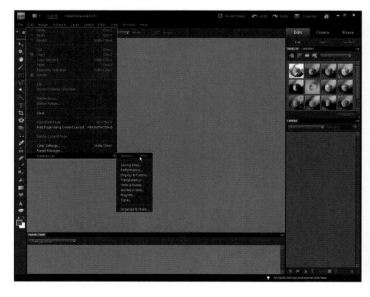

To make other changes, you will need to change the Photoshop Elements Preferences. To do this, from the Menu bar (at the very top of the screen), choose Edit>Preferences>General
(Mac: Photoshop Elements>Preferences>General).

General Preferences Changes

Uncheck-Allow Floating Documents in Full Edit Mode. This will save your sanity!

Check-Zoom with Scroll Wheel. This will allow you to use the scroll wheel on your mouse, or your fingers on a Wacom Bamboo Craft Pen & Touch tablet (and others) to scroll in addition to using the Zoom tool (Z).

The other items are checked by default. In Photoshop Elements 7 & 8 you were able to adjust the lightness and darkness of the User Interface, but that has been removed on this version. I apologize in advance for the darkness of my screenshots in this book.

Click OK.

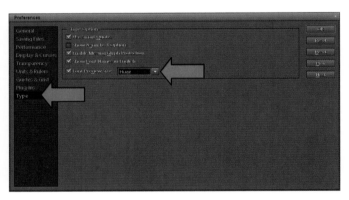

Type Preferences Changes

Change-Font Preview Size from Medium (default) to Huge. Laugh now, all my students do…but you'll like it. Having the default setting at medium confirms to me that the development team at Adobe is young with great eyes!

If you're into tiny and don't mind squinting, leave it at the default setting. Shown below is the Font Preview list available in the Type tool. The medium (default) setting is shown below on the left; huge is on the right.

Project Bin File Names

The Project bin is located at the bottom of your screen, and by default does not show the names of your open files.

To show File Names, right click (Mac>Ctrl Click) in an empty area of the Project bin and choose Show File Names.

Eyedropper Tool Change

Click on the Eyedropper tool icon on the Tool bar, or type the letter I. On the Options bar, click to drop down the Sample Size drop down list. Choose 3 x 3 Average. This change will help when editing photos.

Clone Stamp and Healing Brush Change

Click on the Clone Stamp tool icon on the Tool bar, or type the letter S. On the Options bar, click on the last icon to the right to display options for displaying clone overlay. Uncheck Show Overlay.

To change this setting on the Healing Brush tool, click on the icon that looks like a Band Aid, or type the letter J. There are two different Healing Brush tools nested in this icon. Click and hold on the black triangle on the bottom right side of the icon to display the Healing Brush (icon is a Band Aid with no loop). Uncheck Show Overlay.

Brush Change

Click on the Brush tool icon on the Tool bar, or type the letter B. On the Options bar, click on the brush presets drop down list (black and white squiggly line – this is a technical term).

Click and drag the bottom right corner to the right, as shown by the red arrow to make the box bigger. The brush previews will still be tiny.

Click on the tiny arrows in the top right area of the screen, shown circled in white. Choose Large Thumbnail (white arrow) from the drop down list.

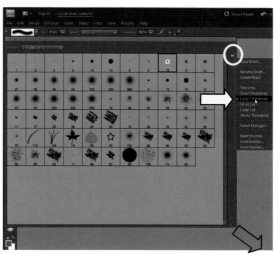

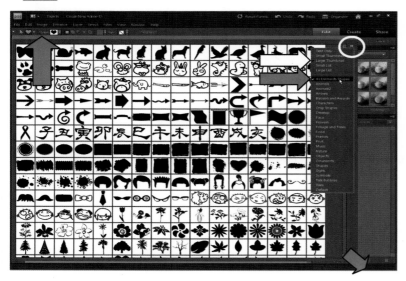

Custom Shape Change

Click on the Custom Shape tool icon (Heart) on the Tool bar, or type the letter U.

If you do not see a heart icon, type the letter U. On the selected tool, click and hold on the black triangle on the bottom right side of the icon to display the seven tools that are nested under this icon.

Follow the steps shown for the Brush tool changes to enlarge the thumbnails and drag out the preview box so you can see all of the shapes at one time.

Click on the tiny arrows on the top right area of the screen (shown circled in white again). This time choose All Elements Shapes so you can see all of the shapes available for you to use.

Cookie Cutter Changes

Click on the Cookie Cutter tool icon (Star) on the Tool bar or type the letter Q. Follow the steps above to enlarge the thumbnails, show all Elements Shapes, and drag out the preview box so you can see all of your choices.

Show Effects Names

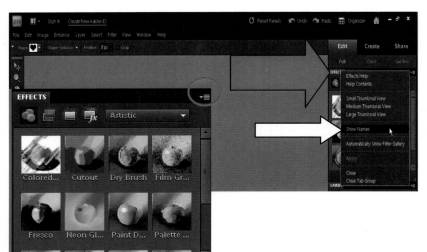

The Effects panel is located near the top right corner of the screen, as shown by a red arrow in the screenshot. The names of your effects may be turned off.

To turn on the names, click on the tiny drop down arrow at the top right area of the screen (shown circled in red). It's dark and sometimes hard to see.

Click on Show names (white arrow), and your names will appear under the Effects thumbnails as shown circled in white.

Organizer Changes

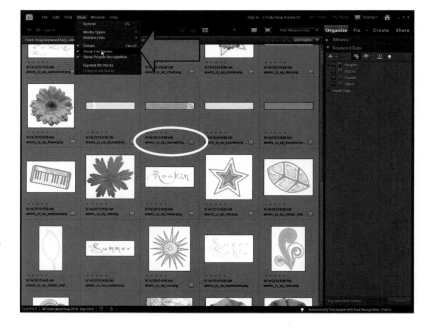

Click on the Organizer icon located near the top right corner of the screen. The Organizer will start up.

On the Menu bar, click on View>Show File Names and Details if it's not checked.

The file name will now show underneath the image thumbnail. If you are unsure what an element is intended for, check the file name. Some designers include what the image is in the file name. The example shown is Amy Teets' Super Sonic kit, which can be found on the *Photoshop Elements Basics & Beyond* DVD. Note that she has included the element type in her file names.

Techie Stuff

Keep reading…don't turn the page, there are a few important things you need to know in this chapter.

Don't worry, as hard as I try, I'm not a Techie, and I still don't have a computeristic brain. I'd love to be a geek, but it's just not in me, and unfortunately we don't have any computer geeks in the family either. Even when I dress up as a computer geek at our Boot Camps, I have a large warning on the back of my shirt professing that I'm not a Techie.

My student's eyes glaze over when I start talking about this stuff. Like I said, I'm not a techie, but I know what works and what doesn't. I don't have to understand all the complicated theories behind it all, and you don't either, but there a few things you do need to know. I've found quite by accident that a magic wand purchased at a party goods store can help me instill faith in my students, if by no other means than being funny. When a student gets stuck and I can't figure it out, I've been known to wave the wand over the computer. The funny thing is, sometimes it works, probably just because we laugh and relax for just a minute. While my students like the wand, a couple of TSA agents who have searched my carry-on computer bag don't find it humorous at all.

Pixels

Digital images are made up of pixels. A pixel is a unit of measure, just like an inch, a centimeter, or a point, only pixels are used to measure digital images. In this example, I zoomed in as far as I could on a photo. Each individual square is a pixel. Many of the Photoshop Elements tools search for pixels based on their color like the Magic Wand, Magnetic Lasso, and the Magic Eraser tool

A megapixel is 1 million pixels; the camera I use is a 10.1 mega pixel camera. My camera takes photos that are 3888 pixels wide and 2592 pixels high which is a total of 10,077,696 or 10.1 million pixels rounded off.

To see the size of your images, from the Menu bar, choose Image>Resize>Image Size or File>File Info>Camera Data. Cameras may display the resolution at different settings as the examples below show (circled in white). My 10.1 megapixel camera shows the resolution at 72 ppi (pixels per inch) while my 6.3 megapixel camera shows it at 180 ppi. Don't worry, this won't affect anything.

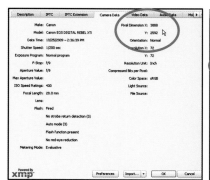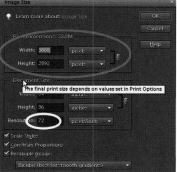

Is a higher megapixel camera better? In my opinion? No. The skill of the photographer and the lens comes into play more than the size of the image within reason. Of course a 6.3 megapixel camera will take a better image than a cell phone camera, but my 6.3 mega pixel camera usually takes better photos than the 10.1 megapixel camera.

Resolution

When purchasing digital scrapbooking supplies, be sure that you only purchase products that were created at 300 ppi (pixels per inch). This will assure that any time you print these products the print quality will be great.

I can't count the number of times my students have told me that their pages have printed horribly, even though they used a good photo processor. The first thing I ask them is where they got their papers and embellishments. Most of the time, they have downloaded freebies from the internet that were created at 100 ppi. If you are going to spend the time making a scrapbook page or other project, be sure that you use high quality art or you're wasting your time.

When you first set up a new project, as explained in *The Basics* chapter, always set the resolution at 300 ppi and everything will work out great.

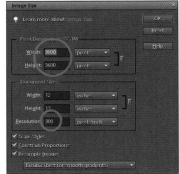 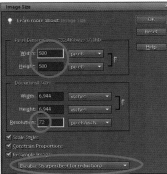

Any image that is displayed on the Internet will need to be resized to 72 ppi. To post a scrapbook page in a gallery on your favorite digital scrapbooking website, you will need to resize it. To do this, open the image and from the Menu bar choose Image>Resize>Image Size. My original scrapbook page is shown on the left in the example. Check the boxes for Scale Styles, Constrain Proportions, and Resample Image; also choose Bicubic Sharper (best for reduction) from the drop down list.

Change the resolution to 72, and then change the width to the maximum size that the gallery allows (most are between 400 and 600 pixels). Notice how once you enter the width, the height box changes automatically. Save this image adding 500x500 or Low_Res at the end of it so you will remember that it's a low resolution copy for posting on the web and should not be printed.

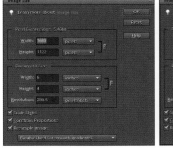 

Just because you resize an image to make it bigger it doesn't mean it will print well. If you use the Transform command (Ctrl>T) and drag the corner sizing handle of a button to increase the size 200%, it may look pixilated so be careful. If you have an image that you want to make into a larger print or poster you can try this method. If you want to increase the size dramatically this can take a long time, but it usually works pretty well.

From the Menu bar, choose File>Duplicate so that you are working on a copy of the image. When the Duplicate Image dialog box appears, rename the image. From the Menu bar, choose Image>Resize>Image Size. As shown on the left, my original image is 6" x 4". From the Width drop list, choose percent instead of inches and type 110. The height box will automatically change to 110 percent. Choose Bicubic Smoother from the drop down list. Click OK. Repeat as necessary. Check the Graffi's Action folder on the *Photoshop Elements - Basics & Beyond* DVD for an action that will do this for you automatically.

PPI or DPI what's The Difference?

PPI is pixels per inch, DPI is dots per inch. Dots per inch are how many dots (round) are actually printed per inch, leaving empty space around them. Pixels (square) per inch is the amount of pixels per inch in a digital image, they have no space around them. As my printing friend explained to me, when your image is printed the pixels are changed into dots and a 300 PPI image will become a 150 DPI printed photo. Many people use the terms interchangeably, but they're not the same.

File Types

As a Photoshop Elements user, you will be using different kinds of files. This is just a little bit of information about the type of files you will probably encounter. I usually use just three types of files: JPEG, PNG, and PSD.

JPEG-Joint Photographic Experts Group
JPEGs or JPGs are the most common file type you will encounter, think of them as your film negatives. Photos are JPEGs, (unless you shoot in Raw) as are most of the digital scrapbook paper files. Every time you save a JPEG file, it loses a little bit of its data. However, just opening a JPEG does not harm it. JPEGs cannot have transparent areas. If you try to save an image with a transparent area, it will automatically be filled with white. Organizer tags can be permanently attached to JPEG files. This is why when you buy papers from *www.TheDigitalScrapbookTeacher.com* the tags are already applied for you. To print an image at a regular photo processor, it must be saved as a JPEG file.

PNG-Portable Network Graphic
PNGs are used by designers to make elements such as brads, rivets, and doodles, etc., because they can have a transparent background. Unfortunately, at the time this book was written, tags from the Organizer cannot be attached to PNG files. This is why the embellishment files that are sold by *www.TheDigitalScrapbookTeacher.com* do not have the tags applied to them, as the JPEG and PSD files do.

GIF-Graphics Interchange Format-CompuServe Gif
GIFs can also have transparent areas and are used a lot on the internet. GIFs only store 256 colors. Text looks sharper in a GIF format. If you want to edit a GIF file in Photoshop Elements, you will first have to change its mode from Indexed Color to RGB. To do this, from the Menu bar, choose Image>Mode and choose RGB.

TIFF-Tagged Image File Format
TIFF files can be color, grayscale, or black and white and retain layers. Sometimes when you use a scanner, your image will be saved in a TIFF format. TIFF files do not lose any data when they're saved. Some digital scrapbooking online stores and scrapbookers save their layered files as TIFF files. Organizer tags are written directly to a TIFF file.

BMP-Bitmap Image
Bitmapped graphics, also known as raster graphics are made up of bits, which are dots. These graphics do not size well, and don't work well for web graphics or photos.

PSD-Photoshop Document
PSD files store your image with layers, masks, text, etc. so that you can open the file and go back to work where you left off. Always save your scrapbook pages in PSD format so that you can go back and make changes later on. You cannot upload a PSD file to a regular photo processor for printing; it must be converted to a JPEG first. All PSD files sold by *www.TheDigitalScrapbookTeacher.com* are also pre-tagged for you to save you time.

PSE-Photo Project Format
This file format is essentially a folder with Photoshop Document (PSD) files inside it. PSE files are created when you make a Photo Creation using the Create Menu like Adobe's photo book. You can still individually edit each PSD and convert them to a JPEG if you want to upload them to a regular photo processor.

PSB-Photoshop Big
This is a Photoshop file that is used for files 2GB and larger.

PDD-Photo Deluxe Document
Photo Deluxe is an Adobe program that was replaced by Photoshop Elements. PDDs were a type of a Photoshop Document file supported by Photo Deluxe.

Raw-Photoshop Raw

If you take photos with your camera set on the Raw setting it will produce images in several different formats, such as DNG, CRW, NEF, or others depending on the camera that took the photo. The file size is much larger than that of a JPEG image, but shooting in Raw gives you many other options for editing the photo. When a RAW image is opened, it opens in the Adobe Raw converter. After you make changes, click the Open Image button to open it in Photoshop Elements. To open a regular JPEG image into the Raw converter, from the Menu bar choose Open As.

Modes-Color and Image

Image Modes are a way to describe color. Before you change the mode of any image, always make a duplicate copy.

The image modes supported by Photoshop Elements are:

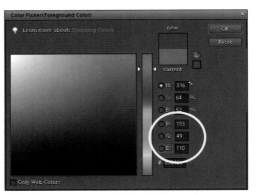

RGB

RGB (Red-Green-Blue) is the default mode for photos you import from your camera or a new image like a scrapbook page you make. Televisions and computer monitors display images in RGB color. Each color is assigned an intensity number from 0 to 255. Black is 0 and White is 255. RGB mode can display 16 million colors. This example displays the RGB values circled.

Images that are printed by professional print shops should be in CMYK mode which Photoshop Elements does not support, however a printer should be able to convert it for you.

Bitmap

A Bitmap image is black and white only. To convert a color image to a Bitmap image, you must first convert it to a Grayscale image.

Grayscale

A Grayscale image includes 256 shades of gray. Grayscale images have a brightness value from 0-255. Black is 0 and White is 255, just like in the RGB mode.

Indexed Color

Indexed Color images can have up to 256 colors. To edit an Indexed Color Image, you will need to temporarily change it RGB mode.

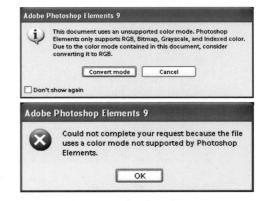

CMYK

CMYK (Cyan, Magenta, Yellow, Black) is used by traditional 4 color professional presses, and is supported by Photoshop, but not by Photoshop Elements. If you try to open a CMYK image you will get a warning box suggesting you to convert the mode to RGB. Click on the Convert mode button to open in RGB mode. If you click the cancel button, the image will not be opened.

When you view a CMYK image on a computer monitor, you are viewing it in RGB mode. A professional printer should be able to convert a RGB file to CMYK.

Software

This book covers how to use Photoshop Elements 9, but can be used for previous versions as well. I am often asked if the tutorials and tips in this book will also work for Photoshop, the answer is yes that most of it will work. Many times I have students who want to come to class with Photoshop. Usually they have a graphic designer friend who put it on their computer and they want to learn how to use it. Here's my advice: first of all, don't use pirated software, it's just not worth it. As a general rule, if you use the program to make a living, use Photoshop. If not, use Photoshop Elements. One of the main reasons I like Photoshop Elements so much is because the Project bin keeps me neat and organized. Photoshop also does not come with the Organizer, although I can use my Photoshop Elements Organizer with Photoshop. After you get the hang of Photoshop Elements and want to try Photoshop, download a free 30 day trial version and check it out.

The Photoshop Elements box lists the minimum hardware requirements to run the program. These are just the minimum requirements and the program may not work as fast as you would like it to. To check your computer: right click on Computer or My Computer and click on Properties. Information about the drive can be found by right clicking on the drive. From the Menu bar, choose Help>System for even more information.

Equipment

Remember, I told you right off the bat in the beginning of this chapter that I'm not a techie! I'll give you the very basics of what you need to get started.

Camera

Obviously you need a camera to take photos, but notice that I didn't say a digital camera? Several of my students still shoot with their film cameras and have the negatives digitized and put on a CD for them. If I wouldn't have dropped my film camera and smashed it to smithereens, I'm sure I would have held out longer, but in hindsight I'm glad the old film camera bit the dust! Do you need the big digital SLR with a wide assortment of lenses to take photos? No…unless you told your husband you do. Is a zillion mega pixel camera the best? No…it may be overkill for what you need. The camera you need is the camera you will use all the time. Because we spend a lot of time on airplanes, I have found that I now bring my pocketsize camera with me more than the big SLR because I'm limited to the number of bags I can carry on. I checked a camera in a suitcase once...never again because even though I packed it well, it was damaged beyond repair. If you have a camera you don't know how to use, read your manual (heaven forbid!) or take a camera class at your local camera store or community college. Buy extra media cards and an extra battery so you don't run out at inopportune times. Write your name and phone number on your media card so that if you lose it, someone can find you to give it back to you. Invest in an inexpensive tripod so that you can occasionally be in your photos and to help when taking panorama and group photos.

Cell Phone

My boys rarely use a real camera to take a photo preferring to use the camera on their cell phone. I, on the other hand, rarely use my phone to take pictures. Cell phones used to take horrible photos, but they're improving dramatically. As shown in the example on the Organizer's Properties panel, some cell phones now take photos with the GPS coordinates imbedded in the file. This means if you post pictures of your jewelry for sale on Craig's List or your precious children on the internet, someone with a little bit of finesse can pinpoint your location. There are several things you can do to remedy  this including disabling this feature on your phone (read the manual) or editing the photo in Photoshop Elements. To edit the photo, check the size of the photo (Image>Resize>Image Size) and create a new blank document in that size and drag the photo onto it with the Move tool. Save the image as a JPEG and the GPS and other information is removed. Instead of creating the new blank document, you can also drag the photo on top of another photo taken by your cell phone and save the files as a JPEG. While the photo will show the jewelry, the GPS coordinates will show another location (like your local Police Department).

Computers
The general rule is to buy the fastest computer with the largest hard drive you can afford and a little bit more. Always leave a minimum of 10% of your hard drive's space free, 15% is better. Don't overload your hard drive or your computer will crash. If your hard drive is getting full, purchase an external hard drive and copy some of your files on it.

In class I'm always asked if I prefer Mac or PCs. To me this choice depends on the individual. I can use both platforms. The only real difference, now that the Mac version of Photoshop Elements has the Organizer, is changing the keys for the shortcuts. If you read a PC shortcut that says to use the Ctrl key, Mac users will use the Cmd key; instead of using the Alt key, Mac users will use the Opt key. Mac users will use Delete instead of the Backspace key. Because the Organizer is new for Mac users, some features are missing that Windows users have available, but I will bet they will be added with future versions. I often see new Mac users who are frustrated because they can't right click with their mouse. On a Mac, Ctrl clicking is the same as right clicking. To change this, from the Apple menu select System Preferences> Keyboard & Mouse>Mouse. Set the right mouse button as the Secondary Button. If you don't have this option, check with the Mac store.

The same goes for a laptop or a desktop. While a laptop is portable, I prefer to work on a desktop at home with two monitors and a complete keyboard. In the past I've had my laptop hooked up to a monitor and keyboard, it's all in what works for you. While some of the small laptops are great for carrying around, they are not too easy to view photos while you're editing with Photoshop Elements, so think about that before you run out and purchase one. Many of them also do not have enough RAM to run the program. If the images on your screen look different than the photos that are printed by a reputable photo processor, it may be time to calibrate your monitor. You can purchase a program to do this yourself, or take it to a professional.

The biggest problem I see in hands-on classes is people trying to use the touch pad on a laptop to work with Photoshop Elements. Get a wired mouse, or better yet a Wacom tablet to save you some frustration. I suggest a wired mouse instead of wireless because I've seen a lot of problems caused by a wireless mouse.

Backup Systems and External Hard Drives (EHD)
Backing up files means nothing more than making an additional copy so that in the event of a problem you have copies of your files safe and sound. This problem could be a hard drive failure, fire, theft, or other type of catastrophe. If you have a lot of photos, and especially if you are a digital scrapbooker, buy an external hard drive with at least 500 GB of storage. An external hard drive is an additional hard drive that you plug into a USB port in your computer. Adding an external hard drive is like adding an extra file cabinet or desk to your work area. Purchase a portable external hard drive so you don't need to plug it into an electrical outlet. Office supply stores, electronic stores, and places like Costco all sell EHDs at affordable prices, often with coupons or rebates. While 2 GB flash drives are great for transferring files from one computer to another, they aren't big enough to backup your computer, the same goes for DVDs and CDs. The key part of making a backup copy of your files is to keep the EHD in another location like your place of work or at a friend's house. If your house burns down (and it happens) and both the computer and EHD are damaged, there wasn't really any point in making the backup.

I've had students tell me not to worry about them because they keep all of their photos and digital scrapbooking supplies on an EHD so that they can work between computers. This is OK, but you also need to back them up on another EHD because the chances of dropping an EHD or losing it are higher than if the files were on your computer. While you're investing in an EHD, also invest in a padded case for it to soften the blow if you drop it.

Using an online backup system is a good idea but there can be some downsides, including the cost and any limits to the amount of files you can backup. Make sure that the service you are looking at also backs up EHDs if you use them, because not all of them do. One thing to understand is that when you backup your files online, it may take a long time. Even with a fast internet connection, 2-3 GB of files is probably the maximum amount of files you can upload in a day. Using one of the well known services, and without turning my computer off other than restarting every few days, it has taken me 168 days to backup 401 GB of files with 14 GB still to go. I've had issues with the program running in the background and using up computer resources, which caused my computer to grind to a halt while writing this book.

Beyond that here's the clincher: If I need to get my files back, I can download only 2-3 GB of files a day to reconstruct my hard drive. On the plus side, while I also back up to an EHD, I have been able to remotely grab a file I needed, which was the real reason I opted for this service and it worked great,.

Printers
Do you have to buy a wide format printer to be a digi-scrapper? No, it's nice to have one but not mandatory. Wide format printers have come down pricewise, so if you haven't looked at one in awhile, look again. I use an Epson R1900 and love the borderless pages it prints. I've found by experience that it's important to use the paper and ink recommended by the manufacturer. If I use a different brand of paper I don't get the best results. Because I like my scrapbook pages to look like real paper instead of photo paper, I use their two sided 12" x 12" Scrapbook Matte paper.

You can also print 8" x 8" pages on a regular color printer, but be sure that you purchase a printer that uses several different color cartridges. While it may be a pain in the neck to keep an extra color cartridge on hand, it's much better than throwing away a single three color cartridge when only one of the colors is empty. I also don't refill my ink cartridges after seeing what can happen firsthand when a friend tried this and had to throw her printer away. Check to see if your ink is archival at *www.wilhelm-research.com* because you want your prints to last a long time. After printing your pages or photos, be sure to let them breathe for a few days before you put them in a plastic page protector or frame because they may fog it up. Other options for printing are to use a commercial printer like *www.PersnicketyPrints.com, www.PolkaDotPotato.com,* your local scrapbook store, or Costco. If you want to print your pages into a bound book, there are many online companies to choose from.

Scanners
I actually own four different scanners: an Epson 3170 Photo (photos, negatives, and memorabilia), a Canon MF4350d (sheet fed, all in one for scanning business documents), a Plustek Optic Film 7600 (negative and slide scanner), and a Canon CanoScan LiDE90 (small and portable).

Do you need that many? No, of course not! I actually didn't realize I had four scanners until I just counted them! If you take good care of your scanner, it will last a long time. Each scanner is set up a little bit differently but the important thing to remember is to always scan regular items at 300 pixels per inch. Check your scanner manual as negatives and slides will need to be scanned at a higher resolution. If you are scanning smaller items you can increase the resolution, but remember, if you are trying to scan to capture the details and there are no details in the original item (like a photo), scanning at a higher setting won't help you. Read your scanner manual for cleaning information. Don't spray glass cleaner or any other liquid on the scanner glass to clean it. Use a soft damp cloth to wipe any dust off the glass and if you have any large particles on it, blow it off before you wipe it clean to keep from scratching the glass. Cover the glass with clear plastic wrap or a clear piece of plastic like an inkjet overlay to protect the glass if you scan food or something sharp that can scratch the glass. If you scan bumpy items, close the lid, turn out the lights, and cover the scanner with a black jacket or cloth before scanning to keep the light out. I use my scanners for a variety of tasks, but most of all, to scan memorabilia.

To save time, scan multiple photos and/or memorabilia at one time and use Photoshop Elements to split them up for you. To do this, place all of the items face down on the scanner glass. The items do not have to be laid out straight, but they can't be touching each other or the edges of the scanner bed for this to work correctly. Photoshop Elements sometimes get confused when dividing images, so I help it along by taping a black piece of cardstock to my scanner lid. If I didn't do this, the large invitation on the right may be broken into several images. Scan the items and save the file as a JPEG and open it into Photoshop Elements. From the Menu bar, choose Image>Divide Scanned Photos and they will be automatically divided up into separate images. As shown in the bottom example, if you end up with a chopped up image, check to make sure that the item was not touching another item or the edge of the scanner bed. Cover the items with a piece of black cardstock, scan it again, and then try it again in Photoshop Elements.

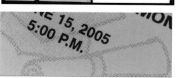

If you want to scan paper scrapbook pages that you have made to make additional copies or as a backup for disaster planning, you can do this with a standard scanner. Because the pages won't fit completely on the scanner bed, scan the pages starting with the top right corner placed on the top right corner of the scanner bed and save the file as a JPEG. Scan the top left corner of the page on the top left corner of the scanner bed and repeat for each corner of the page. To stitch the page together follow the directions in the *Stitching Photos Together with Photoshop Elements* in the *Cool Stuff with Photos* chapter.

Wacom Tablet

A tablet replaces your mouse or a laptop touchpad and is basically like an electronic version of a note pad and pen. My hand and wrist get fatigued using a mouse all the time, but I don't have that problem when using a tablet. Wacom has many different models of tablets available, but the one I use is the Bamboo Craft Pen & Touch which works with either a pen (stylus) or by touching it with one or two fingers. All examples below show this tablet. Getting used to using a tablet takes some time, but it's worth the effort. The best way to get used to the tablet is to hide your mouse…seriously! Practice doodling, writing your name, playing tic tac toe, solitaire, or hangman, just to get the hang of it. Watch the monitor as you practice, not your tablet. For tips, videos, contests, and more visit *www.PenScrappers.com*.

To use the tablet, first install the software provided on the disc in the box. There is also a great manual on the DVD that you can print out or look at if you have questions. Included in my box were two other DVDs that include software, tutorials, and kits.

When the software is installed, watch the video that shows you quickly how to use the tablet. With my tablet I can use the stylus or my fingers. Tapping once with my finger or stylus is the same as left clicking my mouse. Tapping twice is the same as double clicking with the mouse. Clicking on the top button on the stylus, or tapping two fingers is the same as right clicking a mouse.

Hold the stylus as you would a regular pen, but be aware that the tip of the pen (nib) does not have to actually touch the tablet; it can be 3-5 mm above it. Instead of using the Eraser tool (E) flip the pen over. Don't leave the pen lying across the tablet, or standing in a pencil can where the nib can be damaged. The key to scrolling, zooming, and rotating is to spread your two fingers apart so that the tablet knows you're using two fingers. If you don't like the touch feature, click on the top ExpressKey (see arrow below) to toggle it off.

One of the coolest features of the tablet is that I can customize it for my specific needs. To change the ExpressKeys on the side of the tablet, or the way the stylus buttons work, all you need to do is change the tablet program settings which is easy. For Windows: Click on the Windows Start button and choose All Programs or Programs. Click on Bamboo and then click on Bamboo Properties. For Mac: Open System Preferences from the Dock, Apple Menu or from the Applications folder. Click on the Bamboo icon.

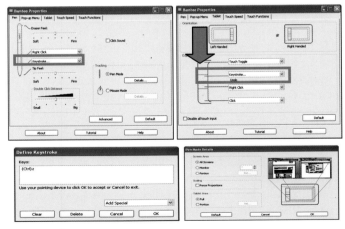

In my examples, I clicked on the drop down list for the pen and the second ExpressKey and choose keystroke from the list. A Define Keystroke dialog box opened and I typed the Ctrl and then the letter Z key which is the PC shortcut for Undo. This way, whenever I want to Undo instead of typing Ctrl>Z on my keyboard, I can click or tap ExpressKey or click on the bottom button of my pen. Try this and enter the shortcuts you use often to speed up your workflow. For a list of my favorite shortcuts, see the *Speed it Up!* chapter.

I like the small size of the Bamboo Craft Pen & Touch and it works great using two monitors. If you want to change the mapping or tracking of the tablet click on the Pen Properties tab (see where to find it above) and then on the Tracking Details button and make changes there.

The Editor

Inside the Editor is where you will edit photos and create digital projects like scrapbook pages, cards, brochures, etc.

To get to the Editor, when the Welcome screen appears after you launch the program, click on the Edit button.

There are three different options for editing: Full, Quick, and Guided. The Windows Full Edit workspace is shown below. A portion of the Mac Full Edit workspace showing the differences between the Windows version is shown at the bottom of the page. The Quick and Guided workspaces (shown circled below) are shown on the next page. Photo credit Madeline Arenas Cubrix Photography.

Full Edit

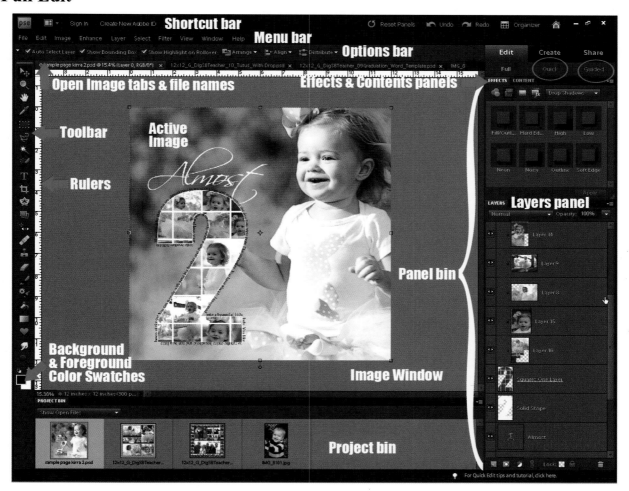

The big difference between the PC and Mac version is that the Menu bar and Shortcut bar are in opposite places. The Mac also has a New File and Save icon on the Shortcut bar which is really nice!

Quick Edit (Quick Fix)

Quick Edit is a fast way to make simple edits to your photos by using a limited number of tools, and by clicking buttons or moving sliders on the right. To fully see the difference your edits make, display a before and after view of your photo by clicking on the drop down list, shown circled. See the *Cool Stuff with Photos* chapter to see how to use Quick Edit to edit photos. Many of the options in Quick Edit can also be done in the Organizer.

Guided Edit

To help learn how to use Photoshop Elements, check out the Guided Edit tab. Instructions for making changes are listed step by step so you can get the hang of it. There are also some great options for turning your photos into works of art. For most of the options, you can also display a before and after view by clicking on the drop down list shown circled.

See the *Cool Stuff with Photos* Chapter for many Guided Edit examples.

Bins & Panels

As shown in the example on the right, all bins and panels can be moved anywhere you would like to place them. Click and drag by the tab to a new location, including nesting them under other panels. Normally I choose the default settings. In some of my examples I may have moved some of my panels to give you a better point of view. To hide/show your active panels, tap the Tab key.

To place a panel back in the bin, drag it to the bin and hover until you see the blue outline as shown in the example below on the right. To return the panels to their default positions, click on the Reset Panels button at the top of the screen (circled), or choose Window>Reset Panels from the Menu bar.

To collapse/open a panel or bin, double click on the tab. To close a panel, click on the drop down list at the top right corner of the panel and choose Close, or if the panel is removed from the bin, click on the X on the corner.

Project Bin

The Project bin is located at the bottom of the Editor workspace and displays all open images.

Double click on a thumbnail in the Project bin to display it as the active image (big image). The active image will be highlighted in the Project bin. To collapse/open the Project bin, double click on the line to the right of the words Project Bin (you may do this by mistake at times).

If you are working on a project and don't want to close Photoshop Elements because you will have to reopen all of the files again, you can save the files in the Project bin as an Album in the Organizer. To do this, click on the drop down list circled above and choose Save Bin as an Album. To open the Album, click on the drop down list under the words Project Bin. If you have trouble and don't see the images you were expecting to see in the Project bin, drop down the list and check to make sure you have selected the right option.

Panel Bin

The Panel bin is located on the far right area of the workspace. To add panels to the Panel bin from the Menu bar, click on Window and the list shown on the right will be displayed. The ✓ indicates that the panel is active. The panels that can be added to the Panel bin are highlighted in red.

Tools Panel

The Toolbar, also known as the Toolbin, Toolbox or Tools panel is located on the left side of your workspace and is on by default. There are tools that you'll probably never use on the Toolbar, and there are others you'll use all the time. Forty nine tools are available in Full Edit; eight are available in Quick Edit. The Foreground and Background color swatches are located at the bottom of the Toolbar. The Toolbar is explained in full detail on the first pages of the *Tools and Tips* chapter.

Color Swatches Panel

To add the Color Swatches panel to the Panel bin, choose Window>Color Swatches. There are several sets of swatches you may choose from, or you may make your own which is explained in detail in the *Tools and Tips* chapter following the Eyedropper tool section.

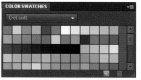

Navigator Panel

To add the Navigator panel to the Panel bin, choose Window>Navigator. The Navigator panel is similar to the Zoom and Hand tools combined. The Navigator is explained in detail in the *Tools and Tips* chapter following the Hand tool section.

Undo History Panel

The Undo History panel displays the last fifty steps done for each image. To add the Undo History panel to the Panel bin, choose Window>Undo History. The Undo History panel is explained in detail in *The Basics* chapter.

Info Panel

The Info panel is used to measure color and location. To add the Info panel to the Panel bin, choose Window>Info. For more information about using the Info panel to measure color and mark locations, see the *Tools and Tips* chapter following the Eyedropper tool section.

Histogram Panel

The Histogram panel displays a graph where you can check the different channels of colors. I normally use the histogram in the Levels Adjustment layer, or in the Camera Raw dialog box. To add the Histogram panel to the Panel bin, choose Window> Histogram.

Favorites Panel

The Favorites panel will be empty until you add something to it. To add one of your favorites from the Contents or Effects panels, right click on the thumbnail and choose Add to Favorites. Unfortunately, there appears to be no way to add a name under the thumbnails at this time. To add the Favorites panel to the Panel bin, choose Window>Favorites.

Layers Panel

The Layers panel appears in the Panel bin by default. If you don't see it, click the Reset Panels button or choose Window>Layers.

The Layers panel is the most important panel. You will use it every time you use the Photoshop Elements Editor. It is also the single most feared aspect of Photoshop Elements. I can't even begin to count the number of people who have said to me: "I just don't get the layers thing".

If you're afraid of layers, or have had trouble mastering them, the easiest way to learn to work with them is to relate digital layers to real paper layers. If you stack one paper photo on top of another paper photo, it will cover up the photo below. It's the same exact thing with Photoshop Elements.

A photo, a piece of digital paper, or digital embellishment is one layer, while a layered template will have several layers. You can have many layers in a document, and I'm sure you'll never exceed Adobe's limit, which the last time I researched, was 8,000 layers.

The more layers in your project, the larger the file size will be, and your computer may slow down while you're working on your project.

When saving your project, you are given the choice to save the file with all of the layers intact as a PSD or TIFF file. You may also choose to save your project as a JPEG file so that you may upload it to be printed by a photo processor. Saving as a JPEG will flatten all of your layers into one single layer.

It's important when saving your files that you save as a PSD file with all your layers intact so that you can easily make modifications in the future. I'm a firm believer in Murphy's Law…it seems like every time I didn't save my file as a PSD file in the past, there was something that needed to be corrected on it.

Layer Names
When you open a photo or digital paper, or make a new document (File>New) the layer name will always be Background. As you add layers to the document, each layer is given its own name. The name of the layer will depend on how it was added to your document.

If you use the Move tool (V) to drag your image **down** into the Project bin to your file, the layer will be named Layer 1, Layer 2, etc. If you drag your image **up** to the file, the layer will be named with the image file name. As you can see by the example above, the file name as the layer name helps you identify where the file came from if the designer names it accordingly. It's really nice that DeDe Smith named her files with the Goodeatz kit name. There are some problems associated with dragging some files **up,** so be sure to read about the Move tool in the *Tools & Tips* chapter.

Renaming Layers
Renaming a layer can help you document the supplies used in a project. A Layer name can also help you remember the methods used on that layer like adding the name of the filter you applied to that layer.

To rename a layer, select the layer, and do one of the following to highlight the layer name: Double click on the layer name, right click on the layer and choose Rename Layer, from the Menu bar choose Layer>Rename Layer, or click the drop down list on the Layers panel and select Rename Layer.

Once the layer name is highlighted, type the new layer name.

Selecting Layers
To select a layer, click on it in the Layers panel. Once selected, the layer will turn a darker color as shown by the example below. Selected layers are also called active or targeted layers. If the Auto Select Layer box is checked on the Move tool Options bar, you can also click on the image on your scrapbook page and the appropriate layer will be highlighted in the Layers panel. A selected layer may also be called a targeted or active layer.

To select the layer above the active layer, choose Alt>] (Bracket key), (Mac: Opt>]). To select the layer below the active layer, choose Alt>[(Bracket key), Mac: Opt>[).

To also select the layer, above the selected layer, choose Alt>Shift>] (Bracket key), Mac: Opt>Shift>]). To also select the layer below the selected layer, choose Alt>Shift>[(Bracket key), Mac: Opt>Shift>[).

To select the top layer choose Alt>->, (Mac: Opt>-,) (hyphen>comma). To select the bottom layer, choose Alt>->. (Mac: Alt>->.) (hyphen>period).

Sometimes you need to select more than one layer at a time to move, merge, link, etc. There are two different ways to do this. In the Layers panel, to select several layers in a row, click on the top layer and then Shift click on the bottom layer and all the layers will be selected. To select several noncontiguous layers, click on the top layer and then Ctrl click (Mac: Cmd click) on all of the other layers. All of the layers you clicked on will be selected.

On a multi-layered file (with the Auto Select Layer box checked on the Move Tool Options bar), click on one layer/element, Shift click on the next one, and they will be highlighted in the Layers panel.

To select all layers with the exception of the Background layer, choose from the Menu bar, Select>All Layers. To select similar layers (like all of your Text layers), select one Text layer, and then choose Select>Similar Layers. To deselect, choose Select>Deselect Layers.

Rearrange Layer Order
As you work with Photoshop Elements, you will need to change the order of your layers. There are several ways to rearrange layers.

As shown on the right, click and drag the layer in the Layers panel to a new location. When you reach the point where you want to move the layer, hover over the area until the line between the layers darkens just slightly, and let go of the mouse. This may be confusing the first couple of times you do it, but after that it's very easy.

Another way to rearrange layers is to select the Move tool (V) and click on the Arrange drop down list on the Options bar. Choose an option to move the selected layer.

Shift>Ctrl>] (Bracket key) (Mac: Shift>Cmd>])	Bring to Front (Top)
Ctrl>] (Bracket key) (Mac: Cmd>])	Bring Forward (Up one layer)
Ctrl>[(Bracket key) (Mac: Cmd>[)	Send Backward (Down one layer)
Shift>Ctrl>[(Bracket key) (Mac: Shift>Ctrl>[)	Send to Back (Bottom, but above Background layer)

Layer Thumbnail
The Layer thumbnail is the small square image to the left of the layer name. As shown in the example, all layer types have a different looking thumbnail. See the next page to see how to change the Layer thumbnail to help you see small layers like brads and buttons.

To make a selection (marching ants) of the layer contents, Ctrl click (Mac: Cmd click) on the thumbnail. This is a trick you will use over and over again, so try to remember it.

Layers Panel Options

As show on the example on the left, the default setting for the layer thumbnail contents is Entire Document. If you are working with a small element like a brad or a cookie (circled), it's difficult to see what is on the layer. You may spend unnecessary time renaming your layers just so you know what's on them.

If you would prefer to see larger images in the thumbnails, as shown in the example on the right, it's easy to change it.

Click on the drop down list on the top right corner of the Layers panel (circled above), and choose Layer Bounds to change the Thumbnail Contents. Now I can actually see that my selected layer is a cookie.

I work with Layer Bounds as Thumbnail Contents setting 95% of the time. When I change back to Entire Document, it is because I want to know the location of the layer on my page when I 'm working on a Montage or template. As shown in the Entire Document example on the left I can see that the cookie, even though it's tiny, is located on the bottom left corner of my page. On the Layer Bounds example on the right, I can definitely see that it's a cookie, but I can't tell by the thumbnail where the cookie is located on my page.

If you want to, you can also choose to adjust the size of the layer thumbnail. The default setting works well for me, but you can try different sizes. While the larger size may be tempting, it requires you to scroll more to see your layers, which takes more time.

Hide Layers (Visibility Toggle/Layer Visibility Indicator)

To hide/show a layer, click on the eyeball icon to the left of the layer thumbnail. If the eyeball is turned off, the layer is "hidden" and there is an empty box where the eyeball was.

There are several reasons you may want to hide a layer: you're working on its duplicate, you're not sure that you will use it on your page but don't want to delete it quite yet, or you created a Text layer with notes to yourself on things that you want to remember regarding the construction of your project.

The Digital Scrapbook Teacher puts a hidden instruction layer on all of our layered templates so that you can easily turn it on if you need to read it.

When you save your scrapbook page as a PSD file, your hidden files are saved intact. If you save as a JPEG file your hidden layers are flattened with all of the other layers. Hidden layers don't print if you are printing from a PSD file.

Alt click (Mac: Opt click) on the eyeball icon on one layer and all of the visible layers in your file are hidden except for the layer you clicked on originally (previously hidden layers remain hidden). Alt click again on the eyeball icon and the layers are shown again. You may also right click on the eyeball icon on one layer and choose Show/Hide all other layers to do the same thing.

Types of Layers

Background Layer

The layer name for a photo, scanned image, digital paper, or any other JPEG file is Background. As indicated by the tiny padlock symbol to the right of the layer name, a Background layer is always locked. The Background layer will always be the bottom layer, its stacking order cannot be changed in the Layers panel. You cannot change the blending mode or opacity, nor can you rename a Background layer. While the Background layer is locked, it has different properties than regular Locked Layers, which you can read more about in this chapter.

There are several ways to change a Background layer to a regular layer. With some methods you get the option to rename the layer and change the blending mode and opacity or use the previous layer to create a clipping mask.

Double click on the Background layer, or choose Layer>New>Layer from Background to display the New Layer dialog box. By default, the new layer will be named Layer 0, the Mode (Blending) will be Normal, and the Opacity will be 100%. If desired, make changes and click OK. Hold the Alt key (Mac: Opt key) and double click to bypass the New Layer dialog box. Using the Background Eraser tool (E) on a Background layer, it will automatically change to a regular layer.

Adding a Background from the Contents panel will automatically replace the existing Background layer. This is another reason to always begin your project with a new blank file, as explained in the beginning of the *How to Use* chapter. If your Background layer is a layer you want to keep, change it into a regular layer first and then add a background from the Contents panel.

To change a layer into a Background layer, select the layer, and choose Layer>New>Background from Layer from the Menu bar. If there are any transparent areas in the layer, they will be filled with the Background color.

Duplicate an Image

You may want to Duplicate a document/file consisting of just a Background layer, or a file containing more layers in your Project bin as a means to avoid working on your original files.

To Duplicate an Image: Right click on the image in the Project bin and choose Duplicate Image, or from the Menu bar, choose File>Duplicate. The Duplicate Image dialog box allows you to type a new name for the duplicated image, or you may keep the default name which is the original file name with the word copy added to the end of it.

Image Layers

An Image layer is also called a Regular layer. An Image layer is made up of pixels and can be blank; it can be a photo or a digital scrapbooking element. The layer name and thumbnail will change, as explained earlier in this chapter.

Raster and Vector Layers

You'll probably never need to understand what Raster or Vector images are, but just in case you run across the term, you'll have a tiny bit of an understanding what they are.

Raster images are made up of pixels. When you zoom into a raster image, you can see all of the pixels that make up the image. Raster images are best used for photographs and digital scrapbooking elements. Vector graphics are made up of paths which have a mathematical relationship with points, and beyond that I'm pretty well lost! Vector graphics are used for text and shapes because they keep their sharp edges.

Text/Type Layers

Text layers are added automatically when you type with the Type tool (T). Text
layers can be adjusted to any size and still keep their detail. It's a good idea to
use the Anti Alias setting to keep the sharpness around the edges. Text layers are
vector based. The example on the right shows a regular text layer on the bottom
and a simplified text layer on top. With the regular text layer you can edit the
text or enlarge it dramatically without any change in quality. Word art that
comes with many digital scrapbooking kits is simplified text that you can't edit.

Simplifying a layer is rasterizing a vector layer…a term that scared me to death when I first started learning
Photoshop Elements. Basically, you are changing a vector layer (paths and points) to a raster layer (pixels).

There are several ways to simplify a layer: Right click, click on the Layers panel drop down list on the top right
corner of the panel, or choose Layer>Simplify Layer from the Menu bar. If you try to use a tool or add a filter
prior to simplifying a layer, a dialog box will appear asking you if you wish to simplify the layer. Choose OK
and you don't need to manually do it yourself.

You must Simplify a text layer to use the Paint Bucket, Red Eye, Cookie Cutter, Eraser (All), Brush (All),
Pencil, Healing Brush (All), Clone Stamp (All), Gradient, Blur, Sharpen, Smudge, Sponge, Dodge, Burn tools,
or add filters. As shown on the preceding page, a Simplified Text layer Thumbnail will show a transparent
background. The text layer name displayed will be the first characters or spaces that you type, depending on
your screen size. When a text layer is simplified, unless you rename it manually, it will keep its original name.

Shape Layers

Shape layers are made automatically when you make a shape with any of the
Shape tools (U). Shape layers can be adjusted to any size and still keep their
detail and smooth edges. As shown on the right, a Simplified Shape Layer
Thumbnail will show a transparent (checkerboard) background. The Shape layer
name displayed will be Shape 1, Shape 2, etc. as designated by the order they
were added to the project. When a Shape layer is simplified, it will keep its
original name unless you rename it manually.

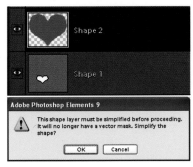

You must Simplify a Shape layer to use the Red Eye Removal, Cookie Cutter,
Eraser (All), Brush (All), Pencil, Healing Brush (All), Clone Stamp (All),
Gradient, Blur, Sharpen, Smudge, Sponge, Dodge, Burn tools, or add filters. A
Simplified Text Layer Thumbnail will show a transparent (checkerboard)
background. The Text layer name displayed will be the first characters or spaces
that you type, depending on your screen size. When a Shape layer is simplified, it
will keep its original name unless you rename it manually.

Smart Object Layers

Smart Object layers allow you to resize them without loss of quality. Graphics
and Backgrounds added through the Content panel are Smart Object Layers. As
shown in the example on the right, the green button and photo became Smart
Object layers when I chose File>Place from the Menu bar to add them to my
project. Had I opened the button files and used the Move tool to drag them onto
my project, they would have become a regular image layer.

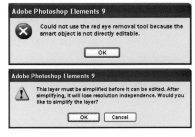

You must Simplify a Smart Object layer to use the Paint Bucket, Red Eye
Removal, Cookie Cutter, Eraser (All), Brush (All), Pencil, Healing Brush (All),
Clone Stamp (All), Gradient, Blur, Sharpen, Smudge, Sponge, Dodge, Burn tools, or add filters.

Fill Layers

Fill layers allow you to fill a layer with a color, gradient, or pattern. Fill layers are often called Adjustment layers. To add a Fill layer to a document, click on the Create Adjustment Layer icon (circled), or from the Menu bar, choose Layer>New Fill Layer>and choose Solid Color, Gradient, or Pattern.

Fill layers do not affect the layers below them like Adjustment layers do. You can change the blend mode, opacity, and stacking order of a Fill layer.

Fill layers include a Layer Mask, unless you have changed the setting in the Panel Options (see example). To paint on a Fill layer with the Brush tool (B) or Paint Bucket tool (K), you must Simplify it first, or you will be painting on the Layer Mask. A better option would be to create a new transparent layer, and paint on that layer instead of the Fill layer.

When adding a **Color Fill layer,** you are given the opportunity to pick a color with the color picker. If you don't choose a new color, the layer will be filled with the existing Foreground color. To see more about using a Color Fill layer, see the *Change It* chapter.

A **Gradient Fill layer** allows you to choose the gradient, style, angle, scale %, reverse, dither, and if you want, to align it with the layer. To see more about using a Gradient Fill layer, see the *Cool Stuff with Gradients* chapter.

A **Pattern Fill layer** allows you to choose the pattern, scale %, if you want to link it with the layer or snap to origin. To see more about using a Pattern Fill layer, see the *Make Your Own* chapter.

Other methods to fill a layer or selection with a color or a pattern are to use the Paint Bucket tool, or from the Menu Bar, choose Edit>Fill Layer/Selection. To fill a layer or selection with the Foreground color, use the shortcut Alt>Backspace (Mac: Opt>Delete). To fill a layer or selection with the Background color, use the shortcut Ctrl>Backspace (Mac>Cmd>Delete). To fill a layer with a gradient, create a new layer, select the Gradient tool, and click and drag at an angle of your choice (the Fill layer specifies the angle).

If your layer has transparency in it, filling the layer or selection with any of the methods above will fill the layer entirely with a pattern, gradient, or color. From the Menu bar, choose Layer>Create Clipping Mask to clip a Fill layer to the layer below it so that the transparency is retained.

To fill a layer with the Foreground color and preserve the layer's transparency, use the shortcut Alt>Shift>Backspace (Mac: Opt>Shift>Delete). To fill with the Background color and preserve the layer's transparency, use the shortcut Ctrl>Shift>Backspace (Mac: Cmd>Shift>Delete).

If you are using the Edit>Fill Layer/Selection command to fill a layer with transparency, be sure to check the Preserve Transparency box (circled).

The advantage of using a Fill layer instead of filling the layer with a color, pattern, or gradient with the Paint Bucket tool, Edit>Fill command, or Gradient tool, is that a Fill layer makes it easier to make changes. To make changes to a Fill layer, double click on the thumbnail and the boxes shown above on the left will reappear.

Adjustment Panel

The Adjustments Panel is added to the Panel bin automatically when an Adjustment layer is added or by choosing Window>Adjustments from the Menu bar. The example on the right shows the Adjustments panel that was added when I added a Levels Adjustment layer to a photo.

Shown below are five tiny icons located at the bottom of each Adjustment layer panel. The first icon from the left will clip the Adjustment layer to the layer below it. The second icon from the left (eyeball) will toggle on/off the Adjustment layer. The third icon from the left (eyeball and arrow) will show the previous state. The fourth icon from the left (circle with arrow) will reset the Adjustment layer to the default settings. The trashcan icon on the right will delete the Adjustment layer.

Adjustment Layers

There are many advantages to using Adjustment layers. The biggest advantage is that any changes made to the layer are not permanent and can be easily changed or deleted. You can use multiple Adjustment layers on an image. You can also restrict the changes made by an Adjustment layer by the use of a selection or mask that is included with all Adjustment layers.

Adjustment layers are saved intact when you save your file as a PSD file, enabling you to make changes to them anytime. If the effect of the Adjustment layer is too strong, you can lower the layer Opacity. To make changes to the Adjustment layer, double click on the Adjustment layer thumbnail and a dialog box will appear.

One way to add an Adjustment layer to a layer (or a selection on the layer), is to select the layer and then click on the Create Adjustment layer icon (half black, half white circle) located at the bottom of the Layers panel to display a list. There are eight different Adjustment layers to choose from, (the first three choices on the list are Fill layers and were covered on the preceding page).

An Adjustment layer will affect **all** the layers under it. If you want the Adjustment layer to affect only the first layer underneath it, clip it to that layer with a Clipping Mask by clicking on the tiny icon at the bottom of the Adjustment layer panel. You can also do this by choosing Layer>New Adjustment Layer from the Menu bar. After you choose the Adjustment layer you want, the New Layer dialog box will appear. Check the box to create a Clipping Mask so that the Adjustment layer affects only the layer below it. If you have already created an Adjustment layer, click on it and choose Layer>Create Clipping Mask (Ctrl>G, Mac: Cmd>G) to clip it to the layer directly below it. You may clip the Adjustment layer to multiple layers.

To make changes on an Adjustment layer, double click on the layer thumbnail (circled) and the Adjustments panel will be displayed allowing you to make changes.

Moving images and/or layers with Adjustment layers can sometimes be tricky, be sure to read about this in the Move tool section of the *Tools & Tips* chapter.

Levels Adjustment Layer

If you are used to the Auto Levels command on the Enhance menu or in Quick Fix, click the Auto button. If you don't like the results, try moving the sliders inward until they touch the edges of the graph (histogram). As the black and white slides move inward, you will see more contrast in the image. A Levels Adjustment layer allows you to adjust shadows, highlights, and mid tones independent of each other by sliding the three sliders at the bottom of the Histogram. You can also change a color cast using RGB (Red, Green or Blue) Channels. The Output Levels Sliders make your darkest pixels darker and your lighter pixels lighter. To make corrections, click on the white eyedropper, and then click on a white area in the image.

Brightness/Contrast Adjustment Layer

A Brightness/Contrast Adjustment layer can help with a drab photo. To adjust brightness/contrast to all or a selected portion of an image, adjust the sliders. Sliding either slider to the right increases Brightness/Contrast, sliding to the left decreases it.

Hue/Saturation Adjustment Layer

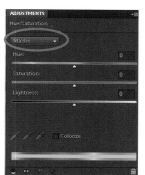

Use the Hue slider to adjust the color of your photos or scrapbook supplies. Adjust the Saturation slider to make colors more vibrant or muted. Moving the Saturation slider all the way to the left removes all color. Check the Colorize box if you are working with a black and white photo. If you are working with a color image like a scrapbooking element and want to match the Foreground color, check the Colorize box and move the Saturation slider to the right. To adjust part of the image, click on the drop down list that says master (circled), and choose a color to adjust. This is very helpful when changing the color of digital scrapbooking elements.

Gradient Map Adjustment Layer

Choose the gradient you want to use from the drop down menu. Shadows are mapped to the starting color of the gradient on the left. Midtones are mapped to the midpoint of the gradient, and highlights are mapped to the ending color of the gradient on the right. Choosing Reverse will do the opposite. To change the mapping of the gradient, click inside the box and the Gradient Editor will open. Drag the color stops to make changes. To smooth the transition between the gradient bands, choose Dither. See the *Cool Stuff with Photos* chapter for tutorials showing how to use this Adjustment layer to create sepia and black and white photos.

Photo Filter Adjustment Layer

Choose one of the twenty preset filters by clicking on the drop down arrow, or click on the Color button and choose your own color to use as a filter. Set the Density by sliding the slider or entering a percentage. The higher the Density, the more color is applied. The image will be darkened with the color unless you keep Luminosity checked.

Invert

There are no options for the Invert Adjustment layer. This Adjustment layer inverts (swaps black for white, etc.) the colors in your image. Your photo looks like a negative when you use this filter. If you have scanned and used a true black and white negative, you can make a black and white positive, which is a black and white photo with this Adjustment layer. The Invert filter will not work with color negatives because of the orange mask that is on them, so use a scanner that is capable of scanning color negatives.

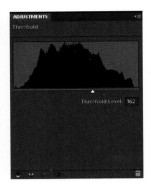

Threshold Adjustment Layer

The Threshold Adjustment layer turns the image to true black and white only. Sliding all the way to the right turns the image completely black, and all the way to the left turns it completely white.

Posterize Adjustment Layer

A Posterize Adjustment layer makes your image look like a cartoon image because it reduces the number of continuous tones. Level 4 is the default, but you can choose 2-255 levels.

Creating a New Layer

There are several ways to make a new transparent layer. As new layers are created, they are added in numerical order to a document. The layer name and stacking order can be easily changed. It's important to add brushwork and stroke outlines to their own layer so that they can be edited independently.

When you create a new transparent layer in one of the following ways: Alt (Mac: Opt) and tap the New Layer icon, Layer>New>Layer (shortcut Shift>Ctrl>N, Mac: Shift>Cmd>N), or click on the drop down arrow on the Layers panel and choose New Layer, the New Layer dialog box appears which gives you the option of changing Blend Modes, Opacity, and Creating a Clipping Mask with a previous layer

Clicking on the New Layer icon located at the bottom of the Layers panel creates a new transparent layer without displaying the New Layer dialog box. The shortcut is: Shift>Ctrl>Alt>N (Mac: Shift>Cmd>Opt>N).

When making a new layer by any method, the new layer automatically becomes the active layer. A new layer is added on top of the layer you previously selected. To add a new layer under the selected layer, Ctrl click (Mac: Cmd click) on the New Layer icon. To add a new layer under the selected layer and to display the New Layer dialog box, Ctrl>Alt click (Mac>Cmd>Opt) on the New Layer icon.

When you drag an element onto your scrapbook page with the Move tool (V), it automatically becomes a new layer, so you don't have to make a new layer for it yourself. When working on a scrapbook page or other project,   it's important to have the top layer selected when adding elements to the page so that you can see them when they're added and they're not buried by other layers on top of it. Adding Text, Shapes, or Fill and Adjustment layers also creates new layers on your document.

Duplicating Layers or Selections

Before my students leave a beginning photo editing class, they know the shortcut to duplicate a layer or selection because it's a great timesaver. A good habit to get into is to duplicate a layer that you will make changes to, like adding a filter, removing wrinkles, simplifying text, etc.

To duplicate a layer or selection without displaying the Duplicate Layer dialog box, select the layer and choose one of these options: from the Menu bar, choose Layer>New>Layer via Copy, use the shortcut Ctrl>J (Mac: Cmd>J), or drag the layer thumbnail to the New Layer icon at the bottom of the Layers panel.

As shown above, if you are working on a single layer file, the layer name for the duplicate will vary depending on how the layer was created. If you choose the shortcut (Ctrl>J, Mac: Cmd>J) first, and then drag the Background layer thumbnail to the New Layer icon, the first layer will be named Layer 1, the second one will be named Background copy. If you reverse the order and use the shortcut second, they will be named Background copy and Background copy 2. It's the same thing and can be confusing, so don't worry about it if you notice it.

To duplicate a layer and display the Duplicate Layer dialog box, which allows you to rename the layer and send it to another file, select the layer and choose one of these options: from the Menu bar, choose Layer> Duplicate Layer, or right click on the layer and choose Duplicate Layer, or click on the Layers panel drop down list and choose Duplicate Layer.

By selecting a document as a destination, I copy and paste this image onto another document; similar to if I had used the Move tool to drag it there.

One of my favorite ways to duplicate layers is to select the Move tool (V) and Alt click and drag on a layer like a brad or button to duplicate it (Mac: Opt click). Change it to Shift>Alt click and drag, and the elements will be copied in a straight line (Mac: Shift>Opt click). The layer will be copied exactly and placed above the original layer in the Layers panel. The new layer name will be the original layer name followed by the word copy, if you make several copies, numbers will be added to the layer name.

To copy a selection onto its own layer, make a selection and from the Menu bar choose Layer>New>Layer via Copy. Only the selected area is added as a new layer directly above the original layer.

Copying a selection by choosing Layer>New>Layer>Via Cut from the Menu bar (Shift>Ctrl>J, Mac: Shift>Cmd>J) will put the selected area on its own layer. It will also leave a hole in the original layer where the selection was cut. If the original layer is a Background layer the hole will be filled with the Background color.

Delete Layers

There are several ways to delete a layer. Most methods ask you to confirm that you want to delete the layer, but the warning box can be disabled by clicking in the Don't show again box.

Select the layer(s) you wish to delete and: click on the Trashcan icon (doesn't work for Shape layers), choose Layer>Delete Layer from the Menu bar, click on the Layers panel drop down list and choose Delete Layer, right click on the layer and choose Delete Layer.

To delete the layer without showing the warning box, drag the selected layer to the Trashcan icon or Alt click (Mac: Opt click) on the Trashcan icon (also doesn't work for Shape layers).

Instead of deleting the layer, you may want to hide it by clicking on the eyeball icon to the left of the layer thumbnail. Hiding the layer makes it invisible on your document, but the layer will still remain in your Layers panel in case you need it later.

Blending Modes

To blend pixels from the selected layer with the layers below it change the blending mode (white circle). See the *Filters and Blending Modes* chapter for more information.

Adjust Layer Opacity

Click on the word Opacity to activate a scrubby slider shown on the right. Click and drag to change the opacity of the selected layer. You can also click on the Opacity drop down arrow and, when the slider appears, slide it or click on it or just type a percentage number in the box. For a solid opaque layer, the opacity is 100%. Instead of hiding a layer you could change the opacity to 0%. As you lower the opacity of a layer it becomes transparent. An easy way to make a vellum type paper is to lower the opacity on the layer.

The only type of layer where you can't adjust the opacity is a Background layer. The shortcut to adjust the opacity for an active layer is to quickly type 9 for 90%, 8 for 80% etc. To set the opacity to 35 %, type 35 quickly, type 0 for 100%.

Clipping Masks

A clipping mask sounds like a pretty scary complicated thing to work with, but it's not! When I clip an image to a shape or text, the image is cut into the shape of the text or shape layer, similar to what a die cut machine would do with real paper items. Instead of creating a clipping mask, I could use the Cookie Cutter tool (Q) or a selection to crop an image, but the clipping mask gives me a lot more options. Once I clip the image, I can still resize and adjust both the bottom layer and that part of the image on the top layer that shows through, something I can't do with the other methods.

One thing to remember is that the bottom layer has the control over the clipping mask. It determines the shape and size (it can still be resized/transformed). The opacity and blending mode is also determined by the bottom layer. If you want to add a layer style, such as a drop shadow or bevel, it must be added to the bottom layer. Adjustment layers affect **all** layers under them. In some situations you may want to clip the layers together.

Using a layered template is a fast and easy way to make a scrapbook page without having to do any of the design work yourself. All you need to do is open the template and some photos. Clip the photos to the template pieces and you're done. After completing a couple of templates, you'll have clipping masks mastered!

Prior to Photoshop Elements 8, Adobe used the term Group with Previous, but changed it to Create Clipping Mask. If you are using Photoshop Elements 7 or older, be aware that Group with Previous and Create Clipping Mask are the same thing. The commands Ungroup and Release Clipping Mask are also the same thing.

To clip two or more layers together, make sure your selected layer is directly above the layer you want to clip it to. From the Menu bar, choose Layer>Create Clipping Mask (Ctrl>G, Mac: Cmd>G). As shown in the example, the paper layer (Layer 1) has stepped to the right and a bent downward facing arrow points down to the layer it's clipped to, which now has its layer name underlined (Shape 1). By moving Layer 1 after I clipped it to the shape, I was able to show different areas of the paper to create a beautiful custom heart embellishment. The paper on the heart is from the Farmhouse kit by Royanna Fritschmann which is included on the *Photoshop Elements - Basics & Beyond* DVD.

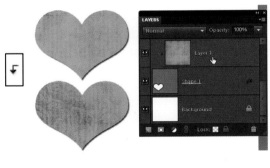

You do not have to cover all of your shape. If you only want to cover part of a shape or text with a digital scrapbook paper, drag it over part of the shape and then choose Layer>Create Clipping Mask (Ctrl>G, Mac: Cmd>G). As shown in the example, repeat the same steps with another paper as I did with Amanda Rockwell's cute Happy Hollydays kit, which is also included on the *Photoshop Elements - Basics & Beyond* DVD. Notice that I made the digital paper pattern smaller in the bottom heart and also on the text. I also added a stroke around the text. Step by step instructions for this technique can be found in the *Cool Stuff with Text* chapter.

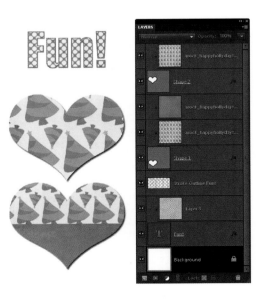

Multiple layers may be clipped together. Layers that are clipped must be stacked directly on top of each other in the Layers panel. As shown in the example, once clipped, the bottom layer name is underlined and the upper layers are indented and identified by a bent downward facing arrow. If you want to move the clipped group up or down in the Layers panel, you will need to select all of the clipped layers and move them together, or better yet, link them together and then move them, or they will become unclipped.

Another shortcut to create a clipping mask is to Alt click (Mac: Opt click) on the line dividing the two layers you want to clip together. You will see a symbol with a black and white circle and a left facing arrow. Click and they are clipped; click again to release the clipping mask.

To release a clipping mask without changing the layer order, choose Layer>Release Clipping Mask (Ctrl>G, Mac: Cmd>G). Rearranging the layers in the Layers panel will also release the clipping mask.

Layer Groups

One of the reasons Group with Previous was changed to Create Clipping Mask is because it conflicted with the Group term within Photoshop. The circled layers in the example above are actually a Layer Group that was created in Photoshop. Basically it's a folder of layers that can be opened in Photoshop. To use a layer group in Photoshop Elements, you must simplify it first which merges all of the layers within the group. This probably isn't what you want.

Linking Layers

Linking layers together is helpful when working with a multi-layered project. Think of linking layers together as using temporary adhesive to keep them stuck together. By linking layers together, you can move, copy, paste, and size them all together. Linked layers do not have to be stacked directly on top of each other; they can be spread out throughout the Layers panel. The Digital Scrapbook Teacher links all of our template shapes so that you don't inadvertently move one of them out of alignment. When using a template, if you want to move or resize the template shapes to make your own special creation, just unlink the template pieces.

There are several different ways to link layers. Select the layers in the layers panel by clicking and Ctrl clicking (Mac: Cmd clicking) or Shift clicking if the layers are next to each other, and: click on the link symbol, right click and choose Link Layers, or click on the Layers panel drop down list and select Link Layers.

Another way to select layers is by Shift clicking on several layers on your scrapbook page when the Auto Select Layer option of the Move tool (V) is activated.

As shown in the example, once the layers are linked, a link symbol will show to the right side of the layer name. The sample Layers panel is for a scrapbook page I created using the Project B Designs Num13ers kit which can be found on the *Photoshop Elements - Basics & Beyond* DVD. I have linked the layers for the photo and frame elements. The only time the link symbol will be visible is when at least one of the linked layers is selected.

To unlink a layer, select one linked layer in the Layers panel and click on the Link icon on the bottom of the Layers panel, and only that layer will be unlinked. To unlink all linked layers, you will need to select all of the linked layers. A trick to selecting all linked layers is to click on one, and then right click or click on the Layers panels drop down list and choose Select Linked Layers. To unlink all of the linked layers after you have selected them: click on the Link icon, Right click on one of the layers and choose Unlink Layers, or click on the Layers panel drop down list and choose Unlink Layers.

To delete linked layers, select one of the linked layers and click on the Layers panel drop down list and choose Delete Linked Layers. All of the layers that were linked to the selected layer will be deleted. If you have another set of linked layers that was not linked with the selected layer, they will not be deleted.

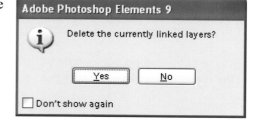

Layer Masks

An exciting new feature for Photoshop Elements 9 is the ability to add layer masks. Adjustment and Fill layers have automatically included a mask, but now you have the ability to add a mask yourself to layers other than a Background layer. Be sure to read the *Cool Stuff* chapters where I have used layer masks extensively.

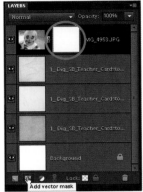

To add a mask, tap the Mask icon (circled above) located at the bottom of the Layers panel, or create a Fill or Adjustment layer. Remember, an Adjustment layer will affect all layers underneath it in the Layers panel. As previously explained in this chapter, to restrict changes to just the layer below it, you will need to clip it to the layer (Layer>Create Clipping Mask).

Using a layer mask allows you to make non-destructive changes to your image. If you have used the Eraser tool in the past to cut away parts of an image, you know that if you make a mistake and cut away too much, you have to Undo any changes and Redo it again. If you have saved and closed, the image you're out of luck! What makes this new feature so exciting is that with a mask, you can easily make changes at any time.

By default, masks are white, which means they conceal everything on the layer below them. Applying black to the mask will reveal 100% of the layer below. Applying shades of gray will reveal different degrees of the layer below. Darker grays reveal more of the layer below, lighter grays reveal less. Another way to reveal more or less of the layer below when using the Brush tool is to adjust the opacity on the Brush tool Options bar.

The simplest way to use a mask is to paint on it with the Brush tool with black. To do this, create the mask as shown above and:

Type the letter D to set your Foreground and Background colors located at the bottom of the Toolbar to the default settings. Your Foreground color should be black, and your Background color should be white.

Select the Brush tool, (normally I use a soft round brush). Click inside the mask on the Layers panel. Paint (click and drag) on your active image over areas you wish to conceal. You may also use the Gradient tool (G) on the mask to softly fade in the pink background. When using the Gradient tool, choose the Foreground to Background gradient, or the Black and White Gradient. *See the Cool Stuff with Photos* chapter, to see how I used a gradient with a mask, to edit a photo that was too dark in some areas.

As shown in the example, I am painting away areas of the photo to reveal the pink paper below. Notice on the layer mask that black was added when I painted on the mask. If I paint away too much of the photo, I will type the letter X to swap my Foreground color to white and I will paint back in the photo, which makes this much more forgiving than using the Eraser tool. Note: All papers used in this example are from the Springtime Paper & Embellishment kit available at *www.TheDigitalScrapbookTeacher.com.*

Speaking of the Eraser tool, you can use it just the same as you would the Brush tool, except that you will need to reverse the colors. When using the Eraser tool on a mask, set the Foreground color to White to reveal and Black to conceal.

If you see painting on your photo in the color of your Foreground color like the example on the right, this means you forgot to click inside the mask before painting. Undo, click inside the mask, and try it again.

To softly paint away the right side of the photo, I selected the Brush tool, the color black and a large soft round brush. You can see the black areas I painted on the mask (circled). When I erased too much of the baby, I switched to white to paint him back in. Adjusting the size of the brush is also helpful in fine tuning the end result. The beauty of using the mask is that I can save this as a PSD file, close it, reopen it later, and still make adjustments. If I move the image, the mask moves with it. If I want to move only the mask, click on the link between the image and mask thumbnail.

Masking Tips

If you have been working on an image and want to start over, you can delete the mask and add a new one, or you can fill the existing mask with white. To do this: click inside the Mask, type D (sets the Foreground color to Black and the Background color to white), type the shortcut Ctrl>Backspace (Mac: Cmd>Delete).

To fill a layer mask with black and conceal everything: click inside the Mask, type D (sets the Foreground color to Black and the Background color to white), type the shortcut Alt>Backspace (Mac: Opt>Delete).

To use a mask with a selection, create the selection first and then add the layer mask by clicking on the Layer Mask icon at the bottom of the Layers panel. The selection will automatically be revealed, and the rest of the image will be masked away.

As the example on the right shows, I used the Elliptical Marquee (M) tool to make an oval selection. I feathered the selection 125 px (Select>Feather) and then added a layer mask. Only the area selected inside the oval is revealed. I can fine tune the revealed area with the Brush tool if desired.

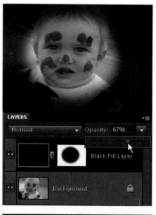

You can also use a layer mask to add a dark vignette around an image. As the example on the left shows, I created a new transparent layer and filled it with black. I used the Elliptical Marquee tool to make an oval selection (it may be helpful to temporarily hide the black layer when you do this) and feathered the selection 125 px (Select>Feather). I Inversed the selection (Layer>Inverse), so that the area surrounding the oval was selected. I added a layer mask by tapping the Layer Mask icon at the bottom of the Layers panel. I adjusted the opacity for the black fill layer. If I want to, I can fine tune the revealed area with the Brush tool.

To see only the mask layer, Alt click (Mac: Opt click) on the mask thumbnail. All other layers are hidden and the layer mask is displayed in black and white. Repeat to return to normal. To see the layer mask in red, Shift>Alt click (Mac: Shift>Opt click) on the mask thumbnail. All of your other layers remain visible, but the mask is red. If parts of your image are red or pink, it's pretty hard to see.

To see the layer mask as a selection, Ctrl click (Mac: Cmd click) on the mask thumbnail, or right click on the mask thumbnail and choose Add Mask to Selection. To toggle your layer mask off/on, Shift click on the mask thumbnail, or right click on the mask thumbnail and choose Disable Layer Mask. A large red X is placed over the thumbnail and it's turned off on your image. To delete a layer mask, right click on the mask thumbnail and choose Delete Layer Mask, or click and drag the mask thumbnail to the trash can icon at the bottom of the Layers panel where you will be asked to confirm that you want to apply or delete the mask. To apply the layer mask which would essentially permanently cut away any of the dark areas on the mask, right click and choose Apply Layer Mask.

If you are using a mask on an Adjustment layer, it's a good idea to link the Adjustment layer and image layer together so that if you move or size one, they are both moved or resized/transformed together.

Merging Layers

Merge layers only if you are sure you won't need to make any changes to the individual layers in the future. If I'm working with a lot of small elements like brads and rivets, I'll merge them together in one layer after I'm sure they're placed in the right position. By merging layers I decrease the number of layers in my Layers panel, which makes the file easier to work with, and sometimes it reduces the file size. Note: the example on the right currently displays the term Merge Layers. This can change depending on the layer selected in the Layers panel. It may say Merge Linked, Merge Down, or Merge Clipping Mask.

To merge layers, select the layers in the Layers panel and do one of the following: From the Menu bar, choose Layer>Merge Layers, use the shortcut Ctrl>E, (Mac: Cmd>E), right click on one of the selected layers and choose Merge Layers, or click on the Layers Panel drop down list and choose Merge Layers. After merging, all of the selected layers are combined into one layer. The new layer retains the name of the original top layer.

To merge a single layer with the layer below it, select the layer in the Layers panel and do one of the following: From the Menu bar, choose Layer>Merge Down, use the shortcut Ctrl>E, (Mac: Cmd>E), right click on one of the selected layers and choose Merge Down, or click on the Layers Panel drop down list and choose Merge Down. After merging down, the layers are combined into one layer. The new layer retains the name of the original bottom layer. You must have a layer below your selected layer for this to work. Merge down is not available if the lower layer is a Shape, Text, Fill or Adjustment Layer that has not been simplified.

Merging Visible Layers
To merge all visible layers into a single layer **and** retain the original layers (this comes in handier than you think it might) type the shortcut Ctrl>Shift>Alt>E (Mac: Cmd>Shift>Opt>E). The new combined layer will be placed above the layer that was last selected. If you choose Merge Visible from the Menu bar by right clicking, or from the Layers panel drop down list, it will merge all visible layers into one layer, naming it the selected layer name.

Merging Linked Layers
To merge linked layers, select one of the linked layers and do one of the following: From the Menu bar, choose Layer>Merge Linked, use the shortcut Ctrl>E, (Mac: Cmd>E), right click on one of the selected layers and choose Merge Linked, or click on the Layers Panel drop down list and choose Merge Linked. After merging linked layers, the layers are combined into one layer. The new layer retains the name of the originally selected layer. One word of warning about merging linked layers, any of the layers that the selected layer was linked to will also be merged together. Instead of selecting Merge Linked Layers, select the layers yourself and link them.

Merging Adjustment and Fill Layers
Adjustment and Fill layers can't be used as the bottom or target layer in a group of layers that you merge. To permanently apply an Adjustment or Fill layer, merge it with the layer below it. Once an Adjustment layer is merged with the layer below it, the lower layers are no longer affected by the Adjustment layer. Clipping (Layer>Create Clipping Mask) an Adjustment layer to the layer below it restricts the changes only to the layers it is clipped to. This may be a better option than merging Adjustment layers; because once the layers are merged you no longer have the Adjustment layer to make adjustments. If the layer is at the bottom of a Clipping Mask group, select the layer and right click, or click on the Layers panel drop down list and choose Merge Clipping Mask. If the bottom layer is a shape or text layer, you will need to simplify the layer first.

Flatten
I don't flatten! I had the opportunity to attend a Photoshop class taught by Dave Cross (he's a wonderful teacher). Dave called Flatten "the F Word of Photoshop" and I agree. When you flatten, all layers are combined into one layer, any hidden layers are deleted, and any transparent areas are filled with white. Essentially, the same thing happens if you save your files as JPEGs for printing. My advice to you is to always save all your layers in a PSD file so that all your layers are retained. To Flatten: from the Menu bar choose Layer>Flatten, or right click on the layer, or click on the Layers panel drop down list and choose Flatten.

Lock Transparent Pixels

Locking transparent pixels locks only the transparent (checkerboard) area of a layer. The actual item on the layer is still able to be painted or filled with color. To lock/unlock transparent pixels, select the layer and then click on the Lock Transparent Pixels icon circled above. A lock symbol will appear to the right of the layer name when the transparent pixels are locked.

If you duplicate a layer with locked transparency by choosing from the Menu bar Layer>Duplicate or by right clicking and choosing Duplicate, the duplicated layer will also have the transparency locked. However, if you use the shortcut Ctrl>J (Mac: Cmd>J) the transparency will not be locked. The transparency in shape and text layers is automatically locked until the layer is simplified.

To fill a layer with the Foreground color and preserve the transparency, use the shortcut Alt>Shift>Backspace. (Mac Opt>Shift>Delete). To fill a layer with transparency with the Background color and preserve the transparency, use the shortcut Ctrl>Shift>Backspace (Mac: Cmd>Shift>Delete).

Lock All/Locked Layers

To lock/unlock a layer, select the layer and then click on the Lock All icon circled above, or type the shortcut / (forward slash) key. The lock will appear on any layer that is locked. The Background layer by default is locked. To unlock it, convert it to a regular layer. Locked layers can be moved up and down in the Layers panel, except for the Background layer. You can crop or straighten locked layers, but that's pretty much it, unless it's a Background layer. If you have a layer that you don't want to move or make changes to, lock it.

Content Panel

The Layers panel appears in the Panel bin by default. If you don't see it, click the Reset Panels button or choose Window>Content.

The Content panel includes backgrounds, frames, graphics, shapes, and text options that you can use on your projects. The backgrounds and graphics are added as smart object layers, allowing you to resize them without worrying about them becoming pixilated.

To add a background, click on the drop down list and choose background. Make a new file (File>New>Blank File), select a background and tap the Apply button, or double click on one of the Background thumbnails. The new background replaces any Background layer that previously existed in your document, which can be aggravating.

Most of the backgrounds work great, but occasionally you'll run into one, like the first one on the list, that won't fit the document you're working on, as shown by the map of Africa on the right

My favorites are the frames, but I would suggest adding them to a photo before dragging them onto another document to avoid frustration.

If you ever wondered what Miss DST dresses like for a night out on the town, I've used some of the graphics to give you a visual you'll probably never forget.

Clicking on a thumbnail with a gold ribbon on it requires a Plus membership to use it. If you don't have one, a box will pop up allowing you to sign up for it by paying a fee to Adobe.

Effects Panel

The Effects panel appears in the Panel bin by default. If you don't see it, click the Reset Panels button or choose Window>Effects. If you don't see names under your effects, go back and read the *First Things First* chapter.

The four icons across the top of the panel are for Filters, Layer Styles, Photo Effects, and All Effects. The filters can also be added to images by choosing Filters from the Menu bar and choosing a filter group. Each category has its own list of options. In the example on the right, I have selected Drop Shadows from the Layer Styles drop down list.

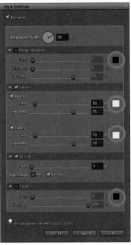

There are many Effects to choose from. The ones I use most are the Drop Shadows, Bevels, and Inner and Outer Glows. Since I use these often, it would be a good idea to add them to the Favorites panel as explained earlier in this chapter.

To apply an Effect, do one of the following: double click on the Effect thumbnail, click once on the thumbnail, and then tap the Apply button, or click and drag the thumbnail to the image. At least one Layer Style from each category can be applied to a layer, which means that each layer can have several layer styles applied to it. When you apply a layer style to a layer, a small *fx* symbol is added to the far right side of the layer in the Layers panel, as shown in the example. Layer styles cannot be applied to a Background layer.

To Remove a Layer Style, do one of the following: right click on the *fx* symbol on the layer and choose Clear Layer Style, drag the *fx* symbol to the trashcan, click on the Effects drop down list and choose Clear Layer Style, from the Menu bar, choose Layer>Layer Style>Clear Layer Style.

To adjust a layer style, double click on the *fx* symbol on the layer in the Layers panel or from the Menu bar, choose Layer>Layer Styles>Style Settings.

Make adjustments by sliding the sliders or entering amounts for pixels or percentages in the appropriate boxes. Adjusting the lighting angle can be done by typing an angle into the Lighting Angle box, or rotating the angle in the circle. While the Style Settings dialog box is open, dragging the drop shadow will also produce the same effect. To change the color of a drop shadow, glow, or stroke, click inside the boxes shown circled and choose a new color.

I will normally start with a Low Drop shadow and change both the Size and Distance from 20 pixels to 5 pixels for most layers to make it look more realistic. If I'm really particular about the specific project, I'll change the Drop Shadow color from black to a darker color of my bottom layer. Watch the size of your shadows; it's easy to spot a new digi-scrapper by the size of their shadows!

To speed up my workflow after I have adjusted a Layer Style, I copy it from one layer and paste it onto the rest of my layers. To do this, click on the Effects panel drop down list, or right click on the Layer name (not the *fx* symbol) and choose Copy Layer Style. Select all of the layers you want to copy the Layer Style to, and then choose Paste Layer Style the same way. The Layer Style will remain copied until you close the program.

Stroke is similar to a Stroke (Outline) Selection, except that you cannot choose a location, which means it doesn't have square corners. There is no option to add this stroke to its own layer. But, because it's a Layer Style, you can remove it in the future without Undoing all of your prior steps.

To temporarily hide all applied Layer Styles, from the Menu bar choose Layer>Layer Style>Hide All Effects. To turn them back on, choose Layer>Layer Style>Show All Effects. To scale the size of the Layer Style on the selected layer, choose Layer>Layer Style>Scale Effects. To make the Layer Style a permanent part of the layer, Simplify the layer.

Tools, Tips, & Commands

The Toolbar, also known as the Toolbin, Toolbox or Tool panel is located on the left side of your workspace. There are tools that you'll probably never use on the Toolbar, and there are others you'll use over and over again. Forty nine tools are available in Full Edit, eight in Quick Edit.

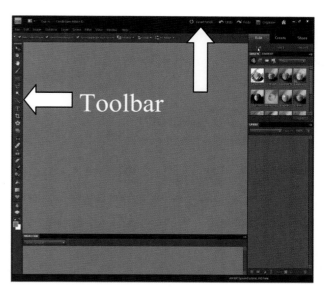

The Toolbar may be moved to another position on your screen if you prefer, but I like it right where it is. To move it, click on the two lines at the top of the panel, hold and drag it to a new location. To put it back, click on the Reset Panels button at the top of your screen at the top of the white arrow in the example on the right.

The Toolbar may also be displayed as a double wide column of tools. Drag the Toolbar away from the left side and double arrows (circled) will be displayed at the top of the panel. Click once, and it changes to a double wide panel, click again and it goes back to single wide.

If the Toolbar extends off the bottom of your screen and hides the Foreground and Background color chips, it would be helpful to change it to the double wide panel.

To close the panel, click the X in the top right corner. Click on Reset Panels to open it again.

Currently the Move tool (V) is selected (I know it's dark!). To select another tool, click on another icon on the bar.

A ◢ symbol on the bottom right corner of the tool icon indicates that there are other tools nested or hidden under the icon. Click and hold, or right click (Mac: Ctrl click) on the ◢ to display the other tools.

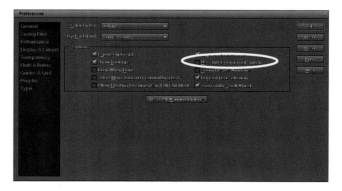

With a nested tool, hold the Shift key and type the tool's shortcut key to toggle through all of the nested tools. If this doesn't work for you, change your program preferences Edit>Preferences>General (Mac: Photoshop Elements>Preferences>General) and ✓ Use Shift Key for Tool Switch. This will work regardless of what tool you currently have selected.

Hold the Alt key (Mac: Opt key) and click the tool icon on the Toolbar to toggle through all of the nested tools.

Hold the Ctrl key (Mac: Cmd) to temporarily activate the Move tool (V) while any other tool is selected (with the exception of the Hand (H) or Shape tools (U)). This is a great shortcut I use all the time.

Toolbar Full Edit (Tools with * are also available in Quick Edit)

Move (V)

Zoom (Z)*

Hand (H)*

Eyedropper (I)

Marquee (M)
Rectangular & Elliptical

Lasso (L)
Regular, Magnetic, & Polygonal

Magic Wand (W)

Quick Selection Brush (A)*
Quick Selection & Selection

Type (T)
Horizontal, Vertical, Horizontal Mask, Vertical Mask

Crop (C)*
Crop & Recompose

Cookie Cutter (Q)

Straighten (P)

Red Eye Removal (Y)*

Spot Healing Brush (J)
Spot Healing & Healing Brush

Clone Stamp (S)
Clone Stamp & Pattern Stamp

Eraser (E)
Eraser, Background Eraser, Magic Eraser

Brush (B & N)
Brush (B), Impressionist (B), Color Replacement (B), Pencil (N)

Smart Brush (F)
Smart Brush, Detail Smart Brush

Paint Bucket (K)

Gradient (G)

Custom Shape (U) Shape Selection, Rectangle, Rounded
Rectangle, Ellipse, Polygon, Line, Custom Shape

Blur (R)
Blur, Sharpen, & Smudge

Sponge (O)
Sponge, Dodge, Burn

Foreground & Background colors
Swap Foreground and Background colors (X)

Default Colors (D)

Hover your mouse over a tool icon to see the name. The shortcut for the tool will appear in parentheses as shown in the example below.

To access Adobe Help for a particular tool, click on the blue tool word displayed while hovering over the tool icon. To turn this feature on or off, go to: Edit>Preferences>General>Show Tool Tips (Mac: Photoshop Elements>Preferences>General>Show Tool Tips.

Every time you select a different tool the Options bar will change to reflect the options available for that tool.

Pressing the Tab key will show/hide the Toolbar and all other panels.

If your Toolbar disappears, press the Reset Panels button at the top of your screen. If this doesn't work, choose Window from the Menu bar and make sure Tools has a ✓ by it.

Navigation and Measuring Tools

The Move Tool (V)

You will use this tool the most when digital scrapbooking. To temporarily activate the Move tool (V) while using another tool other than the Hand or Shape tools, click and hold the Ctrl key (Mac: Cmd key).

Use the Move Tool to:

Move/Copy photos or digital scrapbook elements onto a scrapbook page, card or other photo.
Move/Copy a selection to another location (this is helpful for putting your head on the body of a beauty queen).
Copy photos and elements-even in a straight line if you know the special trick.
Move your layers up and down in the Layers panel.
Align and space photos & scrapbook elements perfectly with the click of your mouse.

Auto Select Layer
Imagine your scrapbook page, click on a button (or any other layer) and you will be able to move the button, it's as easy as that. What you may not notice is that once you click on the button on the page, the button layer is highlighted in the Layers panel. Uncheck this option and you will need to click on the button layer in the Layers panel first to move it. Once this box is unchecked, you will not have to click directly on the button to move it which is helpful for small, hard to grab elements. To toggle on/off hold the Ctrl key (Mac: Cmd key) while the Move tool is selected.

Show Bounding Box
The Bounding Box shows the boundaries of the selected layer when the Move tool is active. Drag by the corner of the Bounding Box to activate the Transform tool to resize/transform a layer. The Bounding Box is shown below surrounding the green button.

Show Highlight on Rollover
Auto Select Layer must be checked for this feature to work. A bright blue rectangle will surround the layer you are hovering over, unless it is the Background layer or the selected layer. I un-check this option because I don't like it. The black button shows the highlight.

Arrange
Select a layer in the Layers panel, and then choose Bring to Front which will bring it to the top of the Layers panel.

For me, once I select the layer in the Layers Panel, it's just as easy to drag it to position myself, so I don't use this option.

Align
Want all the buttons to line up in a straight row? Select all of the button layers in the Layers panel and

choose an option. I chose Bottom Edges.

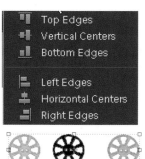

Distribute
Want the buttons evenly spaced apart? Select all layers in the Layers panel and chose an option. I chose Horizontal Centers.

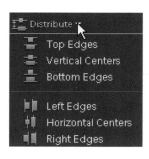

Tips for Using the Alignment Option
The key to getting this to work correctly is to highlight all of the layers you want to align in the Layers panel. Know that Photoshop Elements will choose the "most" image to Align to. For example, using the Bottom Edges option will align all of the buttons shown in the preceding example with the Bottom "most" button which is the black one.

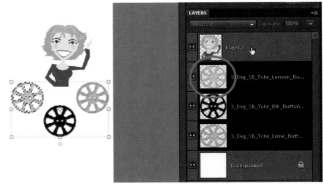

You may override the way that Photoshop Elements automatically aligns layers by selecting the layer you would like the other layers aligned with. To do this, Ctrl click (Mac: Cmd click) on the layer thumbnail (red circle) in the Layers panel. The layer will be selected and will be surrounded by marching ants. Now, because the yellow button layer is selected, Photoshop Elements knows you want to align the black and green button layers to the yellow button layer. Click on Align and choose an option.

Move/Copy a Photo or Scrapbook Element to another File
There are several different ways to add layers to a file to build a scrapbook page or other project. The next two examples are the methods my students have found the easiest.

#1
Make a new file and open the files you wish to use on your page using the methods outlined in *The Basics* chapter.

Double click on the first file you would like to add to your project so that it is displayed as the active image.

With the **Move tool** selected, click (in a solid area), hold, and drag the paper (or other file (s)) DOWN in the Project bin onto your plain white page. Do not click on a transparent area (checkerboard) or you will not be able to move the file.

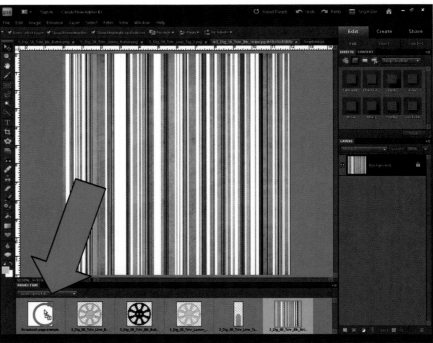

The cursor for Windows users only (sorry Mac users) will display a + sign on it once you touch the plain white page in the Project bin.

Release the mouse and the new layer will be dropped in the center of the plain white page. Multiple layers can be moved at one time if they are selected or linked in the Layers panel.

If you release the mouse before you've made contact with the file in the bin you will receive the message to the right. This has nothing to do with a locked layer and everything to do with the fact that you let go of your mouse too soon.

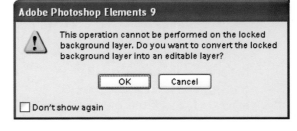

#2

Make a new file and open the files you wish to use on your page using the methods outlined in *The Basics* chapter.

Double click on your blank scrapbook page so that it is displayed as the active image.

With **any** tool selected, click, hold, and drag one of the **single layer** thumbnails in the Project bin UP onto the plain white file. Your cursor will turn into a closed hand and until you let go and for just a second you will see a rectangle as shown in the example. If you do this with a multi-layered file all of the layers will be flattened. Text files, like text paths will be simplified (rasterized), which makes them uneditable.

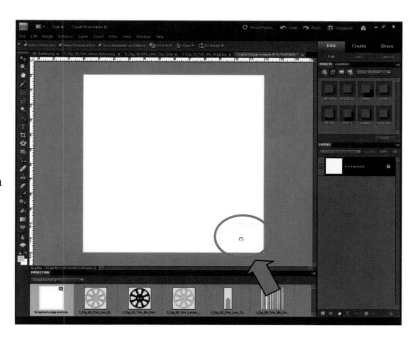

If you release the mouse too soon, you will have switched to the file you clicked on instead of dragging it onto the plain white layer. If you do this, try again.

This method will only work **correctly** if you are using Photoshop Elements 9, 8, or 5. If you have another version, use method #1.

Where are my Files?
When using either method, be aware that your files will be dropped right in the center of the page. In my example, the buttons are all the same size. When I look at my screen, I only see the yellow button because the black and green button are exactly the same size and are stacked directly below it.

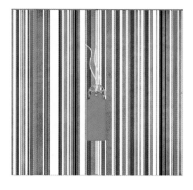

What's the Difference?

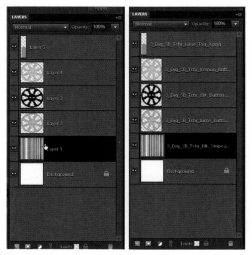

Dragging DOWN into the Project bin (#1) will name your layers with inventive names like Layer 1, Layer 2, etc. (left example).

Dragging UP from the Project bin (#2) will name the layers with the file names. If you routinely submit pages to online galleries, this can help you keep track of where you've purchased your supplies, providing that the designer has named their files with their name. You must save your project as a PSD file to save the layers.

Dragging files UP from the Project bin (#2) sometimes takes longer than dragging files DOWN, but you don't have to switch to the Move tool to do it.

Dragging files UP from the Project bin (#2) flattens multi-layered files and simplifies (rasterizes) text files, like text paths, which make them uneditable.

To me, method #2 has more advantages most of the time. Use either method you are most comfortable with.

Moving a Layer with an Adjustment Layer to another File
If you use tools like the Detail Smart Brush or Smart Brush tools to edit a photo, you may not realize that an Adjustment layer is automatically added to your photo. Adding Adjustment layers yourself, rather than editing directly on the photo is also a great way to edit photos, because you can make adjustments to your changes at any time.

The problem comes when you try to move the photo file including the Adjustment layer onto a scrapbook page or other project. If you drag the photo UP from the Project bin (Method #2 on preceding pages) all of the layers on the photo file will be moved onto the page but will be flattened, which may or may not be what you wanted, as shown in the example below.

 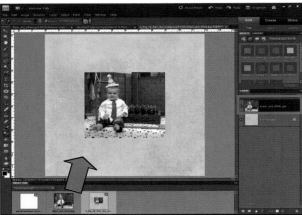

If you are completely done editing the photo, and don't plan to make any changes on the scrapbook page, the flattened layer is OK. Just remember to save the photo with all of its changes as a PSD file in case you need it later. However, if you think you may want to make future changes on the photo, it's better to have the separate Adjustment layer on your page.

In order to move the photo and Adjustment layer, you must select or link **all** layers on the photo file and drag DOWN onto the scrapbook page with the Move tool (V).

If the Adjustment layer includes a mask that is blank (all white, as shown in the example below), you will not be able to move it because it's transparent. Hold the Ctrl (Cmd) key as you drag, or uncheck the Auto Select Layer option on the Move tool Options bar and this will solve this problem.

Adjustment layers affect all layers underneath them. In the middle example shown below, you can see that the paper has been changed by the black and white Adjustment layer. To correct this, select the Adjustment layer in the Layers panel. From the Menu bar, choose Layer>Create Clipping Mask (Ctrl>G Mac: Cmd>G). Note: If you are using Photoshop Elements 7 or lower, choose Layer>Group with Previous (same command, new name).

  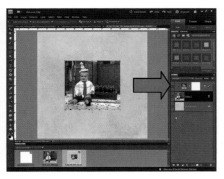

How to Move an Image on a Scrapbook Page

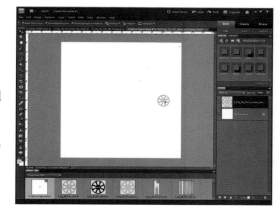

With the Move tool (V) selected, click, hold, and drag on any solid part (not transparent (checkerboard) area) of a layer to another area of the scrapbook page. You can also click on a layer and use the Arrow keys to nudge it where you want it, which is helpful for small items like brads. Every time you tap an Arrow key once, the layer moves one pixel. Hold the Shift and tap the Arrow key to move it ten pixels. If the Arrow keys don't work type Ctrl>T (Mac: Cmd>T) to activate the Transform tool and then you can nudge with the Arrow keys.

Several layers can be moved at one time if they are all selected or linked in the Layers panel.

Move/Copy a Selection from One File to Another

In this photo I've made a selection (marching ants) around my tea cup using the Magnetic Lasso (L) and Selection Brush (A) tools. How to use these tools is covered in the Selection Tools section of this chapter.

To move the tea cup onto a scrapbook page, select the Move tool, click inside the selection border and drag it down into the Project bin onto the scrapbook page. While it appears that you are cutting a hole in the tea cup photo, you are not. You are just copying the selected area to the scrapbook page and the tea cup photo remains unchanged. The cutout area is white, because that is the Background color. On the tea cup photo, tap the Esc key or Ctrl>D (Mac: Cmd>D) to Deselect the tea cup and remove the marching ants (selection border).

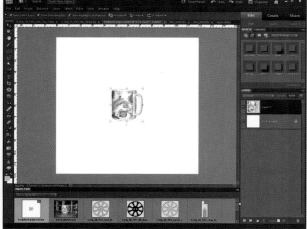

Moving a Selection Border

In this example I used the Elliptical Marquee tool (M) to make a selection, but I want to move the selection border (marching ants).

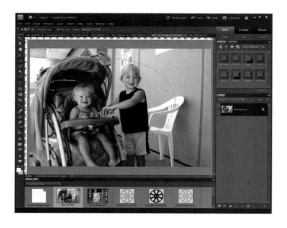

With the Marquee tool still selected, let go of the mouse and hover inside the selection. The cursor changes to the symbol shown on the right.

Click, hold, and drag inside the selection to move the selection border. To move the selection, switch to the Move tool and click, hold, and drag the selection to a new location.

Copying with the Move Tool

This trick is very useful when using scrapbook elements such as eyelets, brads, and buttons that you use multiple times on a scrapbook page. You will see how using this method can really speed up your workflow.

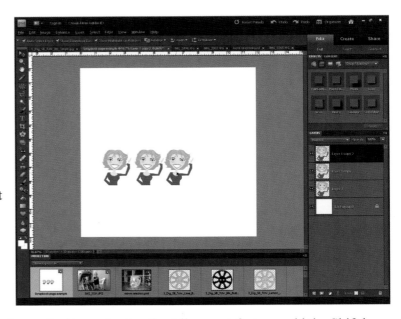

Drag an image (I'm using my logo) onto a scrapbook page and select the Move tool. Hold the Alt key (Mac: Opt key), click on the image to be duplicated, hold, drag, and release. Repeat for a new copy.

 As soon as you Alt click on the image, the cursor changes to a double headed arrow as shown on the left.

To drag out the new images in a straight line, and save the time of using the Alignment feature, add the Shift key along with the Alt key (Mac: Opt key) while clicking and dragging.

To copy the image and move it over one pixel so that you have a blur type effect, press the Alt key (Mac: Opt key) and one of the Arrow keys, depending on which way you want the image to move. It's an interesting effect, but not one that you may use. To copy and move the layer over ten pixels, Press Alt (Mac: Opt), Shift and Arrow key. Watch your Layers panel, because you'll probably end up making a lot more layers than you realize.

Arranging Layers and Editing Layer Styles with the Move Tool (V)

With the Move tool selected, right click (Mac: Ctrl click) on a one of the sizing boxes on the bounding box.

To change layer order choose: Bring to Front, Bring Forward, Send Backward, Send to Back. These options are also available on the Options bar under the Arrange Menu.

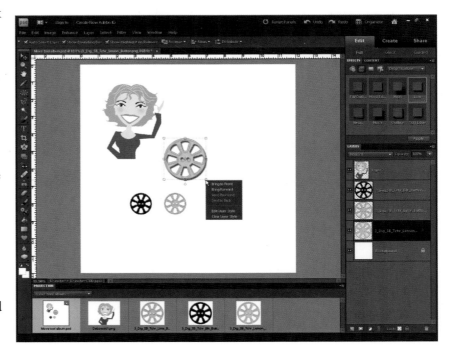

Choose Edit Layer Styles to display the Style Settings Dialog box to make changes to any Layer Styles applied to the selected layer. This may also be done by double clicking on the FX symbol on the selected layer.

Choose Clear Layer Styles to remove any Layer Styles applied to the selected layer. This may also be done by right clicking on the layer in the Layers Panel.

Transform Command (Ctrl>T) (Mac: Cmd>T)

The Transform tool/command can be used to resize/transform photos & scrapbook elements and/or rotate photos or scrapbook elements. To activate this command, choose Image>Transform, type the shortcut above, or activate it while using the Move tool (V), this is the method I use.

Drag an image onto a scrapbook page. Activate the Move tool and make sure that the Show Bounding Box option is checked. Hover over one of the four corner sizing boxes.

Notice that when you hover right over one of the sizing boxes, the cursor is a two headed straight arrow as shown in the example on the left. Click and the transform tool is activated. Click and drag a **corner** handle in or out to size the image proportionally. Dragging a side handle will also size the image but not proportionally. To look thinner and taller, drag a side handle inward slightly.

Hover the cursor out slightly past any of the sizing boxes and the cursor turns into a two headed rounded arrow. Click and the Transform command is activated. Click and drag to rotate the image from the center. Clicking on the handle located at the bottom center of the image will also allow you to rotate.

Once the Transform command has been activated, the Options bar changes from the Move tool Options bar to the Transform Options bar as shown below.

This is the same Menu bar that you will see if you choose Image>Transform>Free Transform (Ctrl>T), Skew, Distort, or Perspective.

To resize an image when another Tool is active, type Ctrl>T (Mac: Cmd>T) and resize/transform. As soon as you check the checkmark, you are automatically returned to the previous tool. If you are transforming a Shape layer, go to Image>Transform Shape>Free Transform.

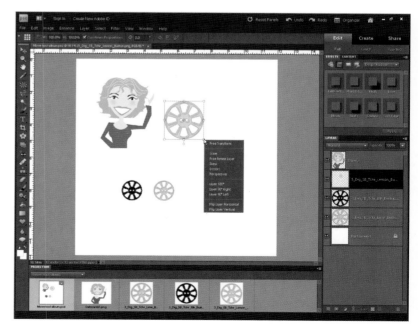

With the Transform tool active, right click (Mac: Ctrl Click) on a corner sizing handle and you'll also get additional options for Free Transform, Scale, Free Rotate Layer, Skew, Distort, Perspective, and Rotate Commands: Layer 180°, Layer 90° Right, Layer 90° Left, Flip Layer Horizontal, Flip Layer Vertical.

More Rotate Commands can also be found on the Image Menu.

How to Resize/Scale a Layer
Click on one of the **corner** sizing boxes and drag outward/inward to resize the image. By dragging one of the **corner** sizing boxes you are constraining the proportions, which means the image will not be distorted. Check the green ✓ when you're finished.

Notice that the width and height numbers change together on the Transform tool Options bar shown above. When dragging by the **corner** sizing box the ✓will remain in the Constrain Proportions box.

Drag by a **side** sizing box and the
Width and Height numbers no longer
match and the ✓ is removed.

I generally try not to resize my layers more than 120% to keep them from looking pixilated. Sometimes the image will appear fuzzy when enlarging until you check the green ✓.

To resize from the center, hold the Alt key (Mac: Opt key) and drag from a corner sizing box.

Once you click on any of the sizing boxes, whether you sized an image or not, you will need to commit your changes. This is the #1 reason for what appears to be a frozen program, but really isn't, once you commit the changes the program will work fine.

If you want to accept your change, you can either click on the ✓, tap your enter key once, or double click in the Bounding box. If you don't want the change, click on the ⊘ or tap the Esc button.

If you are sizing a photo with a mat, etc., you can select several layers in the Layers panel or link several layers together by linking them in the Layers panel. They will be sized and/or rotated at the same time.

Rotate a Layer on a Scrapbook Page
There are two ways to rotate images with Photoshop Elements. Choose an option from the Image>Rotate menu shown on the right, or use the Transform tool to rotate.

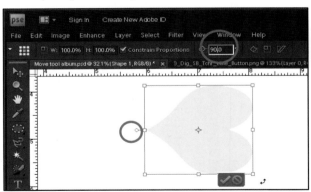

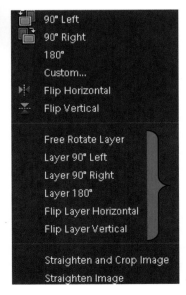

When using the Image menu to rotate, be sure to read exactly what you've chosen to rotate. If I don't actually read my choices, I will normally pick one of the actions from the top section of the list, which will rotate my entire document. If you only want to rotate one or more layers, select the layer(s) and then choose one of the commands that has the word "layer" in it in the middle section of the list shown above.

To rotate using the Transform tool, click or hover on the rotation handle on the bottom center of the Bounding box (it will change to image on right) or hover over a corner sizing box until you see the two headed rounded arrow and click, hold, and drag. As you rotate, the angle will change on the Options bar. If you know you want to rotate the layer 90°, type this amount on the Options bar (shown circled).

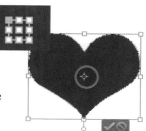

Reference Point Box

By default, all images will rotate from a center anchor point (shown circled in red).

To change the anchor point, click on one of the nine boxes in the Reference Point Box on the Transform tool Options bar. In this example, I've selected the top right box so the image will rotate from the top right corner. Every time an image is rotated, the rotation point is returned to the center default location.

Do You Really Want to Rotate That Image?

When building a scrapbook page, it makes the page look better if the subjects are looking into the page instead of off of the page. Rotating photos is usually an easy fix. Pay attention before you rotate a photo, and make sure there will be no tell tale signs that it's been rotated.

In this photo, both of my sons have on clothing with writing on it, which is now backwards. This is a pretty obvious example, but I see this problem a lot!

Skew, Distort, & Perspective

Choose Image>Transform to activate these commands, or with the Transform tool active, right click (Mac: Ctrl Click) on a corner sizing handle and choose Skew, Distort, or Perspective. When working with a Shape layer, choose Image>Transform Shape from the Menu bar.

If you have disabled the Show Bounding box option on the Move tool Options bar, the Bounding box will appear when using these commands. When these commands are applied to a Background layer it is automatically changed to a regular layer.

If you're not sure which command to use, try each one and Undo if you don't like it.

Skew slants the layer vertically or horizontally. Skew can be applied to all types of layers. To activate Skew, click on the icon on the Transform tool's Options bar, choose Image>Transform>Skew, or hold the Ctrl> Shift (Mac: Cmd >Shift) keys while dragging a sizing box.

Distort twists and stretches the layer. To activate Distort, choose Image>Transform>Distort or hold the Ctrl key (Mac: Cmd>key) while dragging a sizing box. A type layer must be Simplified (Layer>Simplify Layer) prior to using the Distort command.

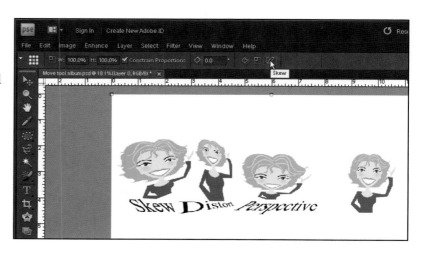

Perspective makes the layer appear to have three dimensions. Choose Image>Transform>Perspective, or hold the Ctrl>Alt>Shift (Mac: Cmd>Opt>Shift) keys while dragging a sizing box. A type layer must be Simplified (Layer>Simplify Layer) prior to using the Perspective command.

Zoom Tool (Z)

Plain and simple, I rarely use this tool. I found out early when teaching classes that this tool frustrates new Photoshop Elements users. This tool can be found in Full and Quick Edit and in some filter dialog boxes.

In the *First Things First* Chapter, you should have set up your mouse scroll wheel so that you can scroll in and out. This is what I use rather than the Zoom tool. Students in my classes also like the scroll wheel better than the Zoom tool. After scrolling or zooming to show the full screen, double click on the Hand tool (H) icon or use the shortcut Ctrl>0 (Mac: Cmd>0), this is the number zero not the letter O. If you use the wrong shortcut, the Open menu will be displayed.

When using another tool: Ctrl>+ (Mac: Cmd>+) zooms in where you've clicked and Ctrl>- (Mac: Cmd>- zooms out. Hold the Ctrl key (Mac: Cmd key) and drag it over the percentage box above the Project bin or type the percentage yourself and click on the image. To zoom into a specific area, hold the Cmd key (Mac: Cmd key) and spacebar and click and drag out a window with your mouse.

How to use the Zoom Tool:
Click to zoom into a specific area. To zoom out, click the Zoom out button shown below. Hold the Alt key (Mac: Opt key) to switch between zooming in and out rather than clicking on the Options bar. Click and drag out a box with your mouse to zoom into a specific area. Double click on the Zoom tool icon on the tool bar to display the image at 100%.

Zoom In
Click the area to zoom into. The more you click, the closer you zoom in.

Zoom Out
Click to zoom out. The more you click, the farther you zoom out.

Zoom Percentage
This amount is automatically filled depending on the amount of zoom selected. You may manually enter any amount between 1% and 3200% by typing it in the box.

Resize Windows to Fit
Because I work with only one image window open at a time, it doesn't matter if this setting is on or off. In the *First Things First* chapter, I unchecked Allow Floating Documents in the Preferences dialog box and chose to display only one window at a time.

Zoom All Windows
If you want to work with multiple windows, choose this option to see changes in all windows.

1:1 – Actual Pixels
Click on the Options bar, or choose View>Actual Pixels or type the shortcut Ctrl>1 (Mac>Cmd>1) to see the online size of the image. This is very helpful when working on images that will be seen on the web.

Fit Screen
Click on the Options bar, or choose View>Fit on Screen or type the shortcut Ctrl>0 (Mac: Cmd>0) to fit the image to the full screen size. This setting allows you to see the entire image at the largest size possible. I use this shortcut all the time.

Fill Screen
Click on the Options bar to fill the screen with the image in a large size. This basically zooms in for you, but you will not see the entire image.

Print Size
Although it's not foolproof, click on the Options bar, or choose View>Print Size to see the image in its print size.

Cool Zoom Trick

Have you ever wanted to see the project you're working on in two different views? Maybe you would like to zoom in to edit a photo on a scrapbook page, but still want to see the scrapbook page full size without having to zoom in and out constantly.

You can do it! Open the image. From the Menu bar choose View>New Window for (your file name).

There will now be two images displayed in the Project bin with the same file name. Zoom in close on one of the files to see the details you can't see in the fit on screen setting. Double click on the thumbnail in the Project bin to switch between views. Make changes on one file and it's automatically changed on the other file.

Notice that the thumbnails in the Project bin look exactly the same, even though on one of them I have zoomed in very close.

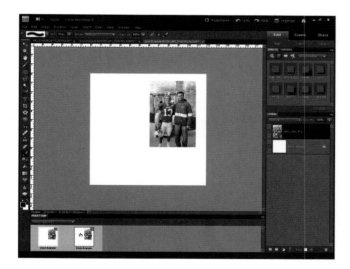
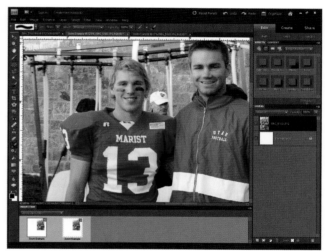

Other Ways to Move Around

On the bottom right area of your keyboard are several keys that can also help you move around. Be aware that to use these keys, you may have to use the Shift or Function (Fn) keys. My desktop computer requires me to also hold the Shift key while using the Home, Page Up, End, and Page Down keys. My laptop requires me to hold the Function (Fn) key while using the Home and End keys.

Page Up/Page Down moves screen up.
Ctrl>Page Up/Page Down moves screen left or right (Mac: Cmd>Page Up/Page Down).
Home key moves to the upper left corner, think of this as the beginning (Home) of the file.
End key moves to the lower right corner, think of this as the end of the file.

Hand Tool (H)

The Hand tool is used to move/pan around an image that is larger than the image window. This tool can be found in Full and Quick Edit, and in some filter dialog boxes. Double click on the Hand tool icon on the Toolbar to fit the image to the screen.

I do use this tool from time to time, but I save time by holding the spacebar to temporarily activate this tool instead of changing tools. Once the spacebar is released, you are automatically returned to the previously selected tool. Once the Hand tool is selected, the cursor will change to a hand symbol.

When using the Hand tool you can temporarily switch to zoom in by holding down the Ctrl key (Mac: Cmd key) or zoom out by pressing Ctrl>Alt (Mac: Cmd>Opt).

Scroll All Windows
Choose this option to see changes in all windows if you work with multiple windows, which I do not. To use multiple windows, click on the Arrange button (shown circled below) near the Photoshop Elements icon at the top of the screen.

Actual Pixels
Click on the Options bar, or choose View>Actual Pixels, or type the shortcut Ctrl>1 (Mac>Cmd>1) to see the online size of the image. This is very helpful when working on images that will be seen on the web.

Fit Screen
Click on the Options bar, or choose View>Fit on Screen, or type the shortcut Ctrl>0 (Mac: Cmd>0) to fit the image to the full screen size. This setting allows you to see the entire image at the largest size possible. I use this shortcut all the time.

Fill Screen
Click on the Options bar to fill the screen with the image in a large size. This basically zooms in for you, but you will not see the entire image.

Print Size
Click on the Options bar, or choose View>Print Size to see the image in its print size, but it's not foolproof.

Navigator

The Navigator isn't really a tool, but I include it in this section because it's like the Hand and Zoom tools combined.

There is no Navigator icon on the Toolbar. To display or close the Navigator, choose Window>Navigator from the Menu bar, or press F12 at the top of your keyboard. The Navigator will be added to your Panel bin. To remove the Navigator from the Panel bin, click on the ◢ on the top right area of the panel and choose Close.

When you first open the Navigator, you may not notice the red rectangle around your photo because it's at the edges of the photo. Adjust the zoom, and the cursor becomes an arrow. The Navigator's red rectangle will enlarge and reduce your active image view to only what's inside the Navigator's rectangle. If you want to change the location on your image, click inside the red rectangle and move it to another location of the image. When you click inside the red rectangle your cursor becomes a hand.

The default color for the Navigator rectangle is red. If you want to change this color, click the ▾ button on the top right corner of the Navigator panel, and then choose Panel Options. Changing the color of the rectangle is the only option. Click the drop down arrow for the default colors, or, click in the big color block, or choose Custom to pick a custom color.

Eyedropper Tool (I)

With this tool you have the ability to copy/sample a color taken from another image or a color swatch, something you can't do in traditional scrapbooking. You can copy/sample from an image you have opened in Photoshop Elements, from the internet, or other program. You can also create a set of custom color swatches that can be saved for future use.

While using the following tools, hold down the Alt key (Mac: Opt key). This activates the Eyedropper tool to change the Foreground color, but only until you release the Alt key (Mac: Opt key).

Cookie Cutter (Q)	Color Replacement (B)	Paint Bucket (K)	Straighten (P)
Pencil (N)	Shapes (U)	Brush (B)	Gradient (G)

With the Eyedropper tool selected, hold the Alt key (Mac: Opt key) to change the Background color.

To select a color from the active image, click on the Eyedropper tool icon and click on the color to copy/sample. It is helpful to zoom into the area to choose a color, because once you zoom in you will see that there are many shades of the same color that you didn't notice before you zoomed in. Once the mouse is released, the Foreground color at the bottom of the Toolbar changes.

To select a color from an image in the Project bin, click anywhere in the active image and drag it down to the image in the Project bin. Let go of the mouse and the Foreground color will change. Because it's difficult to get a good color sample from a tiny thumbnail, it would be better to select the image and then switch back to the original image you were working on.

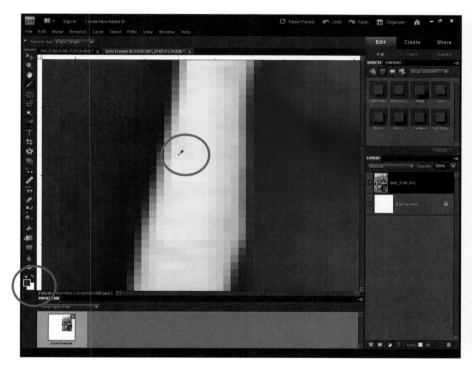

Sample Size
The Eyedropper tool Options bar has only one option which is Sample Size. Change this option on the Options bar or right click (Mac: Ctrl click) on the image when the Eyedropper tool is active, as shown on the next page.

The default Sample Size is Point Sample. Click on the image and the Foreground color will change to the exact color of the point you clicked on.

Choose the 3 x 3 Average Sample Size and Photoshop Elements will average a block of nine pixels (3 x 3 = 9). This is a good change to make and I have listed it in the *First Things First* Chapter.

Choose the 5 x 5 Average Sample Size and Photoshop Elements will average a block of 25 pixels (5 x 5 = 25).

By changing the Sample Size setting for the Eyedropper tool, you are also changing the way the Magic Wand tool selects color.

Choose a Color from another Program

To choose a color from another program or the internet, you must be able to display both programs on your monitor. One way to do this is to click on the Restore button on the top right corner of the Photoshop Elements screen.

Windows Internet Explorer 8 Screenshot

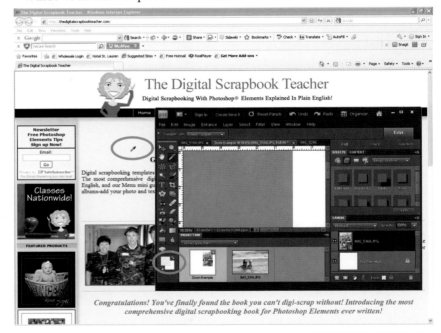

Open the other program at the same time. If the Photoshop Elements screen is too large, click on one of the corners and drag inward to shrink it down.

Click on the Eyedropper tool icon on the Toolbar. Click on the Photoshop Elements screen, hold, and drag to the area on the webpage or program that you would like to copy, release the mouse and the Foreground color will change to the color you selected. To save as the Background color, hold the Alt key (Mac: Opt key)

To put Photoshop Elements back to full screen, click on the same button in the top right corner which will now say Maximize when you hover over it.

Copy Color as HTML

Locate this option by right clicking on your image when the Eyedropper tool is activated as shown above. You can then either paste (Edit>Paste or Ctrl V (Mac: Cmd>V)) this information onto your page using the Text tool or onto a word document. This is the hexadecimal color formula that would be used for Web projects. An example of exactly what it prints out is: color="#72c1d0".

Foreground & Background Color Swatch

The Foreground & Background color swatch is located at the bottom of the Toolbar. The top swatch is the Foreground color, and the bottom swatch is the Background color.

To display the default colors (Foreground-Black, Background-White) type the letter D, or click on the tiny black and white swatch located above the swatch.

To swap the Foreground and Background colors, type the letter "X" (except when you have the Text tool active), or click on the rounded two headed arrow located above the swatch.

Use the Eyedropper Tool (I), Color Picker or Color Swatches to change the Foreground and Background colors.

Foreground Color
The Foreground color sets the color for the Brush, Color Replacement, Pencil, Paint Bucket, and Shape tools. The Gradient tool, set to default setting, uses the Foreground and Background colors. To fill a layer or selection with solid Foreground color, use the shortcut Alt>Backspace (Mac: Opt>Delete). To fill a layer with transparency with the Foreground color, use the shortcut Shift>Alt>Backspace (Mac: Shift>Opt>Delete).

Background Color
The Background color is shown when you use the Eraser tool to erase on a Background layer. It is the default color for increasing your canvas size when choosing Image>Resize>Canvas Size. The Gradient tool, set to the default setting uses the Foreground and Background colors. To fill a layer or selection with solid Background color, use Ctrl> Backspace (Mac: Cmd>Delete). To fill a layer with transparency with the Background color, use the shortcut Shift>Ctrl>Backspace (Mac: Shift>Cmd>Delete).

Using the Color Picker
To use the Color Picker to change the Foreground/Background color, click inside the appropriate swatch and the Color Picker will appear.

If you don't see the color you want, click in the color slider to be directed towards the color you want, or drag the white triangles up or down the bar. Click in the Color field box or on the bar to select a new color. A small circle marks the spot where you chose the color. The top color is the new color, and the bottom color is the current color. Click OK to confirm the change and the swatch will change at the bottom of the Toolbar.

You may also manually enter a color by typing in the Hexadecimal Number, or Hex # in the bottom box. Enter this number in the box to the right of the # symbol. Designers use these numbers, and if you're working with someone on a joint project, it would be helpful to use the Hex # so that your colors will match. Be aware that your colors will match as long as you print both at the same place and at the same time.

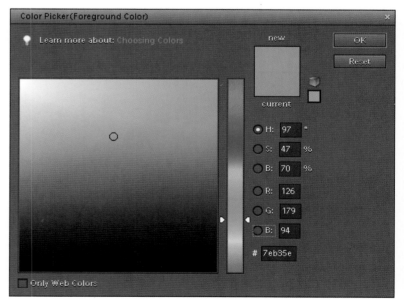

HSB Color
HSB stands for Hue, Saturation, Brightness. Saturation and Brightness are entered as percentages (%). Hue is entered as an angle degree (°) that matches a spot on the color wheel. This is sometimes referred to as Hue, Saturation, Intensity (HSI), and is shown below circled in white.

RGB Color
RGB stands for Red, Green, Blue. Values from 0 to 255 are entered in the appropriate boxes as shown below circled in black. The lower the number, the less of that color. The higher the number, the more of that color. For example, a true red would have the following settings Red 255, Green 0, Blue 0. The settings for white are Red 255, Green 255, Blue 255. The settings for black are Red 0, Green 0, Blue 0. If all of the settings are the same number between 1 and 254 you will get varying shades of gray. The higher the number, the lighter the gray. The lower the number, the darker the gray.

Hexadecimal Values
This is a color number that is used to identify an exact color, and is shown below circled in red. Using the example of the color white: the RGB settings are Red 255, Green 255, and Blue 255. The Hexadecimal Value for White is ffffff. The Hexadecimal Value for Black is 000000.

If you are taking a class, your instructor may refer to a color as Hexadecimal #, Hex #, or just #. This is the number they are referring to. If you have a Hex # you can enter it in by typing the number in the circled box in my example.

You don't need to understand how they come up with the numbers, (because I sure don't) but just understand that if you want to match a color with someone you're working with on a joint project, use the same Hexadecimal Values for the predominant colors in your project. Use the same printer and your colors will match. Because all printers print a little bit differently, even though you use the same Hexadecimal Values, your colors may not match exactly because they were printed on two different printers, even if they are the same model.

Only Web Colors
If the selected color is not safe for the Web, you will see a multi-colored box that says "Warning not a web safe color" when you hover your mouse over it. Hover your mouse over the bottom box and it says "Click to select web safe color". If you check Only Web Colors, you won't have to worry about this!

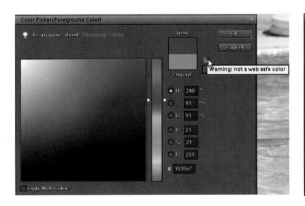
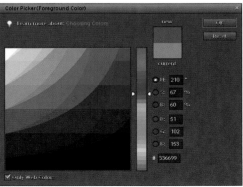

Viewing Color Values with the Info Panel
The Info Panel can be added to the Panel bin by
choosing Window on the Menu bar and clicking on
Info. Click the Reset Panels button to remove it from
the Panel bin, or choose Close when clicking on the ▾
symbol on the top right side of the panel.

With the Info Panel open (shown circled in red), and
any tool selected, drag the cursor over the paper and the
RGB numbers will change in both readouts.

In my Info Panel Options menu, the default options are
set as RGB Color Readout for the first box and Web
Color for the Second Color Readout. To change these
settings, click on the ▾ symbol on the top right corner
of the Info panel and choose other settings.

The box on the area with the (+) indicates the x and y coordinates of the cursor. My example shows X 37.896
and Y 24.399. In plain English this means X is the distance from the right edge and currently I am 37.896 inches
from the right edge of the image, Y is the distance from the top edge and currently I am 24.399 inches from the
top edge. I know my measurement is in inches because in the options I've chosen my Mouse Coordinates Ruler
Unit as Inches.

If I had drawn a selection with the Marquee tool the box with the W & H would show the size of a selection
drawn. Read about the Marquee tool in the Selection tools section.

Color Swatches
To View the Color Swatch panel, choose Window>Color Swatches, the panel will appear
on your Panel bin. To remove it from the Panel bin, click on Reset Panels, or choose
Close when clicking on the ▾ on the top right side of the panel.

Clicking in a color box will change the Foreground color. Ctrl click (Mac: Cmd click) in
a color box will change the Background color.

Clicking on the drop down arrow next to Default will show the
other Color Swatch libraries that are preloaded.

Click on the ▾ on the top right side of the panel and choose a
different display setting. I chose Large Thumbnail.

Make Your Own Color Swatch
Open the Color Swatches panel and change the display option to
Large List. Open the image that you want to use for your color
swatch. This can be a photo, scrapbook paper, etc.

Select the Eyedropper tool by clicking on it on the Toolbar, or typing the
shortcut I. Click once on a color to add to the swatch set. The Foreground color
changes to the sampled color. Hover over the Swatch panel and the cursor turns
into a paint bucket. Click and a dialog box (shown on the next page) appears
with the new color swatch and the name Color Swatch 1. Type a name for the
swatch in the blue highlighted area.

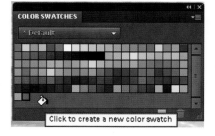

Another way to make a new swatch is: click on the Create New Color Swatch from Foreground button on the bottom right of the Color Swatches Panel, as shown circled to the right. A new color swatch has been added at the bottom of the list. If you want to rename the Color Swatch double click on the color name and type a new name.

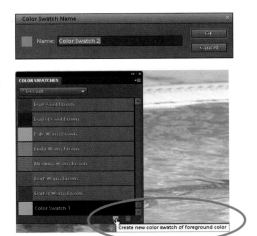

Still, another way to make a new swatch is to click to choose a color and choose New Swatch after clicking on the ▼at the top of the Swatch panel. Type the swatch name in the blue highlighted area.

Saving a Custom Set of Swatches
If you take the time to make a custom set of swatches, you probably will want to save them for future use.

To save a swatch set, click on the ▼at the top of the Color Swatches panel and choose Preset Manager.

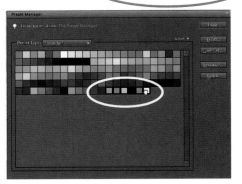

When the Preset Manager opens, the Save Set button will be grayed out.

Click on the first swatch you made, which is near the end of the set. Hold the Shift key and click on the last swatch you made. The selected swatches will have a dark outline around them (shown circled in white). Click on the Save Set button.

When the Save box opens, type a name for the set in the File name box. I named my set Swimming Pool Swatches. Click on the Save button. This set is being saved in the Photoshop Elements program Preset folder. If you are concerned about saving this for future use, you may also want to save this file in another location such as a Swatches folder that you make yourself and back up regularly.

When you return to the Preset Manager, click the Delete Button to delete the new swatches that were added to the existing swatch set. Once the new swatches are deleted, click the Done Button.

Restart Photoshop Elements for the new swatch to show in the Color Swatches drop down list.

Remove a Color Swatch
To remove a single color swatch, Alt click (Mac: Opt click) on the swatch and the cursor turns into a pair of scissors and deletes the swatch. Every time you delete a swatch, the trashcan on the bottom right area of the panel lights up for just a second. You may also drag a swatch to the trashcan, but this is more labor intensive because you must confirm each swatch that is deleted by clicking OK in the dialog box.

To delete an entire Swatch Library, delete the file from the program Presets folder. More information can be found about this in the *Where Do I Install the Extras* Chapter.

Make a Color Swatch of 256 Colors to Match an Image

Most images will be in RGB mode, and to make a swatch this way the image must be in Index Mode. If you are using an image from the web that has been saved as a GIF file, you do not have to change the image to Indexed Color Mode. If the image is RGB, open (File>Open) the image and duplicate it (File>Duplicate) and choose Image>Mode>Indexed Color.

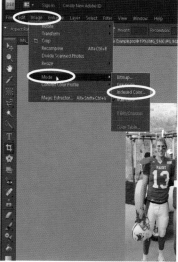

Change the settings to Palette: Local (Perceptual), Colors: 256 (can be lower if desired), Forced: None, Transparency: checked, Matte: None, Dither: None Click OK.

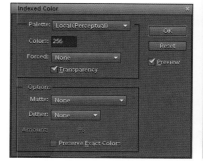

Choose Image>Mode>Color Table

Click the Save button.

Type a File name. Click the Save button. Click OK when you return to the Color Table.

If you are concerned about saving this for future use, you may also want to save this file in another folder in a different location that you made yourself and back up regularly, such as a Swatches folder.

 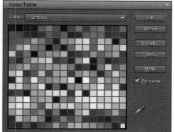 

Close the image you used to make the Color Table. Say "No" to save changes.

Choose Window>Color Swatches and click the ▾ at the top of the Color Swatches panel and choose Replace Swatches. The Load dialog box will be displayed. Don't panic when you don't see the Color Table you just made. Click the drop down list for Files of type (red arrow) and choose Color Table (*.ACT).

Click on the file name to load. Click the Load button and the swatches will be displayed.

Color Tables (.ACT file) are saved in a different format than Color Swatches (.ACO file). If you decide to switch back and use one of the swatches like the default Color Swatch, the new Color Table will disappear from the list and will need to be reloaded.

To avoid this, display the Color Table and save it as a Color Swatch set as explained on the previous page in the *Saving a Custom Set of Swatches* section.

Some great color swatch websites are: www.kuler.adobe.com, www.colorschemer.com, and www.colourlovers.com.

Selection Tools

What's a Selection Anyway?

In techie terms, a selection is an area you select with one or more of the Selection tools, and coincidentally is surrounded by a selection border. You should see the look on a newbie's face when I say that in a hands-on class! Don't panic and stop reading now because you really need to learn how to use Selection tools! Whenever I teach a hands-on class, the first thing everyone wants to know how to do is how to cut something out of a photo. To do this you will probably use one of the Selection tools.

When you make a selection, you select only the pixels (part of the image) that you want to work with. Normally, any changes you make are applied to an entire layer. With a selection, changes are made just to the selected area while the rest of the layer remains unchanged. The selection becomes the active area of the layer. You can add a filter, duplicate, rotate, size, change the color, paint, lighten or darken a selection.

In the top examples, a selection was made with the Rectangular Marquee tool and a brush was stamped inside the selection. The tea cup was selected with the Magnetic Lasso and Selection Brush tools so that it could be cut out from the background and added to a project. The paper in the second row shows how the Magic Wand tool can be used to change color in part of an image. The original paper, from Amy Teets' Super Sonic kit which can be found on the *Photoshop Elements - Basics & Beyond DVD*, is the green one. These are just some of things can be done with selection tools.

Selection Border
Surrounding the selection is a selection border which is commonly called marching ants, dancing ants, or a flashing border of black and white lines. In the first example, the selected area is the inner square. The outside square is selected in the second example, and the tea cup is selected in the photo. I know this because I can still see the selection border, although is a little bit more difficult to see in the paper examples.

Which Selection Tool to Use?
If you're a gardener, you know that some tools work better for trimming plants than others do. The same is true for Selection tools. You can make a selection with any of the Selection tools; the key is to learn which tool will do the best job, in the least amount of time. To make a vignette, choose the Elliptical Marquee tool. To select a red apple sitting on a white plate, choose the Magic Wand tool. To put my head on a beauty queen's body, I'll probably have to use the Magnetic Lasso and Selection Brush tools and spend a little bit of time fine tuning it. As you experiment with these tools you'll quickly find your favorites, you'll also learn that many times you need to use more than one Selection tool to make a good selection.

Good, accurate selections take time and practice. With practice, you'll learn which selection tools work better to make a particular type of selection. With more experience you will begin to shoot your photographs differently. If I am truly going to put my head on the body of a beauty queen, I want to be able to select my head reasonably easy. Taking my picture in front of a white wall would make more sense than taking my picture in a group of people at a party. The white wall would make it easy to select me with the Magic Wand tool, otherwise to select my head from a busy background it's going to take some time with the Magnetic Lasso tool.

In cases like the white wall example, it's easier to select the part of the layer that you don't want and then invert your selection. In the example of the tea cup on the preceding page, my selection is the cup inside the marching ants. If I were to inverse (Select>Inverse), I would be selecting the area around the tea cup. The marching ants would still be around the cup, but they would also surround the edge of the photo.

To make a soft edged selection use Anti-Alias, Feather, or use a soft brush with the Selection Brush tool (A).

Once you make a selection, you can save it forever as long as you save your image as a PSD file. You can also temporarily hide your selection in the event you find it distracting.

Stray pixels are areas of an image that are left over after you cut (extract) something from an image. Often times you thought you made a nice clean selection, but they show up when you print the image. There are several ways to check for stray pixels. Depending on the colors of your image, putting the selection on top of a black or white background temporarily can show stray pixels that need to be erased. Another way to spot stray pixels is to apply a High Drop Shadow to the selection. Still another way is to add a Stroke (Outline) Selection. All of these methods are shown in the *Cool Stuff with Strokes* chapter.

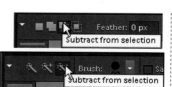

Take photos specifically to use as embellishments on your scrapbook pages. This will save you money on supplies, and make extra special pages at the same time.

Selection Tool Options

Listed below are the choices you will find on a selection tool Options bar. Not each command will be found on each tool.

New Selection-This is the default setting when you first use a selection tool. Every time you click, or click and drag, a new selection is made.

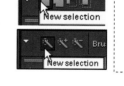

Add To Selection-After you have created a selection, choose Add to Selection to add more to it. You must click outside the first selection to add to, it but the selections do not have to touch. To activate the shortcut, create the first selection, and then hold the Shift key. As shown circled in the example, when Add to Selection is active, you will notice that a + (plus sign) has been added to the cursor.

Subtract From Selection- After you have created a selection, choose Subtract from Selection to remove some of it. You must click inside the first selection to subtract from it. To activate the shortcut, create the selection first and then hold the Alt key (Mac: Opt) key. As shown circled in the example, when Subtract from Selection is active you will notice that a - (minus sign) has been added to the cursor. I use this option often when creating borders, as shown in the Border #2 example that follows in this chapter.

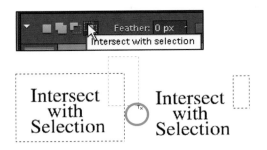

Intersect with Selection-As shown in the example on the right, use this option when you want to select an area that intersects between two selections. To activate the shortcut, create the selection first and then hold the Shift and Alt keys (Mac: Opt>Shift) keys. When Intersect with Selection is active, you will notice that an (x) has been added to the cursor. This option is not available on the Selection Brush or Quick Selection tools.

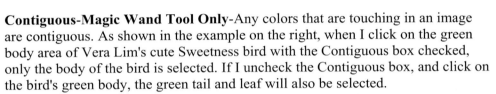

Anti Alias-To smooth the edges of curved selections so that they aren't jagged, check the box for this option. It is not needed for rectangular selections, so it is grayed out when the Rectangular Marquee tool is active. I keep this box checked all the time. This option is not available on the Selection Brush or Quick Selection tools.

Auto Enhance-Quick Selection Tool Only-Selecting this option automatically refines the edges of the selection. If you aren't happy with the result, uncheck this option and try Refine Edge.

Brush-Click on the brush drop down list to choose a different brush to use for the Selection Brush or Quick Selection tools. To make a soft feathered selection, choose a soft round brush. Enter a size for the brush, up to 2500 px, or use the Right Bracket key] to enlarge the brush, or the Left Bracket key [to make the brush smaller.

Contiguous-Magic Wand Tool Only-Any colors that are touching in an image are contiguous. As shown in the example on the right, when I click on the green body area of Vera Lim's cute Sweetness bird with the Contiguous box checked, only the body of the bird is selected. If I uncheck the Contiguous box, and click on the bird's green body, the green tail and leaf will also be selected.

Contrast-Magnetic Lasso Tool Only-To specify the sensitivity to edges in an image, enter a percentage between 1% and 100%. A higher number is for edges that contrast a lot from the area around them, a lower number is for edges that don't contrast as much. The default setting is 10%.

Feather-To soften, fade, and blur the edge of a selection, feather it. A selection can be feathered 0.2-250 pixels. To feather a selection, choose one of the following options: From the Menu bar, choose Select>Feather, use the shortcut Alt>Ctrl>D (Mac: Opt>Cmd>F), or right click on the selection and choose Feather. The dialog box shown above will appear when feathering with these methods. Enter an amount and click OK. Experiment with the amount of feather you apply, if you don't like it Undo and try a different amount.

The Options bar for the Marquee and Lasso tools also have a box where you can enter a feather amount, but I don't recommend it because I've had a lot of students come to class thinking their Marquee tool was broken. Their problem was that they forgot they entered an amount in the feather box on the Options bar. Feathering this way doesn't clear automatically like the Select>Feather command does.

The example on the right shows the effect of feathering an oval selection made with the Elliptical Marquee (M) tool. In the top example I did not feather the selection, it looks like I used an oval paper punch to punch out the selection. In the bottom example, I feathered the selection 200 px to produce a soft dreamy effect. Feathering also helps blend images together. Feathering selections was used many times in vignette examples in the *Cool Stuff with Photos* chapter.

Frequency-Magnetic Lasso Tool Only-To specify how far apart the anchor/fastening points are automatically set, enter a number between 0 and 100. The lower the Frequency number, the farther apart the anchor/fastening points are, the higher the number, the closer they are to each other. Anchor/fastening points are marked by small squares. The last point added is a solid square; the previously added points are a square outline. The default setting is 57.

Hardness-Selection Brush Tool Only-Hardness sets the opacity and the edge sharpness, and is similar to feathering. Another way to adjust the hardness of a selection is to use a soft edged brush.

Mode-Normal-Elliptical & Rectangular Marquee Tools Only-Normal allows you click and drag a selection of any size.

Mode-Fixed Ratio-Elliptical & Rectangular Marquee Tools Only-Fixed Aspect Ratio lets you click and drag out a selection with a perfect ratio. Entering the same number in the width and height boxes will produce a square or circle, depending on whether the Elliptical or Rectangular Marquee tool is selected. If you know the exact size of a selection you want, choose the Fixed Size option.

Mode-Fixed Size-Elliptical & Rectangular Marquee Tools Only-Enter the size of a selection you want to make, and with a click of the mouse, it's done. Right click in the width or height boxes to display a drop down box that lets you specify a different unit of measurement, like inches, pixels, points, etc.

Mode-Selection-Selection Brush Tool Only-Selection is the default mode. Once you click and drag, your selection is surrounded by a selection border (marching ants).

Mode-Mask-Selection Brush Tool Only-To cover the selected areas with a red mask, choose the Mask option. Sometimes it's easier to use the mask to make a good selection, because the red overlay makes it easier to see spots you have missed. When Mask is selected, two more options appear on the Options bar: Overlay Opacity and Overlay Color. The default setting for Overlay is 50% which normally works well. Red is the default color. To change the color, click inside the box and choose another color when the color picker dialog box is displayed. If you are working on an image with a lot of red in it, it might be useful to change the color of the overlay, but normally I leave mine set at red. You can switch between Selection and Mask to make a selection.

Refine Edge-To smooth, feather and contract or expand the edge of a selection, click on the Refine Edge button and the Refine Edge dialog box will appear. Click on one of the five icons to change the view of the selection to a mask, black background, etc. This option is available from the Menu bar by choosing Select>Refine Edge.

Tablet Pressure-Magnetic Lasso Tool Only-To control how far the Magnetic Lasso tool searches for edges choose this option. To decrease the edge width, press harder.

Tolerance-Magic Wand Tool Only-The default Tolerance setting is 32. The range of settings is from 0-255. If you enter 0, the Magic Wand will choose only the exact color you have clicked on. If you enter 255, the Magic Wand will select every color in the image. If you are having trouble making a selection with the Magic Wand tool, adjust the Tolerance setting. As shown in the example on the right, when I click on the green body area of Vera Lim's cute Sweetness bird, with the Tolerance setting lowered to 5 (Contiguous is unchecked in this example), only a portion of the green body is selected. To select all of the green body, I will need to increase the Tolerance setting.

Sample All Layers-To select matching color pixels from all of the layers in your image, choose this option. Using this option would be helpful if you decided you want to change the color of several elements on a project.

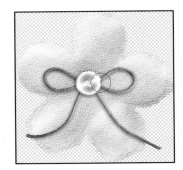

Width-Magnetic Lasso Tool Only-To detect images a certain pixel width away from your cursor, enter an amount between 1 and 256 pixels in the Width box. As seen in the example on the right, tapping the Caps Lock key allows me to see the width distance by changing the cursor from the Lasso symbol to a circle with a + inside it, as I try to extract the button from Farrah's Creations Sweet Dreams cute flower. The default setting is 10 pixels.

Rectangular and Elliptical Marquee Tools (M)

The Marquee tools are among the easiest selection tools to use. They are used to create rectangular or oval selections. To toggle between the Rectangular and Elliptical Marquee tools, type the letter M. This works for all tools that have nested tools as, long as "Use Shift key for Tool switch" box is unchecked in the General Preferences (Ctrl K, Mac: Cmd>K).

Marquee tool Options bar information can be found on pages 79 to 81.

How to use the Marquee Tools:

To create an oval selection, select the Elliptical Marquee tool from the Toolbar. Click, hold and drag the mouse. Your starting point will become a corner and you may drag in any direction (the example below shows clicking and dragging down towards the right). To create a perfect circle selection, click and hold the Shift key as you drag out a selection. To drag an oval selection from the center, click and hold the Alt key (Mac: Opt key). As shown in the example below, to create a perfect circle selection from the center, hold the Shift and Alt key (Mac: Shift and Opt key), as you drag out a selection.

To create a rectangular selection, select the Rectangular Marquee tool from the Toolbar. Click, hold and drag the mouse as you drag. Your starting point will become a corner; you may drag in any direction. To create a perfect square selection, click and hold the Shift key as you drag out a selection. To drag a rectangular selection from the center, click and hold the Alt key (Mac: Opt key). To create a perfect square selection from the center, hold the Shift and Alt key (Mac: Shift and Opt key) as you drag out a selection.

Once you release the mouse, a selection border will appear (marching ants). To add to, subtract from, or intersect with the selection, choose the appropriate box on the Options bar.

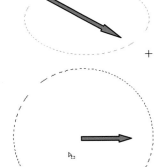

When making a square or circle selection, let go of the mouse before you let go of the Shift key. When creating a selection from the center, let go of the mouse before you let go of the Alt key (Mac: Opt key).

To reposition the selection border **before** you let go of the mouse, hold the Spacebar and drag. To reposition the selection border **after** you let go of the mouse and while the Marquee tool is still selected, click inside the selection and move it. The cursor will change as shown in the circle example on the right.

To remove the selection border (marching ants), from the Menu bar, choose Select>Deselect (Ctrl>D, Mac: Cmd>D), or tap the Esc key which will work for most people.

Use the selection you created to create borders, vignettes, photo mats, crop images, and more. Inverse a selection you made to select the outer edges of an image to darken or recolor it.

Lasso and Magnetic & Polygonal Lasso Tools (L)

There are three different Lasso tools: Lasso (Regular), Magnetic Lasso, and the Polygonal Lasso, they all use the (L) shortcut. All three Lasso tools allow you to make freehand selections by clicking and dragging around an area. Use your mouse or, to make a more precise selection, use a Wacom Tablet. I use the Lasso tools to cut people and objects out of a photo so that I can add them to another photo. I also cut out objects to be used on my scrapbook pages or other projects as embellishments.

The Lasso tools work best with well defined edges and color definitions. Remember, good selections take practice! The Lasso tool cursor looks like a lasso that you would use to rope a bull at a rodeo! Using the Magnetic Lasso tool takes a lot of practice and is probably the most frustrating Photoshop Elements tool to master. Just remember, a rodeo rider had to practice a lot to use his lasso well. You won't be any different.

Lasso tool Options bar information can be found on pages 79 to 81.

Regular Lasso & Polygonal Lasso tool Options bar

Magnetic Lasso Options bar

How to Use the (Regular) Lasso Tool (L)

Select New Selection, and make any other changes necessary on the Options Bar. Click, hold, and drag around an area. Once the mouse is released, a selection is created. If you are not happy with your selection, tap the Esc Key and start over. To toggle back and forth to the Polygonal Lasso tool (L) which makes straight line segments, hold the Alt key (Mac: Opt key) and release the mouse. Click where you want your straight line to end (watch the cursor change, the option bar will not change). Release the Alt key (Mac: Opt key) to return to the regular Lasso tool.

I normally use the Lasso tool and/or the Polygonal Lasso tool to create a very fast selection, like an alpha or other embellishment from a contact sheet, as shown on the next page.

How to Use the Polygonal Lasso Tool (L)

Select New Selection, and make any other changes necessary on the Options bar. Click once to set an anchor point, and click again where you want your first straight line segment to end, setting another anchor point. Keep clicking to add straight line segments. To remove an anchor point, tap the Delete or Backspace key. Toggle back and forth to the Lasso Tool by holding the Alt key (Mac: Opt key) and dragging the mouse (watch the cursor change, the Option Bar will not change). To close a selection, click on the starting point (a circle will appear when you hover over it). To close a selection if you are not over the starting point, Ctrl click (Mac: Cmd click), or double click.

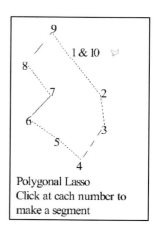

Polygonal Lasso
Click at each number to
make a segment

If you are not happy with your selection, to cancel at anytime and start over, tap the Esc key.

How to Use the Magnetic Lasso Tool (L)
You will either love or hate the Magnetic Lasso tool (L). The Magnetic Lasso clings/snaps to high contrast edges on your image. A white golf ball on bright green lawn would be the perfect image to use the Magnetic Lasso on. The Magnetic Lasso will cling to the edge of the golf ball while you drag around it because of the dramatic color differences. Dragging slowly usually works better than dragging quickly. Using a tablet works better than using a mouse or touchpad.

Select New Selection, and make any other necessary changes on the Options bar. Click once to set your anchor point, drag your mouse without clicking and the Magnetic Lasso should start to set anchor points automatically. The number of anchor points added will depend on the Frequency setting on the Options bar, the higher the number, the more anchor points added. The anchor points snap to the edges where color changes, like the edge of a white golf ball on the green lawn example. Click if you want to set an anchor point. Tap the Backspace or Delete keys to remove an anchor point. Hold the Alt key (Mac: Opt key) if you want to toggle on/off the Polygonal Lasso tool to make straight line segments (watch your cursor because the Option Bar will not change). To close a selection, click on the starting point (a circle will appear when you hover over it). To close a selection if you are not over the starting point, Ctrl click (Mac: Cmd click), or double click.

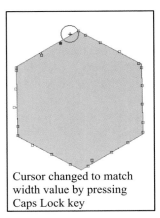

Cursor changed to match width value by pressing Caps Lock key

If you are not happy with your selection, to cancel at anytime and start over, tap the Esc key.

Lasso Tips
Zoom in with the mouse scroll wheel or Zoom tool (Z) to help make a good selection. It's best to have your image in full screen (Ctrl>0, Mac: Cmd>0) or closer. If you come to the edge of your screen and can't see where to go from there, hold the Spacebar so the Hand tool (H) is temporarily selected and you can move your image around in the screen. Let go of the Spacebar and the Lasso tool is still active.

To toggle your cursor on/off to a crosshair instead of the Lasso tool, press the Caps Lock key (Lasso & Polygonal Lasso only). Pressing the Caps Lock key while the Magnetic Lasso tool is active will change the cursor to a circle with a + in the center that shows the area of edge detection.

Press the Backspace key to remove an anchor point. Click the mouse to add an anchor point (Magnetic & Polygonal Lasso Only).

Ctrl click (Mac: Cmd click) or double click to close a selection border without clicking on the starting point of the selection. Use the Selection Brush tool (A) to fine tune selections. The Esc key will delete any full or partially drawn selections.

If you are working with items like alphas or other embellishments that are all on one layer and want to select only one item, make a selection around it with the Lasso tool. In this example I used the Polygonal Lasso tool to create a selection around the A from Amy Teets' Super Sonic kit.

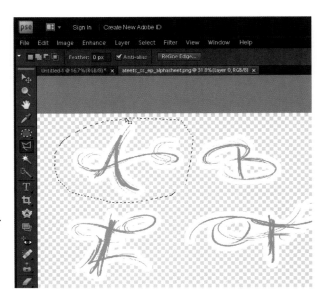

Now select the Move tool (V), click **on** the A (not on a transparent area), and drag it down onto your scrapbook page or other project in the Project bin.

To make your selection conform (stick to it) to your element exactly, hold the Ctrl key and press the up Arrow key (↑).

To save your selection for later use, from the Menu bar, choose Select>Save Selection and name it. Save the file as a PSD file so that you will be able to use the selection again.

To save the selected image by itself on a transparent layer, delete the unselected areas. The fastest way to do this is to put the selection on its own layer. To do this, type the shortcut Ctrl>J (Mac: Cmd>J). Delete all the other layers and save your image as a PSD or PNG file to keep the transparent background.

The Magic Wand Tool (W)

Lasso tool Options bar information can be found on pages 79 to 81.

The Magic Wand tool (W) makes selections based on similar colors. Click on an image with two solid colors and it selects one color perfectly. Click on an image with many different colors or shades of the same color and unless you make some adjustments on the Options bar, it might not work as well.

The Magic Wand tool is affected by the Sample Size setting on the Eyedropper tool Options bar. If the Sample size is set at the default setting of Point Sample then the Magic Wand tool will search by just one pixel at a time instead of a 3 x 3 or 5 x 5 Average. If you're having trouble with the Magic Wand tool, try adjusting this setting.

How to Use the Magic Wand Tool (W)
From the Toolbar select the Magic Wand tool, the cursor will change to a magic wand. Click on a color in an image to select pixels of the same color range, like a stripe in a paper. If Contiguous is checked on the Options bar, only pixels of the same color that are touching will be selected. If Contiguous is not checked, all pixels of that color will be selected. Increasing the tolerance setting will increase the shades of color selected. Check the Sample All Layers box to select pixels from all layers, otherwise only pixels from the active layer will be selected. As shown in the example on the right, the selection you make will be surrounded by a selection border (marching ants). Usually you will need to click your mouse more than once to complete the selection you want.

As shown in the example above from The Orient kit from Anita Richards, which can be found on the *Photoshop Elements - Basics & Beyond* DVD, I wanted to select the pretty flowers and bird. I started with the Magic Wand tool set at the default settings (shown above) and unchecked the Contiguous box. I zoomed in and clicked once on the design, which selected some of it. To select more, I clicked on the Ad to Selection button on the Options bar and clicked again. If I want to use just the design on a page, I can duplicate the selection by typing the shortcut Ctrl>J (Mac: Cmd>J) which copies the selected area onto its own layer.

The Selection Brush Tool (A)

The Selection Brush tool (A), creates a selection by painting with a brush. The selection can also be displayed as a mask. This tool is available in Full and Quick Edit and is nested with the Quick Selection tool. This is one of the selection tools that I use the most. As shown in the example on the next page, I often use the Magnetic Lasso tool (L) to make a selection and then use the Selection Brush tool to clean it up.

Selection Brush tool Options bar information can be found on pages 79 to 81.

How to Use the Selection Brush Tool (A)
Click, hold, and drag/paint over an image to create a
new selection. The selection will be marked with a
selection border (marching ants) if you have
Selection (default setting) selected as the Mode on
the Options bar. Click and drag again to add more to
the selection automatically. To subtract from the
selection, click on the button on the Options bar or
hold the Alt key (Mac: Opt key) and click on the
image again.

With Mask Mode selected on the Options bar, click
and drag/paint over an area you wish to **exclude**
from the selection. It will be marked with a red
mask (or other color you have chosen for the mask).

To make a larger selection when you drag/paint, increase the size of the brush by one of the following methods:
click on the word Size to activate a scrubby slider, click on the Size box drop down list and slide the slider, type
a new number in the Size box, click on the brush drop down list and choose a new brush, or tap the Right
Bracket key several times (my favorite method).

As shown on the previous page, the default brush is a 13px hard brush. To create soft edged selections that are
easier to blend, choose one of the Soft Round brushes from the brush drop down list or change the Hardness
setting on the Options bar. If you make a selection using a hard brush and later wish you had used a soft edged
brush, just feather the selection (Select>Feather) or refine the edge (Select>Refine Edge).

To draw a selection in a straight line, hold the Shift key as you drag your mouse or click,
and then Shift click at the end of your selection. As shown in the example on the right, to
remove an area from selection in a straight line, Alt click (Mac: Opt click) on one side of
the selection, and then Alt>Shift (Mac: Opt>Shift click) click on the other side.

The Quick Selection Tool (A)

The Quick Selection tool is like combining the best of the Magic Wand and Selection Brush tools into one tool.
This tool is available in Full and Quick Edit, and is nested with the Selection Brush tool.

Quick Selection tool Options bar information can be found on pages 79 to 81.

How to Use the Quick Selection Tool (A)
Click, hold, and drag/paint over an image to create a new selection. The tool will select a larger area than the
brush size, because it's selecting areas of matching color and texture. The selection will be marked with a
selection border (marching ants). Click and drag again to add more to the selection automatically. To subtract
from the selection, click on the button on the Options bar or hold the Alt key (Mac: Opt key) and click on the
image again.

To make a larger selection when you drag/paint, increase the size of the brush by clicking on the brush drop
down list and make changes, or tap the Right Bracket key several times (my favorite method). You may also
adjust the hardness of the brush from the brush drop down list. From the Options bar, click on the Auto Enhance
button to automatically smooth edges or on the Refine Edges button to smooth them manually.

Magic Extractor

The Magic Extractor isn't actually a tool, but it can be useful in making extractions. One nice thing about using this command is that the instructions for using it are written right across the top of the dialog box.

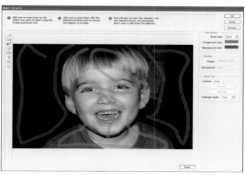 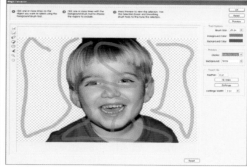

How to Use the Magic Extractor

Open an Image. From the Menu bar choose Image>Extractor to display the Magic Extractor dialog box. Click on the Foreground Brush located at the top of the Magic Extractor Toolbar and paint over the areas of the image you want to keep. The default color for the Foreground brush is red, but it can be changed by clicking in the Foreground Color box on the right of the screen.

Click on the Background Brush tool, which is the second tool on the Magic Extractor Toolbar, and paint over the areas of the image you want to remove. The default color of the Background Brush is blue, but it can be changed by clicking in the Background Color box on the right of the screen.

As shown above on the right, to see a preview of the changes, tap the Preview button. Use the Foreground and Background brush tools to add or delete areas of the image and tap the Preview button again.

To reset the image, hold the Alt key (Mac: Opt key) and tap the Cancel button. Use the Smoothing Brush or the Touch up section to fine tune the extraction. The Preview box allows you to change the Background to help you spot imperfections. Use Fill Holes to fill holes that were removed in error. Defringe will smooth jagged edges, as will the Smoothing Brush. Set this between 1 and 50 pixels.

Other Selection Commands, Shortcuts, and Tips

Cropping with a Selection Tool

Once you drag an image onto a project, you're not able to crop it with the Crop tool (C) because it will crop all the layers of the document. If you do it by mistake, you will be left with the cropped photo and all the other layers cropped to the same exact size. It's usually easier to crop your photos before you drag them onto your project, but because you don't always have a clear vision of the final result, sometimes that's not feasible.

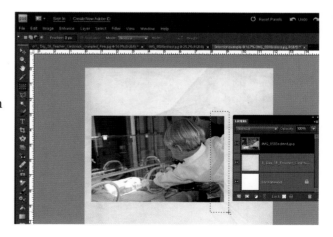

After you have moved the image onto a new file, select an area that you want to remove with a selection tool, tap the Delete key and the selected area will be deleted as long as it is not the Background layer. If you do this on a Background layer, the selected area will be filled with the Background color.

In the example above, I selected an area on the right side of the photo to crop off with the Rectangular Marquee tool (M). Tapping the Delete key or Edit>Cut from the Menu bar will remove the selected area. If I had chosen Image>Crop from the Menu bar, the only part remaining would be the area selected inside the rectangle, just as if I used the Crop tool.

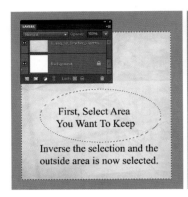

To keep only part of a layer, make a selection around the part that you want to keep, inverse the selection Shift>Ctrl>I (Mac: Shift>Cmd>I) and tap the Delete key to delete it. Verify that you are on the right layer in the Layers panel when you are doing this, or you may crop the wrong layer.

Another way to crop with a selection is to make a copy of the selected area (Ctrl>J, Mac: Cmd>J). This puts the copy on its own layer. Hide the original layer if you will need it again, or delete it. I use this technique a lot when I use a single paper to make several photo mats.

Select All-Use this when you want to select everything on a layer like the entire photo. To Select All, choose one of these options : From the Menu bar, choose Select>All, use the shortcut Ctrl>A, (Mac: Cmd>A), or Ctrl click (Mac: Cmd click) on the layer thumbnail.

Deselect-Once you make a selection you eventually have to get rid of it. To Deselect, choose one of these options: From the Menu bar, choose Select>Deselect, use the shortcut Ctrl>D (Mac: Cmd>D), right click on the selection border and choose Deselect, or tapping the Esc key will work for most Photoshop Elements users.

Reselect-If you remove your selection and then decide you still want it, you're not out of luck. To Reselect, choose one of these options: From the Menu bar, choose Select>Reselect, use the shortcut Shift>Ctrl>D (Mac: Shift>Cmd>D), or you can also try Undo Ctrl>Z if you Deselected recently.

Inverse-When you Inverse a selection, you swap the selected area with the unselected area. As shown in the example above, first I selected the oval area, and then I inversed the selection so that I could delete the outside area, leaving me with just the oval. To Inverse a selection, choose one of these options: From the Menu bar, choose Select>Inverse, use the shortcut Shift>Ctrl>I, (Mac: Shift>Cmd>I), or right click on the selection border and choose Select Inverse. To save time, select the easy parts of an image and then inverse it.

Selecting Layers-To select the contents of a single layer, Ctrl click (Mac: Cmd>Click) the layer thumbnail. To add to the current selection, Ctrl>Shift click (Mac: Cmd>Shift click) the other layer thumbnail(s). To subtract from your current selection, Ctrl>Alt click (Mac: Cmd>Opt click) on the other layer thumbnail(s). To Intersect with your current selection, Ctrl>Shift>Alt click (Mac: Cmd>Shift>Opt click) on the other layer thumbnail(s).

Select All Layers-To select all layers but the Background layer, choose one of these options: From the Menu bar, choose Select>All Layers, or click on one layer in the Layers panel and Shift click on the last layer to select them all (you can include Background layer this way).

Deselect Layers-To deselect all layers, from the Menu bar choose Select>Deselect Layers, and no layer will be selected in the Layers panel.

Select Similar Layers-To select all layers that are similar, choose from the Menu bar, Select>Similar Layers. For example, if you click on a Text layer, all of the Text layers will be selected.

Defringe Layer-If you are left with a fringe or halo around the edges of your selection after you move it to another location, you might want to try defringing the selection. Defringing does not remove pixels from your selection, but changes their color so that they blend better with the image you've placed them on top of. If you selected a white golf ball from a green lawn, you may have some extra green pixels attached to your golf ball. If you were to place the selection of the golf ball on a photo of a blue sky you would see the green around the edge of the ball. Defringing will take the green around the white golf ball and blend it to match the sky better.

To Defringe, first deselect, and then from the Menu bar choose Enhance>Adjust Color>Defringe Layer. Experiment with the width, but I usually use 2 pixels.

Refine Edge-To smooth, feather and contract or expand the edge of a selection, click on the Refine Edge button available on several of the selection tool's Options bars. Clicking on one of the circled icons gives you the opportunity to preview the selection on black, white, as a mask, etc. which can be very helpful. Once the Refine Edge dialog box appears, enter changes and click OK.

Border #1-To add a soft edged border that gently fades into your image, select the image (Ctrl>A, Mac: Cmd>A). From the Menu bar, choose Select>Modify>Border and enter a width for the border size and tap the OK button. Create a new blank layer by clicking on the new layer icon at the bottom of the Layers panel, or type the shortcut Shift>Alt>Ctrl>N (Mac: Shift>Opt>Cmd>N). With the new transparent layer selected, from the Menu bar choose Edit>Fill>Selection and choose a color or pattern you want for your border. Click OK. Since you put your border on its own layer, you can adjust the opacity and add blending modes and filters to it at any time.

Border #2-To create a border that does not have a faded edge, use the select the image (Ctrl>A, Mac: Cmd>A). Select the Marquee tool (M) and hold the Alt key (Mac: Opt key), or from the Options bar choose Subtract from selection. Click and drag out an area that you want removed from your selection to make the frame/border. Using grids or guides may help you keep the border even.

Create a new blank layer by clicking on the new layer icon at the bottom of the Layers panel, or type the shortcut Shift>Alt>Ctrl>N (Mac: Shift>Opt>Cmd>N). With the new transparent layer selected, from the Menu bar choose Edit>Fill>Selection and choose a color or pattern you want for your border. Click OK. Since you put your border on its own layer, you can adjust the opacity and add blending modes and filters to it at any time.

Stroke (Outline) Selection-To put a solid outline around a selection or layer, first select the layer (Ctrl>A, Mac: Cmd>A). Create a new blank layer by clicking on the new layer icon at the bottom of the Layers panel, or type the shortcut Shift>Alt>Ctrl>N (Mac: Shift>Opt>Cmd>N). From the Menu bar, choose Edit>Stroke (Outline) Selection.

Enter a width for the stroke in pixels or inches. If you wanted to add a ¼ inch stroke on a 300 ppi scrapbook page or other project, you would enter 75 px or .25 in. The color will default to the Foreground color. To choose another color, click inside the color box to display the Color Picker dialog box.

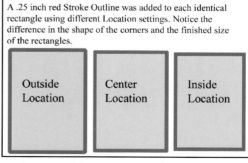

A .25 inch red Stroke Outline was added to each identical rectangle using different Location settings. Notice the difference in the shape of the corners and the finished size of the rectangles.

Outside Location   Center Location   Inside Location

If you are outlining an image with a rectangular corner and wish to maintain a crisp corner, you will need to choose Inside Location. As shown in the example below, choosing Center and Outside Location will slightly round the corner. If you are outlining an image without rectangular corners, you may choose any one of the locations. Inside Location puts the stroke on the inside of the selection which may cover up part of your image. Center puts the stroke centered on the selection border (marching ants), and Outside puts the stroke on the outside of the selection. The Stroke Outline follows the outline of your selection border exactly.

You have the opportunity to change the Blending Mode and Opacity on this dialog box, but since you're putting the Stroke Outline on its own layer, you can change that later if desired. Uncheck the Preserve Transparency box because we are putting our stroke on a transparent layer. Click OK and your Stroke Outline is placed on its own layer.

It is a good idea to link the Stroke Outline layer with the layer that you're outlining. Select both layers and link them by clicking on the Link icon at the bottom of the Layers panel.

To feather a Stroke Outline, make a selection, from the Menu bar choose, Select>Feather and enter an amount to feather the selection. Create a new transparent layer, and from the Menu bar choose Edit>Stroke Outline, enter a size and choose a color. Depending on the size and color of the stroke, this may produce a dark vignette or inked edge type of effect.

Because most digital cameras do not take photos in standard photo print sizes like 4" x 6", it's important that if you intend to print just a photo (not add it to a scrapbook page or other project), that you crop it first with the Crop tool to the correct size, and then add the stroke. To add a white edge around your photos like photo labs offer, add a 50 px white stroke.

For other ways you can use the Stroke (Outline) Selection command read the *Cool Stuff with Strokes* chapter.

Smooth-To clean up jagged edges on selections made by the Magic Wand tool (W), choose from the Menu bar, Select>Modify>Smooth. This command smoothes out edges by finding similar colored pixels by the number of pixels you entered in the dialog box. You can also smooth a selection made by the Rectangular Marquee (M) tool to make a rounded rectangle selection by entering 100 px (the highest amount).

Expand-To expand a selection by an amount of pixels that you enter (100 maximum), from the Menu bar, choose Select>Modify>Expand. If the selection has rounded edges it keeps the same shape, which makes this a good choice for making photo mats. If your selection has rectangular corners, they will be rounded.

Contract- To contract a selection by an amount of pixels that you enter (100 maximum), from the Menu bar, choose Select>Modify> Contract. When you contract a selection with rectangular corners they stay square, unlike the expand command. Contracting your selection by one pixel will sometimes smooth out a rough selection that you've made with a tool, like the Magic Wand (W) or Magnetic Lasso (L).

Grow-To add more of the same contiguous color pixels, from the Menu bar, choose Select>Grow. Your selection might not keep the same shape depending on the image you are working on. No dialog box is displayed after you select Grow and Photoshop Elements automatically selects the same colored contiguous pixels.

Similar-To add all pixels of the same color (not just the contiguous ones like Grow does) select from the Menu bar Select>Similar. Your selection might not keep the same shape depending on the image you are working on. No dialog box is displayed after you select Similar; Photoshop Elements automatically selects the same colored pixels.

Save Selection-To save a selection so that you can use it at another time, make a selection with one of the selection tools. From the Menu bar, choose Select>Save Selection. Type a name for your selection and click OK. The selection is saved only if you save your file as a PSD file. More than one selection can be saved for an image, and you can also Add to, Subtract from, or Intersect with a selection. I have saved selections on the Motion Blur and Blur Distracting Photo files included on the *Photoshop Elements - Basics & Beyond* DVD that are shown in the *Cool Stuff with Photos* chapter.

Load Selection-To Load a Selection that you previously saved, open the image, and from the Menu bar, choose Select>Load Selection. If you have more than one selection saved for this image, to find the one you are looking for click on the drop down list. You are also given the opportunity to Invert the selection by checking the box. If you want to Add, Subtract, or Intersect with the previously saved selection, you can draw a new one and then Load your selection and choose one of those options.

Delete Selection-To delete a selection you no longer need, open the image and then choose from the Menu bar Select>Delete Selection and click OK.

Fill Selection/Fill Layer- From the Menu bar, choose Edit>Fill Selection or Layer to fill a selection/layer with Foreground color, Background color, Color (from Color Picker), Pattern, Black, 50 % Gray, or White.

If you have an active selection, you will be filling a selection instead of a layer and the dialog box will say Fill Layer, even though the command said Fill Selection. I suggest adding a new transparent layer to help with editing along the way. If you do this, you will need to uncheck the Preserve Transparency box on the Fill Layer dialog box.

The shortcut to fill a selection/layer with the Foreground color is Alt>Backspace (Mac: Opt>Delete). The shortcut to fill a selection/layer with the Background color is Ctrl>Backspace (Mac: Cmd>Delete).

Paste into a Selection- If you are using a single layer template with overlapping openings it's much easier to use the Paste into Selection command than try to fit them underneath the template. To Paste into a Selection: Make a selection on the image. In the example of a PNG scrapbook page template, click once in an opening with the Magic Wand tool (W). Create a new blank layer by clicking on the new layer icon at the bottom of the Layers panel or type the shortcut Shift>Alt>Ctrl>N (Mac: Shift>Opt>Cmd>N).

Select the photo or other image that you want to paste by choosing from the Menu bar Select>All or Ctrl>A (Mac: Cmd>A). From the Menu bar, choose Edit>Copy or use the shortcut Ctrl>C (Mac: Cmd>C). Go back to the original image and from the Menu bar choose Edit>Paste into Selection, or use the shortcut Shift>Ctrl>V (Mac: Shift>Cmd>V) to paste the image into the selection.

Hide Selection-It may be helpful to hide a distracting selection but still keep it active. This command is a little bit quirky. The key is to remember to hide it and not to switch to another tool that cancels your selection. I usually can hide/show my selection and use other tools except for the Type tool (T). If you have hidden a selection and are experiencing problems with other tools check to see you have hidden a selection which may be causing the problem. It is probably best to save a selection rather than hide it. To hide/show a selection use the shortcut Ctrl>H (Mac: Cmd>H).

Move a Selection Border-To move a selection border (marching ants) one pixel at a time use the Right, Left, Up, Down Arrow keys. Hold the Shift key to move ten pixels each click. This moves only the selection border (marching ants) not the selected image.

To drag selection borders made with the Lasso (L), Marquee (M), or Magic Wand (W) tools, select New Selection on the Options bar, and click inside the selection and drag it.

To Move a Selection-To move a selection one pixel at a time activate the Move tool (V) and use the Right, Left, Up, Down Arrow keys. Hold the Shift key to move ten pixels each click, or drag it with the cursor. This moves the marching ants and the selected image you've selected.

Type Tools

Horizontal &Vertical Type and Horizontal & Vertical Type Mask Tools (T)

To add journaling or other information to your projects and scrapbook pages you will need to use one of the Type tools. With Photoshop Elements, you can add beautiful professional looking text every time. Never again worry about your special markers drying up or running out of letter stickers. While your special markers never exactly matched the colors of your supplies, with Photoshop Elements you can easily create a perfect match. You can cut text out of photos or digital scrapbooking papers, and create patterns from text that you type. This tool may be called the Type or Text tool in various tutorials you read.

There are four different Type tools: Horizontal Type, Vertical Type, Horizontal Type Mask and Vertical Type Mask, they all use the same shortcut (T). To toggle between the Type tools, type the shortcut T. Toggling works for all tools that have nested tools, as long as "Use Shift key for Tool switch" box is unchecked in the General Preferences (Ctrl K, Mac: Cmd>K).

One thing to remember is that if you get stuck while using the Type tool and can't get the program to move on, you probably haven't checked the green checkmark ✓ on the Type tool Options bar to confirm the text.

Horizontal Type Tool (T)-This is the normal Type tool you'll use most of the time to type from left to right. Using the Horizontal Type tool is similar to using a word processing program or typing an email.

Vertical Type Tool (T)-This tool is designed for Chinese and Japanese Characters and types from top to bottom. Sometimes you can use vertical text for a title, but it's often difficult to read.

Horizontal Type Mask Tool (T)-Instead of typing text, this tool types a selection of horizontal type. When active, as soon as you click on your image to type, the page turns pink. The type appears as part of your image until you check the green checkmark ✓, and then it turns into a selection (marching ants). The selection can be used to cut letters out of images. To do this, see the step by step instructions in the *Cool Stuff with Text* chapter.

Vertical Type Mask Tool (T)-This tool works the same as the Horizontal Type Mask tool except that it adds text vertically.

Font Family-To choose a font for your text, click on the Font drop down list and click on a font. Myriad Pro is the default font, and will appear when you reset the Type tool. The Font drop down list shows all of the fonts that are installed on your computer. Fonts come automatically installed on your operating system and are also installed when you install other programs like digital scrapbooking or card-making programs. Thousands of fonts are available from stores and on the Internet and can be easily installed by following directions from places like *www.Dafont.com*.

A shortcut to find the font you are looking for is to double click in the font box to select the current font name (it will turn blue) start typing the font name. When the font name appears tap the Tab key to move to the next box on the Options bar. Type just a single letter and then click on the drop down arrow. If you entered the letter "T" you will be automatically taken to the first font that starts with the letter "T". Once the font name is highlighted, slide the slider on the side or tap the arrow keys to move up or down in the font list. Click the mouse or press the Enter key when you find the font you want.

As shown in the example on the preceding page, if your font samples are smaller than mine, go back and read the *First Things First* chapter. Because I have installed different fonts than you have, my font list will look different than yours does. Beware that installing a lot of fonts on your computer can slow it down or even grind it to a halt. A corrupt font can crash your computer, so only download fonts from reputable places.

If you are following a tutorial that tells you to select a fat, thick, or wide font, what the author means is a font that is wider than most, like **Impact.** To cut words out of a photo, use a fat font to display parts of the photo.

Font Style-Not all fonts have different styles, especially free fonts. The example shows the styles available for Myriad Pro, which has more styles than most fonts. If the drop down arrow is gray, there are no extra styles available, use the faux styles instead.

Font Size-Type the size you want for your font. Sizes from 6 to 72 points are listed on the drop down list, but any number between .01 and 1296 can be entered manually. 72 points is an inch. I suggest adding journaling not smaller than 12 pts. To see your type size displayed in millimeters or pixels, from the Menu bar choose Edit>Preferences>Units & Rulers (Mac: Photoshop Elements> Preferences> Units & Rulers) and change it there.

An easy way to change the font size is to select the text (double click on layer thumbnail) and select the font size option box (double click in it). With both of them selected, roll your mouse wheel, or tap the up and down arrow keys to increase or decrease the font size. As you do this, the text changes size. To confirm the text, check the green checkmark ✓ on the Type tool Options bar.

The shortcut to decrease/increase the size of your text by 2 pts (if pts is your selected unit of measurement) is Ctrl>Shift (>or<) (> (greater than sign) for increase and < (less than sign) for decrease) (Mac: Cmd>Shift (>or<). Add the Alt key (Mac: Opt key) to change to 10 pts.

Another way to size text is to type Ctrl>T to activate the Transform command or select the Move tool, and drag a corner sizing handle to size text in proportion. To resize the text without regards to proportion to fill in an area for titles or journaling, drag a top or side sizing handle. Some fonts respond better to this technique than others, so try it out. The example shows the same size text created with the Scriptina font with the bottom copy made wider by dragging to the right; the type is no taller, just wider.

Anti-Aliased-Keep this turned on (default setting) to smooth out the edges of text. The "S" on the right has Anti-Aliased turned off. Turning this on/off applies to the entire layer. In this example, I had to make two separate layers to have one with and one without Anti-Aliased.

To turn it on/off do one of the following after you select the layer: click on the AA button on the Options bar, right click on the layer name in the Layers panel, right click on the text, or from the Menu bar, choose Layer>Type>Anti-Alias On or Anti-Alias Off.

Faux Bold Style-If your font does not have a bold font style; Photoshop Elements can create a fake one for you for most fonts. Faux Bold can change the proportions of your font and not always for the better, so be careful when using this style. Click on the Bold T on the Options bar after clicking to add text or right click when adding text to add Faux Bold. Text with Faux Bold cannot be warped; if you try to warp text with Faux Bold, you will be asked if you want to remove Faux Bold. The short cut to toggle Faux Bold on/off is to first select, and then type the shortcut Ctrl>Shift>B (Mac: Cmd>Shift>B).

Faux Italic-Faux Italic works just the same as Faux Bold. The short cut to toggle Faux Italic on/off is to first select the text, and then type the shortcut Ctrl>Shift>I (Mac: Cmd>Shift>I).

Underline-To underline text, select this style. This style can be used with faux bold, faux italic, and strikethrough. Remember, if you don't want the spaces between your words underlined, turn it off on the spaces. The shortcut to toggle Underline on/off is to first select the text, and then type the shortcut Ctrl>Shift>U (Mac: Cmd>Shift>U).

Strikethrough-To strike through your text, click on this icon on the Options bar. Even though I've never used it, you might. This style can be used with faux bold, faux italic, and underline. Remember, if you don't want the spaces between your words with the strikethrough; turn it off on the spaces. The shortcut to toggle Strikethrough on/off is Ctrl>Shift>/ (forward slash) (Mac: Cmd>Shift>/).

Text Alignment-Choose an option to align your text. If you have chosen one of the vertical type tools, you will see the drop down list on the far right. Just like a word processing program, you have the normal Text Alignment boxes with the exception of Justify, but I can show you a little trick on how to Justify your text.

Left Align Text-With this option and one of the Horizontal type tools selected, when you click and start typing, the text starts at the insertion point and types to the right. When you press enter (return key) to type a second line, it aligns with the left edge of type. With Paragraph Type, your type lines up on the left edge of the bounding box. When using the Vertical text tools, the text lines up on the top. The shortcut for Left/Top Align Text is to first select the text and then type the shortcut Ctrl>Shift>L (Mac: Cmd>Shift>L).

Center Align Text- With this option and one of the Horizontal type tools selected, when you click and start typing, the text centers from your first insertion point. When you press enter (return key) to type a second line, it will center below the first line of text. Sometimes this is a little bit confusing, so try it out. With Paragraph Type your type is centered in the bounding box. When using the Vertical Text tools the text lines up Center Vertical. The shortcut for Center Align Text is to first select the text and then type the shortcut Ctrl>Shift>C (Mac: Cmd>Shift>C).

Right Align Text- With this option and one of the Horizontal type tools selected, when you click and start typing, the text starts at the insertion point and types to the left. When you press enter (return key) to type a second line, it aligns with the right edge of type. With Paragraph Type, your type lines up on the right edge of the bounding box. When using the Vertical Text tools, the text lines up on the bottom. The shortcut for Left/Top Align Text is to first select the text and then type the shortcut Ctrl>Shift>R (Mac: Cmd>Shift>R).

Justify-To justify text like in a newspaper column, first select the Text tool, and then click and drag to create a text box, (more about creating a text box is explained later in this chapter). Type the text. Double click on the text layer thumbnail to select all of the text. Type the shortcut Shift>Ctrl>J (Mac: Shift>Cmd>J). If the last line of the paragraph doesn't justify and you want it to, select all of the text and type the shortcut Shift>Ctrl>F (Mac: Shift>Cmd>F).

Leading-Leading is the distance between the lines on which the type line sits, basically it is line spacing. Eons ago they poured hot lead in between rows of type, which is where the term leading originated.

To keep the bottom descending parts of letters (like y, g, and j) from colliding with the tops of the letters on the next row, Photoshop Elements automatically adds 20 percent of space between rows of text. Leading can be easily adjusted by clicking on the Leading drop down list.

When working on a project, I can't look at my type and say to myself "Gee I think the leading should be 36 pts". What I do is select the text (double click on layer thumbnail), and then select the Leading option box (double click in it, it will turn blue). With both of them selected, roll your mouse wheel, or tap the up and down Arrow keys to increase or decrease the leading until you like the way it looks. To confirm the text, check the green checkmark ✓ on the Type tool Options bar.

Color-The color box determines the color of your text. To change the color, click on the drop down list and choose from one of the swatches. To choose your own color, click inside the color box and the Color Picker dialog box will be displayed. To match a text color to an exact color on your image, click inside the color box and then click on the color on the image. For more information, read about the Eyedropper tool in the *Tools* chapter.

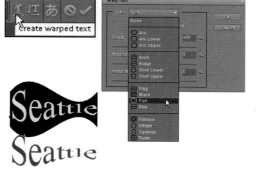

To change the color of the text after it's already been added, select the text (double click on layer thumbnail), and choose a new color. To confirm the change, check the green checkmark ✓ on the Type tool Options bar.

Create Warped Text
Using warped text is a fun and easy way to make scrapbook page titles and other interesting text. Text that you have applied the Faux Bold style to cannot be warped.

To warp text, type the text, select the text (double click on layer thumbnail), and click on the Create Warped Text icon on the Options bar. Choose a Style from the dropdown list, and then have fun playing with the Bend, Horizontal and Vertical Distortion sliders. If you're happy with the change, click the OK button. If not, hold the Alt key (Mac: Opt key) to change the Cancel button to a Reset button and start over. To confirm the text, check the green checkmark ✓ on the Type tool Options bar.

As shown in the example on the right, once the text is warped, the layer thumbnail will change to show the warp symbol.

Other ways to warp selected text are to: right click on the text, right click on the layer name in the Layers panel or, from the Menu bar, choose Layer>Type>Warp Text. Warped text is still editable.

To remove the warping, select the layer that is warped and click on the Warped Text icon on the Options bar to display the Warp Text dialog box. Click on the Style drop down list and choose None. Click OK.

Change the Text Orientation-To change horizontal text to vertical text and vice versa, click on this icon on the Options bar. This is a fast way to see if you want to change the direction of your text. Another way to do this is to select the layer and Right click on the text after you commit it, choose Horizontal or Vertical or, from the Menu bar, choose Layer>Type>Horizontal or Layer>Type>Vertical.

Asian Text Options-(Faux Tracking)-Tracking is available only in Photoshop, but we can still cheat and adjust the spacing in between our characters.

In Photoshop Elements you can't change the tracking in a normal way, but you can kind of cheat. Notice that in the bottom row, the letters are actually touching. I did this by adjusting the Tsume in the Asian Text Options.

From the Menu bar, choose Edit>Preferences>Type (Mac: Photoshop Elements>Preferences>Type) and check the box Show Asian Text Options to add this option to the Type tool Options bar.

In the example on the preceding page on the bottom row of type, I selected all of the letters and changed the Tsume percentage to 100%. Do not check the Tate-Chuu-Yoko or Mojikumi options. The text remains editable.

Style-Click on the drop down list to add a layer style. The layer styles are the same styles that appear when you choose layer styles from the Effects panel, which is the way I normally apply them.

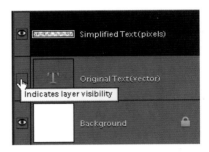

Simplify a Text Layer-To apply filters, paint, gradients, patterns, or to use the Eraser tool (E), Healing Brush tool (J), Clone Stamp tool (S), or Paint Bucket tool (K), you must simplify the text first. Because simplified text cannot be edited, my recommendation is to make a copy of your text (Ctrl>J, Mac: Cmd>J) and simplify the copy. Before you simplify your text, make sure it is the final size you want, because simplified text does not re-size/transform well. Hide your original layer by clicking on the eyeball in the Layers panel. This way, if you don't like how your filter or other effect came out, you can simply delete that layer and don't have to retype the text. Simplified text (pixel based) does not print as crisp as your original text (vector based).

To Simplify a text layer, first select the layer and then do one of the following: From the Menu bar, choose Layer>Simplify Layer, right click on the layer and select Simplify Layer, click on the Layers panel drop down list and choose Simplify Layer.

Shift Happens-There is no spell check in Photoshop Elements. One thing you can do is copy and paste your journaling into a word processing program, and run spell check there. Remember, spell check finds words spelled incorrectly. I can tell you that as I was writing this book I was copying and pasting the Inverse command (Shift>Ctrl>I). I was horrified to realize I wasn't typing Shift, but a similar word minus one letter. My word processing program didn't pick up the problem, so be warned, it could happen to you too!

How to Use the Type Tool-(Click and Type aka: Point Type) Select the Type tool (T) from the Toolbar. Make changes to any of the options on the Options bar. (These were explained on the preceding pages). Click where you want your type to start, your cursor turns into a flashing I beam (shown circled on the right). A small square is added to your page; this is your insertion point. When you click on the image, a new text layer is automatically added in the Layers panel. The new text is underlined as you type. Before you run off the edge of the page, tap the Enter/Return key and you are returned to the line directly under the insertion point.

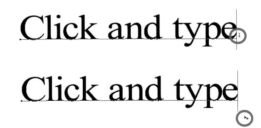

To type a line or two this method works well, but if you're typing more than that, use the paragraph method on the next page. Use this method to add small sections of text. To add more text close by, hold the Shift key as you type, or Photoshop Elements will try to edit the existing text layer.

To move the text before you have confirmed it, move away slightly from the text and the cursor will turn into the Move tool cursor (as shown circled in the bottom example), click and drag the text. To move your text after it has been confirmed, select the layer and hold the Ctrl key (Mac: Cmd key) to temporarily activate the Move tool, or activate the Move tool and drag it that way.

To confirm the text, check the green checkmark ✓on the Type tool Options bar, or select another tool when you're done typing to commit your type. As soon as you commit the text, you will see that the name of your text layer is approximately the first 25 characters of what you typed, depending on your monitor size.

How to Use the Type Tool (Text Box aka: Paragraph type)-When I'm journaling or typing a large amount of text, it's easier to create a Bounding Box to put my text in so I spend less time trying to line everything up. To do this, select the Type tool from the Toolbar and click and drag a text box. Use any of the sizing handles to change the size of the bounding box. Hold the Ctrl (Mac: Cmd key) to resize/transform the text and text box at the same time. Hold the Shift key to keep the text box in the same proportion. Depending on the text alignment box you have selected, your cursor may be on the right, left, or center of the bounding box. The example shows Center Text Alignment.

The little square insertion box shown in the click and type method is not added when you create a text box. As soon as you drag out the bounding box, a new text layer is added in the Layers panel. Your type will be contained in the Bounding Box and will automatically return to the next line, so you don't need to tap the Enter/Return key.

If you type more text than will fit in the bounding box, as I have in the example, a + (plus) will be added to the bottom right corner box of the bounding box (circled). If you can't see the text in the bounding box, it will not be visible on anything you print.

To correct this problem, you can select the text (double click on text layer thumbnail) and change the size of the font or the leading. You can also drag one of the sizing boxes to resize the text box. To move the text box, select the layer and press the Ctrl key (Mac: Cmd key) to temporarily activate the Move tool, or select the Move tool from the Toolbar and drag it.

Create a Text Box in an Exact Size-Alt click (Mac: Opt click) on an image to display the Paragraph Text Size dialog box. Enter the size of a box you want, and it automatically converts it to points for you. A bounding box in the correct size appears on your image.

Adding Text Effects from the Content Panel-To add a text effect to a text layer, do one of the following: double click the effect thumbnail, select the effect thumbnail and click the Apply button, or drag the thumbnail to the image. The effect will be applied after you check the green checkmark ✓on the Type tool Options bar.

You can also double click on the effect thumbnail on the Content panel and a new text layer is added to your Layers panel. Centered on your image are the words "Your Text Here". Type your text. Check the green checkmark ✓on the Type tool Options bar and the effect should be applied. Some of the gradient effects are pretty nice, but the patterns leave a lot to be desired, especially on large letters.

How to Edit Text-There are several ways to select text: My favorite way to select all of the text on a single layer is to double click on the text layer thumbnail (circled), with any tool selected.

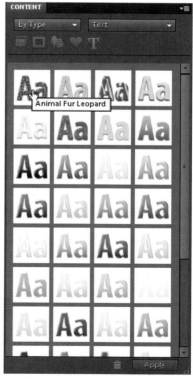

With the Type tool selected: double click on a word and the word is selected, triple click on a word and the whole line is selected, quadruple click on a word and the whole paragraph is selected. Click and drag over the text and whatever you drag over is selected. Click in the text and right click, and choose Select All to select all text on the layer. If you don't click in the text first, when you right click, it will say Edit Text.

In the event you need to add another letter or space, with the Type tool selected, clicking once in the text gives you the ability to start typing immediately without wiping out the original text. To select one character to the left or right after you've clicked in the text, use Shift and the left or right Arrow keys. You will add another character every time you press the keys. To select one line up or down, use Shift and the up or down Arrow key. This adds another line each time you press the keys. To select one word to the left or right, use Ctrl>Shift (Mac: Cmd>Shift) and the left or right Arrow key. You will add another word each time you press the keys.

To move the cursor one character to the left or right, use the left or right Arrow key. To move the cursor up or down one line, use the up and down Arrow keys. To move one word left or right use the Ctrl (Mac: Cmd) and the left or right Arrow key.

With the Type Tool (T) active, and with your text layer selected, click inside your text and tap the "Home" Key on your keyboard to move your cursor to the start of the line. To move the cursor to the start of the text on this layer, type Ctrl (Mac: Cmd) and the "Home" key. To move the cursor to the end of the line, click the "End" Key on your keyboard. To move the cursor to the end of the text on this layer, type Ctrl (Mac: Cmd) and the "End" Key.

To make changes to several text layers with the Type tool selected, select one layer and then Ctrl click (Mac: Cmd click) on the layer (not layer thumbnail) to select the others. Make changes on the Options bar and all of the selected layers will automatically change at the same time. To quickly select text layers, from the Menu bar choose Select>Similar layers.

Smart Quotes-As shown in the example on the right, there are different options for quotation marks. The quotation marks shown in the top option are the default option. In the event you want to change your quotation marks to mark a measurement, you will need to make a change in the Type Preferences. To do this, from the Menu bar choose Edit>Preferences> Type (Mac: Photoshop Elements>Preferences>Type) and uncheck the box that says Use Smart Quotes.

"Quotation Marks"
"Quotation Marks"

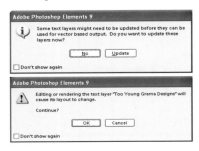

Update **Text Layer**-If you open a PSD file that was created on another computer, or with a different version of Photoshop Elements, you may get the following warning: "Some text layers might need to be updated before they can be used for vector based output. Do you want to update these layers now?" I always check No and haven't had any problems, but will occasionally see the next box when I select a layer on a file that I didn't update that says: Editing or rendering the text layer will cause the layout to change. Continue? I click OK and it is fine.

Missing Fonts-If you open a PSD file that was created on another computer, you may get a message that says the some text layers contain missing fonts. As shown circled on the right, the affected text layers will show a yellow warning symbol on the layer thumbnail. You have several options: Install the font that was used to create the file (if you know what and where it is), or select the text and choose another font yourself. To change the font to Myriad Pro (default font), from the Menu bar, choose Layer>Type>Replace All Missing Fonts, or click the OK button when the font substitution dialog box appears.

Cropping Tools

The Crop Tool (C)

The Crop tool cuts images into preset or custom sized rectangles. It is available in Full, Quick, and Guided Edit. In Full Edit, the Crop tool is nested with the Recompose tool, and they both share the shortcut (C).

Because most digital photos are taken in a 4 x 5.3 aspect ratio, portions of the photo will be cut off if you print the photo in a 4" x 6" size. Use the Crop tool to crop your images before you have them printed to alleviate this problem. You may also be able to change this setting in your camera, or use a photo processor that prints photos in a 4" x 5.3" size. When you use the Crop tool on a multi-layered file, it crops all of the layers at once. This is helpful when making a double wide scrapbook page, but not at other times. If you want to crop only one layer at a time, use the Rectangular Marquee tool to select an area and then delete it. When you crop your photos, crop out distractions, but remember to leave some of the background area intact. Think of how much fun it is to look back at photos taken in the 1950's and see the cars, toys, buildings, etc. For more information about cropping, be sure to read *Cropping with Photos* in the *Cool Stuff with Photos* chapter.

How to Use the Crop Tool (T)-Open a photo and select the Crop tool (C). Select a preset aspect ratio from the drop down list or keep the No Restriction default setting. If you are going to print the photo at a photo processor, be sure that you have cropped the image in a size that they print. If you are cropping a photo to add to a scrapbook page or other project, you do not have to choose a specific size. You can also choose to crop a photo in a specified size. To do this, enter the width and height on the Options bar, as I have. If you will be using the cropped image on a scrapbook page or other project created at 300 ppi, enter 300 in the Resolution box.

Click, hold, and drag over the area you wish to keep. To reposition the crop before you let go of the mouse hold the Spacebar. A dark shield will cover the area to be cropped off. Resize by dragging a sizing handle or drag the selection to a new location by clicking and dragging. To confirm the crop, check the green checkmark ✓.

In my example above, I have entered the numbers shown on the Options bar example above. If I decide that I want my photo 4 inches wide and 5 inches high, instead of retyping the numbers, I can click on the double set of arrows (circled) between the Width and Height boxes to swap the numbers. I can also click on the Aspect Ratio drop down arrow and choose another option.

Aspect Ratio-Click the drop down list to choose from six standard photo print sizes. If you are printing an 8" x 10" photo, it's imperative that you crop it yourself, or you will probably be disappointed by the print that the technician or machine automatically cropped for you.

No Restriction-Allows you to crop a photo with any dimensions that you want to. When I'm working on a scrapbook page, this is the option I normally use.

Use Photo Ratio-To crop the photo in the same ratio as the original image, choose this option. This option would work well if you actually print your photos in a 4" x 5.3" size.

If you have trouble with the Crop tool, try resetting the tool by click on the Reset Tool ▼ on the left end of the Options bar. Also check to see if you have Snap to Grid or Snap to Guides selected, which sometimes aggravates the Crop tool. To do this, from the Menu bar choose View>Snap to Guides or Grids.

If you prefer not to see the dark shield when using the Crop tool, you can toggle it off/on by typing the / (forward slash key) and it will be replaced by a selection border (marching ants). To change the color, and/or opacity of the Crop tool shield or turn it off, from the Menu bar, choose Edit>Preferences>Display & Cursors (Mac: Photoshop Elements>Preferences>Display & Cursors). The default color is black at 75% opacity. In the example on the right, I have changed the shield color to red and the opacity to 100% which creates a dramatic difference.

The Recompose Tool (C)

The Recompose tool (C) allows you to remove portions of your photo by painting over it. This can be an unneeded portion of the photo or an actual person in the photo if they're positioned correctly. The Recompose tool is available in Full and Guided Edit and can be used when making photo books and other projects in the Create Menu. Be sure to also read the *Recompose a Photo* tutorial in the *Cool Stuff with Photos* chapter.

How to Use the Recompose Tool-Open a photo and select the Recompose tool. As soon as you click on the Recompose tool icon, a box pops up with these easy to follow instructions. Highlight the areas you wish to keep with the green protect brush and then highlight the areas you want to discard with the red remove brush. Next, drag the handles on the side of the photo inward.

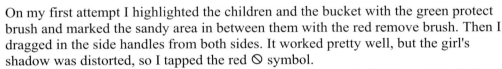

On my first attempt I highlighted the children and the bucket with the green protect brush and marked the sandy area in between them with the red remove brush. Then I dragged in the side handles from both sides. It worked pretty well, but the girl's shadow was distorted, so I tapped the red ⊘ symbol.

To correct the shadow problem, I painted over the shadow with the green protect brush and dragged the side handles in from both sides. As you can see by the example on the right, it worked much better the second time.

For even better results, right click on the image and choose Use Quick Highlights. Enlarge the brush and drag over the areas you want to keep and they are filled in like a highlight marker. Drag the sides inward.

Highlight Skin Tones-This highlighted sand, not skin in this image.
Preset-Choose a preset ratio and Elements automatically resizes the photo, which may or may not work well.
Width & Height-Enter a width & height similar to the Crop tool.
Amount-Keep at 100% to minimize distortion.

Cookie Cutter Tool (Q)

The Cookie Cutter tool crops images into shapes. If you are a paper scrapbooker, think of it as your own personal die cut machine, corner rounder, or punch. The Cookie Cutter tool and the Custom Shape tool share the same shape libraries. You can use the Cookie Cutter tool to create your own embellishments as I have below with paper from a digital scrapbooking kits or, by making your own paper.

How to Use the Cookie Cutter Tool: Open an image and select the Cookie Cutter tool from the Toolbar. I am using a pretty orange paper from the And Many More kit by SuzyQ Scraps which can be found on the *Photoshop Elements - Basics & Beyond* DVD.

From the Options bar, click on the Shape drop down list and choose a shape. If your shape library doesn't look like the example below, go back and read the *First Things First* chapter. Click on the Shape Options drop down list and choose:

Unconstrained allows you to drag out a shape in any proportion.

Defined Proportions will keep the shape in the proportions of the example.

Defined Size will crop the photo in the size that the designer created it. You won't know what size that is until you release your mouse.

Fixed Size crops to the exact dimensions you enter. Size can be entered as inches, centimeters, or pixels.

From Center will draw the shape outward from the center. From Center can be selected with all the other options too.

Feather - Enter a number here from .2-250 pixels to soften the cropped edge of the image.

Crop- Check the box to have the entire image cropped to the size of the shape. If you are using the Cookie Cutter tool on a multi-layered file like a scrapbook page, you want this option **un**checked.

To Cut the Shape: If you have Unconstrained or Defined Proportions selected, click, hold, and drag across the image to crop the shape in a size of your choice. If you have Defined Size or Fixed Size selected, click on the image to crop the shape in the specified size.

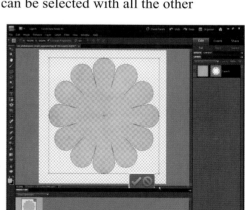

As soon as you let go of the mouse, a checkerboard pattern representing transparency surrounds the shape. The transparency is the area that will be deleted as soon as you check the checkmark. The Options bar is now the Transform tool and the thumbnail in the Layers panel shows a dark grey background. As explained in the Move tool (V) section of this chapter, you can now resize/transform, rotate, or skew the shape now by using the sizing handles. While it appears that the shape is actually already cut, it is not until you check the checkmark. To confirm the crop, check the green checkmark ✓.

As soon as you check the checkmark, the Cookie Cutter Options bar appears again, and the thumbnail in the Layers palette now has a transparent (checkerboard) background.

The Straighten Tool (P)

The Straighten tool (P) quickly and easily straightens photos whether they were taken with a camera or scanned. See the *Straightening a Photo* tutorial in the *Cool Stuff with Photos* chapter for complete step by step instructions for using this tool. The Straighten tool is available in Full and Guided Edit.

How to Use the Straighten Tool-Open a photo and select the Straighten tool from the Toolbar. Choose an option from the Canvas Options drop down list. If you are working on a multi-layer file like a scrapbook page, uncheck Rotate All Layers. If you are working on a photo with multiple layers like Adjustment layers, check the Rotate All Layers box.

Click, hold, and drag across the photo along the horizon or something that should be horizontal, (in my example I'm using the painted lines on the field) and Photoshop Elements does the rest. Shown below are the three different Canvas Options. I normally use the Crop to Remove Background option because it straightens and cleans up the edges.

Grow or Shrink Canvas to Fit   Crop to Remove Background   Crop to Original Size

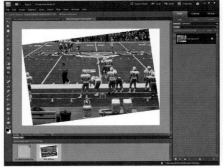      

In the left and right examples above, the area added to maintain the image size is white because it is the current Background color. There are two other ways to straighten images that you can try but they don't always work as well. From the Menu bar choose: Image>Rotate>Straighten Image or Image>Rotate Straighten and Crop Image.

Retouching Tools

The Red Eye Tool (Y)

The Red Eye tool removes red eyes in your photos caused by the camera's flash bouncing off your subject's retina. Red eye is usually worse with blue eyes and photos taken in a darkened room. Turning on your camera's Red Eye feature helps limit this problem, but it can be annoying. Other ways to minimize red eye are: turn on a light in the area, move to a better lighted area, aim your flash towards the ceiling so that the light bounces off of the ceiling, or have your subjects look away from the camera.

When is Red Eye not really Red Eye? In some instances, the presence of a golden/white glow reflected by a camera flash in a child's eye indicates Coats' disease or Retinoblastoma (an eye cancer). My niece was diagnosed with Retinoblastoma when she was just six months old. For more information see *www.knowtheglow.com*.

The Red Eye tool is available in Full, Quick and in the Perfect Portrait option of Guided Edit. You can also automatically fix red eyes from the Menu bar by choosing Enhance>Auto Red Eye Fix (Ctrl>R, Mac: Cmd>R). Because Photoshop Elements sometimes doesn't automatically fix red eyes the way I would like it to, I disable this option when I import photos from my camera. For more about fixing red eyes, see the complete *Red Eye* tutorial in the *Cool Stuff with Photos-Cosmetic Surgery* chapter. The Red Eye tool will also not fix pet eye, but there is a complete tutorial about that in the *Cool Stuff with Photos-Cosmetic Surgery* chapter.

Spot Healing Brush & Healing Brush Tools (J)

The Spot Healing Brush and Healing Brush tools remove imperfections from your photos. Use the Spot Healing Brush to fix smaller areas and the Healing Brush tool to fix larger areas. Both tools are available in Full Edit and in some of the Guided Edit options. In Full Edit, the tools are nested together and share the shortcut (J).

The big difference between the two tools is that the Spot Healing Brush automatically fixes the area under the cursor. In the Wrinkles example in the *Cool Stuff with Photos-Cosmetic Surgery* chapter, this tool covered my wrinkles with different wrinkles. The Healing Brush tool allows you to choose the area to fix the image by Alt clicking (Mac: Opt clicking) first, and then clicking on the areas on the photo to be corrected.

See the *Cool Stuff with Photos Cosmetic Surgery* chapter for several examples using these tools.

How to use the Spot Healing Brush Tool-Open an image and select the Spot Healing Brush tool from the Toolbar. Choose a Type of match from the Options bar (see below for explanations). Duplicate the layer (Ctrl>J, Mac: Cmd>J) so that you are not working on the original layer. Choose a brush from the Brush drop down menu that is about 10% larger than the area to be fixed. Click, or click and drag, and the "bad" area is fixed.

Type-Proximity Match-the area around the "bad" area is blended to fix the spot. This works well if you are fixing an area on a cheek, but as shown in the example, if you are fixing something near an eye or mouth you may have problems.

Type-Create Texture-the area around the "bad" area is blended into a texture to fix the spot. If this doesn't work, try it a second time or try the Healing Brush tool.

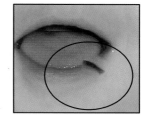

Type-Content Aware-Choose this new option and Photoshop Elements decides what pixels would be the best match for your image. Try it and if you don't like it select, the Healing Brush tool.

Sample All Layers-When not selected, Photoshop Elements will use only the active layer to heal. It's a good idea to create a new transparent layer and paste your editing on it when fixing wrinkles, etc. When doing this, selecting this option to sample all layers in the image will help you.

How to use the Healing Brush Tool- Open an image and select the Healing Brush tool from the Toolbar. On the Options bar select Sampled. Duplicate the layer (Ctrl>J, Mac: Cmd>J) so that you are not working on the original layer. Choose a brush from the Brush drop down menu that is about 10% larger than the area to be fixed. Alt click (Mac: Opt click) on a "good" area of the image and click or click and drag on the "bad" area to fix it. As you work on an image, you may need to select/sample a new "good" area several times.

Mode determines how your patch is going to blend with existing area. Start with Normal. Replace preserves film grain and textures. For more information on blending modes, see the *Filters & Blending Modes* chapter.

Source-Sampled-Uses pixels from your image to fix your problem area. Use this option to fix your photos.

Source-Pattern-Click the Pattern Picker drop down list to choose a pattern. You can make your own custom pattern (like a fabric texture) from another photo to use when fixing a photo.

Align-After Alt clicking (Mac: Opt clicking) to set a sample/copy point, a crosshair appears and moves along with the cursor to sample as it moves. By watching the crosshair you can see the area that is being copied.

Align Not Selected-Alt click (Mac: Opt click) once to set a sample point. Photoshop Elements will use this same sample for all of the areas you fix no matter how many times you click and drag.

Clone Overlay Options-If you find it annoying that the clone overlay is shown, go back and read the *First Things First* chapter where I showed you how to turn it off.

Healing With Two Different Photos
You can use the Healing Brush tool (J) to sample from another photo. To do this you will need to open both photos. Alt click (Mac: Opt click) on the photo you want to sample from. Switch to the second photo and click on it to paste the area from the first photo. Color modes must match to do this unless one is Grayscale mode.

Clone Stamp & Pattern Stamp Tools (S)

The Clone Stamp tool copies/samples pixels from one area of an image and pastes them onto another area. The Pattern Stamp tool copies and pastes patterns that you have created yourself, or are included with Photoshop Elements. You may fill a layer or a selection with either tool. Both tools are nested together on the Full Edit Toolbar and share the shortcut (S). Other ways to fill layers or selections with patterns include using the Paint Bucket tool (K), Layer>New Fill Layer>Pattern, or by adding a Pattern Fill layer.

How to use the Clone Stamp Tool-Choose a brush from the brush drop down list. Adjust the brush size by sliding the slider bar or typing in the size you want. You can also adjust brush sizes by using your Bracket keys. The left Bracket [key reduces the brush size and the right Bracket] key increases the brush size. Alt click (Mac: Opt click) on an area to copy, your cursor will change to look like the example on the right.

As shown in the example, click and drag over the area you wish to cover up. As I drag the mouse, the orange intruder is replaced by water.

Mode-determines how your patch is going to blend with existing area. Start with Normal. Replace preserves film grain and textures. For more information on blending modes see the *Filters & Blending Modes* chapter.

Opacity-Drag the slider or type a percentage in the box. A lower setting allows layers below to show through.

Align-After Alt clicking (Mac: Opt clicking) to set a sample/copy point, a crosshair appears and moves along with the cursor to sample as it moves. By watching the crosshair you can see the area that is being copied.

Align Not Selected-Alt click (Mac: Opt click) once to set a sample point. Photoshop Elements will use this same sample for all of the areas you fix no matter how many times you click and drag.

Sample All Layers-When not selected, Photoshop Elements will use only the active layer to clone. It's a good idea to create a new transparent layer and paste your editing on it when adding new items, etc. When doing this, selecting this option to sample all layers in the image will help you.

How to use the Pattern Stamp Tool-Choose a brush from the brush drop down list. Adjust the brush size by sliding the slider bar, typing the size, or using the right and left Bracket keys. From the Options bar, select a Mode, Opacity and Pattern by clicking on the drop down lists. Click and drag on the image to paste the pattern.

Choosing Aligned on the Options bar will stamp the pattern in alignment, un-checking this box will allow you to stamp without aligning the pattern each time.

Checking the Impressionist box will stamp the pattern as if it was painted with paint dabs, not much of your original pattern will remain.

Clone Overlay Options-If you find it annoying that the clone overlay is shown, go back and read the *First Things First* chapter where I showed you how to turn it off.

Cloning With Two Different Photos

You can use the Clone Stamp tool (S) to sample from another photo. To do this, you will need to open both photos. Alt click (Mac: Opt click) on the photo you want to sample from, switch to the second photo and click on it to paste the area from the first photo. Color modes must match to do this unless one is Grayscale mode.

Eraser, Background Eraser, and Magic Eraser Tools (E)

The Eraser tool erases an area when you click on it. The Background Eraser makes it easy to erase the background of an image. The Magic Eraser works like a combination of the Magic Wand tool and the Delete key. All three tools are nested together on the Full Edit Toolbar and share the shortcut (E). Another way to delete part of a layer is to select the layer in the Layers panel and make a selection with a selection tool. From the Menu bar, choose Edit>Delete or tap the Delete key.

The Eraser tool will erase areas of an image wherever you click. As shown in the first image on the right, you will run into trouble if you try to erase parts of a regular photo JPEG file that consists of only a Background layer, or a regular layer that has the transparency locked. When you try to do this, areas that you want to erase are filled with the Background color instead. As shown in the example on the far right, double click on the Background layer to convert it to a regular image layer to see the results.

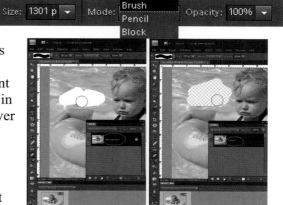

How to Use the Eraser Tool (E)

Open an image and select the Eraser tool from the Toolbar. Select a brush by clicking on the drop down list. To create a soft feathered edge while erasing, choose a soft round brush.

Select a Mode, normally I choose the Brush mode. You may want to choose the Pencil mode which erases with a hard edge, or the Block mode which erases with a 16 px hard square brush which can be limiting. Adjust the Opacity slider if you don't want to completely erase the layer and want part of it to still show.

Click and drag over the area you wish to erase, a checkerboard pattern will appear indicating transparency. Drawing a selection with a selection tool first will allow you to only erase inside the selected area.

How to use the Background Eraser Tool (E)

The Background Eraser tool erases colors similar to the color you click on. Like the example on the right, this tool works best when there is a high contrast between the areas you want to erase and the areas you want to keep. If you are using the Background Eraser on a Background layer it will automatically be converted to a regular image layer.

Once you select the Background Eraser your cursor turns into a circle with a crosshair inside it. The crosshair is called the hotspot. Do not let the hotspot touch any of the area you want to keep. Click the brush drop down list to make any changes to the brush. Use the left and right Bracket keys to adjust the size of the brush. Make other changes on the Options bar as needed.

Contiguous is the default setting and will erase all colored areas that match the hotspot color and are touching. Only the area inside the circle is erased.

Discontiguous erases all colored areas that are similar to hotspot color whether they are touching or not; only the area inside the circle is erased.

Tolerance-Lower the Tolerance setting to select very similar colors to the hotspot color, raise it to select a wider range of colors.

Click and drag over the area that you wish to erase keeping the hotspot on areas to be erased only.

How to use the Magic Eraser Tool (E)

Use the Magic Eraser (E) to erase areas where the colors are similar depending on the Tolerance setting selected. When you click on the image it automatically converts a Background layer to a regular layer.

When working with a regular layer, or if your transparency is locked (checkerboard icon in the Layers panel), the area that is erased is filled with the Background color.

Once you select the Magic Eraser tool, your cursor turns into an eraser with a sparkler on it. Click the brush drop down list to make any changes to the brush. Use the left and right Bracket keys to adjust the size of the brush. Make other changes on the Options bar as needed.

Tolerance-Lower the Tolerance setting to select very similar colors, raise it to select a wider range of colors.

Anti-alias-Smoothes the erased edges, I keep this option selected.

Contiguous is the default setting and will erase all colored areas that match where you click and that are touching. Uncheck to erase the color everywhere in the image. If you are using this tool to remove a white background on clipart, be careful if there is white on the clipart because it will be erased.

Sample all Layers-Uncheck this option if you only want to erase parts of the selected layer, otherwise it samples colors from all visible layers.

Opacity-Keep at 100% to erase completely. Lower this setting to partially erase the pixels.

Click in the color you wish to erase. In my example above, I clicked on the white wall to erase most of it with just one click. Continue clicking until all areas are erased, switch to the Eraser tool if needed.

Blur, Sharpen, & Smudge Tools (R)

The Blur, Sharpen, and Smudge tools do what their names imply they do. They are nested together on the Full Edit Toolbar, and share the shortcut (R). Another way to blur images is by using one of the Blur Filters which can be found by selecting Filters from the Menu bar. Sharpening can be done through the Enhance Menu by choosing Auto Sharpen, Adjust Sharpness, or Unsharp Mask. In Quick Edit, you can choose Auto sharpen or use a slider to adjust the amount of sharpening you want to apply. Sharpening an image too much will make your photo appear grainy. See the *Cool Stuff with Photos* chapter for a tutorial about sharpening a blurry photo. The Smudge tool moves pixels in an image similar to the Liquify Filter.

How to use the Blur, Sharpen, and Smudge Tools
The Blur and Sharpen tools are the opposites of each other. Use the Blur tool to quickly blur out a few wrinkles or a distracting background. Use the Sharpen tool to enhance your subject's eyes or other area of the photo. Use the Smudge tool to tuck in a waistline or double chin.

Choose a brush from the brush drop down list. A soft round brush will create a softer feathered effect. Adjust the brush size by sliding the slider bar or typing in the size you want. You can also adjust brush sizes by using your Bracket keys. The left Bracket [key reduces the brush size and the right Bracket] key increases the brush size.

Mode-Blending Modes change how your blurred/sharpened/smudged area blends with the other areas of the image. See the *Filters and Blending Modes* chapter for more information about blending modes.

Strength-Set the amount of blurring/sharpening/smudging you want with each stroke. The default setting for all three tools is 50%, increase or decrease this as needed.

Sample All Layers-Check this option to use colors from all layers to blur/sharpen/smudge an image. If this option is selected, the active layer is the only layer that will be blurred/sharpened/smudged.

Finger Painting-Available only on the Smudge tool, this option when checked smears the Foreground color at the beginning of the stroke. If it's not checked, only colors from the active layer are used. To see how this works, set your Foreground color to a completely different color than the image you want to smear, and try it. To toggle on/off the Finger Painting option, press the Alt key (Mac: Opt key).

Click and drag over an area to blur, sharpen, or smudge it. To contain the changes to a specific area, make a selection first with one of the selection tools.

The Smudge tool works only on areas with different colors. Nothing will happen if you are trying to smudge an area of just one color until you drag over another color.

Sponge, Dodge, and Burn Tools (O)

The Sponge tool is used to add or remove color from an image. It also increases or decreases the contrast in grayscale images. The Dodge tool lightens, and the Burn tool darkens areas of an image. They are nested together at the very bottom of the Full Edit Toolbar, and share the shortcut (O).

Choose a brush from the brush drop down list a soft round brush will create a softer feathered effect. Adjust the brush size by sliding the slider bar or typing in the size you want. You can also adjust brush sizes by using your Bracket keys. The left Bracket [key reduces the brush size and the right Bracket] key increases the brush size.

How to use the Sponge Tool

It's best to use this tool for small areas. If you want to edit larger areas, from the Menu bar choose Enhance>Adjust Hue/Saturation for color images, or Enhance>Adjust Lighting> Brightness/Contrast for grayscale images. Select the Saturate Mode and try this tool for enhancing lip and eye color.

After selecting a brush, choose Desaturate (default setting) to remove color or Saturate to intensify the existing color or contrast. Adjust the Flow setting as needed. The default setting for Flow is 50%. Adjust this slider higher to increase the rate of saturation/desaturation (depending on mode selected). Enter a percentage amount in the text box or use the slider to adjust the flow.

Click and drag over an area to add or remove color. To contain the changes to a specific area, make a selection first with one of the selection tools.

How to use the Dodge and Burn Tools

It's best to use this tool for small areas. If you want to lighten/darken large areas, it would be easier to use Enhance>Adjust Lighting>Shadows/Highlights.

Try the Dodge tool for whitening the whites of eyes or teeth. See the *Cool Stuff with Photos-Cosmetic Surgery* chapter for a complete tutorial on teeth whitening. The Dodge tool can also be used to create highlights. Use the Burn tool to darken the edges of photos or scrapbook papers or to hide gray hair.

After selecting a brush, choose the Range from the Options bar. Shadows will adjust the dark colors in the image. Midtones is the default setting and is used to adjust the middle tones of color. Choose Highlights to adjust the light colors in an image. Enter an amount for the Exposure box, or leave it at the default setting which is 50%. It's better to start with a lower exposure setting and paint over an area several times.

Click and drag over an area to lighten or darken it. To contain the changes to a specific area, make a selection first with one of the selection tools.

As shown in the examples above, I selected the butterfly with the Magnetic Lasso tool (M) and inversed my selection (Select>Inverse) so that the garden area was selected. Next, I used the tools shown to make changes to the image.

Painting and Drawing Tools

Brush (B), Impressionist Brush (B), Color Replacement (B) and Pencil (N) Tools

The Brush tool is similar to a paint brush or rubber stamp. It is used to stamp or paint brushstrokes, whether it is a simple hard round brush from the Default Brushes library or an intricate brush purchased from a designer. The Impressionist Brush tool paints on your image with stylized brush strokes to give it a hand painted look. The Color Replacement tool is used to replace a color in your image with the Foreground color. The Pencil tool paints with hard edges similar to if you were drawing with a pencil. All four tools are nested together on the Full Edit Toolbar. The Brush, Impressionist Brush and Color Replacement tools share the shortcut (B). The shortcut for the Pencil tool is (N).

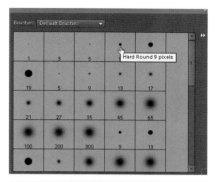

There are many step by step tutorials about using brushes in the *How to Use…, Cool Stuff with Brushes, and Make Your Own* chapters.

Brush and Pencil Tool Options

Show Selected Brush Presets

Choose a brush from the drop down list by clicking on the downward facing black triangle to display the current brush library. Double click on one of the brush thumbnails to select it and close the box. The number under the brush indicates the size of the brush in pixels. You may also load brushes that you have purchased or made yourself. Loading a brush is shown in the *How to Use a Brush like a Rubber Stamp - Single Color* tutorial. If your brushes do not display as shown in the example, go back and read the *First Things First* chapter.

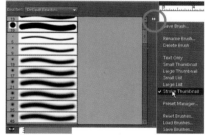

To display the Brush Picker pane when most tools that use brushes are selected, right click on the active image. If it's closed, tap the period or comma keys to switch brushes in the current brush library. You may also change how your brush thumbnails are displayed by clicking on the arrows circled on the Brush Picker pane and choosing a different option.

Size

Brushes can be sized from 1-2500 pixels. 2500 px is approximately 8.33 inches on a 300 resolution scrapbook page. Use the bracket keys (left Bracket key) [to decrease your brush size or] (right bracket key) to increase your brush size. Clicking on the arrow in the box will allow you to use a slider to adjust your brush size, or you can manually enter a size in the box. Brush sizes are entered in pixels only. If your cursor looks like a crosshair, you have the Caps Lock key activated or a very small brush selected.

Mode

Select a Blending Mode by clicking on the drop down list. Normal is the default setting and all Blending Modes are available for use. Blending Modes change how the painted area blends with the other areas of the image. Blending Modes are explained in detail in the Filters and Blending Modes Chapter.

Opacity

The Opacity default is 100%, which means you are painting a solid color. Lowering the Opacity by typing an amount in the box or using the slider will adjust how opaque your painted area is. I suggest you paint on a separate transparent layer. When you do that you can adjust the layer opacity in the Layers panel.

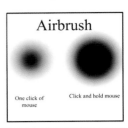

Airbrush
Click on the airbrush icon and a small thin rectangular outline indicates that it's activated. The Adobe airbrush works just like a regular airbrush or aerosol paint can. Click once and a light layer of paint is "sprayed", hold down your mouse button and the paint gets thicker. In this example the brush size was the same for both painted areas. The airbrush is not available for all brushes.

Tablet Options
Using a tablet gives you much more control than a mouse. With my tablet I can press harder to create heavier lines, similar to if I was using a marker on paper. To set the brush options you want to control with pen pressure on your Wacom Tablet, install the tablet drivers, and check the boxes on this drop down list.

Brush Dynamic Options

Fade
Fade options are 0-9999. When set at zero, your brush strokes don't fade. In the example on the right, the Fade option was set at four, and the Spacing was changed to 150%. I clicked and dragged to paint four brush strokes. The first brush stroke is the Foreground color and the next three brush strokes fade out. When using a small brush, set the Fade and Spacing higher to see the effect.

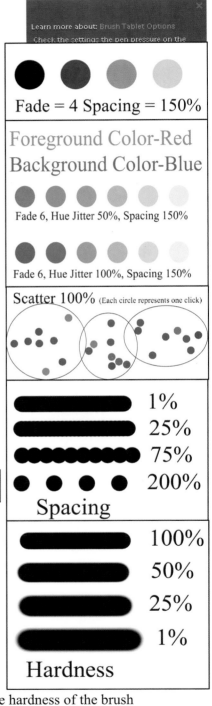

Hue Jitter
Hue Jitter options are 0-100% and specify how the brush stroke switches from the Foreground and Background colors. As shown in the example on the right, the example with the higher setting has more color changes.

Scatter
Increase the Scatter option to scatter your brush strokes when you click. In the example on the right, each circled area indicates where I clicked once. Each time I clicked, my strokes were scattered in a different random order.

Spacing
The spacing percentage sets the distance between the brush strokes. In the example on the right, the same size brush was used to click and drag the same distance. As shown above, the Options bar will change to show the brush spacing. The thumbnail examples shown above are for 1% and 200% spacing.

Keep These Settings for All Brushes
Normally I leave this box (circled above) unchecked because I am only making changes for one brush at a time. If you find that you are having trouble setting your brush options, check to see if you selected this in error.

Hardness
Hardness softens the edges of the brush. The Options bar preview changes with the hardness of the brush selected, but the change is not as obvious as when the spacing is changed. To decrease the hardness of the selected brush use the shortcut Shift>[(Left Bracket key) or increase the hardness use Shift >] (Right Bracket key. You cannot adjust the hardness on all brushes.

Angle

Rotating the angle of some brushes (not a circle) will change the look of the brush. Enter the angle percentage or drag the arrow to the angle you want. The Options bar brush thumbnail also changes when you change the brush angle.

Roundness

Roundness changes the ratio between the length and width of the brush. The roundness can be changed by dragging the dot on the angle icon. The Option Bar brush thumbnail changes to reflect the change in the brush roundness.

Saving a Modified Brush

To save a brush for future use, follow the *How to Save a Brush* tutorial in the *Make Your Own chapter*.

How to Use the Brush Tool (B)

Open an image, choose a Foreground color, and select the Brush tool from the Toolbar. Make changes to the Options bar as desired (see previous two pages). To create a new transparent layer to add the brushwork to, click on the New Layer icon at the bottom of the Layers panel, or type the shortcut Shift>Alt>Ctrl>N (Mac: Shift>Opt>Cmd>N). Click once to stamp the brush, or click and drag to paint. To paint in a straight line, click and hold the Shift key. Making a new transparent layer for each brushstroke is a good idea that will save you time.

How to Use the Impressionist Brush Tool (B)

Open an image, select the Impressionist Brush tool from the Toolbar and make changes to the Options bar as desired (see previous two pages). As shown on the right, choose a brush option from the Impressionist brush options list circled above.

To duplicate the layer, from the Menu bar, choose Layer>New>Layer via Copy or type the shortcut Ctrl>J (Mac: Cmd>J). Click and paint over the image. If the effect is too strong, lower the Opacity setting on the Options bar to allow the original image to show through.

How to Use the Color Replacement Tool (B)

Open an image, select the Color Replacement tool from the Toolbar, and make changes to the Options bar as desired (see previous two pages). I chose Color Mode. As shown on the right, brush size and other options are made by clicking on the Brush drop down list. Choose a Foreground color by clicking in the swatch at the bottom of the Toolbar.

From the Menu bar, choose Layer>New>Layer via Copy or type the shortcut Ctrl>J (Mac: Cmd>J) to duplicate the layer.

Zoom or Scroll in so you can see the image well. The cursor is now called the hotspot which is a circle with a + inside it. Click and drag over the area to be changed with the + staying on the area to be changed to keep the color in the right area. Areas of color with a large amount of contrast are easier to change than similar colors.

Contiguous is the default setting and will change all colored areas that match where you click and are touching. Discontiguous replaces the color under the hotspot.

Tolerance-Lower the Tolerance setting to select very similar colors, raise it to select a wider range of colors.

Anti-alias-Smoothes the edges that are changed, I keep this option selected.

How to Use the Pencil Tool (N)
If you like to sketch with a Wacom tablet, this is the tool to use. Open an image, choose a Foreground color, and select the Pencil tool from the Toolbar. Make changes to the Options bar as desired (see previous three pages). Only hard edged brushes are available from the brush drop down list when the Pencil tool is selected.

Click on the New Layer icon at the bottom of the Layers panel or type the shortcut Shift>Alt>Ctrl>N (Mac: Shift>Opt>Cmd>N) to create a new transparent layer to add the brushwork to. Click once to stamp the brush, or click and drag to paint. To paint in a straight line, click and hold the Shift key. Making a new transparent layer for each brushstroke is a very good idea that will save you time.

Auto Erase
Auto Erase doesn't really mean Auto Erase! This option paints with the Background color over the Foreground color that's been drawn with the Pencil tool (N).

With your Background/Foreground colors set at the defaults of black and white, try this out yourself. In this example the background is white with a blue rectangle. A black (Foreground color) line has been drawn with the Pencil tool on the layer above the rectangle. Switching to Auto Erase and dragging over the black line causes the black line to turn white (Background color). If the blue rectangle wasn't on the white background it would work fine.

The Paint Bucket Tool (K)

The Paint Bucket tool should probably be called the Magic Fill Tool. This tool fills a layer or selection with the Foreground color or pattern by searching for matching color wherever you click (depending on the options selected). The cursor for the Paint Bucket tool is an overflowing paint bucket can. The shortcut is (K).

Other ways to fill layers or selections solid without regard to matching colors are: from the Menu bar choose Edit>Fill Layer, click on the Adjustment Layer icon at the bottom of the Layers panel and choose a Pattern or Solid Color Fill layer, or use the shortcut Alt>Backspace (Mac: Opt>Delete).

How to use the Paint Bucket Tool
Open an image, select the Paint Bucket tool from the Toolbar, and make changes to the Options bar (explanations follow) as desired. Choose a Foreground color by clicking in the swatch at the bottom of the Toolbar. Click on an image to fill it with the Foreground color. The color fill will be solid and will not reflect any of the textures or variations that the original color had.

To make a scrapbook paper, click on the Background layer or make a new blank layer and click to fill the layer with solid color. To change the color of the fill, you will need to change the Foreground color swatch located at the bottom of the Toolbar.

Pattern
Click in the box to fill with a pattern. Click on the dropdown list to choose a pattern. If the dropdown box doesn't work that's because you didn't click in the Pattern box.

Mode-Choose a blending mode here. Blending modes are explained in detail in the *Filters and Blending Modes* chapter.

Opacity-The Opacity default is 100%, which means you are filling with a solid color or pattern. Lower the Opacity by typing in the amount in the box or using the slider to make your fill more transparent.

Tolerance-The default Tolerance setting is 32. The range of settings is from 0-255. If you choose 0, the Paint Bucket tool will choose only the exact color you have clicked on to fill. If you choose 255, it will select every color in the image to fill. If you are having trouble filling an area with color or a pattern try different Tolerance settings and you will probably have better luck.

Anti-alias-Smoothes the edges that are changed, I keep this option selected.

Contiguous is the default setting and will change all colored areas that match where you click and are touching.

Use All Layers-When Use All Layers is checked, the Paint Bucket tool fills the matching color pixels on all the layers in your image. This might be helpful if you decided you wanted to change the color of several elements on your scrapbook page.

Smart Brush and Detail Smart Brush Tools (F)

The Smart Brush and Detail Smart Brush tools are amazing! The tools are nested together on the Full Edit Toolbar and share the same shortcut (F). The only difference between the two tools is that the Smart Brush tool creates a selection automatically based on color from the area you first clicked on, similar to the Magic Wand tool. The Detail Smart Brush tool allows you to make changes yourself.

How to Use the Smart Brush and Detail Smart Brush Tools

Once you click on the tool icon on the Toolbar, the Preset box automatically opens so that you can choose an effect. Double click on the effect you want to select it and close the box

Choose a brush from the Options bar. Click, hold, and drag over the areas of the photo that you want to change. Once you release, you'll notice that several things have happened: The areas you dragged/painted over are changed. An Adjustment layer has been added and there are white painted areas on the mask. A little red square symbol which Adobe calls a color pin is added to the photo where you first started dragging/painting (shown circled below).

A set of three paint brushes also appear on your photo (they have always been on the Options bar). As you click and drag to lighten more areas of the photo, the center brush with the + is active. To paint over your mistakes use the brush on the right with the red – (minus) sign.

Inverse-When you Inverse a selection, you swap the selected area with the unselected area. As shown in the example on the right, if I clicked the Inverse box the majority of the image would change to green and the green area would revert back to orange.

Refine Edge- To smooth, feather and contract or expand the edge of a selection, click on the Refine Edge button and the Refine Edge dialog box will appear.

For complete step by step examples for using these tools to perform popular tasks like lightening part of a photo, changing the color of a shirt, and creating a black and white photo with some color, see the *Cool Stuff with Photos* chapter.

Gradient Tool (G)

The Gradient tool fills a selection or layer with a color that fades into another color or into a transparency. Gradients can be used to make your own papers or elements. The Gradient tool is available in Full Edit and the shortcut is (G).

The default setting for the Gradient tool is Foreground to Background. When you click and drag your mouse with the default selected, you'll be filling with the Foreground color first and fading into the Background color. The point in which the foreground color ends and the background color begins is at the halfway point. Changing these options is easy. Gradients can be used on masks to edit photos as shown in the *Cool Stuff with Photos* chapter. Applying a filter to a Gradient can soften its look or change the look entirely.

How to Use the Gradient Tool

Click on the drop down list and you have a choice of the 15 Default gradients. To match the example, type the letter D to set your Foreground and Background colors (located at the bottom of the Toolbar) to the default settings. Your Foreground color should be black, and your Background color should be white. Hover your mouse over the thumbnail and you can see the Gradient name. The checkerboard indicates that the Gradient fades to a transparency. Click on the side arrow to change the size of the gradient thumbnails, reset, load other gradient sets, save or replace gradients, and display other gradient sets available to use.

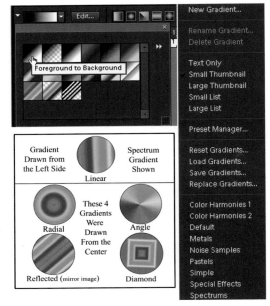

Type-Choose a type of gradient by clicking on the icon on the Options bar (circled above). The default setting is Linear, but you can also choose from Radial, Angle, Reflected, and Diamond. Once you choose one of these options, it will remain your default gradient until you switch to another one.

Gradients will look different depending on the settings you use and the direction from which they are drawn.

The gradients in this example were drawn in a selection made by the Elliptical Marquee tool (M) with the Spectrum Gradient.

Mode-Choose a blending mode here. For more information, see the *Filters and Blending Modes* Chapter.

Opacity-The Opacity default is 100%, which means you are filling with a solid color gradient. Lower the Opacity by typing in the amount in the box or using the slider to make your fill more transparent.

Reverse-Checking this box reverses the colors in your gradient. By checking this box your starting color will become the ending color and the ending color will become your starting color.

Dither-I keep this box checked to make the colors blend together better.

Transparency-Check this box if you have any transparency in your gradient or it won't work correctly. I keep it checked all the time.

Open a new image and make a new layer or selection. It's a good idea to put your gradient on its own layer so you can edit it in the future. Choose your gradient and settings. Click and drag your mouse, when you release your mouse the gradient is drawn. The whole layer or selection will be filled with the gradient.

How you click and drag will affect the gradient. The farther you drag your mouse (even off the edge of your page), the smoother your gradient will be drawn. As shown on the right, I used the same sized heart with the Blue, Red, Yellow gradient from the Default Gradient set.

Because I started dragging my gradient where the arrows begin (beyond the edge of the heart), barely any of the blue color shows. The heart looks different in each example because I dragged the gradient in different directions.

How to Edit a Gradient
To edit a gradient, click on the Edit icon on the Options bar which displays the Gradient Editor dialog box. Here you can choose a gradient and customize it. To adjust a gradient: move, add or delete color and/or opacity stops. You can also change the Smoothness setting from solid to noise.

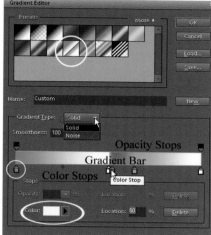

Stops-The tiny icons that look like ink bottles are stops. To change where the opacity changes and where each color starts and stops, drag one of the stops or type a percentage in the Location box at the bottom of the dialog box. In the example on the right, to adjust the Opacity, click and drag one of the Opacity stops or just click and the Opacity Percentage box will no longer be grayed out; then type the percentage number in the box.

The Opacity stops are located on the top of the Gradient Bar and the color stops are located under the Gradient Bar. Once you move one of the stops, the small diamonds appear to mark the exact spot the color/opacity starts and stops. These can be dragged to make changes, then can also be moved by scrolling the wheel on your mouse. To completely delete the blue color from the gradient, click on the blue color stop and then click on the Delete button or drag the color stop down from the Gradient Bar until it disappears. To change a color, double click inside the color on the color stop or in the color box and the Adobe Color Picker is activated; choose a color and click OK. To use a color from your image in the Gradient, hover over the Gradient Bar and your cursor becomes the Eyedropper Tool. Click on the color stop you want to change, and then go to your image and click and the color stop is changed to the color from your image.

To add an additional Opacity stop, click just above the Gradient Bar. To add an additional Color stop, click just below the Gradient Bar and a new stop will be added, which is the color showing in the color box at the time. Double click in the stop to change it.

The Gradient Type can be changed to Solid or Noise. When you choose noise, different options are displayed. Smoothness sets the transition smoothness between the colors.

If you aren't happy with the changes you have made, hold the Alt key (Mac: Opt key) and click on the Cancel button to change it to a Reset button. Once you are happy with the changes, click the OK button. Click and drag the gradient to see if you like it. If you don't like it, edit it again.

When you make a new Gradient, click the New button and your Gradient is added to the thumbnails. If you want to remove it, right click on the thumbnail and choose Delete.

To Save a Gradient, name the Gradient and click on the Save button. You will be saving it in the Gradient Folder located in the Presets Folder, which is in the Adobe Photoshop Elements Program File. I also save mine in a file called PSE Gradients, because if I have to reload my program, they will probably be lost. Restart the program and you can load the Gradient you saved.

Once you make changes to a gradient, the name changes to Custom. To rename it, double click in the field and type a new name. If you forgot to rename it, you can right click on the gradient thumbnail and choose Rename Gradient.

Shape Tools

There are six different shape tools: Rectangle, Rounded Rectangle, Ellipse, Polygon, Line, and Custom Shape. In addition, there is a seventh tool, the Shape Selection tool used to move or resize shapes and all are nested in the third tool from the bottom of the Full Edit Toolbar. They all share the shortcut (U). These tools can be used together or independent of each other.

Shape layers are made automatically when you make a shape with any of the Shape tools. Because they are vector based shape layers, they can be adjusted to any size and will still keep their detail and smooth edges. You must Simplify a Shape layer to use the Red Eye Removal, Cookie Cutter, Eraser (All), Brush (All), Pencil, Healing Brush (All), Clone Stamp (All), Gradient, Blur, Sharpen, Smudge, Sponge, Dodge, Burn tools, or add filters.

Shared Shape Tool Options:
All of the options for these tools are essentially the same, except for a few that are specific to their tool, like Radius for the Rounded Rectangle Tool. Any tool specific option will be listed under the section pertaining to that tool.

Unconstrained-However you drag out the shape, the tool will draw it. If you drag a heart out that is tall and skinny, the Custom Shape tool will draw a tall and skinny heart. If you want to drag from the center, use the From Center setting.

Defined Proportions-This option will keep the shape in the proportions of the example. When you drag out a heart, it will have the same proportions as the heart shown on the shape thumbnail. The Rectangle & Rounded Rectangle tool will show Square and the Ellipse tool will show circle instead of Defined Proportions. From Center can also be selected with Defined Proportions.

Defined Size-To draw the shape in the size that the designer created it, choose this option. You won't know what that size is until you release your mouse. If you don't like the size, you can use the sizing handles. From Center can be selected with Defined Size.

Fixed Size-Fixed Size crops to the exact dimensions you enter. If you enter 2 inches wide by 2 inches high and you pick a rectangle, the Rectangle tool (U) will draw a 2 inch square. Size can be entered as inches, centimeters, or pixels. From Center can also be selected with Fixed Size.

From Center-This option will draw the shape outward from the center. If you want to draw a daisy into a shape, start at the daisy center and draw outward to get it perfectly centered in the shape. From center can be selected with all the other options too.

Create a New Shape Layer- Creates a new shape on its own layer. This option is the default setting. The first shape layer added to a file is named Shape 1.

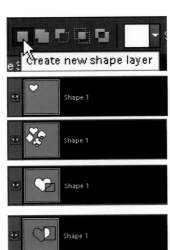

Add to a Shape Area-Adds more shapes to an existing shape layer. All shapes will be on the same layer; the layer thumbnail will also reflect this. Holding the Shift key will also do the same thing.

Subtract from a Shape Area-To subtract from a shape, click on this box and drag over the shape you want to subtract from. This is a little bit confusing because the old shape boundary shows on your screen (when the layer is selected) and layer thumbnail, as does the boundary of the shape you used to subtract with. These lines do not print.

Intersect Shape Areas-The area that overlaps between two shapes is left over. Both of the layer boundaries show on your screen (when the layer is selected) and layer thumbnail, but will not print.

Exclude Overlapping Shape Areas-This is the opposite of intersect shape areas. The areas that do not intersect are filled with color. The layer boundaries show on your screen (when the layer is selected) and layer thumbnail, but will not print.

Color-The Foreground color is the default color for a new shape. With your shape layer active, changing the Color box also changes the color of the shape. Click inside on the drop down list to choose a color, or click inside the color box to activate the Adobe Color Picker. After you have created a shape layer double clicking in the shape layer thumbnail will also display the Adobe Color Picker.

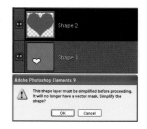

If you have Simplified the shape, you can no longer change the color by changing the Color box. Ctrl click to make a selection border (marching ants) around the shape and then fill the selection by typing the shortcut Alt>Backspace (Mac: Opt>Delete).

Style-To add or remove a Layer Style without having to go to the Effects panel, click on the drop down arrow. The default setting is No Layer Style.

Simplify-Shapes are raster images. In simple terms, the edges of a raster image will remain crisp no matter how big you size them. If you Simplify (rasterize) your shape layer, it is turned into a pixel based layer. When you resize a pixel based layer, the edges will get pixilated.   Simplify a shape layer only when you have to, like when you need to add a gradient, filter, etc. If needed, enlarge the shape before you Simplify it.

If you can't remember if you simplified your shape layer, look at the layer in the Layers palette. As shown in the example, a simplified shape layer will have a transparent background on the layer thumbnail, which is indicated by a checkerboard. The layer name does not change when the shape is simplified. To move a simplified shape, you will have to activate the Move tool (V) as the Shape Selection tool (U) only works on shapes that have not been simplified.

Rectangle & Rounded Rectangle Tools (U)

These tools are used to draw rectangles or squares with straight or rounded edges. To draw a square shape, hold the Shift key when dragging out the shape.

Snap to Pixels-This option, available in the shape options drop down list, moves your rectangle to the edge of a pixel so that you get a sharper shape. Keep this option selected when using these tools.

Radius-The Radius default setting is 10 px. You may enter from 0-1000 px. A 0 px radius is a straight edged rectangle. Holding the Shift key to draw a square and setting the radius at 1000 will draw a circle.

All other options for this tool are explained under Shared Shape Tool Options.

Ellipse Tool (U)

This tool is used to draw ovals and circles. To draw a circle shape, hold the Shift key when dragging out the shape. All other options for this tool are explained under Shared Shape Tool Options.

Polygon Tool (U)

The Polygon tool (U) draws from the center outward by default. Choose between 3 and 100 sides to make your polygon. To round corners, enter an amount in the radius box. On some polygons smoothing the corners will turn it into a circle. To change a polygon into a star by inverting the angles, check the Star box. If you are drawing a star, check the Smooth Indent box to curve the inside edges of the star. All other options for this tool are explained under Shared Shape Tool Options.

Line Tool (U)

To draw lines with or without arrowheads use the Line tool. Normally, if I need an arrow, I use the ones in the Custom Shape tool. Enter a pixel width for your line on the Options bar. The default is 1 px, but any amount between 1 px and 1000 px can be entered.

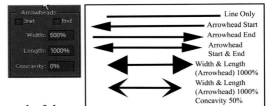

Arrowheads-Start & End-An arrowhead is added at the beginning or end of the line or both. Width & Length-The default setting for Width is 500% and the default setting for length is 1000%. Any amount between 10% and 1000% can be entered to set the Arrowheads size, which is a percentage of the line width. Concavity-The default setting is 0% but a percentage between -50% and +50% can be entered to add a curve to the Arrowhead. All other options for this tool are explained under Shared Shape Tool Options.

Custom Shape Tool (U)

Click on the drop down list to the right of Shape (circled above). This displays the library of shapes that were last used. If you don't see the library you want, click on the small circle with a triangle in it at the top of the current library. It will display all of the libraries that are available. Any shapes that you loaded in from another source will also show up here. Notice the line that says All Elements Shapes. It means only the shapes that came preloaded.

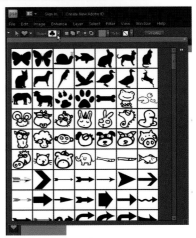

Hover over each individual shape square and a description will pop up. Double click a shape to accept it and close the library box. All other options for this tool are explained under Shared Shape Tool Options.

How to use the Shape Tools (U) Activate the Shape Tool (U) by typing the letter U, or clicking on it on the Toolbar. Choose the shape, size option, color, and layer style preference. Click or click and drag (depending on the shape option chosen) the shape and then release your mouse. The shape will be drawn on its own layer.

To draw several shapes exactly the same, switch to the Shape Selection tool (U) or the Move tool (V) and hold the Alt key (Mac: Opt key). Click, drag, and release your mouse to add each additional shape. To constrain the shapes to a straight line, you will have to use the Move Tool (V) and hold the Shift and Alt keys together.

Shape Selection Tool (U)

The Shape Selection tool is used to select and move shapes without having to switch to the Move tool. This is a time saver. When there is more than one shape on a layer, the Shape Selection tool must be used to move **one** of the shapes. The Move tool will move all of the Shapes on the layer together as if they are linked. If the shape has been Simplified, the Shape Selection tool will no longer work and you'll have to use the Move tool instead.

The **Bounding Box** marks the edges of the shape and the center as soon as you click on the shape. When this box is not checked, there will still be a slight outline around the shape when the shape layer is selected.

Combine-To combine two or more shapes that are already on one layer, click on the Combine button.

How to Use the Shape Selection Tool-Activate the Shape Selection tool (U) and click and drag the shape to move it to a different location. Dragging one of the sizing handles on the sides or corners will transform the shape and the Transform Options bar will be displayed. Check the green checkmark ✓ on the Options bar when you are finished using this tool.

Filters & Blending Modes

Filters

Filters add an artistic touch to your images whether they are photos or scrapbook elements. There are many filters to choose from. Most filters include options that allow you to further customize the filter. All filters can be applied from the Filter Menu on the Menu bar, and many can also be applied from the Effects panel. To apply a filter to just a portion of a layer, make a selection on the layer and then apply the filter.

To apply a filter, open an image and from the Menu bar, choose Filter. Choose a filter from the list which is in alphabetical order. A filter listed with … after its name indicates that some kind of filter dialog box will open allowing you to make changes, otherwise the filter will be automatically applied by Photoshop Elements.

Some filters are affected by the Foreground and Background color, so before applying a filter type D to replace the current colors with the default colors of black and white. To vary the effect of the filter, try different colors to see if it makes a difference.

When applying a filter, duplicate the layer and add the filter to the copy. This way if you change your mind, you can delete the copy layer. Also, by adding the filter to the copy you can blend it with the layer below, creating great effects which can be seen in the *Cool Stuff with Photos* chapter.

After you have applied a filter and want to apply the same filter with the same settings to another image, type the shortcut Ctrl>F (Mac: Cmd>F). To apply the same filter and open the dialog box so that you can make changes, type the shortcut Ctrl>Alt>F (Mac: Cmd>Opt>F).

While the dialog box is still open, to add a filter on top of another filter, click on the New Effect Layer icon circled on the right. To delete additional filters, click on the filter layer and then click on the trash can icon.

The size of an image will affect the filter effect. If you plan to reduce the size of an image, apply the filter to the full sized image first and then shrink it. Filters require a lot of RAM, if your computer is struggling to apply a filter from the Menu bar choose Edit>Clear Undo and Edit>Clear Clipboard.

Filter examples marked with an * (asterisk) on the pages that follow indicate that the layer was duplicated and the filter was added to the top layer, and the blending mode on the top layer was changed to Overlay. Examples marked with ** indicate that a texture was loaded to create the texture. Texture files are PSD files that are located in the Program Presets Texture folder.

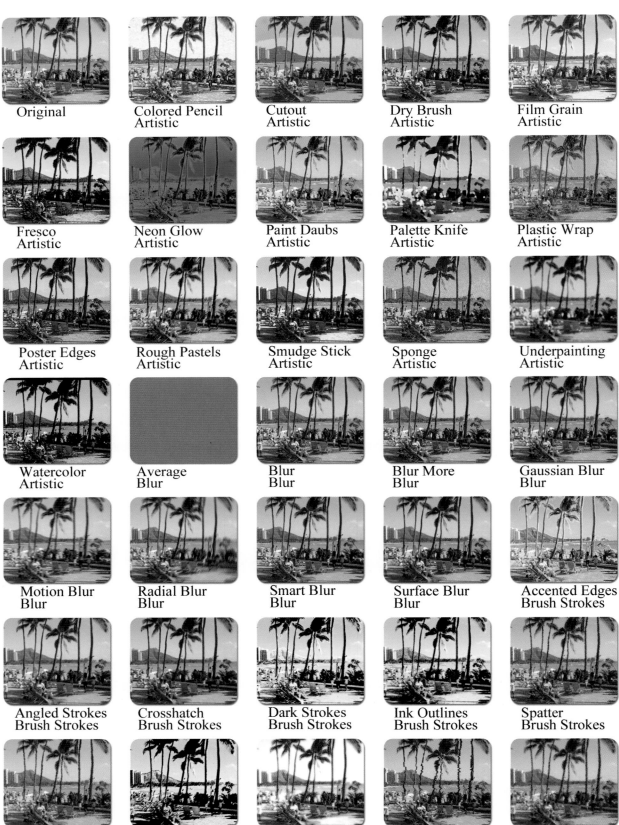

Original	Colored Pencil Artistic	Cutout Artistic	Dry Brush Artistic	Film Grain Artistic
Fresco Artistic	Neon Glow Artistic	Paint Daubs Artistic	Palette Knife Artistic	Plastic Wrap Artistic
Poster Edges Artistic	Rough Pastels Artistic	Smudge Stick Artistic	Sponge Artistic	Underpainting Artistic
Watercolor Artistic	Average Blur	Blur Blur	Blur More Blur	Gaussian Blur Blur
Motion Blur Blur	Radial Blur Blur	Smart Blur Blur	Surface Blur Blur	Accented Edges Brush Strokes
Angled Strokes Brush Strokes	Crosshatch Brush Strokes	Dark Strokes Brush Strokes	Ink Outlines Brush Strokes	Spatter Brush Strokes
Sprayed Strokes Brush Strokes	Sumi-e Brush Strokes	Diffuse Glow Distort	Displace Distort	Glass Distort

Liquify Distort	Ocean Ripple Distort	Pinch Distort	Polar Coordinates Distort	Ripple Distort
Shear Distort	Spherize Distort	Twirl Distort	Wave Distort	Zig Zag Distort
Add Noise Noise	Despeckle Noise	Dust & Scratches Noise	Median Noise	Reduce Noise Noise
Color Halftone Pixelate	Crystallize Pixelate	Facet Pixelate	Fragment Pixelate	Mezzotint Pixelate
Mossaic Pixelate	Pointillize Pixelate	Clouds* Render	Difference Clouds Render	Fibers* Render
Lens Flare Render	Lighting Effects Render	Texture Fill** Render	Bas Relief Sketch	Chalk & Charcoal Sketch
Charcoal Sketch	Chrome Sketch	Conte Crayon Sketch	Graphic Pen Sketch	Halftone Pattern Sketch

* & ** See page 119

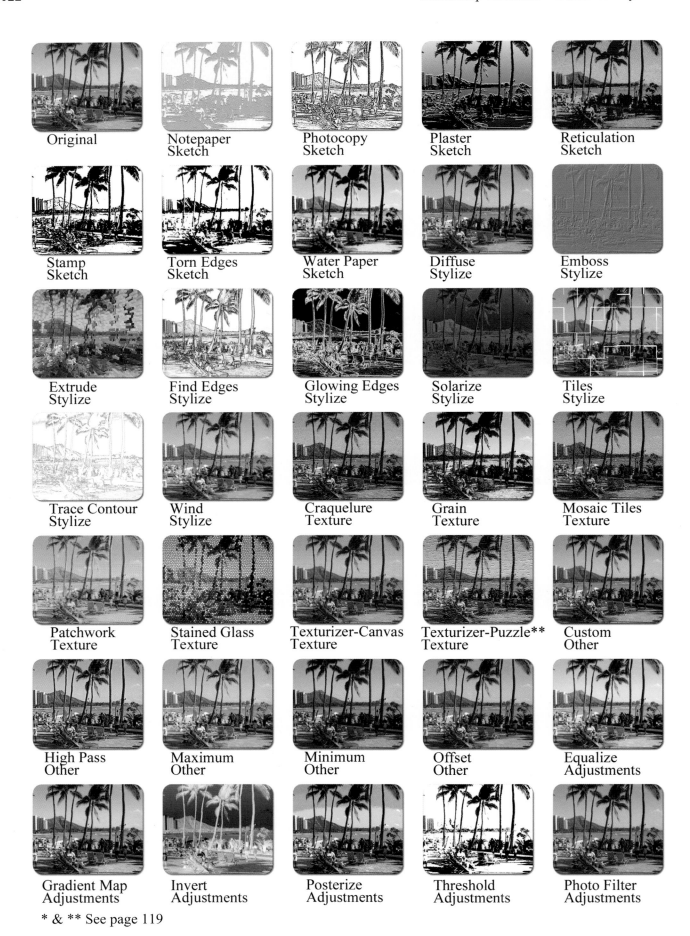

Original

Notepaper
Sketch

Photocopy
Sketch

Plaster
Sketch

Reticulation
Sketch

Stamp
Sketch

Torn Edges
Sketch

Water Paper
Sketch

Diffuse
Stylize

Emboss
Stylize

Extrude
Stylize

Find Edges
Stylize

Glowing Edges
Stylize

Solarize
Stylize

Tiles
Stylize

Trace Contour
Stylize

Wind
Stylize

Craquelure
Texture

Grain
Texture

Mosaic Tiles
Texture

Patchwork
Texture

Stained Glass
Texture

Texturizer-Canvas
Texture

Texturizer-Puzzle**
Texture

Custom
Other

High Pass
Other

Maximum
Other

Minimum
Other

Offset
Other

Equalize
Adjustments

Gradient Map
Adjustments

Invert
Adjustments

Posterize
Adjustments

Threshold
Adjustments

Photo Filter
Adjustments

* & ** See page 119

Blending Modes

For beginners, blending modes are probably one of the most misunderstood and feared aspects of Photoshop Elements. But in reality they're so simple to use that I added them to my Beginning Photo Editing classes so that my students would learn them early and not be afraid of them.

When I tried to learn more about blending, I turned to the Photoshop Elements help menu. This is how they define the Hue (the shortest definition in the list) blending mode: "Creates a result color with the luminance and saturation of the base color and the hue of the blend color". I used to think that someday I was actually going to easily understand what that meant and in return I would understand exactly how blending modes worked. What I have found by experimenting and talking with a lot of people is that I have a few favorite blending modes for specific tasks and if those don't work the way I want them to, I try another one.

Basically, a blending mode changes the way a layer or brushwork blends with the layer below it. For this reason you cannot apply a blending mode to a Background layer. As shown in the example on the right, this is the reason why the blending mode drop down list is grayed out.

As shown in the example on the right, with two or more layers, you are able to click on the drop down arrow to display the list of blending modes.

When using a tool that utilizes brushes, the blending modes are listed on the specific tool Options bar. As show in the example of the Blur tool Options bar on the left, not all of the blending modes may be available for use. Different tools will have different blending mode options.

The default blending mode setting is Normal. Think of two printed photos. If you have them stacked on top of each other, as long as they are the same size you can't see the photo on the bottom. This is how Normal at 100% opacity works in Photoshop Elements.

Change the blending mode and all kinds of fun and weird things start to happen. There are several ways to select a blending mode, the easiest way is to click on the drop down arrow and click on one. Because I often want to try out several different blending modes, it is time consuming to repeat this step.

There are several ways to quickly cycle through the blending mode list depending on your version of Photoshop Elements and your operating system. To cycle through the list, you must first drop down the blending mode list and choose one. Then try one of these options: roll the scroll wheel on your mouse wheel, tap the Up or Down Arrow keys, or tap the Shift and the + and – key. Using one of these methods I can quickly scroll through the list of 25 blending modes. When I reach Luminosity I am at the bottom of the list and need to work my way back up the list to Normal. As you cycle through the blending modes, you will notice that most of them change your image, some dramatically, but some won't change at all. There is also a complete blending mode shortcut list on page 356 in the *Speed It Up* chapter.

When you have a few minutes, the best way to start using blending modes is to just play around with them. Try blending a photo with a digital paper or vice versa as shown in the *Cool Stuff with Photos* chapter.

Adjusting the layer's opacity will also lower the effect of the blending mode. The Opacity box is located to the right of the blending mode drop down list. Different ways to adjust the opacity are: click on the drop down arrow and click on or slide the slider, enter a percentage in the Opacity box, hover over the word Opacity until the two headed scrubby arrow appears, or use the keyboard shortcut of typing 1 for 10% when several tools are active.

Duplicating a layer with a blending mode intensifies the effect of the blending mode. From the Menu bar, choose Layer>New>Layer via Copy or type the shortcut Ctrl>J (Mac: Cmd>J) to duplicate a layer.

As shown on the blending mode shortcut list on page 356 the blending modes are broken up in groups in the drop down list according to what they do. However, don't get frustrated when you select the Lighten or Darken blending mode and expect them to Lighten or Darken your photo. As shown in several examples in the *Cool Stuff with Photos* chapter, you need to try several blending modes until you find the one that works well for you.

My favorite blending mode to lighten a photo is Screen. When I chose Lighten for this photo nothing happened. As you can see by the top example, I added multiple layers set at screen.

As shown in the second example to darken a photo, I use Multiply. When I chose Darken on this photo nothing happened. Sometimes I change by text layers to Multiply to make them look more realistic.

To blend photos with papers or other photos, I use Overlay, Soft Light, Hard Light, or Pin Light. In the third example I used Hard Light and lowered the Opacity to 63%. I also clipped the photo to the mat.

Before you spend the time removing a white background from a layer, try changing the blending mode to Darken or Multiply and see if you like the effect. As shown in the fourth example, I scanned a school announcement and dragged it to a photo taken at the event. Instead of using a tool to remove the white background, I simply changed the blending mode to Darken.

To intensify the color in a drab photo, I use Soft Light.

When using blending modes as shown in the Screen example above, I may have to duplicate a layer several times to intensify the effect, or as shown in the third example I may need to lower the opacity of the layer to lessen the effect. You may apply different blending modes to the same image.

When using a tool with a blending mode option, you may choose a blending mode like Screen and paint directly on a layer. Using shades of gray works well for photo editing. While the result will not be exactly the same, I prefer painting on a new transparent layer so that I have more editing options. To do that, choose the Normal blending mode and paint on a new transparent layer, then change the blending mode to Screen.

How to Use....

So admit it...you've skipped over the rest of the book to this section because you want to get started right now! I know your type...I was just like you. Before you get really frustrated, read over the *First Things First* chapter to save you some grief. When you get stuck...and you will...be sure to read the *What Did I Do Wrong* chapter.

Before you begin any project, make a new blank file. Think of this as starting a traditional paper scrapbook page (or other project), with a piece of white cardstock as your base. The reasons for this are twofold. First you won't save over your digital supplies by mistake, and second you'll be assured that your project is print quality. As a beginner I didn't know better, and as a result encountered many problems that are easily alleviated by this simple step.

How to Make a New Blank File

From the Menu bar choose File>New>Blank file. The shortcut is Ctrl>N (Mac: Cmd>N).

If you are using a Mac, there is also a New File shortcut as shown circled, in the example on the right.

Type a name for your project.

Choose a preset size from the Preset drop down list. I normally enter in my own dimensions because it's faster.

To enter the dimensions, I normally choose inches before I type in the numbers for Width & Height. Enter the dimensions for your project.

Special Note: If you are making a card or envelope, measure the item with a ruler and type in those dimensions. When making an 8 x 8 (or any square size) scrapbook page I enter 12 x 12 inches for the dimensions. Otherwise I have to resize each piece of paper as I drag it on if I want to include the grungy edges of the paper. When it's time to print, I can choose to print it in a smaller size.

Resolution is 300 pixels per inch (ppi) for great print quality. If you are creating something for the Web, only enter 72 pixels per inch.

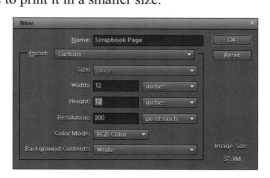

Color Mode is RGB Color.

Background Contents is White. Some people will use Transparent for this setting, but I find it easier to see things with a white background.

If you would rather use Preset options for Scrapbooking to set up your page, there are 3 different sizes available.

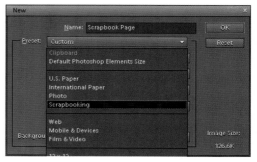

To save yourself time if you normally work with the same size new file, use the shortcut Ctrl>Alt>N (Mac: Cmd>Opt>N) to bring up the dialog box with the same settings as the last page you made.

How to Use a Quick Page to Make a Scrapbook Page

Quick Pages and Ploppers are pages that are put together for you by a designer; all you need to do is add your photo(s) and journaling and the page is done. Many designers make Quick Pages that match their kits so that you will have many options for making your pages quickly. Some designers have their own specialized names for their brand of Quick Pages.

Make a new blank file as explained in the beginning of this chapter. Open a Quick Page. In this example I will be using a Quick Page made by Amy Teets. You can find this file on the *Photoshop Elements-Basics & Beyond* DVD in Amy's folder. The name of the file I am using is: ateets_ss_qp. The checkerboard area indicates that these areas are transparent so that you can slide your pictures underneath and have them show through.

Open two pictures. Select the Move tool (V) on the Toolbar. Click, hold, and drag the Quick Page to the plain white file. As explained in more detail in the Move tool section, this can be done two ways.

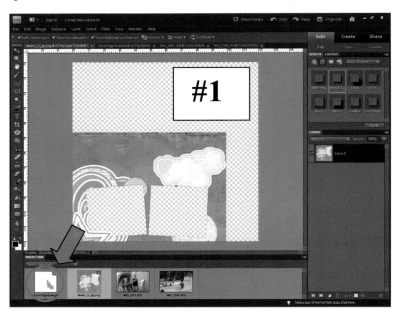

#1 Double click on the Quick Page image in the Project bin to make it the active image (big). With the Quick Page as the active image (big), click, hold, and drag the image **down** into the Project bin to the plain white file. When Windows users see the + sign on the cursor let go; Mac users will not see their cursor change. This method works for all versions of Photoshop Elements. Do not click on a transparent area (checkerboard) or you will not be able to move the file.

Release the mouse and the Quick Page will be added to your new scrapbook page file. The layer name will be Layer 1.

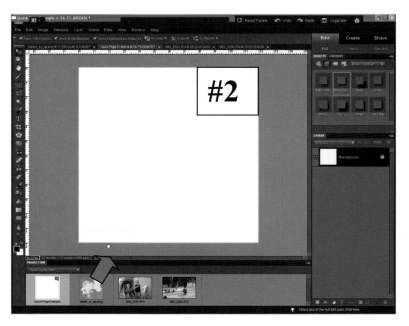

#2 With the plain white file as the active image (big), click, hold, and drag the Quick Page **up** from the Project bin and touch the plain white file.

Release the mouse and the Quick Page will be added to your new scrapbook page file. The layer name will be the actual file name.

Note: method #2 will only work **correctly** with Photoshop Elements 9, 8, & 5.

Currently the Quick Page layer is selected. Click on the Background layer (plain white paper) in the Layers panel to make it the selected layer.

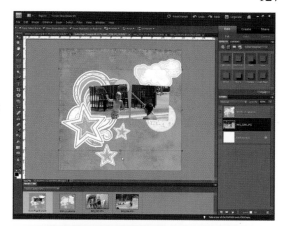

Select a photo in the Project bin and drag it onto your page using either method. The photo will land exactly in the middle of the page. By selecting the Background layer first, the photo will be placed in between the Quick Page layer and the Background layer. Choose File>Save from the Menu bar.

Click and drag a **corner** sizing handle to re-size the photo to fit one of the boxes. Dragging a side sizing handle will cause the photo to be distorted. Don't worry if some of the photo hangs over into the second transparent area. Check the green checkmark ✓ to confirm the transformation.

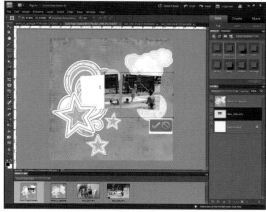

Click and drag the second photo onto the page. Because the first photo was the selected layer, the second photo will automatically come in on the layer above it. It will also drop right in the middle of the page. Save.

Click and drag a corner sizing handle to re-size the photo to fit the second box. Depending on the sizes of your photos, there will be some overhang that will need to be removed in a future step.

If the overhang is distracting, hide one of the photo layers while you adjust the other one. To hide a layer, click on the eyeball icon to the left of the layer thumbnail (shown circled). To turn the layer back on, click in the empty box where the eyeball was and the eyeball and layer will reappear.

To crop off the overhanging photo, select the Marquee tool (M) on the Toolbar (do not choose the Crop tool). Click hold and drag out a box over the part of the photo that needs to be removed.

Select the layer in the Layers panel that needs to be cropped, this is very important!

Choose Edit>Delete from the Menu bar, or simply tap the Delete key on the keyboard to remove the selected area. Save.

To remove the selection border (marching ants) choose Select>Deselect, or use the shortcut Ctrl>D (Mac: Cmd>D). The Esc key will also work for most people.

Add text using the Type tool (T) if desired and save your page. Choose File>Close All (Alt>Ctrl>W Mac: Opt>Cmd>W) from the Menu bar to close all images.

How to Use a Scrapbook Kit to Make a Scrapbook Page

Make a new blank file as shown at the beginning of this chapter.
Open (File>Open or open from the Organizer) the papers and scrapbook embellishments that you plan to use on the page; don't worry about opening up too many because you don't have to use everything you open. Open your photos.

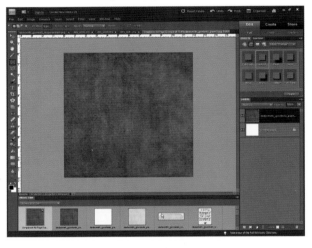

In this example I am using the Good EatZ kit by DeDe Smith from the *Photoshop Elements-Basics & Beyond* DVD. Note: some of these papers will show guide lines on them. If this is distracting to you choose View>Clear Guides

Using method #1 or #2, drag a piece of paper onto the plain white file with the Move tool to begin building the page as shown in the preceding example.

Drag a second piece of paper onto the scrapbook page. This new paper will completely cover the first red paper I dragged on. Save.

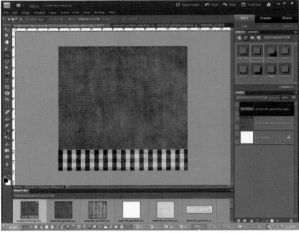

If you only want to use a strip of this paper, choose the Marquee tool and drag out a selection of the area that you want to remove. Once you have a selection, tap the Delete or Backspace key to cut away the portion of the layer you don't want. To remove the selection border (marching ants), from the Menu bar, choose Select>Deselect (Ctrl>D Mac: Cmd>D).

Switch back to the Move tool and drag on another piece of paper. If you would like a border around the page, drag the **corner** sizing handles inward to shrink the layer. To save time, click on the handle and then hold the Alt key (Mac: Opt key) to size the layer from the center. Be aware that sizing this paper will make the pattern smaller on this layer, so it may not work for all of your papers, but on this one it will work fine.

Check the green checkmark ✓ to confirm the transformation.

If desired, with the Move tool selected, click and drag the black checked strip up a little bit.

Save.

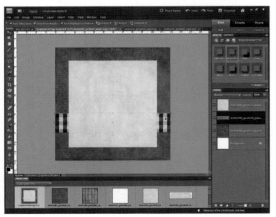

Click on the top layer (yellow paper) in the Layers panel and then drag a photo onto the page using the Move tool. The photo will drop in the center of the page. Reposition it by dragging it. Resize it by dragging a **corner** sizing handle. Repeat for each photo you want to add to the page.

Mat a Photo
There are several ways to mat a photo, but I'll show you the two ways that I normally use.

Because I want the mat paper to be below the photos, I will click on the yellow paper layer in the Layers panel. By selecting this layer, the mat paper will be added to my scrapbook page directly above the yellow paper layer which will be below the photos. If I were to drag the mat paper on with the photo selected above, the mat paper layer would cover two photos. I would have to rearrange my layers in the Layers panel by clicking on the layer and dragging it down below the bottom photo.

As shown in the example below, once I drag the mat paper onto my scrapbook page it will cover up the layers below. Make sure the mat paper layer is selected (red arrow).

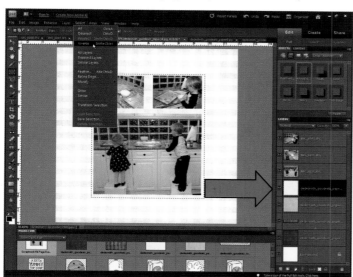

Select the Marquee tool (M) and click and drag a selection the size you would like the mat. Choose Select>Inverse (Shift>Ctrl>I, Mac: Shift>Cmd>I). Once the selection is inversed, the marching ants will surround the outside edge of the page and the area for the mat. Choose Edit>Delete from the Menu bar, or tap the Delete or Backspace key to delete the part of the paper you don't want.

Choose Select>Deselect (Ctrl>D, Mac: Cmd>D) from the Menu bar to remove the selection border (marching ants), or tap the Esc key which will work for most people.

This method works fine for one mat but if I were to make individual mats for all 3 photos, it would take extra time. If you want to mat several photos, try the next method instead.

With the mat paper layer under the photo layers, use the Marquee tool to make a selection around one of the photos. Select the mat paper layer (red arrow) and choose Layer>New>Via Copy (Ctrl>J, Mac: Cmd>J). A mat will be added on a new layer in the Layers panel directly above the mat paper layer. Deselect.

Use the Marquee tool to make a selection around another photo. Select the mat paper layer and choose Layer>New>Via Copy (Ctrl>J, Mac: Cmd>J). A second mat will be added.

Repeat as necessary. If you are having trouble, it is probably because you are not selecting the full size mat paper layer in the Layers panel.

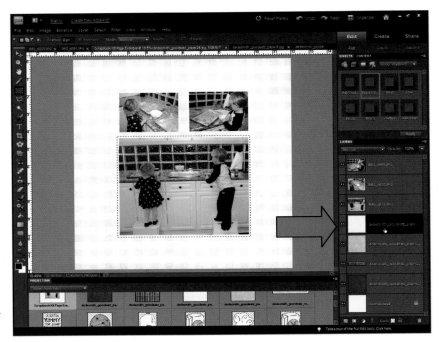

Save.

To see the location of the layers on the page, it may be helpful to switch the Panel Options from Layer Bounds to Entire Document as shown in the *Panels* chapter.

Hide the full 12 x 12 mat paper by clicking on the eyeball icon (circled). If you don't think you'll use it anymore, it can be deleted by clicking and dragging it to the trash can at the bottom of the Layers panel, or right clicking (Mac: Ctrl>Click) and choosing Delete layer.

Using the Move tool, click on the top layer in the Layers panel and drag on embellishments. If you are having trouble moving elements with transparent areas, be sure that you are clicking directly on a solid part of the layer.

Position the embellishments on the page, just as you would on a traditional paper scrapbook page.

To add text using the Type tool, select the top layer in the Layers panel. Choose a font from the font drop down list, click and start typing on the page. To confirm the text, check the green checkmark ✓on the Type tool Options bar (shown circled in red on the next page).

Add drop shadows to each layer by choosing Drop Shadows from the Effects panel drop down list. I normally use a Low drop shadow (shown circled in white).

Double click on the Drop Shadow icon to add the drop shadow.

To read more about adjusting, copying, and pasting Drop Shadows, see the *Panels* chapter.

Save. If you are not printing this page at home you will need to save it as a JPEG file to send to the printer. Choose File>Save As and choose JPEG for the format. More saving information is covered in *The Basics* chapter.

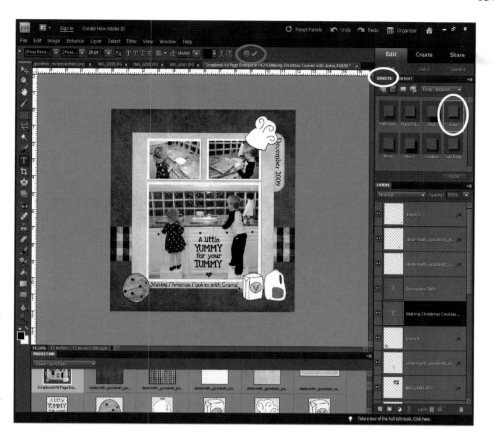

From the Menu bar, choose File>Close All (Alt>Ctrl>W Mac: Opt> Cmd>W) to close all images.

How to Use a Scrapbook Kit to Make a Two Page Layout at One Time

Making a two page layout at one time is really no different than making a single page layout. For me, it's a lot easier to scrap this way. If you are/were a paper scrapper you probably made two page layouts most of the time, so why not do the same thing digitally?

Make a new blank file, but this time change the width dimension to 24 inches.

You may want to add a Guide line or turn on your Grids to mark the center of the page to help you with page layout . In my example below I have added a Guide line at the ruler's 12 inch mark. To turn on the rulers, choose View>Rulers. To add a Guide line, click and drag on the side ruler and an aqua colored guide line will be added to the page. Click and drag it to the center of the page. More information about Guides and Grids can be found in *The Basics* chapter.

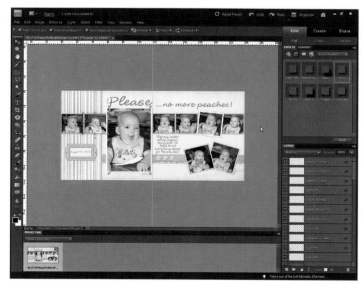

Complete the page as you would a single page layout as explained in the preceding example.

In my example, I am using the following products available at *www.TheDigitalScrapbookTeacher.com*:
24 x 12 #C Template set – Template #04 and Springtime Paper & Embellishment Kit

To print the page, you have a couple of options: Print the page as a 24 x 12 inch page, or crop the page in half and print two 12 x 12 inch pages.

My neighborhood Costco prints pages in a 24 x 12 inch size. At this time, you cannot upload the 24 x 12 inch file to them, you must bring the file into the store which is something I personally don't like to do. While the price for printing one 24 x 12 inch page is less expensive than printing two 12 x 12 inch pages, the big problem for me is that I have to cut the page in half. I'm dangerous with a paper cutter or scissors!

There are several options for printing 12 x 12 inch pages, including PersnicketyPrints.com, PolkaDotPotato.com, your local scrapbook or photo stores, Costco, and many others popping up all the time.

To print the page as two 12 x 12 pages: Save (File>Save) the finished page first as a PSD file. Choose the Crop tool from the Toolbar. This is the one exception where you can use the Crop tool on a scrapbook page!

On the Crop tool's Options bar enter 12 inches in the Width and Height boxes. Enter 300 pixels/inch in the Resolution box.

Starting from beyond the top left corner of the page, click, hold, and drag towards the bottom center off the page. Release the mouse and Check the green checkmark ✓ to confirm the crop.

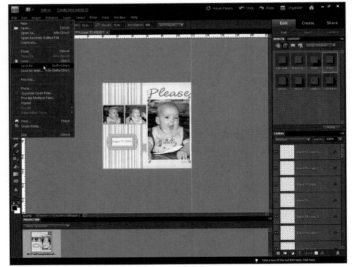

The right side of the page will disappear once you commit the crop. Many of the layers in the Layers panel will now be blank. This is all OK!

If you are printing this page on your home printer you can print it now, you do not have to save it as a JPEG file.

Choose File>Save As from the Menu bar and save the page as a JPEG file (no layers) for printing purposes. You may want to add the word "left" to the file name.

Undo by clicking on the Undo button or using the shortcut Ctrl>Z (Mac: Cmd>Z). Repeat the above steps for the other side.
Undo the crop and save the 24 x 12 inch file again as a PSD. If you would like the full page as a JPEG file choose File>Save As and save it again. Choose File>Close All (Alt>Ctrl>W Mac: Opt> Cmd>W) from the Menu bar to close all images.

How to Use a Scrapbook Kit to Make a Card

If you can make a scrapbook page, you can make a flat or folded card, poster, or decorated envelope. The one thing to remember when making a folded card is that ½ of the card is placed upside down so that when you fold it they both face the right way.

Flat cards can be mailed with or without an envelope. Check the U.S. Post Office website at www.USPS.com to make sure you are using the correct postage. If you are using an envelope that is larger, smaller than normal, or square, be aware that there is an extra charge added to the regular postage. If you want to mail a flat card without an envelope you can do that, all you need is the address and postage on the back. Some people think that you need to purchase the peel off postcard backs that you see in office supply cards to mail postcards but you don't need them. I mail photos all the time as postcards. If you order 4 x 6 inch prints online many printers will mail them to you or someone else free of charge, so you could actually send a postcard without paying for postage!

Paper of any kind can be used to print your cards and postcards, depending on your printer. There are also many companies that now print cards too. I've had better luck with precut and scored cards that I purchase at my local scrapbook store or Michaels or Jo-Ann's. Because when I cut regular card stock and score it myself the edges never quite look finished.

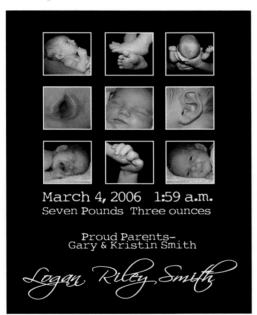

March 4, 2006 1:59 a.m.
Seven Pounds Three ounces

Proud Parents–
Gary & Kristin Smith

Logan Riley Smith

An inexpensive way to make a party invitation or birth announcement is to make a new blank 5 x 7 inch file (File>New>Blank File) and create your card just as you would a scrapbook page. To work faster, use a card template like the example on the left which was created using our Card Templates #A set available at *www.TheDigitalScrapbookTeacher.com*. Print the card at your local photo processor and they're ready to be mailed in an hour!

To help with cutting and scoring, use a regular piece of copy paper cut to the size of your card to make a folding template. Fold the copy paper so that the corners line up correctly and then lay it over your card as a pattern.

I haven't found anything that works better to make a crisp fold than a cheap plastic Chinese spoon purchased at a 99¢ store as shown on the right.

To make a crisp fold using the spoon put your finger in the spoon part and slide it across your fold. The flat bottom of the spoon flattens out the fold better than any of the expensive gadgets I've purchased in the past.

Single Fold Card

To make a single fold card, make a new white blank document (File>New>Blank File) the size you want your card (instructions are at the beginning of this chapter). Add a Guide or turn on your Grids to divide the paper in half (top and bottom). More information about Guides and Grids can be found in *The Basics* chapter. My example will show an 8.5" x 11" inch card. For this card you can use a 5 ¾ " x 8 ¾" envelope which can be purchased very inexpensively at office supply or paper stores. You can make a card any size you want. If you are using a package of cards, I suggest you actually measure them with a ruler and enter those dimensions.

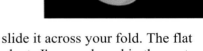

Using a Guide or Grid line as a guide, build the card just like we did in the preceding scrapbook page example.

Open (File>Open) paper, embellishments and photos if desired, to be used on your card.

The big difference between a card and a scrapbook page is that the paper will be larger than the card as shown by the bounding box in the example to the right. If you like the way it looks, it's OK and will print just fine.

Drag a digital paper onto the card so that your card is no longer white. In my example I cheated a little bit…along with the pink diamond paper I also used a Quick Page. All files used on this card are from Meredith Cardall's Cherry Limeade kit which can be found on the *Photoshop Elements - Basics & Beyond* DVD.

I also included my logo (logos are covered at the end of the Cards section) onto the top center of the card. Because the logo will be on the back of the card I flipped it upside down. To flip the logo, choose Image>Rotate>**Layer** 180° from the Menu bar. Move the logo with the Move tool and size it by dragging on the sizing handles on the bounding box if necessary.

I used the Marquee tool to crop out the overlap of the photos and pink diamond paper in the Quick Page holes just as we did in the Quick Page example at the beginning of this chapter. Lastly, I also added a piece of word art from the same kit. Add Drop Shadows if desired.

To add printing for the inside of the card you have two options: The long way is to make another new file, and use a Guide or Grid to locate the center fold in your card to show you where to type your text. Save this as a separate file and print out the card and then print the center printing on the back of the printed card.

A faster way to do this is to hide (click on eyeball icon) all of the layers other than the Background layer (as shown circled in red). Type the text, it will be automatically added on it's own layer. Print the card with just the text layer visible (shown circled in white) for the inside. Hide the inside text layer and then unhide the other layers. Turn the paper over and print on the opposite side of the card. Essentially you have the inside and outside of your card all in one file. As long as you remember that you'll be fine!

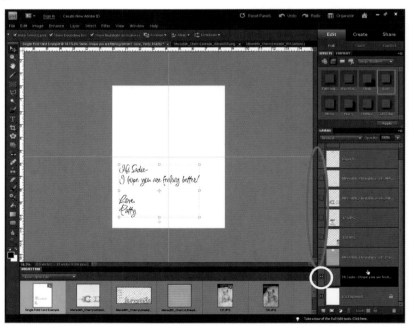

Double Fold Card

To make a double fold card with an 8 ½ x 11 inch piece of card stock, make a new blank file 8.5 inches wide by 11 inches high. Drag out Guide lines or change your Grid Lines (Edit>Preferences>Grid) to a Gridline every 25% with 1 Subdivision. To turn on your Grid Lines, choose View>Grid. In my example I used Guides. In the example on the left, I have used different colors to show the different areas of the card. When making a card like this, the top two sections of the card will need to have the text or image rotated. To do this choose Image>Rotate>**Layer 180°**.

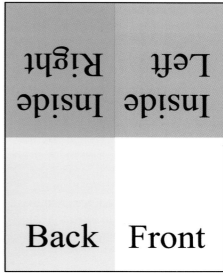

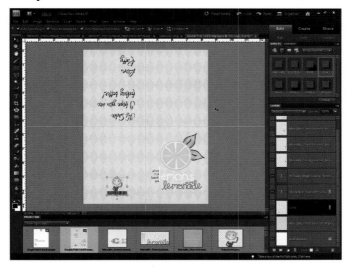

Note Cards

Set up a note card with the above specifications. It is faster to make the card for Card 1 and then duplicate it and move it with the Move tool up to the Card 2 area. An easy way to do this is to hide the paper layers (pink diamond and plain white in my example). Type the shortcut Shift>Ctrl>Alt>E (Mac: Shift>Cmd>Opt>E) and all of the visible layers will be merged into one layer **and** the original layers will still be intact. With the Move tool drag the layer of merged layers into position.

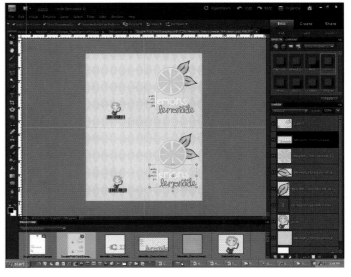

In the example above on the left, I added cut and fold lines for illustration purposes only. With your Grid Lines turned on you will be able to use them for placement. To add text to the inside for a party invitation, make a new template or turn off the layers and make a new text layer for Card 1. Duplicate the text and move it up to Card 2.

Envelopes

Measure the envelope with a ruler and make a new blank file as explained in the beginning of this chapter. I am going to make an envelope to fit the single fold card we made in an earlier example.
The envelope is 5 ¾ " x 8 ¾".

Because the envelope doesn't get folded I won't add Grids or Guides. Drag on elements with the Move tool. Add type with the Text tool. Add Drop Shadows, Save, and Print. When the mail arrives, which envelope will be opened first?

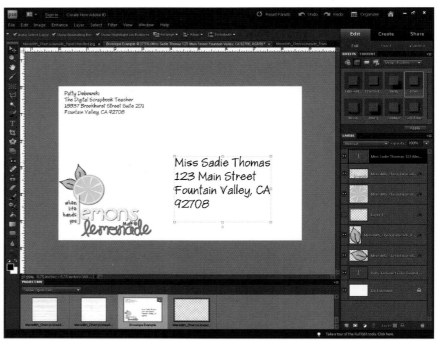

If you are making a lot of envelopes, you may want to make and save the card with your return address and the other elements. Save and Print them, and then use a mail merge program to print the recipient's addresses on them.

Check your printer to see if they have a setting for the size of envelope you're using, but chances are they don't. If they don't, you'll need to enter a custom size yourself. When you enter the custom size for the envelope, type something like "Card Envelope 8.75w" x 5.75h" and save it. This way, the next time you want to print an envelope that size it's already set up in your printer and will save you time.

Printing Cards

In most cases you'll be printing your cards at home. The hardest part of printing a two sided card is figuring out how your printer prints. My advice is to print a test card on regular copy paper, and then print the inside text on the back of it. If it works the first time, you're lucky. My two printers feed paper and print differently. When I finally figured it out I taped notes on them to save paper and frustration.

Card Logo

One of my favorite parts of making my own cards is the logos that I've designed; Hallmark has their own logo so why shouldn't you? Normally I like to design funny logos that make people laugh. Sometimes they do a double take when they realize that I've added a personalized barcode to the card.

To make the bar code, download a barcode font from a free website and type what you want, the barcode and the type are both written at the same time. To make the bar code even more realistic, place it on a white rectangle shape to look like a label. The barcode font I've used in this logo is 2Peas Price Check and was purchased at *www.twopeasinabucket.com.*

To make a logo, make a new transparent file the size you want the logo. Use the Move tool to drag on the pictures or clip art and add type. Save as a PNG file to retain the transparent background, and as a PSD file so you can easily make changes. Name the file with a file name that you will be able to find quickly.

How to Use a Text Path

Text paths are an easy way to add words or journaling to your scrapbook pages. Text paths cannot be created in Photoshop Elements. Text paths that were created in Photoshop can be used in Photoshop Elements. Text paths come in all different shapes to fit the theme of your project. Adding a text path to a page is an easy way to make your journaling a part of the page design, rather than just adding a block of regular text to the page.

A wide assortment of text paths can be purchased on our Edge Template kits available on our website at *www.TheDigitalScrapbookTeacher.com*. When using text paths, be aware that you want to use the PSD file. Sometimes a JPEG file is also provided for a preview so that you can see what it looks like.

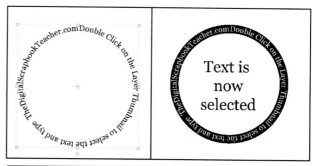

The great thing about text paths is that they are reusable and can be edited at any time. It's easy to change the size of the text path, the font, and/or the size of the type. There are two basic types of text paths, one that is an outline, and one that fills a shape. Both types of text paths are shown in the example to the right.

To use a text path, choose the Move tool (V) and drag the text path onto your scrapbook page. If the text path has several layers, do not drag it **up** from the Project bin to your page because it will merge all of the layers and simplify (rasterize) the text layer and the text will no longer be editable.

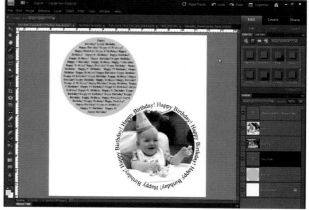

To make the text path larger or smaller, drag one of the **corner** sizing handles.

Double click on the text path layer thumbnail to select the text (so it will be highlighted like the example above). Changing the font now will affect the sizing of the text.

With the text path type selected, start typing. All of the text that was written disappears and your text is shown as you type. Continue typing your text until you get to the end of the path. If you're lucky, the text you type fits perfectly into your text path. If it doesn't (which it probably won't on your first attempt), try one of these fixes:

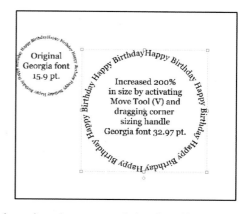

Add spaces in between the words. If you are using a text path that fills a shape, adjust the Leading on the Type tool Options bar, also be sure that Center Alignment is chosen.

Select the text by double clicking on the text path layer thumbnail, select the font size, and roll the wheel on your mouse so that the font size adjusts. I don't recommend adding any Faux Font Styles to your text.

When transforming (resizing) your text path by using the Move tool and dragging the corner sizing handle, you will probably have to resize the font. For example, my 4 inch circle is filled with text that is 15.9 pts in the regular Georgia font. If I transform my circle to approximately 200% of the original size, my font is now 32.97 pts, which may not be the look you want because the text is so big. If you want the circle bigger, but the font smaller, first select the text and then select the font size and make it smaller. If you're making the text smaller, you'll need to type some more text to fill the text path.

How to Use an Edge Template

Ever try to use any of those fancy scissors that I myself could never get to work right? Or, how about one of those fancy cutting systems? Have you ever purchased a large fancy mat to use on a traditional scrapbook page? An edge template will make you look like a paper cutting expert and save you money.

Our website *www.TheDigitalScrapbookTeacher.com* has several sets of edge templates available for purchase that will take up a lot less room in your scrapping room than your fancy scissors, and they'll always work perfectly.

There are two edge templates included in The Digital Scrapbook Teacher's Example files folder on the *Photoshop Elements - Basics & Beyond* DVD.

There are at least 2 ways to use an Edge Template. I prefer Method #1 below, but you can use whichever one works best for you. With both methods, make a blank new 12 x 12 inch white file to begin. In my examples below I have dragged on a piece of digital paper to cover my white background. With the Move tool (V) drag the template onto the page. The template will drop right in the middle of the page, move or size it as needed.

Method #1

With the template layer selected, use the Move tool (V) to drag a piece of digital scrapbook paper onto the page. The paper will completely cover your view of the template. Think of this in a traditional paper sense, you have taken a 12" x 12" piece of paper and covered up a mat. To cut the paper out of the template shape, choose Layer>Create Clipping Mask (Ctrl>G Mac: Cmd>G) from the Menu bar. Note: If you are using Photoshop Elements 7 or lower choose Layer>Group with Previous (same command, new name).

The benefit to using this method is that you are able to move and resize the paper layer as desired.

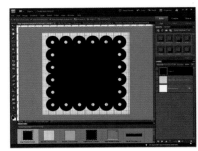  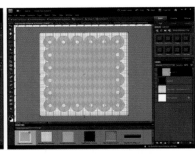

Method #2

With the template layer selected, use the Move tool (V) to drag a piece of digital scrapbook paper onto the page. The paper will completely cover your view of the template. Ctrl click (Mac: Cmd Click) on the template layer thumbnail (circled). There will be a selection border (marching ants) around the template piece. Choose Select>Inverse (Shift>Ctrl>I Mac: Shift>Cmd>I) from the Menu bar. Select the scrapbook paper layer and tap the Delete or Backspace key. The paper will be cut the size of the template. Choose Select>Deselect (Ctrl>D Mac: Cmd>D to remove the selection border (marching ants).

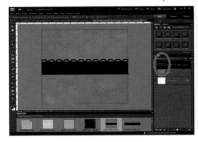  

The papers used in both examples are from Meredith Cardall's Cherry Limeade and Dress Up kit, which can be found on the *Photoshop Elements- Basics & Beyond* DVD. The edge templates are from The Digital Scrapbook Teacher's Edge Templates #B & #C sets which can be purchased at *www.TheDigitalScrapbookTeacher.com*.

How to Use a Layered Word Template

The Digital Scrapbook Teacher's Word Templates are a great way to make a fast and easy page in about a minute flat...after you get the hang of it.

Included in each set are three different file types for each template, PSD, PNG, and a JPEG file which is included only for preview purposes. I have used Photoshop to create these templates so that I can eliminate most of the space in between the letters which I can't do with Photoshop Elements. The word is not editable.

For this example open the Word Template PSD file and a photo.

All of The Digital Scrapbook Teacher's products are created at 300 pixels per inch, and all of our templates include a plain white Background layer. For this reason, you do not have to make a new blank white file yourself to drag the template on.

Because you do not want to save over the original template as soon as you open it choose File>Save As from the Menu bar and save it with a new file name in a new location such as a Scrapbook Pages folder. The format will remain as a Photoshop document (PSD).

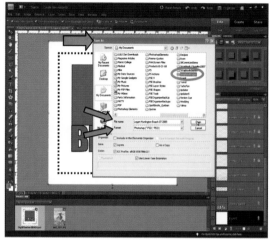

Click on the Word Template layer in the Layers panel so that the layer is highlighted. Click and drag the photo onto the template. Because the Word Template layer is selected, the photo will be dropped in the middle of the page on the layer directly above the Word Template layer. Make sure that the photo layer is directly above the Word Template layer as shown.

With the Move tool (V) selected, click and drag a **corner** sizing handle to quickly enlarge the photo. Holding the Alt key (Mac: Opt key) as you drag the **corner** sizing handle will size the photo from the center which will save you time. The photo should cover the word "BEACH" and the gray rectangle attached to it. You will be able to resize the photo at any time, so don't worry about getting it the perfect size now.

If you are using a tiny photo from the web or a camera phone be aware that the page will not print well.

Check the green checkmark ✓ to confirm the transformation (resizing).

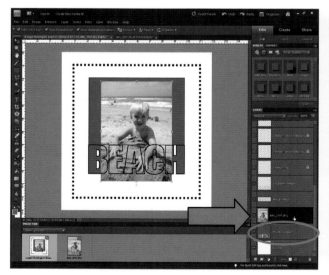
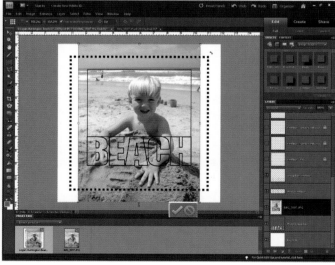

With the photo layer selected choose Layer>Create Clipping Mask (Ctrl>G Mac: Cmd>G) from the Menu bar. Note: If you are using Photoshop Elements 7 or lower choose Layer>Group with Previous (same command, new name).

The photo will now take on the shape of the template layer. If you want to move the photo, use the Move tool to move the photo around while the photo layer is selected. Note that in the Layers panel, the photo layer has moved to the right and it has a bent arrow pointing down to the template layer. This indicates that the photo is clipped/ grouped with the template layer.

There are many outlines that can be used to outline the page. To display an outline, click in the empty box next to the layer shown circled above. To turn off (hide) an outline click on the eyeball icon.

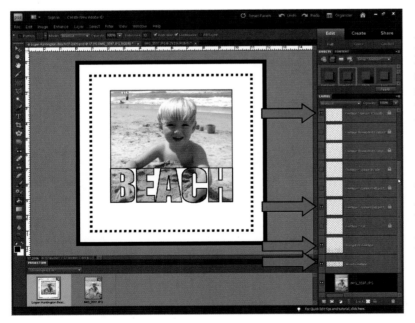

In the example to the left there are 4 outline layers that are active:
Outline Squares (Small)
Outline Square Full Page Thick
Template Outline
Word Outline

Whichever outlines you choose to use is a personal choice. There are hearts, dots, stars, etc. that will work for all of your pages.

To add color to the background, click on the Background layer and either drag on a piece of digital paper with the Move tool (V) or fill it with a solid color. To fill the Background layer with a solid color, click in the Foreground Color swatch at the bottom of the Toolbar and choose a color. With the Background Layer selected, choose the Paint Bucket tool (K) and click on the page, or use the shortcut Alt>Backspace (Mac: Opt>Delete).

To fill an outline with a solid color, choose a Foreground color by clicking in the Foreground color swatch at the bottom of the Toolbar and select the layer in the Layers Panel. Choose Edit>Fill Layer, choose Use Foreground Color, and check the Preserve Transparency box at the bottom of the dialog box. The shortcut to do this is Shift>Alt>Backspace (Mac: Shift>Opt>Delete).

In my example below on the left, I clicked in the Foreground color box and then clicked on the sand bucket in the photo to match the blue color and used the shortcut to fill the Outline Squares (Small) layer.

Add drop shadows to the outline and template layers only. If you add a drop shadow to the photo layer you will not be able to see it.

In the example on the right, I filled my Background layer with black. Because the Template Outline and Word Outline layers are still active, it appears that the word "BEACH" and the rectangle shape are not touching so I will hide those layers.

In my final page, I have turned off all of the outline layers with the exception of the Outline Squares (Small) layer which I have filled with white. I have also added two text layers using the free Scriptina font available at *www.Dafont.com*.

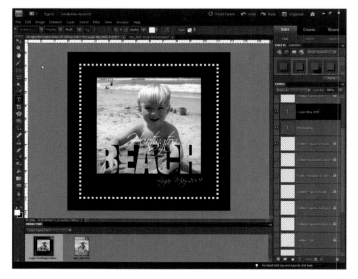

Save. If you are not printing this page at home you will need to save it as a JPEG file to send to a printer. Choose File>Save As and choose JPEG for the format. More saving information is covered in The Basics chapter.

How to Soften the Edges of a Word Template

I've had many students who want to soften the edges of a Word Template so that it isn't so bold looking. This is easy and can be done before or after you complete the page. You will not be able to soften the Template Outline and Word Outline layers.

Click on the eyeball icon (as shown by the red arrow) on the Word Outline and Template Outline layers to hide both layers. Both outline layers should be turned off.

Ctrl click (Mac: Cmd Click) on the Layer thumbnail for the Word Template layer in the Layers panel (black arrow). The Word Template piece will be surrounded with a selection border (marching ants).

From the Menu Bar choose Select>Feather and choose an amount. In my example I used 200 pixels (Maximum is 250 pixels). Click OK.

From the Menu bar choose Select>Inverse (Shift>Ctrl>I Mac: Shift>Cmd>I).

The selection border will now also surround the outside edge of the page. Click on the Word Template layer and tap the Delete key.

Choose Select>Deselect (Ctrl>D, Mac: Cmd>D) from the Menu bar to remove the selection border (marching ants), or tap the Esc key which will work for most people.

If you are not happy with the result, Undo and enter a different feather amount or repeat the above steps to soften the edge more.

How to Use Word Template PNG Files

Also included with our Word Templates is a single layer PNG file. A PNG file is a file that has transparency in it. You can use these templates for a multitude of uses, such as on cards or to add to scrapbook pages or scrapbook pages made from our 12" x 12" (or other size) templates.

To use a Word Template PNG file on a card, open the template file and a photo. Make a new blank white file the dimensions of your printed card, as explained in the beginning of this chapter. Mark the fold line with a Guide.

Drag the template onto the card file with the Move tool (V). Drag **any** sizing handle to resize the template. It's not necessary to resize by the corner because you can size it out of proportion.

Drag the photo on top of the Word Template layer; quickly resize the photo to cover the entire template. If you are using a tiny photo from the web or a phone camera, be aware that the card will not print well.

With the photo layer selected, choose Layer>Create Clipping Mask (Ctrl>G Mac: Cmd>G) from the Menu bar. Note: If you are using Photoshop Elements 7 or lower, choose Layer>Group with Previous (same command, new name). Resize and/or reposition the photo as needed using the Move tool (V). Save.

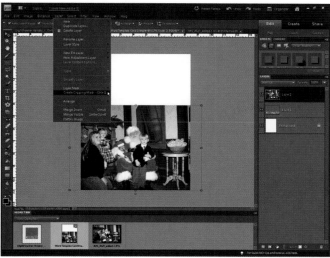

Use the Move tool (V) to drag paper and embellishments onto the card. Add text using the Type tool (T) and you've got a fast and easy card.

All supplies used for this card are available at *www.TheDigitalScrapbookTeacher.com*. Paper and embellishments are from the Wintertime Paper & Embellishment kit, and the Word Template is from the Holiday Word Template Set.

The font is Inspiration and is available for purchase at *www.MyFonts.com*.

In this example I have replaced the two circled template layers on a 12" x 12" template with a Word Template PNG file.

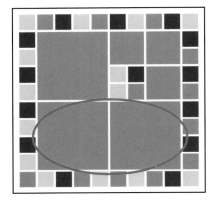

Open a layered template (PSD file) and a Word Template PNG file. Choose File>Save As from the Menu bar and save the template with a new name so you don't save over your original template by mistake.

Select the top layer in the Layers panel.

Use the Move tool (V) to drag the Word Template onto the template. The Word Template will automatically drop in the middle of the page.

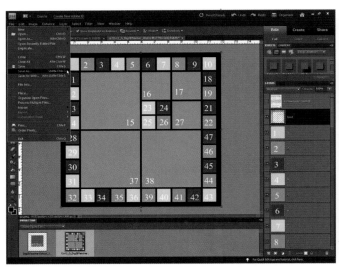 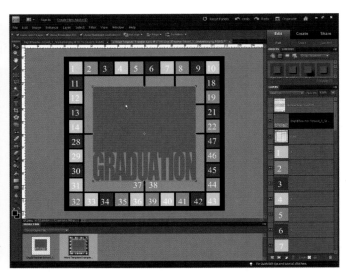

Click and drag the sizing handles to resize the Word Template layer to cover the circled template pieces exactly. Check the green checkmark to confirm the transformation (resizing). In the example below I also turned off the black grid overlay.

Hide the template pieces under the Word Template layer circled above by clicking on the eyeball icon in the Layers panel (circled in red). Save. Complete as you would a regular template as explained in the next tutorial.

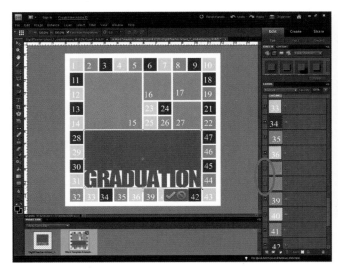 

How to Use a Layered Template

Using a Layered Template speeds up your work because you have the design work all done for you. No thumbing through magazines and books or surfing the web to find the perfect layout you like that will work with your photos. No spacing and measuring everything to make sure all of your photos are balanced.

If you have a lot of photos to scrap, or you're short on time and patience, templates are definitely the way to go. I had a student that attended our Boot Camp in April. When we returned for an Intermediate/Advanced Digital Scrapbooking Workshop the next August she had completed more than 400 pages. When I asked her what her secret was, she told me that she used templates to make her pages. It will take you longer to pick out your template, photos, papers, and embellishments than it will take you to put the template together…after you get the hang of it (don't you hate it when I keep saying that!).

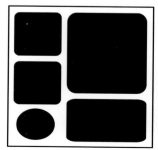 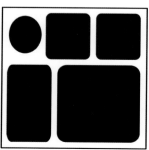 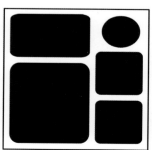 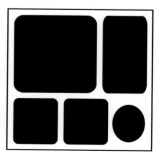

As you can see by the examples above, templates suit any style of scrapbook. Whether you have one photo or 100 to use on a page, you can find a template to use. Templates can be reused and changed to suit your needs as shown in the *Change It* chapter.

By simply rotating a template, you can get up to eight different page options from some templates. Using one template that has been flipped or rotated gives a uniform and balanced look to a two page scrapbook layout.

Rotate a template 90° by choosing Image>Rotate>90° Right (or Left) from the Menu bar.

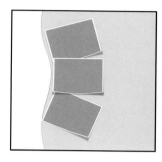 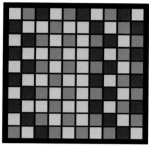 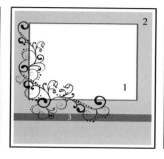 

Flip a template by choosing Image>Rotate>Flip Horizontal from the Menu bar for four different choices.

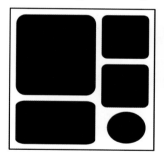 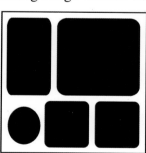  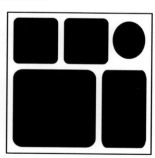

Hide one of the shape layers to add journaling or an embellishment.
Try hiding or deleting a shape layer and adding a different shape
layer. This will give the template a completely different look as
shown in the preceding example with the Word Template.

Layered Templates are available for purchase in PSD or TIFF format
and these instructions will work for both file types.

Just because you're a 12" x 12" scrapper doesn't mean that you can't
use an 8.5" x 11" inch template. Drag the 8.5" x 11" template onto a
12" x 12" scrapbook page and fill in the left over areas with more
photos or digital and/or traditional embellishments.

I have many students who do not own a wide format printer capable of printing 12" x 12" pages. What they do
own is lots of traditional scrapbook paper…oodles of it. What many of them do is make their pages using an
8.5" x 11" template and print it on their color printer. They adhere this and other traditional supplies to their 12"
x 12" papers thus alleviating their guilt over their huge paper stash that they fear they'll never use up.

Included on the *Photoshop Elements - Basics & Beyond* DVD are several templates for you to use. At
www.TheDigitalScrapbookTeacher.com we sell templates sets that are priced way less than most other websites.
Something that other designers don't do but you will find included in each one of our templates is a layer with
easy to understand instructions. When you're done reading the instructions, hide the layer and they disappear.
When you get stuck, turn the instruction layer back on by clicking on the eyeball instead of searching for the
instructions. Each template includes a layered template (we've found they're easier to use especially for
beginners) and a single layered template either in PNG or JPEG format. In addition, all of the template shapes
are numbered and match to the layer number so they're much easier to work with. The shapes are also linked so
that if you want to move them as a group, you can. This helps so that you don't move one shape by mistake and
mess up the design. If you want to unlink the shapes, we've also explained how in our instructions and in the
Change It chapter.

Open the template (layered PSD file), photos, papers, and embellishments you wish to use to complete the page.
Check the template to see that it has several layers to make sure you haven't opened the JPEG file in error. The
template shown in the example is in the Digital Scrapbook Teacher's Examples folder on the *Photoshop
Elements - Basics & Beyond* DVD.

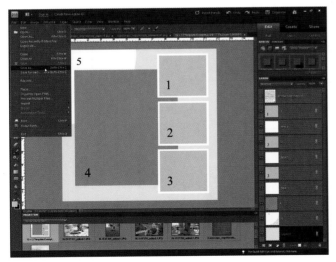

For this page I am using items from the Snips and
Snails kit that can be found in the Kelly Jo's Scraps
folder on the *Photoshop Elements - Basics & Beyond*
DVD.

All of The Digital Scrapbook Teacher's products are
created in RGB Color Mode at 300 pixels per inch, and
include a plain white Background layer. For this
reason, you do not have to make a new blank white file
yourself to drag the template onto.

Because you do not want to save over the original
template, as soon as you open it, choose File>Save As
from the Menu bar and save it with a new file name in
a new location such as a Scrapbook Pages folder. The
format will remain as a Photoshop document (PSD).

Click on the bottom layer in the Layers panel so that the layer is selected.

Select the Move tool (V) and click, hold and drag the paper you wish to use as the background onto the page. If you receive the warning on the right it's because you let go too soon.

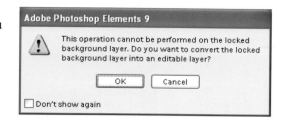

Because you had selected the bottom layer of the template the paper is dropped on top of that layer. Using this trick will help you complete a template quickly.

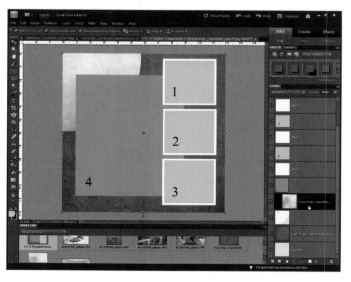

In the Layers panel, click on the layer marked #5 (the quarter circle piece) so that it is the selected layer.

Drag the next paper onto the template file.

The new paper layer will cover up the #5 template piece. In the Layers panel it should be directly above the #5 layer.

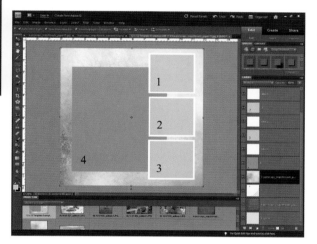

Choose Layer>Create Clipping Mask (Ctrl>G Mac: Cmd>G) from the Menu bar. Note: If you are using Photoshop Elements 7 or lower, choose Layer>Group with Previous (same command, new name).

Once you click on Create Clipping Mask, the paper will be cut into the template quarter circle shape just like a die cut!

Notice that the paper layer in the Layers panel has stepped a little bit to the right and there is a bent arrow pointing down to the layer it's clipped to (red circle).

Now or in the future, because the paper isn't actually cut, it can be moved with the Move tool (V) to display some of the different colors on the paper. Save.

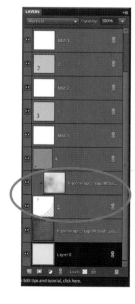

We will repeat the same steps for each layer we wish to fill with paper or photos. You will find that if you pay special attention and select the correct layer you will finish a page in half the time!

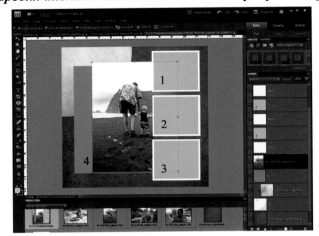

Click on the layer in the Layers panel marked #4 so that it becomes the active image.

Your Move tool (V) should still be selected because we haven't changed tools. Click and drag the photo onto the template page. The photo will be dropped exactly in the middle of the page. Your photo may be larger or smaller than my example. If your photo is tiny, even though you enlarge it, be aware that it will probably not print well.

Click and drag on a **corner** sizing handle to make the photo slightly larger than the template piece. Do not drag the **side** sizing handles or you will distort the photo. Do not make the photo the exact size of the template piece.

Click on the checkmark (red circle) or double click on the photo to commit your change.

Choose Layer>Create Clipping Mask (Ctrl>G Mac: Cmd>G) from the Menu bar. Note: If you are using Photoshop Elements 7 or lower, choose Layer>Group with Previous (same command, new name).

You may adjust the size and position of your photo by clicking on it or using the **corner** sizing handles again. Be sure that the photo covers the gray template piece. Remember to check the green checkmark ✓ to confirm the transformation (resizing), or you will not be able to proceed.

Click on the Mat 3 layer to make it the selected layer.
You have several choices:
Leave the mat white and go on to the next layer.
Fill the mat with the multi-colored paper used for Shape #5 by following the same steps above (you can also open another paper).
Fill the mat with a solid color.

To fill the mat with a solid color, you will need to first choose the color by clicking in the Foreground color swatch at the bottom of the Toolbar. Once you click inside the swatch, the Adobe Color Picker box will be shown.

If the box is in your way, click and drag on the top bar and move it to another area of your screen. You may choose a color by clicking anywhere inside the color box. In my example Red is displayed. (Note the small circle where I clicked to choose red).

If I want blue I, would click in the bar on the right (white arrow) and then blue would be displayed. Click once in the large color square to select a color and then click OK.

To match a color from the page, move the cursor out of the Color Picker Box and it will become an eyedropper. Click anywhere to choose a color. Make sure the new color shows in the top of the box and click OK. Notice your Foreground color swatch has changed to the color you just picked.

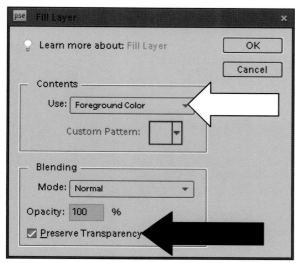

To fill the Mat 3 layer with the new Foreground color, select the layer and choose Edit>Fill Layer. Select Foreground Color (white arrow in my example).

Blending-Normal
Opacity 100%

*Very Important! Check Preserve Transparency (black arrow). If you forget to check this box your whole layer will be filled with your Foreground color instead of just the mat shape.

Honestly…I don't ever fill my layers this way. I use a great shortcut: Shift>Alt>Backspace (Windows) Shift>Opt>Delete (Mac)

Use whichever method works best for you.

Repeat the same steps for each layer as we've done in the preceding examples. Pay attention to what layer you're on to work smarter!

Right now the page is pretty flat, so we will add drop shadows to give it dimension. To add drop shadows you will need your Effects panel open. If your Effects panel is not open, choose Window>Effects or tap the Reset Panels button at the top of the screen.

Click on the Layer Styles icon (red circle) and choose Drop Shadows from the drop down list.

Several drop shadows will be displayed. If the names under the drop shadows are not displayed, see how to turn them on in the *First Things First* chapter.

Drop shadows need to be applied to template pieces, any embellishments added, and possibly text. If you add a drop shadow to a photo layer that has been clipped to a template piece, the drop shadow will not be displayed; you must add it to the template piece. For this reason you could have actually added the drop shadows before you started adding papers and photos.

To add a drop shadow, select the layer in the Layers Panel, and double click on the Drop Shadow icon…it's that easy.

Add drop shadows to each layer using this technique, or you can speed things up a little bit especially if you've customized your shadows.

Once you've added a shadow, right click (Mac: Ctrl Click) on the layer **name** (red circle) and choose Copy Layer Style (red arrow).

Select all layers in the Layers panel that need a drop shadow by clicking on one and Ctrl clicking (Mac: Cmd Clicking) on the others, or using the Shift key to select several layers in a row.

Right click (Mac: Ctrl Click) and choose Paste Layer Style and your work is done very quickly. To save time, add drop shadows to all layers including the photo layers.

Save.

Add the embellishment to the page by clicking on the **top** layer and then dragging it onto your page. Move it to the desired location from the center of the page where it dropped.

Add type using the Text tool (T) if desired. Make sure you are on the top layer in the Layers Panel when adding type or it may be covered up by another layer.

Add drop shadows to the embellishments and add type if desired. Save.

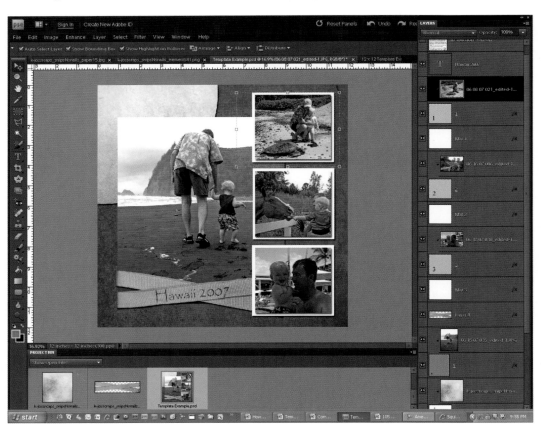

In this example I have expanded the Layers panel so that you can see most of the layers.

The *fx* symbol on the layers indicates that a Layer Style has been added to the layer.

How to Use a Single Layer (PNG) Template

Make a new blank white file, as explained in the beginning of this chapter. Open the template, photos, papers, and embellishments. The template shown in the example is in the Digital Scrapbook Teacher's Examples folder on the *Photoshop Elements - Basics & Beyond* DVD.

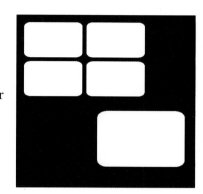

Drag the template onto a plain white file with the Move tool (V). Save. Click on the Background layer to make it the active layer and drag on a photo. Because you selected the Background layer, the photo will be sandwiched between the Background layer and the template layer; right where you want it to be.

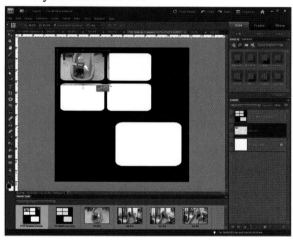

Drag the photo under one of the holes in the template. The photo will land in the center of the page. Use a **corner** sizing handle to transform/resize the photo.

Do **NOT** try to resize the photo to fit the hole in the template by using the **side** sizing handles because you will distort the photo.

To confirm the transformation (resizing), check the green checkmark ✓. Don't worry if the photo also fills all or part of one of the other holes in the template.

Repeat each step for each photo. If the overhang is distracting, hide one of the photo layers while you resize the other one. To hide a layer, click on the eyeball icon to the left of the layer thumbnail (shown circled). To turn the layer back on, click in the empty box where the eyeball was and the eyeball and layer will reappear.

To crop off the overhanging photo, select the Marquee tool (M) on the Toolbar (do not choose the Crop tool). Click hold and drag out a box over the part of the photo that needs to be removed.

Select the **layer** in the Layers panel that needs to be cropped, (this is very important). Choose Edit>Delete from the Menu bar, or simply tap the Delete key on the keyboard to remove the selected area. Save.

To remove the selection border (marching ants) choose Select>Deselect, or use the shortcut Ctrl>D (Mac: Cmd>D). The Esc key will also work for most people.

You may also use the Eraser tool (E) or a Mask to remove the overlapping photos.

To fill the template layer with a solid color, first select the layer in the Layers panel. Click in the Foreground color box at the bottom of the Toolbar and choose a color, click OK. Choose the Paint Bucket (K) tool from the Toolbar and click on the template, or use the shortcut Shift>Alt>Backspace (Mac: Shift>Opt>Delete).

One way to cover the template piece with a digital paper is to select the template layer in the Layers panel; it should be the top layer. Drag the paper onto the page and it will completely cover the page.

From the Menu bar, choose Layer>Create Clipping Mask (Ctrl>G Mac: Cmd>G). Note: If you are using Photoshop Elements 7 or lower, choose Layer>Group with Previous (same command, new name). The paper is now clipped in the shape of the template as shown below on the left.

Another way to cut the paper out of the template layer is to Ctrl Click (Mac: Cmd Click) on the template layer thumbnail (shown circled in red below in the example on the right). Drag the paper onto the template page. Marching ants will now surround the outside edge of the paper and the photo cutouts.

From the Menu Bar, choose Select>Inverse (Shift>Ctrl>I, Mac: Shift>Cmd>I), the marching ants will now surround only the photo cutouts. Tap the Delete key. From the Menu bar, choose Select>Deselect (Ctrl>D, Mac: Cmd>D) to remove the selection border (marching ants), or tap the Esc key which will work for most people.

Add text, embellishments, journaling, and drop shadows (add on template layer only) to the page as desired. Save.

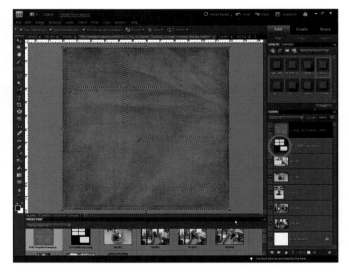

The paper shown is from the Funtime Paper & Embellishment Kit available at: *www.TheDigitalScrapbookTeacher.com.*

How to Use a Single Layer (JPEG) Template

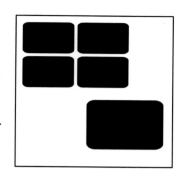

Using a JPEG template isn't ideal, but if it's the only option you have you can make it work. As in typical Photoshop Elements fashion, there is more than one way to do this and I'll explain a few methods below.

First, make a new blank white file, as explained in the beginning of this chapter. Open the template, photos, papers, and embellishments. The template shown in the example is in the Digital Scrapbook Teacher's Examples folder on the *Photoshop Elements - Basics & Beyond* DVD.

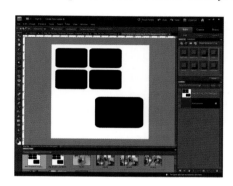

Drag the template onto a plain white file with the Move tool (V). Fill the Background layer with any color besides black or white. This way you'll be able to easily differentiate between layers on later steps. To do this, click on the Background layer in the Layers panel to select it. Choose a Foreground color by clicking in the box at the bottom of the Layers panel. Use the shortcut Alt>Backspace (Mac: Opt>Delete) to fill the layer. In my example I chose red. Save.

Method #1 This method will only work if none of the template pieces are overlapping.

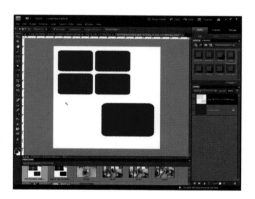

Select the template layer in the Layers panel. From the Toolbar, select the Magic Wand tool (W). On the Options bar, make sure that there is **not** a ✓ in the Contiguous box. Click on a black template piece, marching ants should now surround all black template pieces. Tap the Delete key to remove all of the black template pieces. From the Menu bar, choose Select>Deselect (Ctrl>D, Mac: Cmd>D) to remove the selection border (marching ants), or tap the Esc key which will work for most people. Complete the template as explained in the preceding How to Use a Single Layer (PNG) Template example.

Method #2
Select the template layer in the Layers panel. From the Toolbar, select the Magic Wand tool (W). On the Options bar make sure that the Contiguous box **is** checked. Click on one template piece, marching ants should surround only **one** template piece.

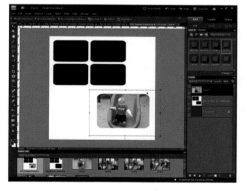

Double click on a photo in the Project bin so that it becomes the active image. From the Menu bar, choose Select>All (Ctrl>A, Mac: Cmd>A), marching ants will surround the photo. From the Menu bar, choose Edit>Copy (Ctrl>C, Mac: Cmd>C) to copy it to the clipboard.

Double click on the template file in the Project bin so that it becomes the active image. Make a new **transparent** layer by clicking on the New Layer icon at the bottom of the Layers (shortcut Shift>Ctrl>Alt>N (Mac: Shift>Cmd>Alt>N).

Choose Edit>Paste into Selection (Shift>Ctrl>V, Mac: Shift>Cmd>V). From the Toolbar, choose the Move tool (V) and drag the **corner** sizing corner to resize the photo. Repeat for each template piece.

Method #3

Select the template layer in the Layers panel. From the Toolbar, select the Magic Wand tool (W). On the Options bar make sure that the Contiguous box **is** checked. Click on one template piece, marching ants should surround only **one** template piece.

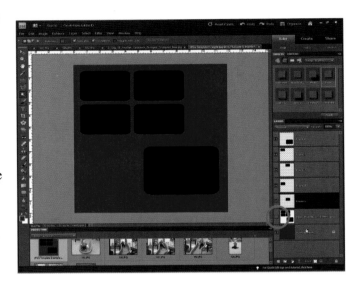

From the Menu bar, choose Layer>New>Layer via Copy (Ctrl>J, Mac Cmd>J). The template piece has been copied onto its own layer. From the Menu bar, choose Select>Deselect (Ctrl>D, Mac: Cmd>D) to remove the selection border (marching ants), or tap the Esc key which will work for most people.

Repeat this step being careful to select the template layer in the Layers panel each time. Hide (shown circled in red) or delete the original template layer. Complete the template as explained in the preceding How to Use a Layered Template example.

How to Use a Folded Corner Template

Open the Corner Template from the Digital Scrapbook Teacher's Examples folder on the *Photoshop Elements - Basics & Beyond* DVD.

Open three pieces of paper. I am using paper from the Springtime and Funtime Paper and Embellishment kits available at *www.TheDigitalScrapbookTeacher.com*. They are not included on the *Photoshop Elements - Basics & Beyond* DVD.

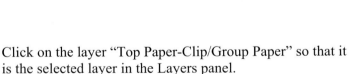

From the Menu bar, choose File>Save As to save a copy of the corner template so that you don't save over it by mistake.

On the Corner Template file select the layer named "Bottom Paper" (arrow in example). Drag a piece of paper onto the template file. The paper will be dropped right above the "Bottom Paper" layer and will become the selected layer. As shown in the example on the right, the paper will show only in the top left corner of the page.

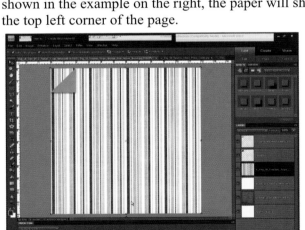

Click on the layer "Top Paper-Clip/Group Paper" so that it is the selected layer in the Layers panel.

Select the paper that you want to use to cover the main part of the page, drag it on to the Corner Template file.

As shown in the example on the left, the paper should cover the entire image. The gray corner piece should be floating above the paper you just dragged on.

Select the second paper layer. From the Menu bar, choose
Layer>Create Clipping Mask (Ctrl>G Mac: Cmd>G). Note: If
you are using Photoshop Elements 7 or lower, choose
Layer>Group with Previous (same command, new name). The
bottom paper (brown in my example) will now show on the top
left corner.

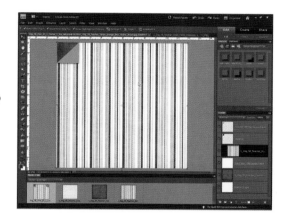

Select the layer named "Corner Fold-Clip-Group Paper". This
layer is at the top of the Layers panel, you are skipping the
Shadow layer.

Drag the third piece of paper onto the template file. The paper
will cover the entire page.

With the top layer in the Layers panel selected, from the Menu bar, choose Layer>Create Clipping Mask
(Ctrl>G Mac: Cmd>G). Note: If you are using Photoshop Elements 7 or lower, choose Layer>Group with
Previous (same command, new name).

The paper will be cut into the corner shape and the bottom two papers will show properly.

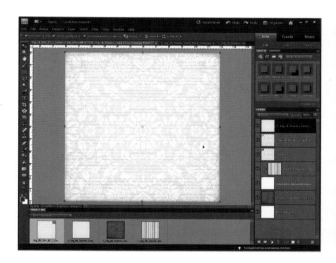

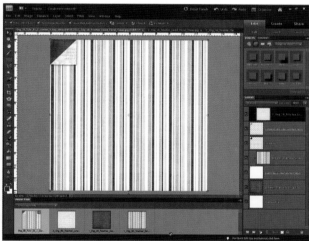

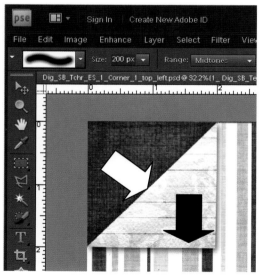

To make the fold look more realistic,
select the paper layer above the "Corner
Fold-Clip-Group Paper" layer and use
the Dodge tool (O) along the folded
edge (white arrow on example) to
lighten up the fold.

The Dodge tool (O) is nested in the last
tool icon on the Toolbar along with the
Sponge and Burn tools.

Use the Burn tool (O) along the bottom
edge (black arrow on example) of the
paper fold to add dimension.

More Corner Fold Templates like this are available at
www.TheDigitalScrapbookTeacher.com in the Essentials #1 kit.

How to Use a Paper Pattern Overlay

Make a new blank piece of white paper to begin building your paper.
From the Menu bar, choose File>New>Blank File.

Type a name for your paper.
Type in 12 x 12 inches for the size
Resolution will always be 300 pixels per inch
Color Mode will always be RGB Color
Choose White for the Background contents.
Click OK

Fill the white paper (Background layer) with a solid color (if desired).
Click on the Foreground Color chip located at the bottom of the Toolbar and
choose a color (I left mine white so it's easier to see in this example).
Choose Edit>Fill Layer.
In the Use box, choose Foreground Color.
Leave the Mode drop down list at the default setting, which is Normal.
Opacity is 100%.
Un-check the Preserve Transparency Box.
Or…after choosing a Foreground color, use the shortcut I use all the time: Alt>Backspace or Opt>Delete for
Mac users.

Open the Paper Pattern Overlay files from the Digital Scrapbook Teacher's Examples folder on the *Photoshop
Elements - Basics & Beyond* DVD. The Paper Pattern Overlays and Texture Overlays sold at
www.TheDigitalScrapbookTeacher.com are OK to use for commercial use in the event you want to make your
own papers and sell them.

Select the Move tool (V), click and drag the
Paper Pattern Template onto the new paper file
you made (file name-
1_MYOPP_4_Dig_SB_Tchr_Circle_Dots_3).

Because most of the paper pattern overlays have
a lot of transparent areas, you will need to click
on a solid piece of the overlay so that you can
move it. If you click on a transparent area of the
overlay you will not be able to move it down
onto your new file. If you are having trouble,
hold the Ctrl key (Mac: Cmd key) when you
click and drag onto your new file, or uncheck
the Auto Select Layer box (circled below) on the
Move tool Options bar.

If you are dragging up (only Photoshop
Elements 5, 8, & 9) from the Project bin you
will not have a problem clicking on transparent
areas.

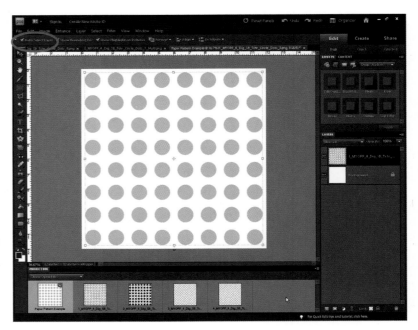

Fill Paper Pattern Overlay with One Solid Color
Select the paper pattern layer in the Layers panel.
To fill with one color, choose the color by clicking in the Foreground color
chip at the bottom of the Toolbar.
Choose Edit>Fill Layer.
In the Use box, choose Foreground Color.
Leave the Mode drop down list at the default setting, which is Normal.
Opacity is 100%.
Check the Preserve Transparency Box. Click OK.

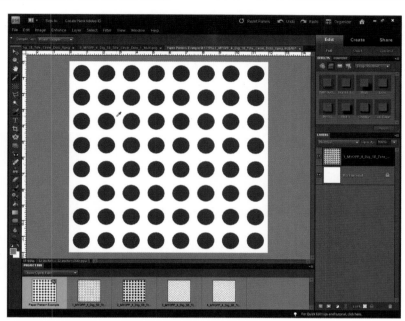

Or…after choosing a Foreground color, use the shortcut I use all the time:
Shift>Alt>Backspace
Shift>Opt>Delete for Mac users.

In my example I filled the pattern with dark
blue (Hex # 343f60). The Hex # can be
entered at the bottom of the Color Picker
box shown circled below.

You may be finished at this point, but you can still add other pattern layers and textures depending on how
detailed of a paper you want to make. Instructions for adding more pattern layers, textures, and pre-made paper
follow this tutorial. Save.

To create many different papers, layer
several paper pattern templates together by
repeating the above steps for each layer.
The key to working efficiently is to always
make sure you are on the correct layer
when filling it with color.

Repeating the same steps as the first layer,
drag another Paper Pattern Template onto
the page (file name-
2_MYOPP_4_Dig_SB_Tchr_Circle_Dots_
4). This pattern is also dots, but in a
different size. Choose a Foreground color
and fill the layer (Shift>Alt>Backspace,
Mac: Shift>Opt>Delete). In my example I
filled the pattern with light blue (Hex #
6b88a0).

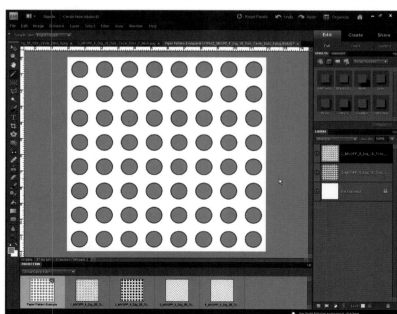

Fill Paper Pattern Overlay with One Solid Color
Repeating the same steps as the first layer, drag another Paper Pattern Template onto the page (file name-3_MYOPP_4_Dig_SB_Tchr_Circle_Dots_4). This pattern includes dots of different colors. While you can fill all dots with the same color, we will fill them with different colors.

Zoom or Scroll in so you can see the different colors. From the Toolbar, select the Magic Wand tool (W). Uncheck Contiguous on the Magic Wand tool Options bar.

Click on the darkest dots, all of the dots of that color should now be selected (surrounded by marching ants).

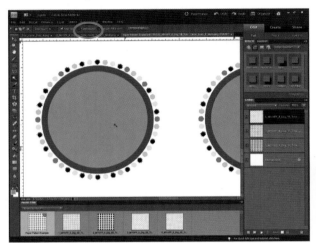

Choose a Foreground color and fill the layer (Shift>Alt>Backspace, Mac: Shift>Opt>Delete). In my example I filled the pattern with red (Hex # 912c22).

From the Menu bar, choose Select>Deselect (Ctrl>D, Mac: Cmd>D) to remove the selection border (marching ants), or tap the Esc key which will work for most people.

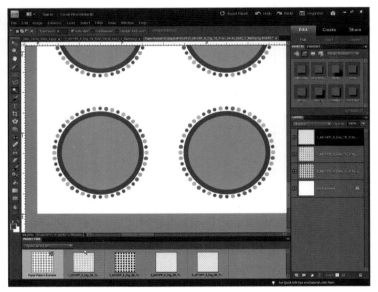

Repeat for each different color dot. If the Magic Wand tool selects more than one color of the dots, lower the Tolerance setting on the Magic Wand tool Options bar.

I also used yellow (Hex # ddb340), green (Hex # 9faf61), and blue (Hex# 3f6288).

Save. To add a real paper look to your paper, you will want to add a texture to it which I will show you how to do after the next example.

Fill Paper Pattern Overlay with Digital Paper
Instead of filling a pattern with solid color which may look flat, you can fill it with a digital paper from one of your kits. The Paper Pattern Overlays and Texture Overlays sold at *www.TheDigitalScrapbookTeacher.com* are OK for commercial use in the event you want to make your own papers and sell them. If you plan on selling the papers you make, and you use digital papers you have purchased to combine with a pattern template, be sure that the papers you use are OK for commercial use as well.

Make a new blank file and drag a paper pattern template from The Digital Scrapbook Teacher's Examples folder onto the page using the Move tool, just like we did in the preceding example. Open a digital paper and drag it on top of the paper pattern layer. I am using papers from the Wintertime Paper and Embellishment kits available at *www.TheDigitalScrapbookTeacher.com*. These papers are not included on the *Photoshop Elements - Basics & Beyond* DVD.

Select the top paper layer. From the Menu bar, choose Layer>Create Clipping Mask (Ctrl>G Mac: Cmd>G). Note: If you are using Photoshop Elements 7 or lower, choose Layer>Group with Previous (same command, new name). Save.

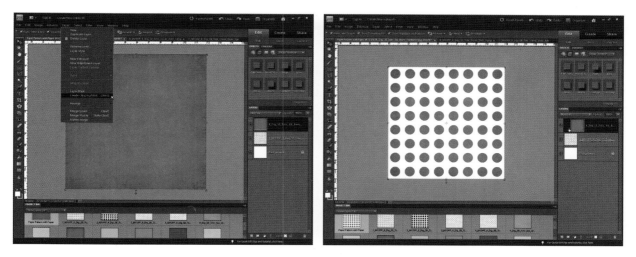

Continue adding pattern layers and digital paper layers, clipping them together following the same steps. This technique will work for all of the pattern layers that are the same color.

Drag the multi-colored Paper Pattern Template onto the page (the file name is-3_MYOPP_4_Dig_SB_Tchr_Circle_Dots_4). This pattern includes dots of different colors. If you want all of the dots the same color, fill all dots with the same paper. In this example we will fill them with different paper.

Zoom or Scroll in so you can see the different colors. From the Toolbar, select the Magic Wand tool (W). Uncheck Contiguous on the Magic Wand tool Options bar.

Select the pattern layer in the Layers panel and click on the darkest dots. All of the dots of that color should now be selected (surrounded by marching ants). Drag on another piece of paper. The paper layer should be directly above the pattern layer in the Layers panel. Marching ants should be visible on the pattern layer surrounding the dark dots as shown below.

From the Menu bar, choose Select>Inverse (Shift>Ctrl>I, Mac: Shift>Cmd>I). The marching ants will remain around the dots as before, but will now also surround the edge of the page. Tap the Delete key to remove the rest of the paper you don't need.

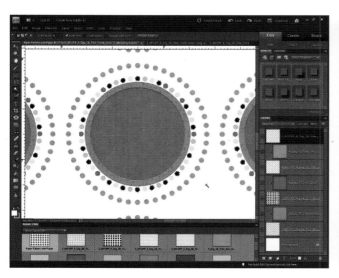
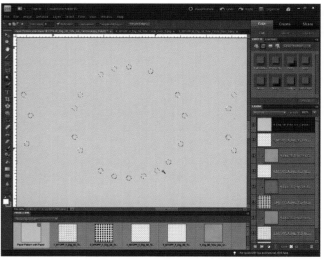

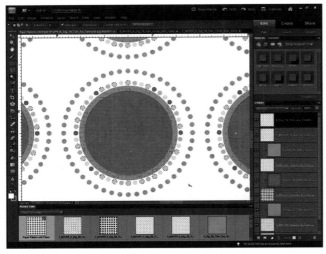

From the Menu bar, choose Select>Deselect (Ctrl>D, Mac: Cmd>D) to remove the selection border (marching ants), or tap the Esc key which will work for most people.

Repeat for each different color dot. If the Magic Wand tool selects more than one color of the dots, lower the Tolerance setting on the Magic Wand tool Options bar.

There are two key things to remember: Select the pattern layer when using the Magic Wand tool. Select the new paper layer before tapping the Delete key.

To create different papers, try changing around the papers to fill different parts of the overlay.

In the example on the right, I have pulled the Layers panel out of the Panel bin so that you can see all of the layers.

As you can see, choosing the Magic Wand to select the paper and deleting the excess is similar to using a Clipping Mask. Either method will work for cutting paper out of a template. I prefer using the Clipping Mask method because if I want to make changes, it gives me more options.

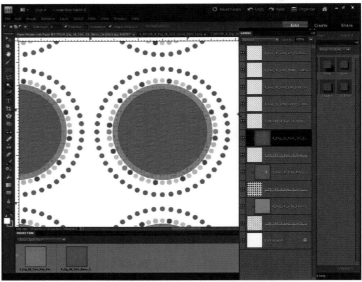

Using Blending Modes with Paper Pattern Overlays

Some paper templates do not have transparent backgrounds and are created in shades of gray. To try and select a specific color from the template and change it as we did in the previous example would be very difficult to do.

By changing the opacity and/or blending mode of a paper pattern layer (with or without transparency), you can achieve many different results.

Note that some blending modes will remove black or white. If your paper pattern template has black or white in it, you may want to replace it using the preceding example.

Make a new blank file and drag a paper pattern template from The Digital Scrapbook Teacher's Examples folder onto the page using the Move tool, just like we did in the preceding example. Fill the Background layer with any color.

In my example I am using yellow (Hex # e7da0e). I am using two paper pattern overlay templates from Paper Pattern Overlay Templates # 3 & #4 which are available from *www.TheDigitalScrapbookTeacher.com*. These paper pattern overlay files are not on the *Photoshop Elements - Basics & Beyond* DVD.

Adjust the blending mode by clicking on the drop down list next to the word Normal (red arrow) at the top of the Layers panel and cycling through the list of blending modes. To quickly cycle through the list, tap the Up and Down Arrow keys.

Click on the Opacity drop down arrow (circled) to reduce the opacity of the layer.

In my example I have chosen the Soft Light blending mode. The opacity is 45%.

Follow the same steps to add another paper pattern overlay. In the example on the left, I have changed the blending mode to Overlay and the Opacity is 79%.

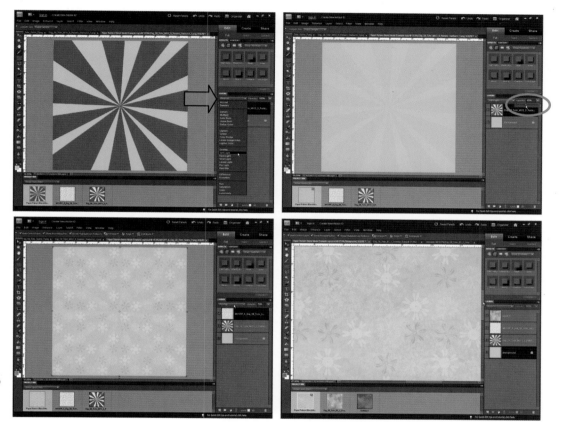

The example on the right shows the paper after we have added a texture layer to it following the steps in the next tutorial. Save.

How to Use a Paper Texture Overlay

Adding textures to your projects give them dimension and make them look like you used real textured paper. Instead of starting with a solid color Background layer like the example on the right, add a texture to it and see how much it improves the final result.

First, make a new blank white file, as explained in the beginning of this chapter. Fill the Background layer with any color. In my example I am using a medium blue color (Hex # 31658c).

Open the texture overlay from the Digital Scrapbook Teacher's Examples folder on the *Photoshop Elements - Basics & Beyond* DVD.

Available from the Essentials #1 kit at *www.TheDigitalScrapbookTeacher.com* this overlay, has transparent areas in it. Texture overlay files sold on our Paper & Photo Texture Overlay kits do not have transparency. Texture overlays you purchase from other sources may or may not have transparent areas.

With the Move tool, drag the texture overlay onto the page. Be sure to click on a solid area, because if you click in a transparent area you may have trouble dragging the texture onto your page. Sometimes you may like the look of the texture layer on top of the colored Background layer as shown in the example on the left. You may also want to adjust the opacity of the texture layer as shown on the example on the right where I lowered the opacity to 30%.

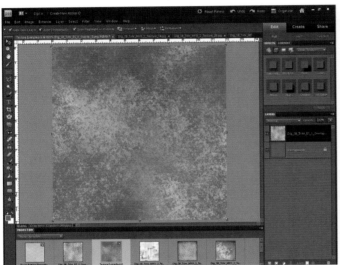 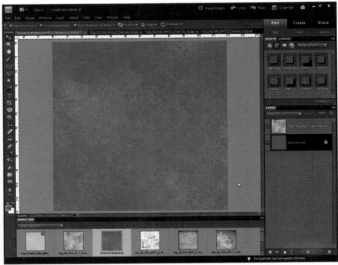

Change the blending mode to Overlay and the opacity to 100% to achieve the same results as the example shown below on the left.

Lower the opacity of the texture layer to 60% to achieve the same results as shown below in the example on the right.

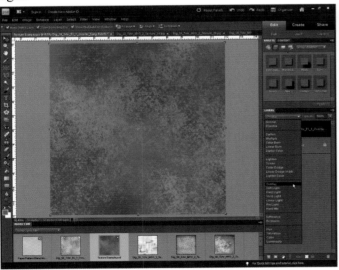 

All of these examples are much more interesting than the plain blue background we started with. Experiment using different blending modes and opacities to make your own one of a kind papers. Adding extra texture layers will add more depth and dimension to your papers, as you can see by the example on the next page.

I used seven different texture layers in this example. The blending mode and opacity for each layer was also changed. The Background layer color was the same as the previous examples.

The additional texture layers I used in the example on the right are from the Paper & Photo Texture Overlay #1 & #2 kits available at *www.TheDigitalScrapbookTeacher.com.* Save.

How to Use a Grunge Edge Overlay

First, make a new blank white file, as explained in the beginning of this chapter. Fill the Background layer with any color. In my example I am using a medium blue color (Hex # 31658c).

Open the grunge edge overlay from the Digital Scrapbook Teacher's Examples folder on the *Photoshop Elements - Basics & Beyond* DVD.

This overlay, available from the Essentials #1 kit at *www.TheDigitalScrapbookTeacher.com* has transparent areas in it.

With the Move tool, drag the texture overlay onto the page (be sure you are clicking on a solid area of the overlay). As shown in the example below on the left, a dark edge will be added to your page. Change the blending mode to Overlay as shown on the example below on the right.

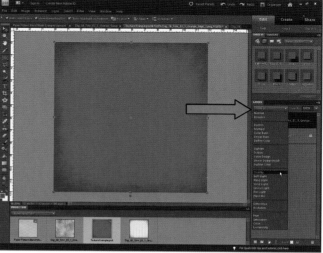

Because the Grunge Edge Template is a transparent file, it can be filled with any color. In the example below on the left, I filled the layer with white to produce a chalked edge effect. To do this, set the Foreground color at the bottom of the Toolbar to white. From the Menu bar choose Edit>Fill Layer. Choose Use Foreground Color and make sure the Preserve Transparency box is checked. Click OK. The shortcut to do this is Shift>Alt>Backspace (Mac: Shift>Opt>Delete). Adjust the opacity and blending mode as desired.

In the example below on the right, I added the Grunge Edge Template to the paper file with seven textures (shown in an earlier example) to darken the edges of the paper.

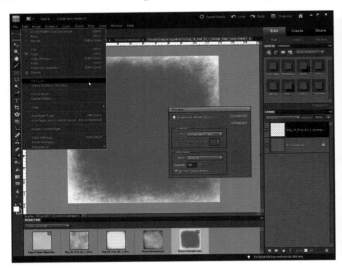 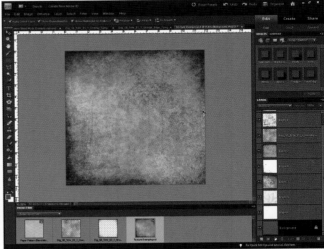

How to Use a Page Blender

Using a Page Blender is a great way to softly blend two papers together.

Open the Page Blender from the Digital Scrapbook Teacher's Examples folder on the *Photoshop Elements - Basics & Beyond* DVD. A Grunge Edge Template can also be used in the same way as a Page Blender.

Open two pieces of paper. I am using paper from the Springtime and Funtime Paper and Embellishment kits available at *www.TheDigitalScrapbookTeacher.com*. They are not included on the *Photoshop Elements - Basics & Beyond* DVD.

First, make a new blank white file, as explained in the beginning of this chapter. With the Move tool, drag a paper onto your new page. Next, drag the Page blender onto the page, followed by the second piece of paper.

With the top paper layer selected, from the Menu bar, choose Layer>Create Clipping Mask (Ctrl>G Mac: Cmd>G). Note: If you are using Photoshop Elements 7 or lower, choose Layer>Group with Previous (same command, new name). Save.

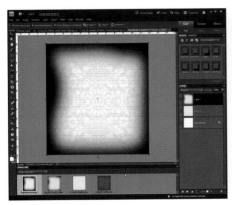 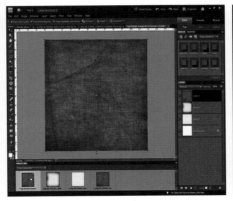 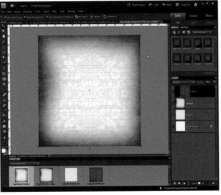

How to Use a Brush like a Rubber Stamp - Single Color

Rubber stamps and I never got along too well. I'd buy them and then want to stamp them in different sizes or in different colors than my stamp pads. Several times I found my stamp pads too late after my children had found them and I had to scrub their multi colored fingerprints off the wall. When I discovered brushes I was in heaven! My color choices are now endless, and I am no longer regulated to stamping in just one size.

Make a new blank white file, as explained in the beginning of this chapter. In these examples we will temporarily load the brush set in the Digital Scrapbook Teacher's Examples folder on the *Photoshop Elements - Basics & Beyond* DVD.

To temporarily load the brush set, select the Brush tool (B) on the Toolbar (shown circled below on the left). There are four tools nested under the Brush tool icon, so click and hold on the small black triangle to make sure the right tool is selected.

Click on the brush picker drop down list (shown circled below, on the right). Click on the two double white arrows (shown circled below, on the right, in white) to pop out more options. Click on Load Brushes.

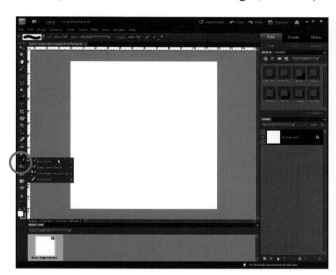
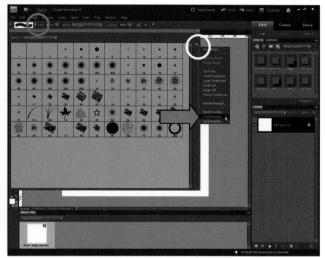

Navigate to the Brush Set folder in the Digital Scrapbook Teacher's Examples folder on the *Photoshop Elements - Basics & Beyond* DVD.

Windows XP Screenshot

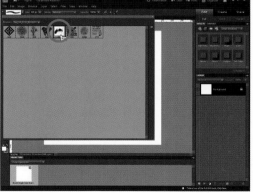

Click on the Dig_SB_Tchr_Brushes-Basics-Beyond file. Click on the Load button and the brushes will be temporarily loaded. Click on the Ant brush (224 pixels); your cursor should now look like a small ant.

Temporarily loading a brush means that if you switch to another brush set you will need to load this brush set again. To permanently load a brush see the Brush tool section in the *Tools* chapter.

One of the Cardinal Rules of using brushes is to always make a new transparent layer every time you stamp a brush. This means if you are stamping four decorative corners on a page, you make a transparent layer for each corner. While it may seem like a lot of extra work, it really isn't. If you stick to this rule, you'll do great and won't have to redo a lot of your work when you make mistakes or want to make simple changes.

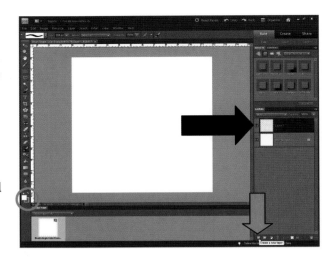

Think of handing me a beautiful traditional paper scrapbook page that you've spent hours working on, and asking me to add some rubber stamping to it. If you're smart, you will ask me to stamp on a piece of transparency that you will slide inside the page protector, if not; I'll ruin your page because my rubber stamping skills are horrific.

To add a new transparent layer, click on the New Layer icon at the bottom of the Layers panel (red arrow). If you are using Photoshop Elements 7 or below, this icon is at the top of the Layers palette. The shortcut to add a new transparent layer is Shift>Alt>Ctrl>N, Mac: Shift>Opt>Cmd>N.

Once the transparent layer (black arrow in the example above) has been added, we're ready to begin. Click in the Foreground color swatch (white in the example above) at the bottom of the Toolbar to choose a color for the brush. In this example I chose red.

To stamp, click once. To paint, click and drag.

The fastest way to resize a brush is to use the Bracket keys located to the right of the P key on your keyboard.
To make the brush bigger, tap the right Bracket key **]**.
To make the brush smaller, tap the left Bracket key **[**.

By using the Bracket keys you can see the brush grow or shrink to the size you need. If you don't like this method, you can always use the slider on the Brush tool Options bar.

While you can't resize your rubber stamps, you can resize your brushes. The example on the right shows the same brush used in different sizes.

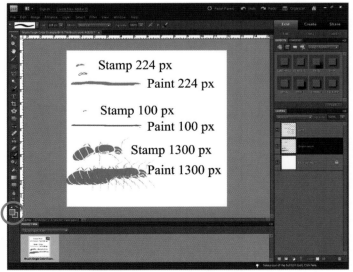

Stamp 224 px
Paint 224 px
Stamp 100 px
Paint 100 px
Stamp 1300 px
Paint 1300 px

You no longer need stacks of ink pads, because your supply of colors is endless! To choose another color, click on the Foreground color swatch (circled in the example on the right) and you're ready to go.

How to Use a Brush like a Rubber Stamp – Straight Line & Evenly Spaced

Follow the instructions to load the Ant brush, make a new blank file, and new transparent layer as explained in the preceding *How to Use a Brush like a Rubber Stamp - Single Color* tutorial.

Click, hold, and drag a line across the page using the ant brush, trying to keep the line straight. If I was making a scrapbook page about ants invading my picnic, this probably wouldn't be the look I had in mind.

To make a straight line, make another transparent layer (Shift>Alt>Ctrl>N, Mac: Shift>Opt>Cmd>N). Click, hold, and drag a line across the page while also holding the Shift key to drag the ants in a straight line. While the result is better, the line does not look like ants marching in formation preparing to abscond with my picnic lunch.

To evenly space the ants, click on the Brush Options icon on the Brush tool Options bar shown circled above. Currently the Spacing for this brush is set at 25%. Change it to 100%. Make a new transparent layer, hold the Shift key and click and drag across the page. Changing the Spacing setting to 100% did not give me the results I wanted so I tried 200% as shown in the example to the right.

To gain confidence, try this with other brushes in the brush set.

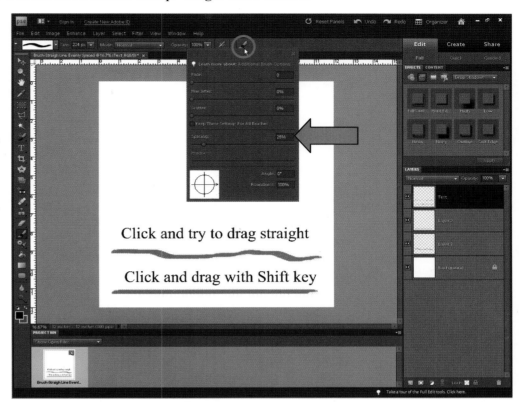

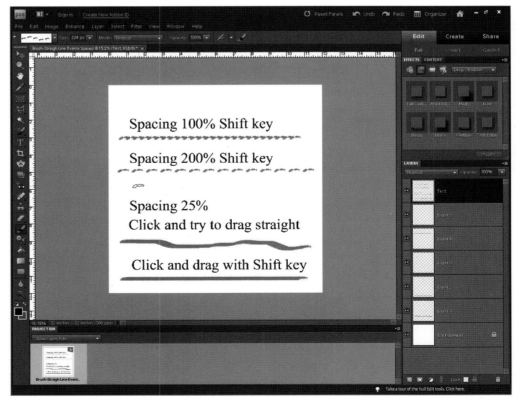

How to Use a Brush as an Eraser to Round Corners

One of the most used tools in my scrapbook stash is my corner rounder punch. As a matter of fact, I've had to replace several corner rounders over my lifetime as a traditional scrapper.

While you can round the corners of a photo or paper using the Rounded Rectangle tool (U) and a clipping mask, this way is faster and easier for me, especially if I don't want to round all four corners.

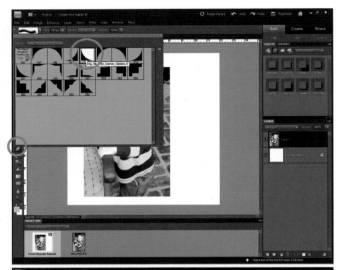

The corner rounding brush I am using is not on the *Photoshop Elements - Basics & Beyond* DVD. This brush set is included on the Essentials #1 kit and can be purchased at: *www.TheDigitalScrapbookTeacher.com.*

Follow the instructions to load a corner brush set, and make a new blank white file as explained in the preceding *How to Use a Brush like a Rubber Stamp - Single Color* tutorial.

Use the Move tool (V) to drag a photo or paper onto the page.

Select the Eraser tool (E) on the Toolbar and choose a brush. I have chosen a brush to crop the bottom left corner.

With the photo layer selected, hover the brush over the corner as shown in the example to the left. Re-size the brush if desired by tapping the left or right Bracket keys (be sure to remember the pixel size). Line up the brush with the photo and click to cut off the square corner.

To round the next corner, rotate the page (Image>Rotate), or choose another corner brush in the same set.

If you re-sized the brush for the first corner, you will need to re-size it the same size for the corners to match.

Depending on the look you're after, round one or more corners. You can round the corners of many things other than photos. Round the corners of accent papers, mats, tags, and anything else that strikes your fancy.

In this example, I've rounded only two of the four corners, and I really like how it looks.

Change It!

One of the wonderful things about digital scrapbooking is that you have so many options available to you. Since you no longer have to spend time cleaning up your scrapping area, you've got more time to complete your projects. If you are/were a traditional scrapbooker, you know that there were many times when you unearthed the perfect paper or other element from the bottom of your stash, only to be disappointed because it wasn't the right color. Maybe you bought a laser cut overlay to use as a grid over your page and the holes were in the wrong configuration. What about when you do have the perfect paper, but you've only got one piece and you need two? If you've experienced any similar issues, you'll be glad to know that with digital scrapbooking you won't have those issues any more.

Digital scrapbooking allows you to re-use and re-color your papers and elements. Templates can be easily modified to fit your needs. You'll use the tricks covered in this chapter over and over.

Change the Color

There are several ways to change the color of items with Photoshop Elements; I'll cover the techniques I use most of the time. My examples below are using items found in The Digital Scrapbook Teacher's folder on the *Photoshop Elements - Basics & Beyond* DVD in the Example Files folder. The papers below are from our Wintertime Paper and Embellishment kit available for purchase at www.TheDigitalScrapbookTeacher.com.

Normally, I will start making a page and then decide that, while I like the paper I have chosen, I would like to change the color a little bit. In my example below, I've started making a scrapbook page and have two layers of paper on top of my plain white paper file.

Change Color-Eyeball It

To change the color of the dotted paper, I select the correct layer in the Layers panel and then choose Enhance>Adjust Color>Adjust Hue & Saturation. I know my layer is selected, because it is a darker color in the Layers panel list. The shortcut for this command is Ctrl>U (Mac: Cmd>U), think of the "u" in Hue to remember this shortcut. If I don't pay attention and choose the correct layer, I will change the color of the wrong layer, which is something I do when I'm tired. If you do this, click on the Cancel button and select the correct layer.

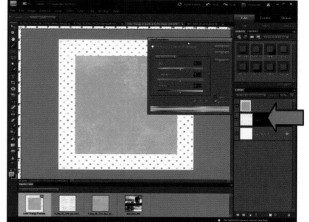

The Hue/Saturation dialog box will open in the middle of the screen; click and drag on the top bar to move it out of the way. The next time you use this command, the dialog box will open in the new location.

Slide the Hue slider to change the color of the entire layer. Slide the Saturation to the left to remove all color, to the right to intensify it. Slide the Lightness slider to lighten or darken the paper. All the way to the left will fill the paper with black, and all the way to the right will fill it with white.

To reset the changes you've made before clicking the OK button, hold the Alt key (Mac: Opt key) to change the Cancel button to a Reset button.

Click OK when you're happy with your results. Because this paper was dragged onto a new blank white file you are only changing the color of it in this file. The original paper is still safe with the original colors that match the kit.

Change Color-Exact Match

Matching an exact color gets a little bit tricky. Using the same papers as an example, I want to change the solid blue paper to the green color in the dotted paper. To do this, I will select the Eyedropper tool (I) and click in one of the green dots. This will change my Foreground color at the bottom of my Toolbar to green.

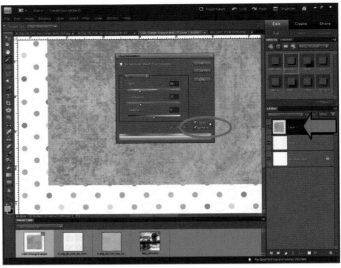

Select the blue paper layer in the Layers panel. Choose Enhance>Adjust Color>Adjust Hue & Saturation. Click in the Colorize box shown circled in the example to the right.

The paper will change to green, but it will not be the exact color match you were expecting. Slide the Saturation slider to the right until the green is the correct shade.

Change Color-Change Certain Colors #1

Select the dotted paper layer in the Layers panel. Choose Enhance>Adjust Color>Adjust Hue & Saturation from the Menu bar.

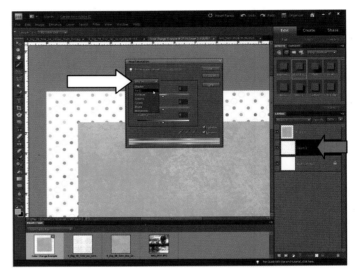

Click on the Master drop down arrow (shown with the white arrow).

Choose Red from the list and slide the Hue slider. Only the red toned colors which are the red and pink dots will change on the paper. Choose Magenta and only the pink dots will change color. To change the color of the green dots, choose Green or Yellow from the drop down list. To fine tune color changes, see Fine Tuning Color Changes on the next page.

Change Color-Change Certain Colors #2

Method #1 above will generally work well, but as you can see when choosing Red from the Hue/Saturation drop down list the pink <u>and</u> the red dots change on the paper. To change only the red dots you will need to select them using the Magic Wand tool (W).

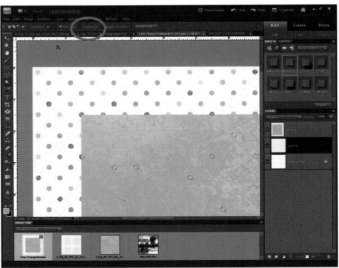

With the dot paper layer selected in the Layers panel, click on the Magic Wand tool icon on the Toolbar. On the Options bar, uncheck the Contiguous box (circled). Click on a red dot and all of the red dots should be selected (surrounded by marching ants). You may need to adjust the Tolerance setting on the Options bar to select more or less of the color.

Choose Enhance>Adjust Color>Adjust Hue & Saturation to change the color of only the red dots.

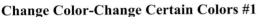

This Quick Page can be found on *Photoshop Elements - Basics & Beyond* DVD in the Kelly Jos Scraps Folder. The kit folder is named: k-josscraps_IBEM.

To change the green mat to another color such as yellow to match the flowers, select the Eyedropper tool (I) and click in the color you would like to use for the mat. The Foreground color will change to this color as shown (yellow in my example).

Select the Magic Wand tool (W). On the Magic Wand tool's Options bar check the Contiguous box (circled). Otherwise, once you click you will select all of the green areas on the Quick Page. By choosing Contiguous you will only select green areas that are touching each other.

The default setting for Tolerance is 32. By increasing this number you will be able select more of the green mat at one time. I have entered 50 for this example.

Click once, and most of the green mat is selected. To add more to the selection, click on the second icon from the left (marked with a red arrow in the example) on the Options bar or hold the Shift key while clicking.

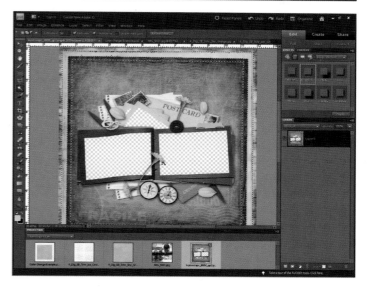

Once you have made a selection that includes the green mat, choose Enhance>Adjust Color>Adjust Hue & Saturation. Remember to click inside the Colorize box and move the Saturation slider to the right as show in the Change Color-Exact Match example on the preceding page.

To remove the marching ants (selection border), choose Select>Deselect (Ctrl>D Mac: Cmd>D). Tapping the Esc key on your keyboard may also work for you.

Fine Tuning Color Changes
When choosing a color from the color drop down list on the Hue/Saturation dialog box, or on an Adjustment layer shown on the next page, you have the ability to specify the range of colors to change.

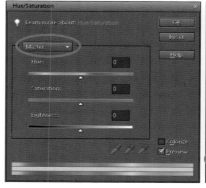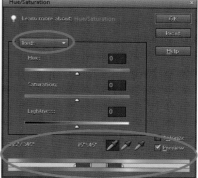

Once a color is selected from the drop down list and Master no longer shows, the bottom section of the box is no longer grayed out and changes may be made.

In this example, I want to change the red dots on the paper. The problem is, even though I chose Red from the drop down list, the pink dots also change color. I can use the Magic Wand (W) tool to select the red dots and change them, or I can use the eyedroppers and bar at the bottom of the dialog box to fine tune the color change.

This box is available from the Enhance>Adjust Color>Adjust Hue & Saturation command, and also on the Hue & Saturation Adjustment layer.

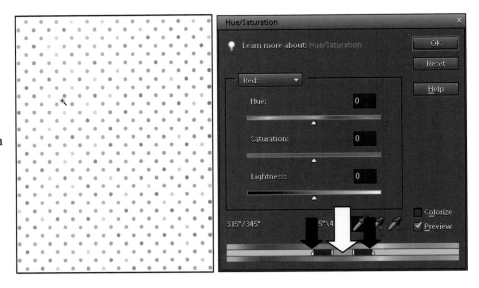

As soon as I choose Red, the first Eyedropper icon on the left is selected and the cursor is now an eyedropper. Click on a red dot on the paper. Notice that the range of color is indicated by the gray area on the middle section of the bar (marked with the white arrow). Click on the eyedropper icon with the minus sign next to it and click on a pink dot. The color range will shift slightly.

Next, click and drag the two sliders (black arrows) toward the center to cover the dark gray area on the bar as shown to the right (inside red circle).

Slide the Hue slider to adjust the color of only the red dots.

As shown circled to the right, the color above the dark gray bar is the selected color (red); the color on the bottom bar is the new color (green).

Remember, to change the Cancel button to a Reset button hold the Alt key (Mac: Opt key).

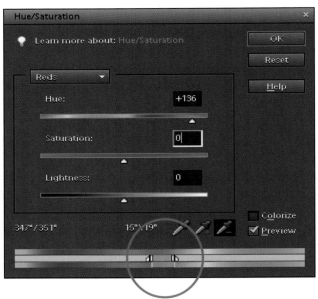

Problems You May Face Changing Colors

Imagine this scenario: you begin to build a scrapbook page. On step 5, you change the color of a paper using the Enhance>Adjust Color>Adjust Hue and Saturation command. On step 40, you decide that you're not happy with the color change and you would like to change it back to the original color or adjust it. Your options…Undo (Ctrl>Z Mac: Cmd>Z) 35 times to get back to the original paper and then basically start over, delete the layer and drag on the original paper again, or you can try Enhance>Adjust Color>Adjust Hue & Saturation and adjust the color again to see if you can get a better match.

To make sure you don't face this issue, use a Hue/Saturation Adjustment layer to make your color change as shown in the next example. With an Adjustment layer you can make changes or revert to the original color at any time.

Color Change-Adjustment Layer
I have selected the blue paper layer in the Layers panel by clicking on it.

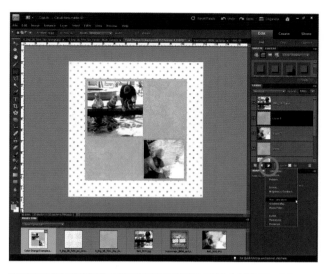

At the bottom of the Layers panel, click on the Adjustment Layer symbol (half black, half white circle) shown circled in red. Choose Hue/Saturation. Note: If you are using Photoshop Elements 7 or lower, these icons are located at the top of the Layers panel.

An Adjustment layer dialog box opens up in the Layers panel. This box appears similar to the Adjust Hue/Saturation command dialog box and, with one exception changes can be made the same way.

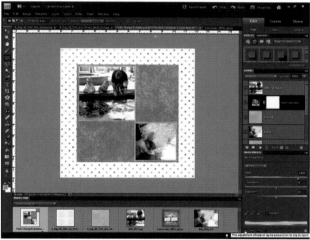

As I slide the Hue slider, all of my layers underneath the layer with the Adjustment layer change colors. This can be good or bad.

I've had many mothers of twins in my classes. They are very busy women with not much time to scrapbook (much like the rest of us!). Using an Adjustment layer, they can very easily make one page and then change the color to make the page look different, especially if they have boy and girl twins. Swap out the photos and change some type and you've made a second page very quickly.

The best part of an Adjustment layer is that you can adjust the color at any time without Undoing anything. Open up the Adjustment layer 100 steps after you've adjusted the color and simply move the 3 sliders back to the center 0 setting and you're back to your original layer.

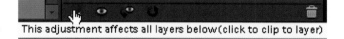
This adjustment affects all layers below (click to clip to layer)

In my example, my photo on the lower right side of my page has now taken on incorrect colors. One fix would be to move the photo layer up above the Hue & Saturation Adjustment layer.

Adjustment layers adjust every layer underneath it. In the example on the left, all layers below the Adjustment layer would be affected by the Hue/Saturation Adjustment layer. To make the Adjustment layer adjust only one layer, you will need to clip it to the layer (center example), or layers (right example) directly below it. At the bottom of the Adjustment layer dialog box are several icons as shown above. Click on the first icon on the left or choose Layer>Create Clipping Mask (Ctrl>G Mac: Cmd>G) from the Menu bar to clip the Adjustment layer to the layer(s) directly below it.

If you find the open Adjustment layer panel as distracting as I do, once you're done with it, tap the Reset Panels button at the top of your screen. To re-open it to make more adjustments, double click in the circled area.

Changing the Color of Part of an Element

As you have seen in the previous tutorials it's easy to change the color of a
layer. As shown on the right, the sunflower from the KDesigns Vintage
Days kit (available on the *Photoshop Elements - Basics & Beyond* DVD) has
a nice yellow center. However, when I change the color of the sunflower all
of it changes, including the center part I wanted to keep yellow.

The easiest way I have found to do this is to add a Hue/Saturation
Adjustment layer as shown in the previous example. On the
Hue/Saturation Adjustment layer, slide the Hue slider to find a color you
like. Because you are using an Adjustment layer you can adjust the color
at any time. After adding the Adjustment layer, from the Menu bar
choose Layer>Create Clipping Mask (Ctrl>G, Mac: Cmd>G). Doing
this will clip the Adjustment layer to the flower so that it does not affect
any other layers below it.

Type the letter D to set your Foreground and Background colors located at the bottom of the Toolbar to the
default settings. Your Foreground color should be black, and your Background color should be white. From the
Toolbar, select the Brush tool (B). Choose a soft round brush from the brush drop down list on the Options bar.
Click inside the mask (circled) on the Hue/Saturation Adjustment layer and then click on the center of the flower
and paint away the center so that the yellow color below shows through.

Adding Color to a Desaturated Image

Some designers sell elements that have the color removed
so that you can recolor them yourself. One way to recolor
an element is with a Solid Color Fill Layer. First you must
change the Foreground color chip at the bottom of the
Toolbar to the color you want the element to be.

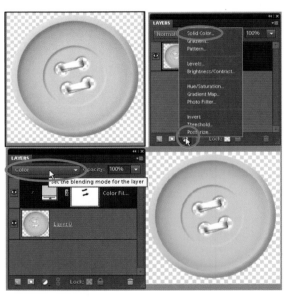

Open the image and click on the Adjustment Layer symbol
(half black, half white circle) at the bottom of the Layers
panel and choose Solid Color. The Adobe Color Picker box
will appear with the Foreground color selected, click the
OK button. The entire layer will be filled with color.

From the Menu bar choose Layer>Create Clipping Mask.
Solid color will now cover only the element (button) but no
definition or shading can be seen on the element. To remedy
this, change the blending mode from Normal to Color. If
there are any areas that you do not want the Color Fill layer
applied to like the stitching on the button holes, follow the
instructions in the preceding example for painting them
away with the Color Fill layer mask.

Changing a Photo or Patterned Paper to a Texture

It's easy to change a digital photo or patterned paper into a texture. In this
example I'm using a paper from Meredith Cardall's Dress Up kit included on the
Photoshop Elements - Basics & Beyond DVD to create an embossed solid
paper. To create a texture, open an image and save it as a PSD file to this folder:

Windows-C:>Program Files>Adobe>Photoshop Elements 9>Presets>Textures
Mac-Applications>Photoshop Elements 9>Presets>Textures

Create a new document (File>New>Blank File). Choose a Foreground Color (in this example I used the Eyedropper tool (I) to sample the aqua color from the paper). Select the Paint Bucket tool (K) (Alt> Backspace, Mac: Opt>Delete) from the Toolbar and click on the page to fill it with color.

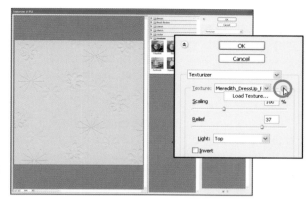

From the Menu bar choose Filter>Texture>Texturizer. Click on the blue arrow to the right of the Texture box to load a new texture. Navigate to the Textures folder where you saved the PSD file and the texture will appear on your document. Adjust the scaling to make the pattern larger or smaller (100% will match the original image).

Increase the Relief setting to make the texture heavier or decrease it to make it more subtle. Change the Light direction or check the Invert box if desired. If you don't like the changes you made, hold the Alt key (Mac: Opt key) and click on the Cancel button to reset the settings. Click the OK button. To add more depth and dimension add a grunge overlay.

How to Keep the Edges When Resizing an Image

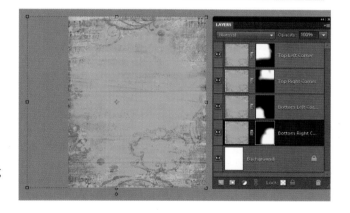

Angel Hartline's paper from the Renewal kit has great edges, but if I try and resize this paper to an 8 ½ x 11" paper I will lose the edges. An easy way to remedy this situation is to drag the paper onto a new blank document, resize the paper so that it is 11" high but it will still be wider than 8 ½" and will be hanging off the side which is good. Duplicate the paper layer so that you have four layers, move each layer to a specific corner of the document, and use a mask to hide some of the edges. It may be helpful to rename each layer with its location (top left corner). I also worked on one layer at a time by hiding the other layers as I worked.

How to Add to an Edge Template

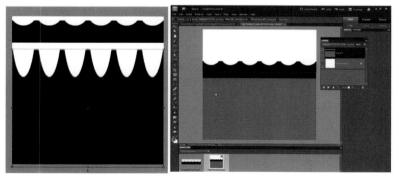

An Edge template is great to add a thin decorative cut out strip along the edge of a scrapbook page or other project. A lot of times you need a wider strip. As shown in the example, dragging a sizing handle distorts the decorative edge which isn't usually the effect you want. Instead of resizing the template to make it larger, you need to add to it which is easy to do.

Open the template which can be found in the Digital Scrapbook Teacher's folder on the *Photoshop Elements - Basics & Beyond* DVD. Create a new blank document (File>New>Blank File). Select the Move tool (V) and drag the template onto the new white document. Select the Rectangular Marquee (M) from the Toolbar. Select the template layer in the Layers panel. Click and drag a rectangle over the area that you want to add to the template making sure that you are overlapping the template shape. Select the Paint Bucket tool (K) and click inside the selection. In my example I have filled my selection with red to make it easier for you to see. You can fill your selection with any color because the color of the template will not show after you clip a paper or photo to the edge template with a clipping mask (Layer>Create Clipping Mask).

Changing Templates

Layered templates are a great way to work faster because most of the design work is done for you. It will take you longer to pick out your photos, scrapbook papers, embellishments, and a template than it will to put the page together after you get the hang of it. Sometimes you want to make changes to the template to fit your photos or mood.

The templates that The Digital Scrapbook Teacher sells have the layers all linked together so that you won't bump a layer and move it out of alignment. This is an extra step we do because we specialize in teaching brand new digi-scrappers and it helps them a lot.

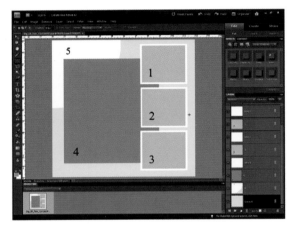

Open file Dig_SB_Tchr_12x12d 047 from The Digital Scrapbook Teacher Example files folder on the *Photoshop Elements - Basics & Beyond* DVD.

Choose Image>Rotate and choose an option to change the look of the template by simply turning it.

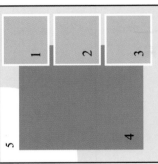

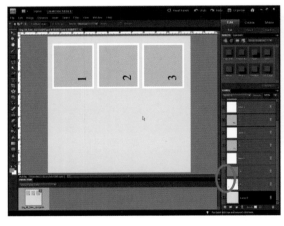

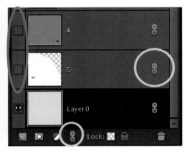

Maybe you only want to use some of the template pieces and don't want to use others. To do this, simply click on the eyeball icon (circled) on the layer in the Layers panel to temporarily hide the layer. You can also drag the layer to the trash can, or right click (Mac: Ctrl click) and choose delete.

In this example I have hidden layers # 4 & 5.

To resize one of the template pieces all you need to do is use the Transform command. If the layers are linked together, you must first unlink the layer from the other layers. To unlink a layer, select the layer in the Layers panel. The link symbol will be displayed as shown above (circled in yellow). Click on the link symbol at the bottom of the Layers panel. The link symbol will disappear from the selected layer. If a linked layer is not selected, the link symbols will not show. Note: the link symbol for Photoshop Elements 7 and below is located at the top of the Layers palette.

To activate the Transform command, type the shortcut Ctrl>T (Mac: Cmd>T) or select the Move tool (V) and drag a corner of the bounding box. Check the green check mark to commit the change.

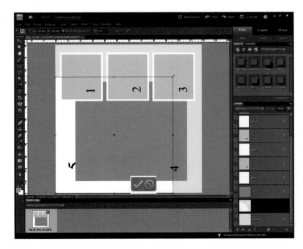

Organizing

Keep an open mind and stick with it. That's my best advice before you start reading this chapter. Know this before you start reading: I've been teaching how to organize images for several years. The feedback from my students is that of all the things I've ever taught them, this is by far the best.

Your eyes may glaze over as you read this chapter; you may think that organizing your images, whether they be photos or digital scrapbooking supplies or both, is an overwhelming task. I promise you the payoff is huge!

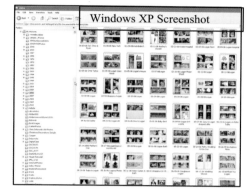

In the course of my lifetime I've taken thousands of photos, maybe even more than a million. Can I find them all if I need one? I have all of my film negatives in a binder in chronological order all the way back to 1986, waiting for the day when I have some free time to scan them, or a lot of money to pay someone to do it for me. Some of the printed photos made their way into scrapbooks, while others reside in plastic tubs in my office closet, begging to be put in a book of some kind. My hope is that when I get the negatives finally scanned, I will scrap them digitally...that's the plan anyway!

My digital photos are fairly organized in individual folders by date. My digital scrapbooking supplies are organized by the stores where I have purchased them. Some people would kill to be this organized; I know, I see their computers every time I teach a hands-on class. If you're not this organized, don't stress out, I'll show you another way to get organized.

Even though I'm well organized, it's not a good enough system for me to easily find the images I'm looking for. Without using the Photoshop Elements Organizer, I have to rely on a lot of brain power to remember exactly where the images are stored. And frankly as I get older, my brain power isn't what it used to be!

The Organizer allows me to tag my photos and scrapbooking supplies so that I can find them by different search criteria. Currently, I have more than 45,000 pieces of digital scrapbooking art that is organized by color, type of element, designer, and theme and it's wonderful! I have more than 25,000 photos organized by date, event, person, favorites, and more.

Is my organizing perfect and up to date? No, but it's a work in progress. As we proceed through this chapter, I'll share lots of tips with you that will save you a lot of time and frustration that I wish I would have thought of years ago.

Beginning with Photoshop Elements 9, Adobe has included the Organizer with the PC and Mac versions. Not all of the Organizer's features have been included in the Mac version yet, but most of what I cover in this chapter will apply to both the PC and Mac version.

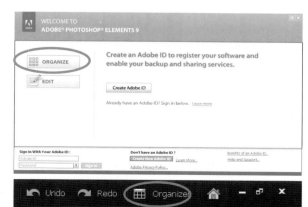

The Organizer is a separate program that works side by side with the Editor. You can also use it in conjunction with Photoshop.

To open the Organizer, click on the Organizer button on the Welcome screen. If you have the Editor open, click on the Organizer icon near the top right corner of the screen.

Not only will my organizing method save you time in the end, it will also save you space on your hard drives because the Organizer doesn't make a duplicate copy of your images as many people believe. Because of this reason, it's important not to move around the images you've imported into the Organizer unless you do it the proper way. We will cover moving images at the end of this chapter.

Why do I say the Organizer will save you space on your hard drive? Because of the things I've seen my students do, and the things I've done myself. Let me tell you about the way I started organizing my digital scrapbooking supplies. I had about 8,000 images and realized that I couldn't remember where anything was, even though I was pretty well organized, or so I thought. I decided that what I needed to do was make folders to hold all of my paper, another for all of the buttons, another for all of the ribbons...you get the idea. The problem was that I didn't want to break up the kit folders because everything in the kit folder was coordinated. What did I do? I duplicated the kit folder and then divided up the pieces by element type. Now I had the kit folders along with paper, buttons, ribbons, etc. folders. Right there I doubled the amount of space I needed to store the items. Did that system work? Sometimes, but I'd hate to think of trying to do that now with more than 45,000 items.

I did the same thing with my photos, keeping them in folders by date and event and then pulling out my favorites in one folder and photos of individuals for another folder with their name on it. This really took up a lot of hard drive space, because if I had a nice family photo it was duplicated several times.

Now if I want to find my favorite photos of my granddaughter, I can find them in seconds flat. If I want to find a piece of red, white, and blue, scrapbook paper with stars and stripes on it I can find it really fast, even though I purchased it more than five years ago and have no idea who the designer is, or what store I purchased it from.

How Many Catalogs?

Think of a catalog as a notebook full of images. A very helpful feature of the Organizer gives you the option to make different catalogs. I have a catalog for my photos, my digital scrapbooking supplies, my commercial use supplies and another for the catalog I use for teaching classes. I do not have a catalog for my scrapbook pages and chose not to keep them in the Organizer because I've found it slows down my Organizer. However, you may not have the same experience. I also have a few other test catalogs that I use for teaching purposes.

From the Menu bar, choose File>Catalog to display the Catalog Manager dialog box where you manage your catalogs.

The default catalog is named My Catalog. To rename it, click on the Rename button and type a new name such as Photos.

To create another catalog, click on the New button and type a name for the new catalog, such as Scrapbook Supplies.

To switch back and forth between two catalogs, select the catalog name in the list and then click on the Open button.

Where Should I Start?

You've got what seems like a million images to organize. It's overwhelming, where do you start? My suggestion is to start with your photos. Start with the current year and work backwards. Write down a plan of action. Print out a screenshot like the one from the first page of this chapter from your computer. Marking off each folder as you tag it is a great way to keep track of where you are. If you don't know how to make a screenshot, see the *What's New* page at *www.TheDigitalScrapbookTeacher.com*. Budget your time. Pledge to spend a certain amount of time organizing, and stick to it, write that down too. Don't overdo it and attempt to tag all your images in a week or you'll get cranky. You need to also have time to create pages and play with your photos. As you get faster at tagging, you'll find that you can tag while you watch TV, sit on an airplane, or wait for your children's soccer practice to finish up. But in the beginning, you'll need all of your brain power.

Make a new Photos catalog or rename the default My Catalog to Photos as shown above. If you have images in your existing catalog that you haven't tagged yet, delete them so you can start fresh. **Do not delete the images from the hard drive**.

How to Delete Images from the Organizer

To delete all of the images in the catalog, choose Edit>Select All (Ctrl>A, Mac: Cmd>A) and then choose Edit>Delete from Catalog or tap the Delete key. You can also select one or more thumbnails and right click and choose Delete from Catalog.

If it's a bad photo, and you would like to remove it from your computer completely, click in the box that says Also delete selected items from hard disk and then click the OK button.

How Do I Get Images Into The Organizer?

There are several ways to get images into the Organizer. When you save an image in the Editor, there is a Save Option to Include in the Elements Organizer. If you choose this option, the image will be saved in the specified folder and an untagged thumbnail will be saved in the Organizer.

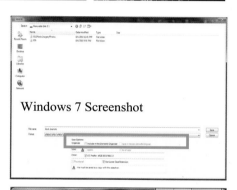

Windows 7 Screenshot

Note: Photoshop Elements uses the term photos. As a digital scrapbooker, I think they should use the term images. It gets confusing when you want to import clip art, buttons, bows, and papers and it says Get Photos and Videos but that is the option you will use.

If you prefer, there is also a command in the Editor that can be accessed by choosing Organize Open Files from the Menu bar, which I don't use.

When Windows users connect a digital camera card or other storage device like a flash drive or external hard drive with images on it to their computer, the Adobe Photo Downloader automatically launches as shown below on the left.

Click on Organize and Edit using Photoshop Elements Organizer 9 to launch the Elements Organizer Photo Downloader.

If you would like this to happen each time you connect a storage device to the computer, click in the Always do this for pictures box at the top of the dialog box (shown circled).

You may also choose File>Get Photos and Videos and choose to get the photos from Camera or Card Reader, Scanner, From Files and Folders, or by Searching. If you have chosen Folder Location from the Display menu, you can right click on a folder and choose Import to Organizer.

If you choose to download images from the Camera or Card Reader, or from the Auto Play dialog box the Elements Organizer – Photo Downloader box will appear. Choose a Subfolder option and if you want to, rename your files (I do not). I do not delete any images from the storage device until I preview them, so I keep the default Delete Option (After Copying, Do Not Delete Originals).

Click on the Advanced Dialog box if you would like to add Copyright and other information.

Click Get Media. When the box appears that says Files Successfully Copied, click the Yes button to import them into the Organizer.

When the box appears that says "The only items in the main window are those you just imported…Click OK.

If you choose File>Get Photos and Videos >From Files or Folders navigate to the folder (see red arrow) and click on it **once** to select it (circled).

Windows 7
Screenshot

I do not check the Automatically Fix Red Eyes because it often makes mistakes on my photos, takes longer to import images, and because there are no red eyes on scrapbooking supplies so why wait the extra time. I do not check the Automatically Suggest Photo Stacks boxes because I don't stack photos.

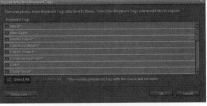

Click on the Get Media button (circled). If there are tags applied to your images you will see the Import Attached Keyword Tags dialog box. All JPEG and PSD images sold by *www.TheDigitalScrapbookTeacher.com* come pre-tagged for you to save you time. Click on the Select All button and then click on the OK button to import the files.

If you send or receive photos from family and friends and, if they use Photoshop Elements, there may be tags applied to them too.

The Elements Organizer dialog box will appear that says: The only items in the main window are those you just imported. To see the rest of the Catalog, click Show All. **Don't click Show All!** We only want to work with this small group of images not the entire catalog. Click in the box that says Don't Show Again to save you time in the future (shown circled), if desired. Click OK.

Before I imported the 14 new photos, the Catalog had 1760 images in it. The only images showing right now are the 14 images I just imported, which is exactly what I want. This helps me work with just these images and tag them. I suggest importing images in small batches (less than 100) so that you don't get overwhelmed. Located at the bottom left corner of the screen (red arrow) is the Catalog Name (Class Example), the number of images just imported (14), and the number of images not shown (1760).

Properties-Metadata Panel

To display the Properties panel, which gives you more information than you will probably ever need, from the Menu bar choose Window>Properties. To add this panel to the bin, click on the symbol shown circled on the right. The General tab displays the image size, star rating, date and time taken (if the camera is set correctly), and the folder location. You can also add notes or captions here. The Metadata tab lists file size, name, type, mode, color profile, resolution, camera data (exif) which includes the camera that took the image and the settings at the time. Depending on your phone, it may also include GPS information, so if you're advertising your jewelry on Craig's List that may be a problem. The Keyword Tags tab will list all keyword tags and albums for this image. The History tab shows import information.

Customizing the Organizer

From the Menu bar, choose View>Details to show the date the image was created under the thumbnail. Choose View>Show File Names to display the files names under the thumbnail. If the designer has put the element type in the file name, it makes it easier to tag it.

Choose Window>Timeline to display the Timeline at the top of the screen (red arrow).

Choose Window> Properties to add the Properties panel to the Panel bin (white arrow).

To make the thumbnails bigger or smaller, slide the slider above the timeline that is almost impossible to see (circled). You can also click on the Small Thumbnail Size and Single Photo View icons on either side of the slider. I normally set the slider in the middle and double click on a thumbnail to make it full size, and then double click again to make it smaller.

Click on the Display drop down list to choose a different view. I prefer to display my Scrapbooking Supplies Catalog as Import Batch.

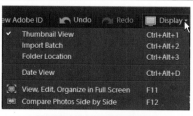

I display my Photos Catalog in Thumbnail View. In Thumbnail View I have the option to display Newest First (my choice) or Oldest First. This drop down list is located below the Undo button.

It's been my experience that if I choose Folder Location, my Organizer slows down dramatically, so I only choose this View when I need to move files or folders. I personally don't ever use Date View.

To rotate an image that came into the Organizer the wrong way, select the image and then click on the Rotate icons at the top of the screen (shown circled in the bottom example). My photos usually import the right way. I admit it, I rotated this thumbnail just to show you how to do it.

Watch Folders

One way to make sure that you don't forget to import your images (photos or scrapbook supplies) into the Organizer is to set up specific folders as Watch Folders. From the Menu bar, choose File>Watch Folder. Add the appropriate folders and Photoshop Elements will notify you when new files not yet imported into the Organizer have been added to that folder. I do not recommend choosing the Automatically Add Files to the Organizer option because if you're like me, you'll forget to tag them.

Photo Tagging Strategy

The reason that you tag photos is so that you can find them when you need them. This could be today when you decide to make a scrapbook page. It could be in 18 years when your newborn baby graduates from high school and you need your favorite baby photo for his yearbook. The need for photos comes up at all times. Not to be morbid, but what happens when someone dies? I know when my mother passed away my sisters and I searched through many boxes for days in search of her best photos to display at her memorial service.

I have listed my tagging strategy below and on the next page. Feel free to modify it for your own needs, but I would suggest you over tag your images in the beginning. When I first started tagging my photos, I thought that tagging the people and maybe an event was great, and it was much better than nothing. I found over time that this was not the most effective way to use this powerful software. As I worked with the Organizer, I wished that I would have added more tags to my photos, especially the star tags to mark my favorites.

Remember, everyone's needs are different. In the course of teaching classes I have met people who had no family or pets and only wanted to tag their travel photos very specifically. I've met people with huge extended families like myself that wanted to keep track of a lot of people. The Organizer allows you to set up a system that works for you, and modify it as things change. I've learned a lot about tagging photos from ideas my students have given me. I firmly believe that my Organization class is the best class I teach. By the time my students leave the class, their minds are on overload just as yours probably is right about now.

It's much less time consuming to add the tags in the beginning than to decide you wish you would have done things differently, and go back and add them later. Tags are easily editable, so if you decide you don't like the name of the tag, that's easy to change.

Apply tags to all people or pets by name in the photo. I had one student who used a general category of Pets, instead of the names of her dogs. She went back later to tag each pet individually by name because her system didn't work for her. If you have a large family, make a list of family members in outline form to begin with, or you can modify your tags in the Organizer as you go.

Apply a year tag. Yes there is a Timeline, but I've found adding a tag for the year works out great and it takes a second to do. **Apply a month tag** (use 01 January instead of January to help keep your months in order). This was a student's idea, and when she first mentioned the idea of tagging by month I thought it was a waste of time, but it's actually a timesaver. As an extra bonus I have created year, month, and holiday tags for you.

Apply special event tags and holiday tags as needed. Add the year tag separately.

Apply star tags. This is something I really wish I would have done in the very beginning to help me find my favorite photos. My criteria is that a 5 star photo is worthy of being in a wedding reception slide show (the best of the best-you know those photos). A 4 star photo is scrapbookable; it may not even be a great photo if I only have one photo of an event. I don't tag photos I consider to be 1-3 star worthy.

Another reason I wish I would have Star tagged my photos is because I take a lot of digital photos. I usually look at them right after I've taken them and identify the best ones that I'll use. When it comes time to scrap the photos, I don't have a clue which ones were the best ones and have to carefully look at a lot of them again. If I would have Star tagged them in the beginning, it would save me time.

Apply tags for special locations. Do you visit a certain place often? Maybe you make a Hawaii tag and that's sufficient for your travels. A real Hawaii buff would need tags for Oahu, Kauai, Maui, Hawaii (Big Island), etc. Make a tag for your children's different schools, or favorite park if you take photos there often.

Instead of tagging your photos with a Christmas 2010 tag, make a Christmas tag and a 2010 tag and tag it with both along with a 12 December tag. In the future you'll be able to pull up all of your Christmas photos by just clicking in the box next to the Christmas tag. Click in both the 2010 and Christmas tags and you'll find the Christmas 2010 photos. By choosing to tag with multiple tags it simplifies things, because in 20 years you would have added 20 Christmas tags. Multiply that by every holiday and it would be a nightmare!

If I take my grandchildren to see Santa at the end of November, do I still tag it with a Christmas tag? Yes, to me this is a Christmas photo; I even tag them with a Santa tag! If I was in Hawaii, I could also add a Hawaii tag (Yes, I know I'm dreaming!) It's all about helping you find the images in the future.

Here's a scenario of what I face when I finally have the time to scrapbook. My daughter gave me photos that were from the month of June 2009. I wanted to make a 2 page layout from the Calendar templates available at *www.TheDigitalScrapbookTeacher.com*, and I wanted to make a double page layout for a month of swimming lessons and the beach. My dilemma? There were more than 500 photos....because digital photos are free, we take a million!

How do I find the photos I want to use for my scrapbook pages? Because I had tagged the photos with the children's names, a June tag, a 2009 tag, a beach tag, a swimming lesson tag,...and very importantly, a star tag, I was able to specify exactly what I wanted and pull up only 40 photos for each child, which narrowed it down from the 500 photos that were taken just by their mother alone, not counting my photos.

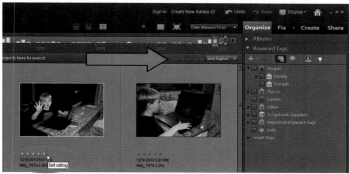

How to Apply a Star Tag

Underneath the image thumbnail are five dark stars. Click on the appropriate star (circled) and you've Star tagged the image. Change your mind? Click on the yellow star again to remove it.

Star tags can also be applied by selecting and right clicking on an image or by choosing Edit>Ratings from the Menu bar.

To search for your star tagged images, click on the Star Search bar (arrow).

Tags or Sub-Categories?

I keep using the term tag, but in reality I use sub-categories much more than I do tags. The act of tagging means applying a tag or sub-category to an image. There are two major differences between tags and sub-categories.

First, tags can have images inserted in them. This can be good and bad. Trying to teach an Organizing class to scrapbookers can be exasperating, because it's all about the little things with us scrapbookers. We want the perfect image to appear in the tag, even though no one but us is going to see it. Because of the image, tags take up more room in the Keyword tags panel, so consequently you have to scroll more to find the tag you're looking for.

Another advantage of sub-categories, other than taking up less space, is that they can step like an outline. Think of setting up your family in a family tree type outline, and you can see where this is important. A tag is the end of the line and you can't step another tag or sub-category underneath it.

In this example of my fictitious family, you can see that my tag is cute but doesn't give me the accountability like the sub-category does where I can list my entire family hierarchy. Looking at this, you know that Thelma and Louise belong to Bonnie and Clyde's family, even without me making the child notation.

Do you think of your family in alphabetical order? No, most people think of their siblings in birth order. The Organizer is going to list your tags in alphabetical order by default. There are two things you can do: Add a two digit number to your tags or sub-categories as I have in this example to indicate birth order. My husband gets to be #01 because he's older than I am.

Or, you can choose Edit>Preferences> Keyword Tags and Albums and change the settings from Alphabetical to Manual for the Keyword Tags and Sub-Categories selections. Making this change allows you to drag your tags and sub-categories into place. I prefer to keep the default Alphabetical settings and number my tags and sub-categories.

How to Install My Instant Tag Files to Save You Time

Included on the *Photoshop Elements - Basics & Beyond* DVD is an instant tag file for you to install into your Photos catalog. This will save you the time of making individual tags for the months, years, and holidays. I figure if I can make the tags for you, then you have more time to tag your images. This is the same reason that we pre-tag all of the JPEG and PSD files in the template and paper kits that we sell at *www.TheDigitalScrapbookTeacher.com*.

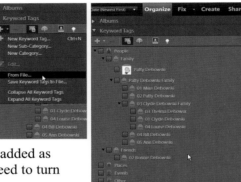

To install the tags, click on the green + under the Keyword Tags heading (not Albums) and click on From File. Locate the Photo Tags file on the *Photoshop Elements - Basics & Beyond* DVD in the Photo Tags folder in the Digital Scrapbook Teacher's folder. Click on Open, and then look at your Keyword Tags panel to verify that the new Time and Holiday & Celebrations Categories have been added as shown. If you have trouble installing this file you may need to turn off your virus protection software.

The category may be collapsed as shown in the middle example, or expanded as shown in the example on the right. To expand the category, click on the ▾ to the left of the Category.

How to Make a New Category

By default, Photoshop Elements has provided you with a People, Places, Events, and Other categories. Sub-categories for Family and Friends are provided under People.

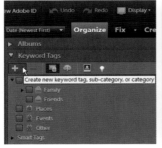

Instead of always using the Other category, it's easy to make a new category. To do this, click on the green + under the Keyword Tags heading (not Albums). Choose New Category. Type the name of the category, my example is Pets. Choose an icon by clicking on it and click the Choose Color button if you want to change the color of the tag edge. The color chosen will also affect any new tags or sub-categories listed under this category.

Click OK. The new Pets category will be added to the Keyword Tags panel. Click and drag it to reposition it in the list if desired.

How to Make a Tag or Sub-Category

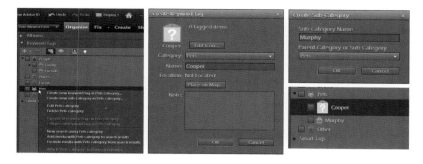

Making a new tag or sub-category is basically the same as making a category. As shown in the example I can click on the green + again, or I can right click (Mac: Ctrl click) on an existing category or sub-category to display my choices.

Because the Pets category is highlighted in the list, the new tag or sub-category will be placed under the Pets category. I encourage you to start with sub-categories instead of tags…yes, I know you like the cute pictures in the tags, but trust me…I'm an expert, that's why you bought this book…right? I know you'll be happier in the end with the sub-categories, besides you can always switch to tags later.

How to Apply Tags & Sub-Categories

The act of tagging involves adding tags and sub-categories to all images (photos or digital scrapbooking supplies). I will use the term tags or tagging, even though I will be applying both tags and sub-categories.

To add a tag or sub-category to an image, click, hold, and drag the tag or sub-category to the image. If you are using tags, the first time you tag an image the ? on the tag will be replaced by the image. As soon as you release the mouse, a tag icon may appear at the bottom of the image, depending on the size of the thumbnail (see examples on the next page). The tag on the image will also disappear.

You can also drag the image to the tag but you'll make fewer tagging mistakes if you drag the tag to the image.

To tag more than one image at a time, select all of the images at once and drag the tag to it. In this example, I have tagged seven photos in the same amount of time it took me to tag one.

To select all of the images in the window, choose Edit>Select All (Ctrl>A, Mac: Cmd>A). As shown on the right, to select several images in a row, click on the first one and hold the Shift key, and click on the last one. Selected images will be lighter in color.

To select several images that are not in a row, click on one and then Ctl click (Mac: Cmd click) on the others.

To select more than one tag or sub-category, repeat the steps above. Selected tags will be darker in color.

The idea is to tag as quickly as you can. In the two bottom examples, I tagged all of the photos with seven tags very quickly. First I tagged the three children and Santa. Next I tagged with a 2010, Christmas, and 12 December tag. Notice, as I drag the tags over, you see more than one tag (circled). I also star tagged one photo.

How Do I Know If I Tagged A Photo?

At the smallest thumbnail setting (left example) you will see the month and year of the photo and a tag icon on the image.

As I increase the thumbnail size, the tags may disappear completely, or differ from image to image (red outline). The best way to see what tags are applied to a photo is to double click on the thumbnail to see it full size and read the tags under the image (shown circled).

How to Find Untagged Items

From the Menu bar, choose Find>Untagged Items and any images without tags will be displayed. If you were interrupted while tagging and only applied half of the tags you intended to, this option won't help you because it will search for images without any tags.

Smart Tags

Smart tags such as High Quality, Low Quality, Blurred, and Shaky are automatically added by the Auto Analyzer. If you want to automatically apply smart tags, choose Edit>Preferences>Media-Analysis and click on Analyze Media for Smart Tags Automatically. I don't need Photoshop Elements to point out if I've taken a blurry photo, so I keep this option turned off. You may also select an image or several images, right click or from the Menu bar, choose Run Auto-Analyzer to apply smart tags. Smart tags can also be dragged and dropped on images. If you have a lot of images to organize, it may be helpful to use smart tags to find the bad photos that need to be deleted. Try it on a few batches to see if it helps you save time.

How to Remove Tags from Images

The example on the right is a close up of the tags applied to the photo above it (my Granddog in a Santa suit). In error, (you will do this too) I applied a Baseball tag to the thumbnail. To remove it, Right Click (Mac: Ctrl>Click) on the tag and choose Remove Baseball Sub-Category Keyword Tag.

If you delete a tag as shown in the example on the next page it will also be removed from the image.

How to Hide Images in the Organizer

If you have any images that you would like to hide so that they don't pop up at inopportune times (like when you're teaching a class), you can easily hide them. Select the photos you wish to hide. From the Menu bar, choose Edit>Visibility>Mark as Hidden. A Hidden file icon will appear on the image.

To actually hide the hidden images, choose View>Hidden Files>Hide Hidden Files from the Menu bar.

To see only hidden images, choose View>Hidden Files>Show Only Hidden Files from the Menu bar.

How to Edit a Category, Tag, or Sub-Category

Change happens all the time, whether we like it or not. We will always be making changes to our Photos or Scrapbook Supplies catalogs. All steps shown below will work for any type of catalog, not just the photo catalog that I'm demonstrating.

Let's say that Bonnie and Clyde split up. You want to remove Bonnie's sub-category from Clyde's Family. There are a few things you can do. Click on the red – (minus sign) below the Keyword Tags heading to delete her. I don't recommend this, no matter how mad you are about the situation. If you choose to delete Bonnie anyway, you will be asked to confirm the change.

Instead of deleting Bonnie click on the green + below the Keyword Tags heading to make changes. Choose Edit, or right click on Bonnie's sub-category and choose Edit 02 Bonnie Debowski sub-category. When the Edit Sub-Category dialog box appears, click the Parent Category or Sub-Category drop down list (circled) and choose another option. In my example I'm being civilized and have chosen Friends. You may want to make a new Enemies category first and put her in there.

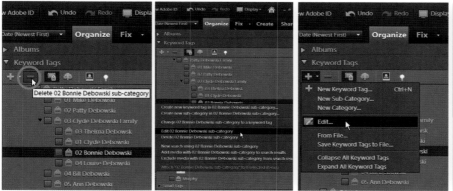

If you have already started tagging your photos, and have decided that using sub-categories instead of tags might be a good idea, don't start over. Right click on the tag and choose the first option to Change XXXX keyword tag to a sub-category.

If you still want to use the tags and want to adjust the photo that shows in the icon, right click on the tag and choose Edit XXXX Keyword Tag. Click on the Edit Icon button.

If the image showing in the tag is too small, drag the corners of the white flashing box (arrow) inward and click OK.

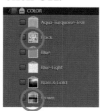

Sometimes when you import tagged images, the original tag thumbnail changes automatically. This can be aggravating, especially on the digital scrapbooking color and elements tags shown later in this chapter.

To change the image completely, click on the Find arrows (circled) to cycle through images that have been previously tagged. You can also click the Import button and choose an image from another location on your computer. Click OK.

Merging Tags

You may merge tags (not sub-categories). If you want to merge sub-categories one way you can do it is to right click and change them to tags temporarily. Select both tags and right click and choose Merge Keyword Tags. Choose the tag you wish to keep, and the other one will be deleted

Face Recognition

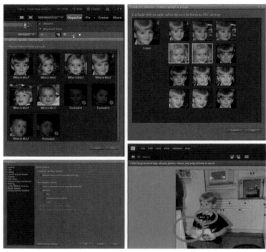

Adobe has improved their face recognition, but it still has its quirks. If you see a box that shows up and says Who is this? you can type in the names and see how it works for you.

Select the images you want the Organizer to recognize. Click on the Start People Recognition icon (circled), or choose Find> Find People for Tagging from the Menu bar and follow the prompts.

In the examples on the right, I added a name on the first screen and then was shown five screens and was asked to exclude the people that don't belong to the group. It was more labor intensive than I thought it would be.

At this time, I prefer to tag my photos myself. To turn off face tagging, choose Edit>Preferences>Media Analysis and uncheck the box. I actually uncheck all of the boxes because I'm not a fan of the Smart tags either.

Photo Stacks

If you have a lot of very similar photos, you may want to stack them. Before you start stacking all of your photos, practice searching for images to see if you achieve the desired results after you have created a few stacks. Many times in hands-on classes, my students have had issues searching for images and the culprit was their photo stacks. To stack images, select them and right click or choose Edit>Stack Selected Photos from the Menu bar. Once a photo stack is created, Photo Stack is added to the image thumbnail. A stacked

photo icon appears at the top right corner and an arrow is added that you can click to unstack and then restack the photos. To Unstack images, right click or choose Edit>Stack>Unstack Photos. If you choose to Flatten a Stack, all of the images except for the top one will be deleted. You can also change the top photo in the stack.

Version Sets

A version set is created when you make changes to an image and choose the Save in a Version Set option in the Save dialog box. Photos are saved together in a group.

From the Edit menu or by right clicking, you may Expand or Collapse a Version Set, Convert a Version Set to Individual Items, Revert to Original, Remove Items from Version Set, Set as Top Item, or Flatten Version Set.

If you choose to Flatten the Version Set, all images except for the top one will be deleted.

Correcting the Date on an Image

If your camera was set with the wrong date it's easy to change with Photoshop Elements. From the Edit menu on the Menu bar or by right clicking, choose Adjust Date and Time and make changes. By correcting the date, the thumbnails will show up in the right order when you have Thumbnail View selected as a Display option.

Write Tags to File

One way to protect the time you have spent tagging your photos is to actually write the tag information into the image itself. To do this, select all of the images you wish to embed with the information. From the Menu bar, choose File>Write Keyword Tag and Properties Info to Photo. Depending on the number of images selected, you may or may not see the Apply Metadata to Files status box below.

This means that I can tag my photos and give them to my friends and they don't have to tag them....of course it would be nice if they returned the favor.

This works great for JPEG images and PSD files like layered templates. At this time it does not work for PNG files like digital scrapbooking embellishments.

How to Search

So you've stuck with me so far and read twelve pages about organizing and tagging and you're asking yourself: OK, so how does it work now that I've applied the tags?

There are several ways you can search for any kind of image (photo or digital scrapbooking supplies): The first way to search is to click inside the empty box to the left of the tag name. Click in several different boxes to narrow down your search. Once you click in the empty box, a pair of binoculars will appear. The second way to search is to double click on a tag name. This will select one box only, because as soon as you double click on another tag, it will clear the first tag. The third way to search is to drag the tag to the Search bar.

To search for images that you have tagged with star tags, click on the appropriate stars on the Search bar.

To clear a tag, you can click on the binocular icon in the box to the left of the tag name, or you can click on the Show All button at the top of the screen. If the Show All button is not there, that means you are already showing all images.

In the top example, I clicked in the box next to Logan's name and all of the images I have tagged with Logan's tag appear.

In the middle example when I clicked on Mike's tag, all of the images I have tagged with Logan **and** Mike's tag appear. Other people may also appear.

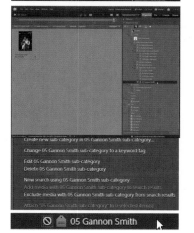

I can choose to exclude images that are tagged with a certain tag by right clicking on the tag and choosing Exclude media with XXX sub-category from search results. In the last example, I have excluded Gannon because I already used another photo of him on my scrapbook page and the search produces just one image. Notice that instead of the binoculars, a ⊘ symbol appears next to his tag.

Tagging Digital Scrapbook Supplies

In order to simplify things I keep my scrapbooking supplies in a separate catalog. I could keep my photos and scrapbook supplies in one catalog but scrolling through a huge list of tags would be overwhelming. Having a large number of images in one catalog may also slow it down.

Included with your book is a DVD filled with more than 3200 pieces of digital scrapbooking supplies which I suggest you tag to help you find the element you're looking for quickly. At the suggestion of a student we now sell our Organizer Back-up DVD at *www.TheDigitalScrapbookTeacher.com* which has all of the 3200+ items pre-tagged for you. This product is a great time saver and helps you set up a good foundation for getting organized. Follow the step by step directions included on the DVD and all the tagging is done for you. Purchase of the book, which already includes the art, is required to purchase the Organizer Back-up DVD because I am selling you my time it took to do the tagging, not the art.

If you would rather spend days tagging the art on the *Photoshop Elements – Basics & Beyond* DVD yourself I have included a set of tags to use. The Scrapbooking Supplies tag set includes more than 300 tags. This file is copyright protected, please do not share it. Before installing the tags file, create a new Catalog (File>Catalog> New) and name it Scrapbook Supplies or something similar. Follow the instructions on page 184 to install the tags. If you have a problem installing the tag file, you may have to turn off your virus protection software first.

Tag your scrapbook supplies following the same steps for tagging photos outlined earlier in this chapter. I also suggest that you add as many tags that apply to your scrapbook supplies as needed to speed up searching.

I've found through lots of experience that I can find anything I need when I tag my digital supplies by:
Kit Name (as a sub-category of the designer)
Element type (paper, buttons, ribbon, kit preview etc.)
Theme (pattern, holiday, etc.)
Color

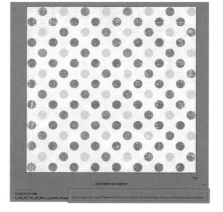

Kit Name is first on the list because it's important to be able to find the entire kit at one time to enable matching papers and embellishments. As you purchase supplies you will discover that similar to other avenues in your life like clothing, furniture, etc you like specific designers. By tagging by the kit name you can quickly find your favorite items designed by your favorite designer.

For example, under the Sub Category Designer make a new sub-category for the designer- TheDigitalScrapbookTeacher.com

Under the Designer's sub-category (TheDigitalScrapbookTeacher.com) make a new sub-category for the kit name-Wintertime Paper kit-The Digital Scrapbook Teacher. Tag the files with the kit name not the designer name. If you want to search for all files made by the designer click on the designer's tag.

I also include the designers name in the kit name to enable more searching options. Years down the road, will you remember that the Wintertime kit was designed by *www.TheDigitalScrapbookTeacher.com*? Probably not!

Tagging by element type is pretty straightforward, but sometimes you can't tell what the item is, so check the file name. Because of the Organizers white background, sometimes you may need to actually open the image in the Editor to see what type of element it is in the event of a white overlay or similar file.

There are many themes available to tag. The more theme sub-categories you tag your image with, the easier it will be to search for the image you need.

Color is listed last on the list because color is easy to change. I take the time to tag by color because my scrapbooking time is so limited. If I need a piece of blue paper, I like being able to click in the Blue and Paper tag boxes to find all the blue papers I have. If I can't find one that I like, I can always recolor another paper.

Because I know how time consuming it is to tag all of your supplies, all of the products that are JPEG or PSD files that the *www.TheDigitalScrapbookTeacher.com* sells are pre-tagged for you. Unfortunately, at this time due to software limitations, I am unable to pre-tag PNG files (files with transparency like buttons, etc.) so you will need to tag those items yourself; hopefully this will change with further software enhancements.

Imported Tags

If you import pre-tagged images (photos or scrapbook supplies) into your organizer, you will be asked if you want to import the attached tags. Click the Select All button and import them to save you time.

As shown in the example, the asterisk indicates that I already have a Keyword Tag with that name and it will be used. Because the Snowflakes and Wintertime Paper kit tags do not have an asterisk next to their name on the list, Photoshop Elements will automatically create a new tag for me.

The new tags will be placed under the Imported Keyword Tags sub-category; you will want to move them so that you can find them later. Right click on imported tags and change them to sub-categories if desired. I Right clicked and chose Edit to change the Snowflake Category from Imported Keyword Tags to Themes.

Albums

Albums are similar to tags except that you change the order of the photos and make projects like slide shows with the Create menu. You may also apply keyword tags to Images in an album. If you wish to back up and synchronize photos on *www.Photoshop.com*, they must be in albums.

Images saved from the Project bin in the Editor become an album. Saving images from the Project bin is helpful if you are working on a large project and want to use the same scrapbooking supplies throughout the book, or, if you don't have time to finish the page. After you save the files as an album, click on the Project bin drop down list to choose an album to open in the Editor.

To create a smart album, click on the drop down arrow next to the green + under the Albums tab. When the New Smart Album dialog box appears, enter the search criteria. New images added to the Organizer that meet the search criteria will be automatically added to the smart album.

Moving and Missing Files

When you import images into the Organizer it keeps track of them by the folder location. Move the image the wrong way and the Organizer gets confused. Select the image and the Organizer will begin searching for missing files while displaying the dialog box shown above. If you have already made this mistake, fixing it could take hours. Before you go to bed, choose from the Menu bar File>Reconnect>All Missing Files and let it run all night to see if will fix itself. If you know where you moved the images, you can click on the Browse button and find them manually.

So that you don't have this problem, choose Folder Location from the Display menu. Click and drag a thumbnail to a folder as shown above or click and drag a folder to a new location. Since my Organizer tends to run slower in Folder Location view, I normally only use this view when moving images.

Converting a Catalog

If Photoshop Elements doesn't automatically convert a catalog for you, it's easy to do yourself. From the Menu bar, choose File>Catalog and click on the Convert button. Select a catalog from the list and click on the Convert button.

Optimizing, Repairing, Renaming, and Deleting a Catalog

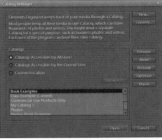

If your Organizer is running slow, from the Menu bar choose File>Catalog, select a catalog from the list and click on the Optimize and then the Repair buttons. To delete a catalog you no longer want, click on the Delete button (another catalog will have to be in use). To rename a catalog, click on the Rename button and type a new name.

Backup Catalog

It's imperative that you backup any catalogs you create. In the event of a hard drive failure, you can lose not only your images (photos and scrapbook supplies) but you will also lose all of the time you spent tagging. My best advice is to back up your catalog to a portable external hard drive and bring it to work or take it to a friend's house. This will also protect you from theft, fire or other types of disaster. From the Menu bar, choose File>Backup Catalog to CD, DVD, or Hard Drive. If you have missing files, you will need to reconnect them before you proceed (see the preceding page). Choose Full Backup and click the Next button. Select a Destination Drive and click on the Browse button to find the folder to back it up into. In my example, I have a folder on my external hard drive named Photoshop Elements Photo Backup. Click the Save Backup button and wait for it to finish.

Make it a habit to backup on a regular basis. I normally save two backup copies just in case there is a problem with the most recent one. When you backup a catalog you are backing up the images and the tagging work.

Moving a Catalog

Many of my students store their photos and scrapbooking supplies on an external hard drive and want to be able to use the Organizer on both their laptop and desktop computers. To do this, all of the images must be on the external hard drive (EHD), see the preceding page to move them correctly. If you're first starting out, make a new catalog. From the Menu bar, choose File>Catalog>New and choose a Custom Location on the EHD where you have made a folder for the catalog.

If you have an existing catalog, make a new folder on the EHD and name it Photoshop Elements (Photo or other name) Catalog. From the Menu bar, choose File>Catalog, select the catalog in the list and click on the Move button. Click on the Custom Location button and then click on the Browse button to locate the folder you made for the catalog. When the Move Catalog dialog box appears, click on Custom Location (the folder location will now show below Custom Location as shown circled in the example above). Click OK.

To access this catalog, click on the Custom Location button and click on the catalog name. When you plug the EHD into another computer, you will be able to find the catalog by choosing Custom Location and browsing for the folder. As long as you also keep all of the images imported into the Organizer on the EHD, this will work.

Restoring a Catalog

To restore a catalog that you have previously backed up, from the Menu bar choose File>Catalog>Restore Catalog from CD, DVD, or Hard Drive. Choose where to Restore From and To and click the Restore button.

What Did I Do Wrong?

On some days, it seems like the first thing I do wrong is get out of bed. We've all had days when everything seems to go wrong, all day long. If this is one of those days....go back to bed! If you don't have the luxury of going back to bed, keep reading!

Learning to use Photoshop Elements was not easy for me. I joke that I have a dent in my home office wall from banging my head against it in frustration over the years. As I look back, I realize that many of the mistakes I made were simple ones. As a newbie I wanted a Photoshop Elements expert to turn to for instant help. This chapter will point out many of the mistakes you'll make and will save you hours of frustration, and dents in your walls! **One more thing…put a paper clip on this page so you can find it quickly.**

Missing Panels

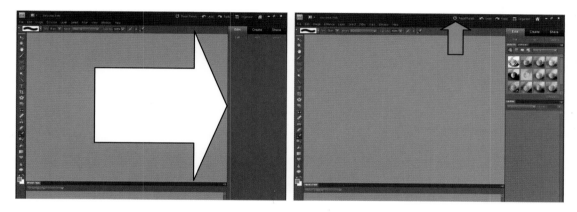

Somehow, you've lost one or more of your Panels (Layers, Content, Effects, etc.) Tap the Rest Panels icon (red arrow) at the top of your screen and the default panels will once again appear.

Missing Project Bin

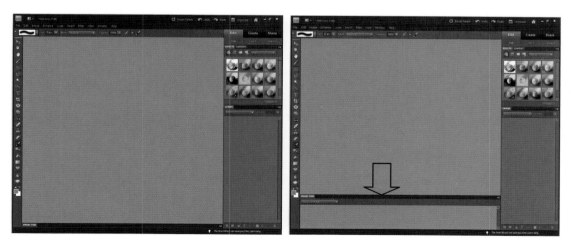

If the Project bin appeared to close by itself don't panic. Double click on the dark area (red arrow) to pop the bin back open. In order to have more room while editing an image, you may want to close the bin on purpose.

Too Many Images are Showing up At One Time in the Image Window

I prefer to work with one image showing at a time in the image window. For me it's much less confusing to work this way. To change this setting, choose Edit>Preferences>General (Mac-Photoshop Elements>Preferences>General) and uncheck Allow Floating Documents in Full Edit Mode. Once you make this change you should see only one image at a time in the image window, if not click on the Arrange Menu at the top of the screen and choose the first option which is Consolidate All.

All of your open files will show in the Project bin. Double click on the thumbnail in the bin to display it as the active image.

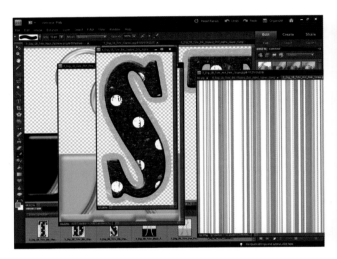 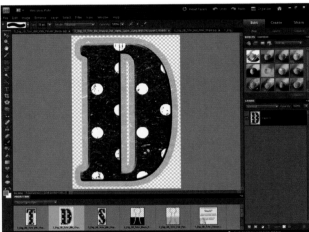

My New Scrapbook Page is Tiny

When making a new scrapbook page or other project from scratch we start with a new blank, white piece of digital paper. If you don't pay attention, the width and height unit of measure may have changed to pixels instead of inches. Close the file and start over. If this happens to you frequently, you may want to use the Scrapbooking Preset on the File>New>Blank File dialog box.

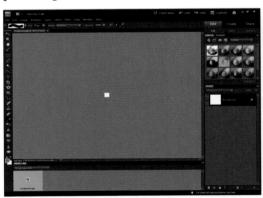 

An easy way to see the size of your document is choose Document Dimensions from the drop down list located at the bottom left corner of the image window.

Where's My Text #1?

You will encounter this issue several times as you learn to use Photoshop Elements. Choose the Type tool (T), click on the page and start typing, do you only see a line and flashing cursor where you were expecting to see text? The problem is before you started typing, the Background layer was selected. You should have selected the layer located at the top of the Layers panel. When you start typing, a new layer is automatically added directly above the selected layer. In my example below, the text is located underneath a 12" x 12" inch piece of paper. It could be located under a talk bubble, journaling mat, or anything that is big enough to cover it up. If you are/were a paper scrapbooker, and you can relate this back to using paper supplies, it will make a lot of sense.

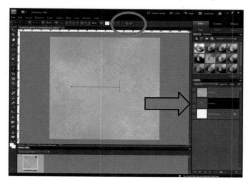

You have two choices:

Check the green ✓on the Type tool's Option bar to commit the type. Click, hold, and drag the type layer above the paper layer in the Layers panel.

Tap the red ⊘ on the Type tool's Options bar to cancel. Click on the top layer and then type the text again. Check the green ✓on the Type tool's Option bar to commit the type.

Where's My Text #2?

So as not to have the same problem that we covered in the example above, you paid attention and made sure that your Text layer is above the Shape layer (or other type of layer) in the Layers panel.

You should be able to see the text, but you can't. The problem is that the color of the Text is the same color as the talk bubble Shape - white. Imagine writing on a white paper talk bubble die cut with a white pen…that's just what's happened here.

Double click on the Type layer thumbnail to select the text and choose a darker color. Check the ✓.

 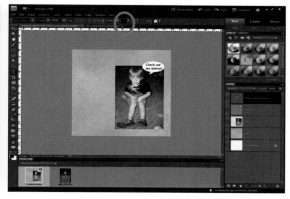

Where's My Text #3

You add text to your project, but it runs right off the end of the image, why? You have two choices: tap the return key when you get close to the edge of the file, or make a text box to hold the text.

Read about the Type tool in the *Tools* chapter for more information.

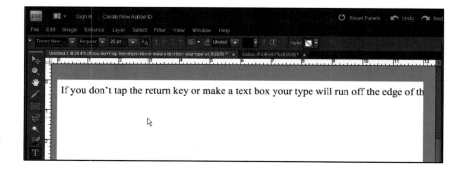

Where's My Text #4

You created a text box with the Type tool and typed your text. The only problem is that some of your text is missing. Where did it go?

Check the lower right corner of the text box. If there is a + in the box, it means that you have overfilled the text box. To correct the problem make the font smaller, or tighten up the leading on the Text tool Options bar. You can also make the text box bigger or put less text in the box.

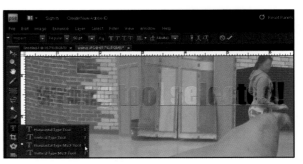

Why Does My Screen Turn Red When I Try to Add Text with the Type Tool?

Relax! You have selected the Horizontal Type Mask tool by mistake. Click on the ◢ at the bottom right corner of the Type tool icon and choose the Horizontal Type tool and you'll be fine.

Where's My Layer?

Always make a point of selecting the top layer before dragging a photo or element onto your project. This way the new added layer will always be added above everything. If you don't pay attention, your new layer will be inserted directly above the selected layer and you may not be able to see it without re-arranging layers.

When you drag images onto a scrapbook page, they all automatically land in the center of the project on top of each other. Check your Layers panel to see if you have a layer for the item you're missing. If they are there, use the Move tool (V) and move them around on your page.

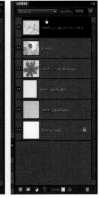

Check to make sure that the layer is not hidden. If the eyeball icon is turned off, the layer is hidden. Turn it back on by clicking in the empty box and you should see the layer.

Is there a larger layer on top of the layer you're missing? Check the Layers panel and see. If it is, drag the missing layer above the larger layer. Think about scrapbooking with real paper products and the layers will make more sense to you.

In the example below, I dragged on a new leaf embellishment. When I did this, I didn't pay attention that I was on the light cropped paper layer, so the new leaf went right above this layer. The problem is, my embellishment is underneath my photo layer and can't be seen. Notice that the bounding box shows where my new embellishment is because it's the selected layer.

Click, hold, and drag the layer in the Layers panel up to the top of the Layers panel so it is sitting on the top of the stack of layers.

My Screen Doesn't Look Like Yours

Read the *First Things First* Chapter and make the changes that I recommend to the default settings, and then your screen will look like the examples in the book.

I Can't Edit/Move My Stroke Outlines or Brushwork, Why?

The page below shows black brushwork and a black stroke outline around the photo. Notice that the Layers panel on the right shows the stroke and brushwork on its own layer. The middle Layers panel is missing these two layers because the black items were added directly to the layers.

Both pages look the same, the difference being that I can adjust the size, opacity, blend mode, and more on the page that has the brushwork and stroke on its own layer. If I decide I want to make changes of the stroke or brushwork on the page without the separate layers, I would need to Undo all of my changes made after they were added to the page....not too much fun!

 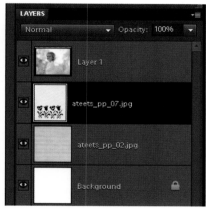 

Why is My Stroke Outline Rounded?

You paid attention and added the Stroke Outline to a separate layer but it doesn't have straight corners, why? This is something that my students ask me about all the time, and it's easy to correct.

When adding the Stroke (Edit>Stroke Outline Selection) choose inside for the Location.

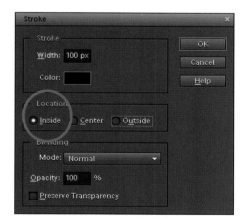

I Can't Undo and I Just Realized I'm Working on My Original!

Hey, at least you realized it now! When I first started out, I ruined my daughter's bridal shower photos by working on the originals. Always have your original images backed up for safe keeping.

By default, Photoshop Elements will allow you to Undo 50 times. This setting can be changed. Choose Edit>Preferences>Performance>History States ((Mac-Photoshop Elements>Preferences>Performance>History States) although I don't recommend it because it will slow down your computer. If you haven't already saved, choose File>Save As (Shift>Ctrl>S Mac-Shift>Cmd>S) and save the file with a new name, thus keeping the original safe. Choose Edit>Revert to Undo all changes if you haven't yet saved.

Editor is Frozen or Busy

Sometimes Photoshop Elements will freeze but, 99% of the time the program is not actually frozen, you've just forgotten to do something. That something is usually checking a green ✓ after sizing, cropping or adding text. If your program won't do anything, or if some of the Menu bar commands are grayed-out (see example to the right) search for the green ✓ and check it. If that doesn't work, try tapping the Enter key.

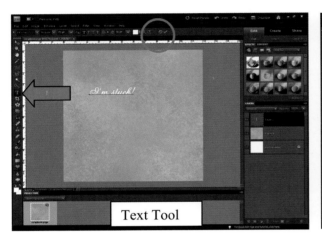

Text Tool

Crop Tool

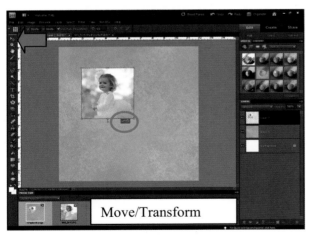

Move/Transform

The green ✓ is located near one of the bottom corners when using the Move tool (V), Transform Command (Ctrl>T, Mac-Cmd>T), Crop tool (C).

When using the Type tool (T) you'll find the ✓ on the Type tool's Options bar near the top of the screen.

When attempting to open an image from the Organizer into the Editor you may encounter a window that pops up and says:

"The command could not be completed because the Editor was busy. Please finish the current operation and try again." Go back to the Editor and check one of the ✓ as listed above and that should solve the problem.

My Paper is not 12"x 12"

You set up a blank new white page to build a scrapbook page, and when you drag a paper onto your page it doesn't cover the entire bottom layer as you expected. There are a couple of possibilities with this issue.

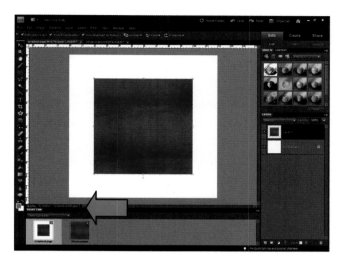

Most probably, the paper you are using is not the correct size. Check the Document Dimensions (marked with red arrow) and make sure that the size is 12" x 12". If it is, check and make sure that it is 300 ppi (pixels per inch). You may have downloaded products that are not 300 ppi. The paper in this example is 12" x 12" but it's 200 ppi. Always purchase artwork that is 300 ppi so that the pages print well.

Many freebies on the web are made at 100 or 200 ppi. If you are purchasing artwork, make sure that the website specifies that their products are created at 300 ppi.

TheDigitalScrapbookTeacher.com sells only 300 ppi products; I have resized our paper for this example only.

If this isn't the problem, make sure that you have created your starting page at 300 pixels per <u>inch</u>. I once had a student in class who created her page at 300 pixels per <u>centimeter</u>. She was from Canada and was used to working in centimeters.

My Layer is Distorted

To resize a layer, choose the Move tool (V) or the Transform Command (Ctrl>T, Mac Cmd>T) and click on the corner sizing boxes on the bounding box surrounding the layer. Drag from the corner only to constrain the proportions of the image. If you drag from one of the side sizing boxes, you will size the photo out of proportion.

If completely by accident, you were to click on one of the side sizing boxes and push slightly inward, the people in your photos would appear taller and thinner. Of course you would never want to do anything like this on purpose, but if you did by it by "accident", remember that a little bit goes a long way. Reducing the width of the photo by more than 5% will probably be pretty obvious. Dragging a side sizing box outward will cause people to look shorter and wider and I know you would never want that!

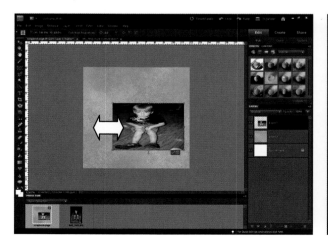 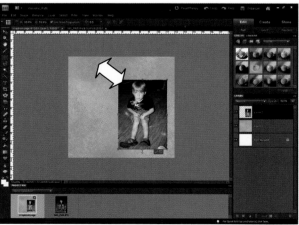

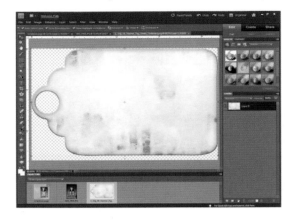

What's the Checkerboard All About?

The checkerboard area is transparent; it will not print when you print your project.

Any transparent areas remaining when you print your project will be printed white. If you save an image as a jpg file, all transparent areas will be filled with white.

To change the grid size or color of the transparent areas in your images, choose Edit>Preferences>Transparency (Mac-Photoshop Elements>Preferences>Transparency).

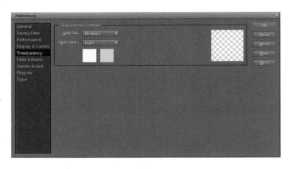

Why Can't I Move a Layer with Transparency with the Move Tool?

You can move a layer with transparent areas using the Move tool. The key is to click right on the item and then drag it. If you click in a transparent area, it will appear that you are trying to move the image with the Marquee tool as shown below. If the item is small and hard to see like a brad or beads, scroll in with the mouse wheel or zoom in with the Zoom tool so that you can make sure you are not clicking on a transparent (checkerboard) area.

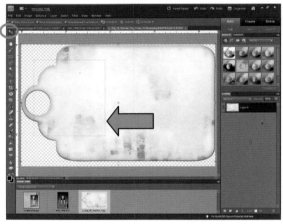

If you are still having trouble, uncheck the Auto Select Layer option on the Move tool (V) Options bar. Holding the Ctrl key when the Move tool (V) is activated toggles Auto Select Layer on/off.

Why Did My Filter Mess Up?

Not getting the expected results from a filter? Before applying a filter, always type the letter D to set your Foreground and Background colors, located at the bottom of the Toolbar, to the default settings. Your Foreground color should be black, and your Background color should be white.

Filters use either the Foreground or Background color to work their magic.

The Colored Pencil filter was applied to the Hawaii photo below. The green photo shows what happens when I set the Background color to green. The Photocopy filter was applied to the sketch photo. When I set my Foreground color to red, the sketch became red.

Why Can't I Drag an Image Onto My New Project-Locked Layer?

This can happen whether you're trying to drag a photo or scrapbook paper onto your new project. The problem is that you're letting go too soon.

Click and drag your active image down to the project in the Project bin. Do not let go until you touch the file in the bin. Windows users (sorry Macs!) will see your cursor change to the regular Move tool cursor with a + added to it as shown to the left.

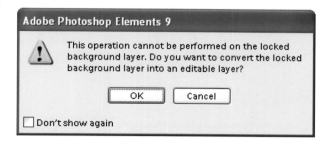

This has nothing to do with the Background layer being locked, it has everything to do with the fact that you let go of the image too soon.

Why Can't I Drag an Image Onto My New Project?

If you've checked the transparency and locked layers issues above, you may be trying to layer files with different Modes.

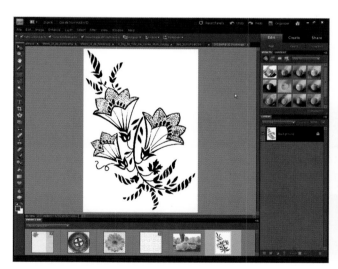

The clip art is a Bitmap image and cannot be dragged onto a RGB image. As you try to drag the clip art image onto the scrapbook page in the Project bin, it appears that it will drag but then the cursor changes to a ⊘.

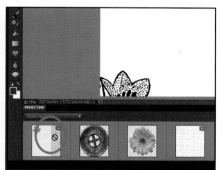

If you are having this problem, check the Mode of the image by choosing from the Menu bar Image>Mode. If Bitmap or Indexed Color mode are checked, and you are trying to add them to a project in RGB Color mode (everything shown in this book), change the mode by clicking on RGB Color.

What Happened to My Layers?

Here's the scenario: You take some time editing your photos using multiple layers. You decide that you're going to use this photo on a card, brochure or other project. You create the project file and drag the photo **UP** from the Project bin on to the new page. As you look in the Layers panel, you see that the photo's layers have been flattened into just one layer.

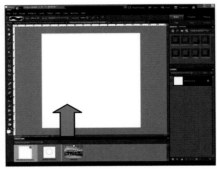

If you were completely finished editing the photo and won't need to edit it anymore this is OK, and you can just leave it the way it is. If you think you may want to edit the photo in the course of completing your project, you need to move it with all of the layers intact. To do this, you will need to select or link the layers of the photo. From the Toolbar, select the Move tool (V). Drag the photo **DOWN** onto the page in the Project bin and all of its layers will be intact. You'll probably have the next problem too, so keep reading!

I Can't Drag My Photo with an Adjustment Layer Down Into the Bin

So…I just told you don't drag an image with an Adjustment layer **up** from the Project bin if you want to keep the layers intact. You follow my directions and try to drag the photo **down** into the Project bin, and it won't work.

The reason this won't work is because the Adjustment layer is transparent, or you are clicking on a white (transparent) area of the mask. As you can see by my example, I only used the Levels Adjustment layer to lighten the entire photo. I haven't painted black on the mask with the Brush tool to conceal anything so there is nothing for me to grab onto when I try to move it.

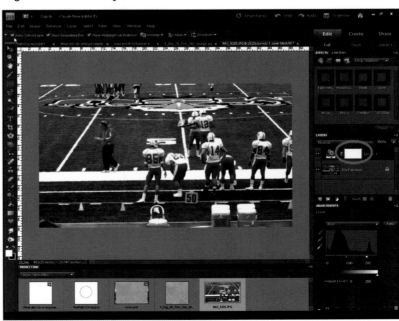

Remember, if you try to move a file with transparency, like a button for instance, you must click on the button, not the transparent areas to move it. But in this instance, when using an Adjustment layer with a blank mask, there is nothing to click on.

What do you do? Two things will work, but first, select both layers in the Layers panel, or better yet, link them together. Choose either method below. I prefer the second one because it's faster:

Uncheck the Auto Select Layer box on the Move tool (V) Options bar, click and drag the photo down into the Project bin to the new file. I like to work with this option on, so be sure to go back and put the check back in the box.

With the Auto Select Layer box checked, hold the Ctrl (Cmd) key (temporarily toggles it off); click and drag the photo down to the new file the Project bin.

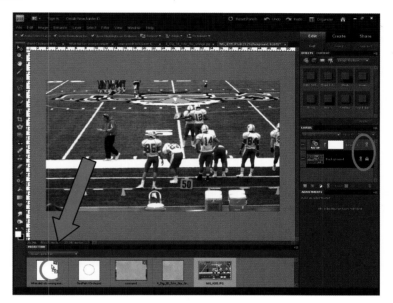

My Photo Adjustment Layer is Messing up My Project

Adjustment layers are applied to **all** layers below them. This is important if you are using them on multi-layered projects like a scrapbook page or card. When I apply a Levels Adjustment layer to the photo layer (example below), and make adjustments, the light blue scrapbook paper is also lightened to the point of being white.

To apply the Adjustment layer to the photo only, clip it to the photo with a clipping mask. From the Menu bar, choose Layer>Create Clipping Mask (Ctrl>G Mac: Cmd>G). Note: If you are using Photoshop Elements 7 or lower, choose Layer>Group with Previous (same command, new name). Your Layers panel should look like the example on the right.

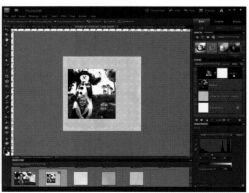

Why Can't I Edit My Text Path?

Here's the scenario: You are making a project, and you want to add a text path to your page so that your text will be in the shape of a circle, as shown on the right.

You drag the text path **up** to your page and your screen will look like the left or center examples below.

When you try to type in the text, you discover that the text is no longer a text layer and is not editable. Your first clue to this is that there is not a Text layer thumbnail in the Layers panel as shown in the example on the right.

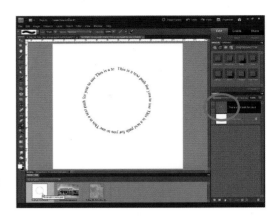

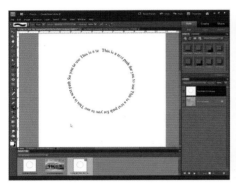
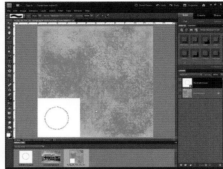
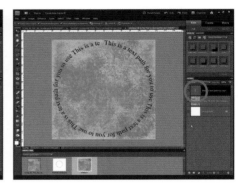

What's the problem? You dragged up from the Project bin to your active image. In order for the text path to remain a Text layer, you must select the Move tool (V) and drag the text path **down** to the file in the Project bin. Follow those steps, and your file will look like the example above on the right.

Why Can't I See Anything on My Layer Thumbnails

You will notice as you go through pages in the book, sometimes I change how my layer thumbnails display. The example on the left is the default display setting. 95% of the time I prefer to work with my layer thumbnails the way they are in the example on the right.

I've had students who tell me they need to rename their layers so they know what's on them. When I show them this they go crazy. Who has time to rename all your layers? Wouldn't you rather see what's actually on your layers?

If I'm working on a template, or a double wide montage page, I may change the Thumbnail Contents setting back to Entire Document, but normally I work with the Layer Bounds option.

To change this setting, click on the ▾ at the top of the Layers Panel. Choose Panel Options from the drop down list. Under the Thumbnail Contents section, click in the Layer Bounds box. I show you how to change this step by step in the Layers section of this book.

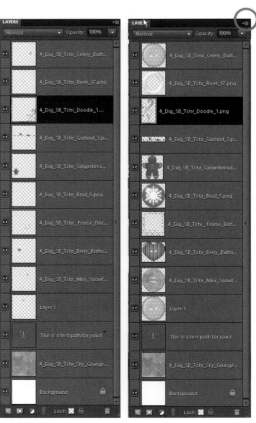

Why Does My Cursor Look Weird?

Many tools use brushes. In the image on the left below, the Brush tool (B) is selected and the cursor displays the selected brush at a size of 1300 pixels. Switch to another tool and the cursor will change. The image on the right below also shows the same brush selected, the only difference is that the Caps Lock key on the keyboard has been pressed. The cursor is now displayed as a + (shown circled) instead of the actual brush. Clicking will produce the same result no matter what the cursor looks like, however I think it's easier to use brushes if you can see the actual brush shape.

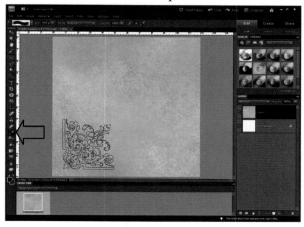

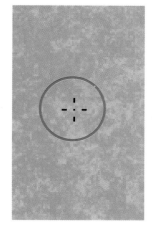

Reducing the size of this brush drastically will also cause the cursor to be displayed as a + instead of as a fancy corner.

If your cursor doesn't look the way you would expect it to, check the size of the brush or try tapping the Caps lock key.

Tools using brushes are not the only tools affected by the Caps Lock key. Activating the Caps Lock key when using the Eyedropper will cause the cursor to change from an eyedropper (default setting) to the cursor shown to the right.

The Marquee, Lasso, Magic Wand, Selection Brush, Quick Selection Brush, Crop, and Paint Bucket tools are all affected by the Caps Lock key.

If tapping the Caps lock key does not change the appearance of the cursor, the Cursor Preferences may have been changed from Normal/Standard to Precise.

To change the settings for your cursor, choose Edit>Preferences>Display & Cursors (Mac-Photoshop Elements>Preferences>Display & Cursors.

What's Wrong With My Brush #1?

If you are using one of the tools that uses a brush, and expected to stamp/paint a brush stroke and instead you see marching ants, you've chosen the wrong tool. The Toolbar icons for the Selection Brush tool and Brush tool are very similar. To stamp or paint, choose the Brush tool (B) shown on the left. To make a selection with a brush, choose the Selection Brush tool (A) shown on the right.

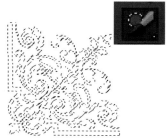

What's Wrong With My Brush #2

I freely admit in my classes that I make mistakes all the time, and not just with Photoshop Elements…don't ask about the gas station story! I was working on something for this book and I made this really dumb mistake, so I decided I should include it in this section. I have to tell you that I really panicked, because I couldn't figure out how I could mess something up so badly. In reality, I didn't mess up anything, I just wasn't paying attention!

I use soft round brushes all the time on masks to softly blend areas. Normally, my Default brushes panel looks like the example on the left. On this particularly panic stricken day, my Default brushes looked like the example on the right. You'll notice I have selected a Soft Round 300 pixel brush in both examples, but the brush on the right definitely doesn't look like it has soft edges.

I'd like to say that I quickly solved my problem, but I didn't. I tried resetting the tool and restarting the program, but nothing happened. Finally, after calling a friend and telling her that I really messed up my program I realized that I had the Pencil tool selected, not the Brush tool. The Pencil tool only paints with hard edged brushes.

This is a classic ID 10 T error that I make when I'm tired!

Notice the tool showing on the Toolbar on the bottom left corner of both examples and you'll quickly see my mistake.

I purposely didn't circle the tools so that you would have to search and see the answer.

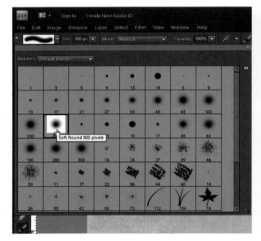
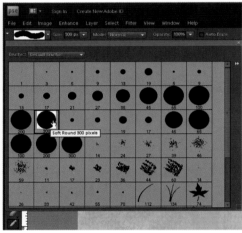

Where Are My Brushes?

Here's the scenario: I load the set of brushes from the *Photoshop Elements –Basics & Beyond DVD* (or any another set) and I use them. I drop down the Brushes drop down list and choose another brush. I go back to use the set I just loaded, and it's gone from the drop down list. Where is it?

Not to worry…When you loaded the brushes, you only loaded them temporarily. The brush set will remain on the drop down list until you choose another brush set. If you want to use it again, click on the double arrows shown circled and choose Load Brushes to load them again temporarily.

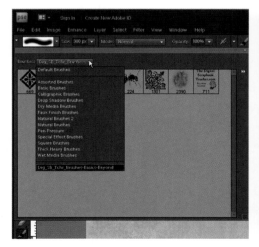
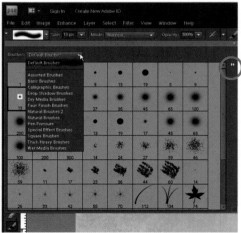

Why Can't I Make a Brush

You have doodled a cute design that you want to make into a brush. You attempt to choose Edit>Define Brush from the Menu bar, but it is grayed out. What's the problem?

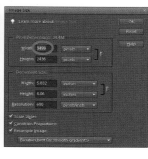

Your image is probably too big. To check and see if that's the problem, from the Menu bar choose Image>Resize>Image Size. Make sure that the height **and** width size is smaller than 2500 pixels.

Why Isn't My Layer Mask Working?

You've made a Mask and things are going well, until you notice instead of masking away areas of the photo, it's as if you're painting directly on the image. You probably are! This can happen with the Brush tool or the Gradient tool. The most common colors you may see are black, white, gray, or red.

In the example on the right, I was painting directly on the photo layer not on the Mask.

To fix this, undo to remove the color. Click inside the Mask thumbnail on the Layers panel (shown circled) and try it again.

Bounding Box, How Do I Get Rid of It?

In class, many of my students are concerned because they have a bounding box surrounding their image.

This means two things: The Move tool (V) is the active tool. The bounding box surrounds the selected layer (red arrow).

If it really bugs you, it can be turned off, but I rarely do this because I use it to re-size/transform my layers.

To turn on/off the bounding box check the ✓ on the Move tool Options bar as shown below.

Missing Open Files in the Editor

You've opened several images, but only a few are showing in the Project bin. I've opened seventeen images from Amy Teets' Super Sonic kit which can be found on the *Photoshop Elements Basics & Beyond* DVD. In the example above, only six of them are showing in the Project bin.

Click on the slider on the right side of the Project bin (red arrow) and you will see two more rows of images as shown below.

If you have opened images and nothing is showing in the Project bin, make sure that the tab at the top of the Project bin says: Show Open Files (red circle).

Oh Crop!

The first time I tried to crop on a scrapbook page I messed up royally.

In the example below, I wanted to crop off part of the photo layer and used the Crop tool (C) to do it. What I ended up with was five layers cropped to the size of the area I wanted to crop off.

On a multi-layered file, use the Marquee tool (M) to drag out a selection and then tap the Delete or Backspace key to delete only that portion on the selected layer.

 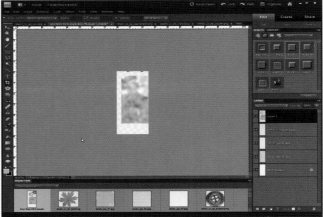

Why Does My Photo Have a Border after Using the Crop Tool?

After cropping a photo you notice that you have a white (or other color) border around one or more sides of your photo. You probably don't realize that you told Elements to do this.

This is how the border gets added:

Drag out a crop selection with the crop tool and let go of the mouse. Once you let go of the mouse, a selection border (marching ants) surrounds the area you want to keep. The darker area (crop shield) is the area that will be cropped off.

Once you see the marching ants, you decide to fine tune the selection and drag one of the sizing boxes off the edges of the photo as shown in the middle example below. To confirm the crop, check the green checkmark ✓.

As soon as you confirm the crop, a white (or other color) border appears. In my example, the border is white because white is my Background color. I show how to do this on purpose in the *Cool Stuff with Photos* chapter.

  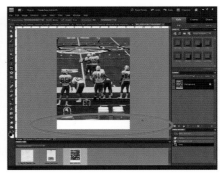

Why Does My Photo Have a Strange Border after Using the Straighten Tool?

After straightening a photo you notice that you have a strange angular border around the photo. The border will be the color of your Background color swatch at the bottom of the Toolbar.

This is really easy to fix. First, Undo. From the Straighten tool's Options bar click on the Canvas Options drop down list and choose Crop to Remove Background. Straighten the photo again, and the photo will be straightened and cropped. If you are having this photo printed, be sure to crop the photo to the correct size.

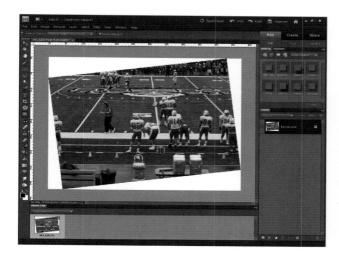
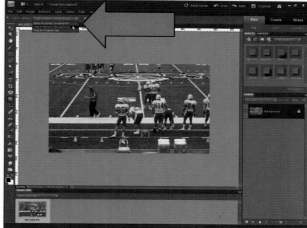

Clone and/or Healing Brush Copying the Entire Image?

If you've used the Clone Stamp tool (S) or Healing Brush tool (J) in previous versions, and notice something is different, check the tools Options bar.

On the Options bar, click on the icon to the right of Sample all layers. If Show Overlay (shown below red circle) is checked, it will appear that you are copying the entire layer. Although confusing, in reality, you are only copying the area covered by the brush.

Why Do I Have a Selection Border (Marching Ants) Around My Layer?

One way to get a selection border around a layer is to Ctrl click (Mac: Cmd click) on the layer thumbnail shown circled. This happens a lot in my hands-on classes when students try to select more than one layer at a time.

To select more than one layer, pay attention and Ctrl click (Mac: Cmd click) on the layer name, not on the layer thumbnail.

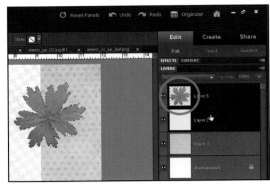

My Layers Are the Wrong Color or Translucent

The screenshot on the left shows the leaf from Amy Teets' Super Sonic kit in the correct color.

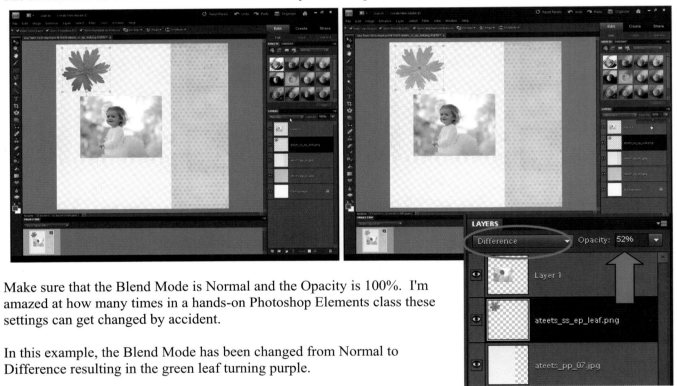

Make sure that the Blend Mode is Normal and the Opacity is 100%. I'm amazed at how many times in a hands-on Photoshop Elements class these settings can get changed by accident.

In this example, the Blend Mode has been changed from Normal to Difference resulting in the green leaf turning purple.

The Opacity has been adjusted from 100% to 52% resulting in a translucent layer.

Grids or Lines Appear on My Image

Many designers use gridlines or guidelines to design their products.

If you open an image that has these lines displayed, it's easy to turn them off.

From the Menu bar choose View>Grid to turn off the Grid Lines.

Choose View>Clear Guides to turn off the Guide Lines.

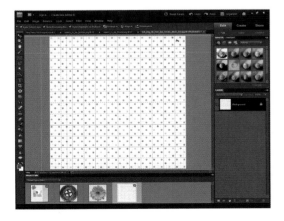

My Computer Crashed and My Project is Gone!

Been there, done that! Unfortunately there is no auto save feature in Photoshop Elements. New in Photoshop Elements 9 is a subtle reminder to save your page.

Notice the file in the Project bin has an icon that looks like a brush in the top right corner. As soon as you choose File>Save the icon disappears. Make it a point to save after each step, and even if you crash you'll be OK.

I Don't Know Where the Computer Saved My Project.

This is probably one of the top things I hear in hands-on classes. The problem is that you do tell the computer where to save your page whether you realize it or not.

Choose File>Save (Ctrl>S – Mac Cmd>S).

Regardless of what Operating System you're using you are given the choice of where to save the file. I cover a lot about getting organized in the *Organizing* Chapter, be sure to read this chapter.

If you don't remember where you saved the file, you might be able to open it again by choosing File>Open>Recently Edited File from the Menu bar. If that doesn't work, use your operating system's search feature.

Why Does Everyone in My Photos Have Black Eyes?

It doesn't happen to me often, but every once in awhile Auto Red Eye Fix goes a little bit overboard! I turn this feature off in the Organizer and when importing photos from my camera card. This is explained in detail in the *Organizing* Chapter.

In the Organizer, choose Edit>Preferences>Camera or Card Reader. Uncheck the box that says Automatically Fix Red Eyes if it's checked.

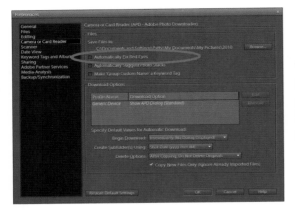

When importing images into the Organizer, make sure the Automatically Fix Red Eyes box is unchecked.

Why Do I Have Photos In My Scrapbook Supplies Catalog?

You've decided after reading the Organizing chapter that you want to keep separate catalogs for your photos and your scrapbook supplies because it's an excellent idea. Somehow, photos keep ending up in your Scrapbook Supplies folder and you can't figure out why.

What is probably happening is this: the last time you used the Organizer you had the Scrapbook Supplies catalog open. You imported photos later, and they were automatically added to the wrong catalog.

How do you fix it? Two ways: Make a point to close the Organizer in the Photos Catalog. Don't import photos into the Organizer unless you're ready to tag them. That way you'll notice right away if they are imported into the wrong catalog.

Missing Files in the Organizer

The Organizer is a great tool as long as you play by its rules. The most important rule is to only move files and folders through the Organizer.

Moving files is explained in detail in the *Organizing* chapter of this book, which I think is one of the most important chapters of the book.

Why is My Project Bin Messed Up?

Here's the scenario: You open some images in the Editor. The image that's showing in your workspace is not in the Project bin. All of the thumbnails that appear in the Project bin are not open. What's the deal?

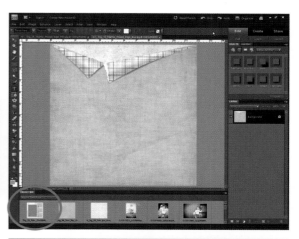

The problem is that at one time you saved the contents of the Project bin as an Album. Files from the Album are showing in the Project bin.

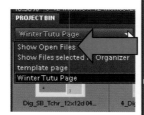

In my example on the right (I enlarged the circled area); the Project bin is displaying the images from the Winter Tutu Page Album. Notice the active image (blue layered torn paper) does not show in the Project bin.

Click on the Project bin drop down list and choose Show Open Files. Now only the open files will appear.

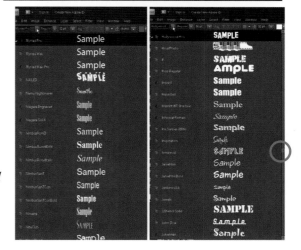

Missing Scroll Bars-Font List & Others

This doesn't happen often, but when it does it will drive you crazy! Without a scroll bar on your font list, you have to use the Arrow keys to move up and down the list, and that is really aggravating.

If you have this problem, go to my website:
www.TheDigitalScrapbookTeacher.com
Click on the *What's New* tab and click on the link *Missing Scroll Bars* to see the fix that Adobe helped me with.

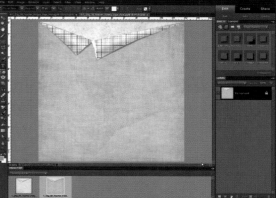

Missing Menu Bar-Organizer

Every once in awhile, I see this problem in one of my classes. The image below is from Photoshop Elements 6, but I've seen the problem in newer versions as well. If you have this problem, go to my website: *www.TheDigitalScrapbookTeacher.com*. Click on the *What's New* tab and click on the *Organizer Missing Menu Bar* link and follow the steps to fix the problem.

Tool Won't Work or Won't Work Correctly

First, check to make sure that you don't have a ✓that needs to be checked somewhere. Switch to another image and try the tool to see if it works on the new image. Try another tool and see if it will work correctly.

Click on the ▼ located at the far left end of the problem tool's Options bar. Choose Reset Tool. This will set the tool back to the default settings and hopefully clear your problem.

Reset All Tools only if necessary. Changes may have been made to other tools options that you would prefer to keep and this will clear them.

If resetting all of the tools doesn't fix the problem, try closing Photoshop Elements and opening it again. The next thing I would try is to shut down your computer completely and turn it back on. In my experience I've found that shutting down is a better option than restarting a computer when Photoshop Elements is misbehaving.

Resetting Program Preferences

If none of the above steps solve your problem, shut down Photoshop Elements.

Open the Photoshop Elements Welcome Screen.

Hold the Ctrl>Alt>Shift (Cmd>Opt>Shift for Mac) keys and click on the Edit tab.

Click the Yes button when asked to Delete the Adobe Photoshop Elements Settings File.

Changes that you have made on tool settings, including changes you may have made from the *First Things First* chapter will have to be done again.

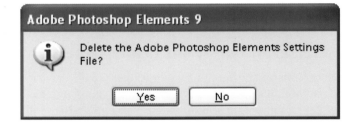

Still Stuck?

Get up and walk away from your computer for a few minutes. Review the tutorial again, did you miss a step? Read each word in the directions carefully, sometimes missing a key word will throw you off.

Did you purchase our video tutorials? If so, play the video and that should help you figure out what's wrong.

Click on Help on the Menu Bar to display Adobe Help.

Call, email, instant message, or text a friend for help. Send a screenshot or take a photo of the screen with your cell phone so they know what your screen looks like.

Check a message board, there are plenty of people willing to help. Before you post your problem, do a search to see if someone has already posted the same problem.

My favorite message boards are:
www.ElementsVillage.com/forums & *www.ScrappersGuide.com/forum*

Cool Stuff

Cool Stuff with Photos

I'll never forget sitting in my booth at the Ontario California Scrapbook Expo in 2008 when a man approached me with a question that was a real eye opener for me. He asked me why people spent so much time and money on their scrapbook pages when their photos looked like garbage. He said that with just a few quick simple edits, most scrapbook pages would look so much better. He caught me off guard and I was busy, so I didn't think much about it until several months later when I realized he was absolutely right. Thinking of our conversation the following year, The Digital Scrapbook Teacher began offering more classes in photo editing. Not only to help the traditional scrapbooker make their photos look better on their traditional pages, but also to help the digital/hybrid scrapbookers and people who just like to take photos as well. In this section I'll share with you some of the tricks we teach in our hands-on classes.

One thing about Photoshop Elements that is both good and bad is that there are many ways to accomplish the same task. For some photos, one method may be better to use than another, so try to keep that in mind when working on your own photos. I'd love to be able to say, to fix a photo that is too dark you must use technique X to fix it, but in reality you may have to use techniques X, Y, & Z. The key is to try out and practice different techniques so you know what will work on your photos.

Always remember, make a duplicate of your photo (File>Duplicate) before you make any changes to it so that you do not save over the original photo. When I first started using Photoshop Elements, I quickly believed that I had become a pro and didn't need to spend a couple of seconds creating a duplicate photo. Hey, my photos looked great on my computer screen so they should look great printed out too…right? If tapping the Quick Edit button once looked good, then maybe tapping it two or three times would make it even better? My daughter's bridal shower photos fell victim to my temporary loss of sanity. For some reason my daughter's mother-in-law's photos got the worst of it (honestly, this was not deliberate). Whenever I look at those scrapbook pages, I'm amazed that: one, they're actually complete and in a book, and, two, I can't believe that I was so ignorant and didn't follow a simple rule that takes only a second to do.

If you get frustrated while working, remember that you are working on a duplicate photo and that you have the Undo key on your side. Try something, and if you don't like it, Undo it. In my classes I tell my students to pretend that they are a four year old child sitting at their computer. A four year old is going to press every button on the keyboard to see what it will do. What do you have to lose? Try changing your attitude and pretend that you are four years old, (sorry, not a size 4) and you will see that you will have a lot of fun. If you don't like what you created on your screen, Undo it.

Always keep a copy of your original photos on another computer, external hard drive, or burned on CD's or DVDs at another location (work, friend, relative, etc.), so that in the event of a computer failure or natural disaster you will always have your original images. This also applies to digital scrapbooking supplies.

Many of my students believe that since they have uploaded their photos to photo processors that they will be able to get back their full sized images if they need them. While you may be able to do this, you will probably have to order and pay for them burned onto a CD/DVD.

Before you get overconfident editing your photos, print out a few and see how they look. What you see on your screen may not be what you pick up from the printer. If your prints are not what you expected, have your photos printed by another photo processor. If the prints still don't look like they did on your screen, check into getting your monitor calibrated. All of the photos used in my examples are included on the *Photoshop Elements- Basics & Beyond* DVD in the Photo Editing Examples folder.

General Photo Fixes

Basic photo editing can be done in either the Editor or Organizer. Some people think that the quick editing tools are a waste of time, but not me. By all means, try the auto buttons to see if they fix your problems before trying more advanced techniques. You will be amazed that they work great on some photos, and you can also use them with other editing techniques.

The photo used in my example was taken at the Roughley Manor Bed and Breakfast in Twentynine Palms, CA, which is a great place to stay. I attended a traditional scrapbook retreat there and it was fabulous! The Innkeepers are one of a kind! Check them out at: *www.roughleymanor.com*.

Editor
In the Editor (shown in the example above), click on the Edit tab and choose the Quick tab to display Quick Fix options. Tap the Auto fix buttons or slide the sliders to make changes to the photo. You can also apply these changes by selecting the same commands from the Enhance menu (red outline above).

For more control editing your images, choose one of the commands inside the white outline above from the Editor's Enhance Menu. Make changes and click OK.

If you are editing a batch of photos with the same problems, fix one and open another image. Hold the Alt key (Mac: Opt>key) as you click on the command or type the shortcut. The dialog box will open with the changes made on the previous photo applied automatically. Make any other changes desired and click OK.

For the best results, use Adjustment Layers to edit photos because they are fully editable, make non-destructive changes, and allow you to have much more flexibility. Adjustment layers are used in many of the tutorials in this chapter. You can read more about Adjustment layers in the *The Editor* chapter.

Organizer
In the Organizer (shown in the example on the right), click on the Fix tab to display the Photo Fix Options. Tap the Auto fix buttons to make changes to the photo. You can also make these changes in Full Screen View (F11) and Photo Compare View (F12). To exit Full Screen View and Photo Compare View, tap the Esc key to return to the Media Browser window. Auto Smart Fix and Auto Red Eye Fix are also available from the Edit menu.

When fixing (editing) a photo in the Organizer, a duplicate copy is automatically created and saved in a version set. Because of this, you don't have to make a duplicate copy yourself, but I do it myself just as an extra safeguard, because those wedding shower photos still haunt me. I will not tell you to duplicate the photo in each tutorial in this chapter; get started now with this good habit.

What Do Those Buttons Do?

Auto Smart Fix
Photoshop Elements automatically makes changes to the entire image, including contrast, color balance and saturation, and lighting issues. You may or may not like what it does to your photo. You may also want to tap the Auto Smart Fix button more than once. In the Editor's Quick Edit, you can adjust the amount of Smart Fix applied to the photo.

Auto Levels
Photoshop Elements automatically corrects photos if they are over or underexposed. You will be amazed at what a difference making a Levels change will do to your photos.

Auto Contrast
Photoshop Elements automatically corrects contrast issues between the dark and light areas of the photo. In the Editor's Quick Edit section, you can adjust the amount of change to Shadows, Midtones, and Highlights.

Auto Color
Photoshop Elements automatically corrects color issues caused by different lighting and camera settings. In the Editor's Quick Edit section, you can adjust the Saturation and Hue.

Auto Red Eye Fix
In the Editor's Quick Edit section, this option is found on the Toolbar. Click to have Photoshop Elements automatically remove red eyes. This will not work on pet eye problems. If this does not work correctly for you be sure to read about the Red Eye tool (Y) in the *Tools* chapter.

Auto Sharpen
Photoshop Elements automatically corrects blurred photos. Apply sharpening at the end of editing your photo. Be very careful and watch how it affects the dark colors in your photos. If you over sharpen the photo and someone is wearing a black sweatshirt, the shirt will look as if it was put through the washer and dryer with some tissue…not a look you really want!

How to Lighten/Darken a Photo

I had a great camera, had…is the key word. When a new improved model of my camera was introduced, I felt that it would be a great investment for me. In an attempt to alleviate my guilt a little bit I asked my daughter if she would possibly want a used camera for her upcoming birthday. Her response: "Your camera? Are you kidding? I'd love to have your camera. Why would you ever want to get rid of your camera? It works great!" I told her my reasons and went ahead and bought the new camera for me, and wrapped up the old camera for her birthday. I'd love to report that we're both thrilled with our cameras, but only one of is. My new camera takes dark photos. I've tried everything to fix the problem. I've compared the setting on both cameras and taken the same photo at the same time, and my camera always takes a darker photo. My old camera (now my daughter's camera) takes great photos almost 100% of the time that rarely requires any kind of editing.

So…I've had a lot of experience lightening up dark photos. To lighten a photo, first I try Auto Smart Fix and/or Auto Levels available from the Enhance menu or in Quick Edit. You can also choose from the Editor's Enhance menu Enhance>Adjust Lighting>Shadows/Highlights or Brightness/Contrast. Once the dialog box opens, adjust the sliders too. If none of these options fix the photo to my liking, I try using a blending mode or Levels Adjustment layer to lighten it up.

Using a Blending Mode to Lighten a Photo

For some reason, blending modes are considered by some people to be an advanced tool which is not true at all. When I decided to start teaching about blending modes in my beginning photo editing classes, several other teachers I know told me I was crazy and that my brand new Photoshop Elements students couldn't possibly understand how to use them. Nothing could be further than the truth. Brand new users are thrilled when they see how easy blending modes are to use.

To use a blending mode, open the dark photo and make a duplicate of it (File>Duplicate). Blending modes affect how two layers blend together, and since your photo has only one layer you can't apply a blending mode to the Background layer. Duplicate the layer by choosing Layer>New>Layer via Copy or better yet, use the shortcut Ctrl>J (Mac: Cmd>J). You will now have two copies of your photos, but nothing will look any different to you. Think of this as a set of double print paper photos stacked directly on top of each other.

With the top layer selected as shown above, click on the blending modes drop down list at the top of the Layers panel that says Normal (red arrow). The lightening blending modes are shown above inside the red outline. Your first choice would be to probably choose Lighten, because you want to lighten the photo. With this photo, when I choose Lighten, absolutely nothing happens. At this point most people would probably give up and try some other editing method than blending modes. Don't give up, instead of Lighten choose Screen.

You'll notice that the photo lightens up slightly when Screen is chosen, but it's not light enough. Duplicate the layer again by using the shortcut Ctrl>J (Mac: Cmd>J) and the photo lightens more. Notice the blending mode on the new layer also says Screen. Continue duplicating the layer until the photo is light enough. In my example below, I have duplicated the layer eight times and have a total of nine layers in my Layers panel including the Background layer. Most photos that I edit using this method normally only require one or two layers.

If the photo is too light after adding an additional layer, and too dark without the extra layer, try adjusting the opacity of the top layer to about 50%. The Opacity slider is located to the right of the Blending Mode drop down list.

While this photo is greatly improved, it will never be a fabulous photo. However, if all of my photos from a special event were like this, I'd be thrilled with the results. I can't tell you how many students have told me in class that they have deleted all of their really dark photos because they didn't think they could ever fix them.

Levels Adjustment Layer to Lighten/Darken a Photo

There are several ways you can adjust Levels in an image. Auto Levels options can be found on the Organizer Fix menu, the Editors Quick Edit menu, and by choosing Enhance>Auto Levels in Full Edit mode.

Choosing Enhance>Adjust Lighting>Levels (Ctrl>L, Mac: Cmd>L) will display the Levels dialog box, but what do you do with it when it opens? For starters, click on the top bar where it says Levels and drag the dialog box out of the way so you can see what you are doing. You can try clicking on the Auto button if you haven't already tried it, but you can see from my examples above that using Auto Levels didn't affect this photo much.

Under the Auto button are three eyedroppers. Click on the white eyedropper (far right) and then click on something that is supposed to be white in the photo. In my photo, I clicked on the tent and the snowman (as shown circled below on the example on the right) to see which changes I liked better. I'll be cropping off the tent portion of the photo, so I'm more interested in the snowman being the right color of white.

Click on different white areas to see which ones make the photo look better. If the white eyedropper isn't working well, try the gray or black eyedroppers.

If the eyedroppers don't produce the results you want on the children and the snowman, slide the white, gray, and black sliders under the histogram shown circled in the example below on the left. Histogram is the technical term for the graph that looks like black mountains on the Levels dialog box. To begin, slide the white slider until it touches the first black mountain which may be the only adjustment the photo needs. If not, slide the other sliders until the snowman and children look the way you want them to. Notice that while the children and snowman look better, the blue sky is now white.

While Levels and Auto Levels may work great on your photos, I recommend using a Levels Adjustment layer instead because it gives you more options.

To add a Levels Adjustment layer, click on the Adjustment layer icon at the bottom of the Layers panel that looks like a half black, half white circle. Choose Levels from the pop out box. Once you click on the word Levels, an Adjustment Layer panel will appear in the Panel bin and a new Adjustment layer will be added above the Background layer.

There are two reasons to use an Adjustment layer rather than making a change with just the Levels command. The first advantage of using an Adjustment layer is, like the photo of the children and snowman in this example, that it comes with a mask so we can apply the Levels change to just part of the photo. We will cover this in the *How to Adjust Part of a Photo with a Mask* tutorial later in this chapter. The second advantage is that I can make changes at any time to the Levels settings. If I used the Levels command, I would have to Undo all of my changes or try to make another Levels change, which may or may not work right.

Adjustment layers are applied to **all** layers below them. This is important if you are using them on multi-layered projects like a scrapbook page. When I apply a Levels Adjustment layer to the photo layer as shown in the center example below, and make changes, the light blue scrapbook paper is also lightened to the point of being white.

To apply the Adjustment layer to the photo only, clip it to the photo with a clipping mask. From the Menu bar, choose Layer>Create Clipping Mask (Ctrl>G Mac: Cmd>G). Note: If you are using Photoshop Elements 7 or lower, choose Layer>Group with Previous (same command, new name). Your Layers panel should look like the example on the right.

How to Lighten Part of a Photo Using the Detail Smart Brush Tool

Select the Detail Smart Brush tool (F) from the Toolbar shown circled. On the Brush tool Options bar, click on the brushes drop down list and select by double clicking the Soft Round 300 px brush shown circled. I have chosen a soft brush because it creates a softer transition. Double clicking selects the brush **and** closes the box.

Click on the Presets drop down list and choose the Lighting option. In the Lighting group, choose Spotlight as shown below on the right.

Click, hold, and drag over the areas of the photo that you want to lighten. Once you release, you'll notice that several things have happened:

The areas you dragged/painted over are lighter.

An Adjustment layer has been added and there are white painted areas on the mask.

A little red square symbol which Adobe calls a color pin is added to the photo where you first started dragging/painting (shown circled).

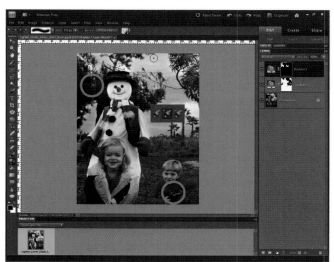

A set of three paint brushes also appear on your photo (they have always been on the Options bar). As you click and drag to lighten more areas of the photo the center brush with the + is active. To paint over your mistakes use the brush on the right with the red – (minus) sign.

To choose a new adjustment, choose the New Selection brush on the left and a new Adjustment layer will be added along with another new color pin in a different color.

In my final example, I have added an additional adjustment called Brighter.

This is a great tool! If you get stuck or want more tips about using this great tool, be sure to read more about it in the *Tools* chapter. I also show you how to use this tool to do some more cool techniques later in this chapter.

How to Lighten/Darken Part of a Photo Using the Dodge or Burn Tool

Using the Dodge and Burn tools (O) is a quick way to lighten or darken areas of photos or scrapbook supplies. These tools can be found at the very bottom of the Toolbar, and are nested with the Sponge tool. Click and hold the ◢ on the tool icon to display all of the nested tools, and choose the Dodge tool.

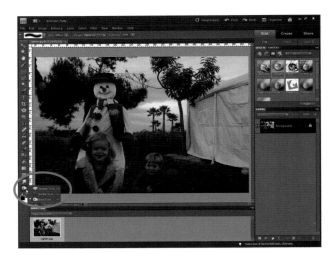

Because these tools make changes directly to the image, make sure you are not working on your original photo. From the Menu bar, choose File>Duplicate to create a copy of your photo. Also, create a duplicate layer of the photo so that in the event you don't like the changes, you can just delete the layer instead of Undoing all the changes.

From the Menu bar, choose Layer>New>Layer via Copy or type the shortcut Ctrl>J (Mac: Cmd>J).

With the Dodge tool selected, choose a large soft brush about 300 px. I used the Bracket keys to resize my brush.

Click and drag over the areas of the photo that you wish to lighten. Click and release often, because if you don't like some of your changes, it will save you time in the long run. Because we are not working with a mask your work must be precise, because your only option to correct it is with Undo. If you lighten an area too much you can paint/drag over it with the Burn tool, but that method isn't always 100%.

Zoom in to fine tune your work. Adjust the size of the brush as needed using the Bracket keys to resize it. If the intensity of the brush is too much and it washes out an area of the photo like the children's faces, lower the Exposure setting on the Options bar, shown circled on the right.

To darken areas of a photo or scrapbook supplies, choose the Burn tool and follow the same steps. In the example below on the left, I have darkened part of the hay roll. In the example below on the right, I have darkened just the left edges of the scrapbook paper by making a selection with the Marquee tool (M) and using the Dodge tool.

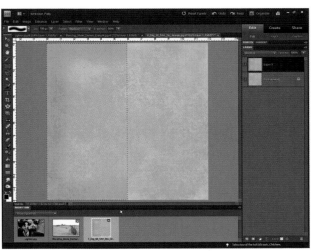

Using a Blending Mode to Darken a Photo

I took this photo on a beautiful fall day in Kentucky. When I had a chance to look at the photo after I returned home from my trip, I realized that the colors in the photo were not the colors I had actually witnessed, and I was disappointed. This technique also works well for photos that are blown out by the camera flash.

To use a blending mode, open the light photo and make a duplicate of it (File>Duplicate). Blending modes affect how two layers blend together, and since your photo has only one layer, you can't apply a blending mode to the Background layer. Duplicate the layer by choosing Layer>New>Layer via Copy or use the shortcut Ctrl>J (Mac: Cmd>J). You will now have two copies of your photos, but nothing will look any different to you. Think of this as a set of double print paper photos stacked directly on top of each other.

With the top layer selected as shown above, click on the blending modes drop down list at the top of the Layers panel that says Normal (red arrow). The darkening blending modes are shown above, inside the red outline. Your first choice would probably be to choose Darken, because you want to darken the photo. With this photo, when I choose Darken, absolutely nothing happens. At this point most people would give up and try some other editing method than blending modes. Don't give up; instead of Darken choose Multiply.

You'll notice that this particular photo darkens a lot when Multiply is chosen.

If the photo does not darken enough, duplicate the layer again by using the shortcut Ctrl>J (Mac: Cmd>J) and the photo will get darker. Notice the blending mode on the new layer will also say Multiply. Continue duplicating the layer until the photo is dark enough. In a previous example, I duplicated a layer eight times to lighten it.

Most photos that I edit using the Multiply blending mode normally only require one or two layers. In my example, adding just one layer makes the photo too dark for what I want.

After adding the additional layer with the Multiply blending mode to it if the photo is too dark, try adjusting the opacity of the top layer down until you like the result. The Opacity slider is located to the right of the Blending Mode drop down list.

How to Adjust Part of a Photo with a Mask

New in Photoshop Elements 9 is the ability to add Layer Masks. This feature is just like the full blown version of Photoshop, which is really exciting. With a mask you can choose what areas of a photo are affected by Adjustment layers, blending modes, and other changes. In this example, we are going to use a Levels Adjustment layer, but you can use this method for fixing all different kinds of photos with any type of Adjustment layer.

This photo has a nice blue sky, but the lower portion of the photo with my husband and grandson is too dark to see them very well.

Add a Levels Adjustment layer by clicking on the Adjustment layer icon (half black, half white circle at the bottom of the Layers panel). Lighten the photo by sliding the white, gray and black sliders in the Adjustment layer panel (shown circled) until you get the desired effect, don't worry about blowing out the sky or top bubble.

 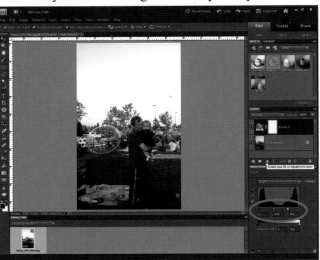

You can also click on the white eyedropper in the Adjustment layer panel (shown circled on the right), and then click on a white area in the photo to correct the lower portion of the photo.

If you are not pleased with the results from using the white eyedropper, try clicking on the black or gray eyedroppers and clicking on an area in the photo that is black or gray.

There are several ways to use a mask. We will use the Brush tool (B) first to paint away areas of the mask we don't want to use.

Choose the Brush tool (B) from the toolbar (shown circled above). Select the default colors by typing the letter D. Your Foreground color should be black, and your Background color should be white as shown on the left. When we paint on the mask, black will reveal the original image and white will conceal it. The mask is now filled with white (circled in yellow) so all of the original image is concealed. If you paint in gray, part of the image will be revealed depending on the intensity of the gray.

On the Brush tool Options bar, click on the brushes drop down list and select by double clicking the Soft Round 300 px brush shown circled. I have chosen a soft brush because it creates a softer transition. Double clicking selects the brush **and** closes the box.

Click inside the mask shown circled in yellow.

Click and drag over the area of the photo that you would like to be darker, which is basically the top portion of the photo.

As you click and drag, the mask will be filled with black, and the sky and top balloon will be painted back in. Continue until you like the way it looks.

If you paint in an area by mistake, switch your Foreground color to white and paint over it. Resize the brush as needed.

My example on the right shows half of the original dark blue sky painted back in, which also reveals the bubble. Notice how part of the mask, shown circled in red, is now black in this example.

The original photo is on the left and, the edited photo is on the right.

If you're having trouble and see black on your photo, it's because you did not click on the mask. In the example below, notice that my Background layer is selected, not the Adjustment/mask layer. Undo and click inside the mask to fix your mistake.

Another way to paint out areas of the mask is with the Gradient tool (G). Choose the Gradient tool from the Toolbar as shown circled. Type the letter D to set your Foreground and Background colors located at the bottom of the Toolbar to the default settings. Your Foreground color should be black, and your Background color should be white.

On the Gradient tool's Options bar, choose the default gradient which is the Foreground to Background gradient. The gradient should show fading from black to white. If it's not, reset the Foreground and Background colors again. Also, choose the Linear Gradient shown circled above which is the default.

Click on the Mask. Click, drag and hold starting at the top of the photo. Release when you get below the sky area. The Mask will fill with a black and white gradient circled below.

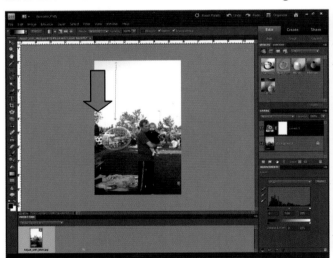 

If the effect is not enough, you can click and drag again, or you can double click on the gradient on the Options bar (shown circled above) to display the Gradient Editor.

The default gradient is shown on the left. Click and drag the Color and Opacity Stops (circled) to adjust the gradient, then click OK. Click on the Mask again, just to make sure you won't paint the picture. Click, hold and drag from the sky downward to fill the mask with the gradient and reveal the blue sky.

Adjusting the Color of a Photo

Bright colorful photos speak to you and tell a story. If you've ever taken a photo that you thought would be wonderful, only to look at it and see a blah photo, you know what I'm talking about. If your photos lack the color you want, Photoshop Elements can help you add it back in. While it can be frustrating to adjust the color in some photos, I'll show you a few of my favorite methods.

If you have old photos from the 1970's, they are most likely discolored. This probably didn't happen because you stored them in your attic (like my Editor does). Those photos were doomed right off the bat by the processing methods used at the time. Some of the colors in the photos have simply disappeared. The first two methods work well if you have scanned these types of photos.

As with all methods of editing photos, you will probably need to adjust more than just one problem on the photo. I normally adjust the lighting and then adjust the color.

Color Variations

Open a photo. Please note that on the adjust_color.jpg file provided on the *Photoshop Elements - Basics & Beyond* DVD I have deliberately blurred out the faces of the girls on the back of the elephant.

From the Menu bar, choose Layer>New>Layer via Copy or type the shortcut Ctrl>J (Mac: Cmd>J) to duplicate the layer. I make changes to the duplicate layer so that I can hide the layer to see my original photo and determine if I like the changes I made. This also saves me time, because if I don't like any of my changes it's easier to drag the layer to the trashcan icon than Undo all of the steps I did.

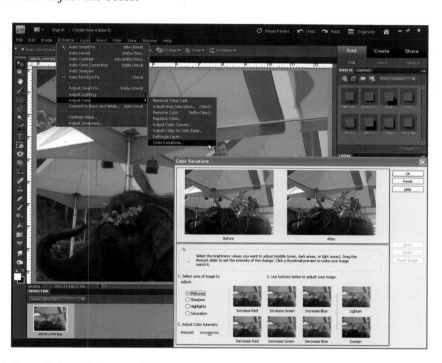

From the Menu bar, choose Enhance>Adjust Color>Color Variations. Basically, pretend you're a four year old. There's a lot of red in the photo because it was taken under a red awning. I begin by tapping the Decrease Red thumbnail. Although not recommended you can tap this several times until the elephant and people turn blue.

Tap the Undo button on the Color Variations dialog box to Undo one click. Click on the Reset Image button to start over. Clicking the Cancel button will close the Color Variations dialog box.

Editing the color on all photos will be a little bit different. Normally, I leave the default settings of Midtones and Color Intensity alone, but try making changes, it only takes a second and you've got the Undo button on your side. You can also choose to click on more than one of the thumbnails for each image.

While you have Before & After previews, sometimes it's hard to see the full result of your changes in the small After window. After you click OK, examine the changes closely to see if they look just as good in full screen view. If you don't like them, Undo or drag the layer to the trashcan icon at the bottom of the Layers panel. I'm not happy with the changes on this photo so I'll try another method.

Remove Color Cast
Open a photo. Please note that on the adjust_color.jpg file provided on the *Photoshop Elements - Basics & Beyond* DVD I have deliberately blurred out the faces of the girls on the back of the elephant.

From the Menu bar, choose
Layer>New>Layer via Copy or type the
shortcut Ctrl>J (Mac: Cmd>J) to duplicate
the layer. I make changes to the duplicate
layer so that I can hide the layer to see my
original photo and determine if I like the
changes I made. This also saves me time,
because if I don't like any of my changes
it's easier to drag the layer to the trashcan
icon than Undo all of the steps I did.

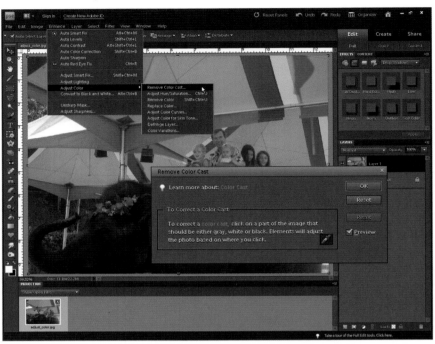

From the Menu bar, choose
Enhance>Adjust Color>Remove Color
Cast. Honestly, when I first began using
Photoshop Elements if I saw something
like the Remove Color Cast dialog box I
would have hit the Cancel button in
seconds flat because it would have
intimidated me.

It's easy to follow the directions. First click
on the gray elephant or my husband's gray shorts. I don't like it so I tap the Reset button. Click on the bottom of
my grandson's shoe which is black, I don't like that either so I reset again. Click on my husband's white sock and
it does a pretty good job.

I use this photo in class, and included it with this book to illustrate that even though you are doing exactly what
Photoshop Elements tells you to do, you get different results. If you know this from the start it will help you
build confidence and have more success with the program in the future.

Intensifying Color with Blending Modes
This is a really fast and easy way to intensify the color
of a photo. Open a photo. From the Menu bar, choose
Layer>New>Layer via Copy or type the shortcut
Ctrl>J (Mac: Cmd>J) to duplicate the layer.

Click on the Blending Mode drop down list at the top
of the Layers panel (circled). To begin with choose
Overlay from the list. Also try Soft Light, Hard Light,
Vivid Light, and Linear Light.

If the effect is too
much, lower the opacity
of the top layer by
clicking on the Opacity
slider at the top of the
Layers panel.

Adjusting Hue & Saturation

Increasing or decreasing the saturation of a photo is easy with a Hue and Saturation Adjustment layer. You can also do the same thing by choosing Enhance>Adjust Color>Adjust Hue/Saturation an Adjustment layer gives you the ability to make color adjustments at any time, which is important.

Click on the Adjustment layer icon (half black, half white circle) at the bottom of the Layers panel and choose Hue/Saturation.

Below are examples using the Adjust_Hue-Saturation.jpg photo provided on the *Photoshop Elements - Basics & Beyond* DVD.

Original photo is shown on the left below.
Second from left: Slide the Saturation slider all the way to the left (-100) produces a black and white photo.
Third from the left: Sliding the Saturation slider to the left (-50) will produce a photo that appears to be tinted.
Far Right: Sliding the Saturation slider to the right (+65) produces an overly saturated photo. This effect is used a lot on scrapbooking layouts featuring football, basketball, skateboarding, etc.

Fluorescent Chalk

If you like the look of grungy, oversaturated photos, try this easy trick. You will see that finding this effect is harder than applying it!

Open a photo. From the Menu bar, choose Layer>New>Layer via Copy or type the shortcut Ctrl>J (Mac: Cmd>J) to duplicate the layer

Open the Effects panel and click on Photo Effects which is the third icon from the left.

To apply the effect Double click on the Fluorescent Chalk thumbnail (circled).

If you see the warning that says "The command "Hide" is not currently available, it's because you didn't duplicate the layer.

Adding/Removing Color with the Sponge Tool (O)

The Sponge tool is nested with the Dodge and Burn tools at the very bottom of the Toolbar. To select the Sponge tool, click and hold the ◢ on the tool icon to display all of the nested tools, and click on the Sponge tool to select it. Think of the Sponge tool as sponging color on/off an image and you'll always remember what it does.

From the Menu bar Mode setting, choose Saturate to add color. The default setting for flow is 50%, so keep that to start.

Open a photo. From the Menu bar, choose Layer>New>Layer via Copy or type the shortcut Ctrl>J (Mac: Cmd>J) to duplicate the layer.

Click and drag over only the areas where you want to bump up the color. In my example, I divided the page in half and used the Sponge tool to increase the color on the right side of the page. The trees on the right now look more like they did when I saw them.

Normally I use this tool to increase the color in small specific areas of a photo. To decrease the color, choose Desaturate from the Options bar. To increase or decrease the intensity of the tool, adjust the Flow percentage.

Adding a Filter to a Photo

A filter is a great way to make a photo look like a work of art. I'm often surprised when I see framed photos for sale how easy it is to figure out what Photoshop filters the photographer has used.

Open a photo. From the Menu bar, choose Layer>New>Layer via Copy or type the shortcut Ctrl>J (Mac: Cmd>J) to duplicate the layer.

Type the letter D to set your Foreground and Background colors located at the bottom of the Toolbar to the default settings. Your Foreground color should be black and your Background color should be white.

From the Menu bar, choose Filter>Artistic>Colored Pencil and the Colored Pencil dialog box will be displayed as shown on the next page.

If you are seeing only a small portion of your photo, click on the bottom left area of your screen to either display Fit on Screen or click the + or – buttons.

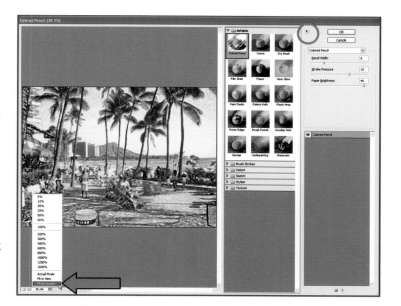

This is where you once again are a four year old child. Drag the sliders for the Pencil Width (6), Stroke Pressure (10) and Paper Brightness (46). My settings are shown in parenthesis but they are not necessarily the right settings. It's your photo, you make it how you like it.

Try other filters by clicking on the other thumbnails. To display other sets of filters, click on ▶ next to the other filter names.

If you would like to see more of your photo, hide the filter thumbnails by clicking on the small round button to the left of the OK button shown circled).

If your photo doesn't look like mine in the large example on the right, check your Background color. In the tiny example on the right, my Background color was set to a dark pink instead of white.

Click OK to apply the filter. In the Layers panel there should be two layers. The top photo layer has the filter applied to it and the bottom layer is the original photo.

Because there are two layers, you can change the blending mode and/or adjust the opacity of the top layer to create some beautiful effects.

Change the blend mode or opacity for the top layer by choosing each option at the top of the Layers panel.

Blending mode and Opacity settings for the photos below are:

Left - Lighten, 100%.   Center - Overlay 75%.   Right - Normal 50%

How to Change a Color Photo to Sepia

Sepia photos evoke a warm feeling when you see them, look great on scrapbook pages or cards, and especially look good in frames on display. Photoshop Elements has many methods for creating sepia photos; I'm sure I won't cover them all!

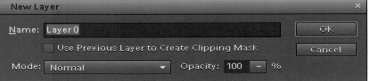

Sepia Photographic Effect
On the Effects panel, click on the Layer Styles icon (shown circled on the left) and choose Photographic Effects.

Double click on the Sepia Tone thumbnail. If you don't see names under the thumbnails that means you didn't read the *First Things First* Chapter.

A warning box will pop up that says that Styles can only be applied to layers. Do you want to make this background a layer? Don't panic!

I've mentioned several times in this book, that one way to have success using this program is to pretend that you are four years old. You're working on a duplicate photo, right? You would never use your original photo, right? What would a four year old do? Press the OK button!

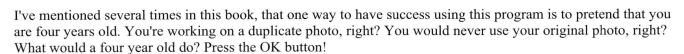

As soon as you press OK, a New Layer dialog box pops up. Don't make any changes and click OK again. Now you have a sepia photo as shown on the right.

Sepia Duotone with the Smart Brush Tool (F)
While I love some of the effects this tool offers, I don't use this one at all!

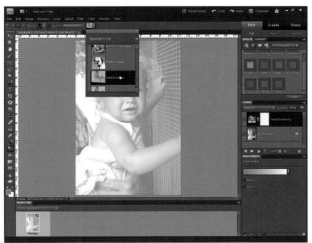

If you still want to try it on one of your photos, choose the Smart Brush tool from the Toolbar. Choose Sepia Duotone from the drop down list on the Options bar and click.

Sepia Monotone Color
On the Effects panel, click on the Photo Effects icon (shown circled on the left) and choose Monotone Color.

Double click on the Tint Sepia thumbnail. If you don't see names under the thumbnails that means you didn't read the *First Things First* Chapter. The Background layer is automatically duplicated and the top layer is now sepia.

Sepia – Hue/Saturation Adjustment Layer
Add a Hue/Saturation Adjustment layer by clicking on the half black/half white Adjustment layer icon at the bottom of the Layers panel shown circled below on the example on the right.

Once the Adjustment layer is added in the Layers panel, click in the Colorize box **first** at the bottom of the Hue/Saturation Adjustments panel.

Slide the Hue, Saturation, and Lightness sliders until you like the effect. In my example the Hue is +40, the Saturation is +38, and the Lightness is -1.

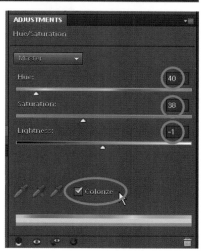

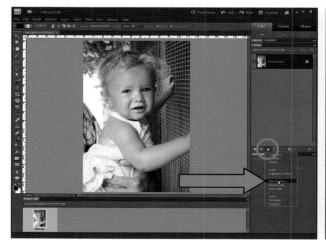 

Sepia – Gradient Map Adjustment Layer with a Custom Gradient
While this method is a little bit more work, I think it produces the best sepia
effect.

Set the Foreground and Background color chips located at the bottom of the
Tool bar to the default colors of black and white. Click inside the Foreground
color chip and choose a warm brown color. I chose Hex # 8c663f.

Add a Gradient Map Adjustment layer by clicking on the half black/half white Adjustment layer icon at the
bottom of the Layers panel, as shown circled below on the example on the left.

The photo will be a
washed out light
brown color. Click
inside the gradient
on the Adjustment
layer, as shown
with the red arrow
on the example
below on the right.

The Gradient Editor dialog box will open. Click under the
gradient bar at the center and a new brown Color Stop will
be added to the gradient (circled in yellow).

Double click on the brown Color Stop at the far left end of
the gradient and the Color Picker box will appear. Choose
black, and click OK (circled in red).

You can see that your photo now has a nice sepia tone to it.
Click OK to close the Gradient Editor.

Sepia – Special Effects Guided Edit
Yet another way to add a sepia effect to a photo is to
open Guided Edit and click on Action Player. From
the first drop down list, choose Special Effects. Next,
choose the Sepia Toning or Sepia Toning with Grain
option. Click the Play Action button. If you like the
effect, click the Done button.

How to Change a Color Photo to Black and White

Just like other types of photo editing with Photoshop Elements, there are many ways to change a color photo to black and white. I've included several methods so you can try them out and choose your favorite. My least used method is shown first and my favorite methods are shown at the end. Try each method and choose a favorite. As you can see by the examples, each method produces a slightly different result. All photos will remain in RGB mode when changing them to black and white with the exception of the first example where the mode is changed to Grayscale.

Change to Grayscale Mode

Many of my students have told me that they use this method to produce a black and white photo. I personally don't think it does the best job, but it's a personal preference. Because you are changing from RGB mode to Grayscale mode, you will not be able to add color to the photo unless you change it back to RGB mode.

From the Menu bar choose Image>Mode>Grayscale. Click OK to discard color information.

Threshold Adjustment Layer or Filter

You would probably want to use this method on a skyline or football type photo. To add an Adjustment layer, click on the Adjustment layer icon (half black, half white circle) at the bottom of the Layers panel. Choose Threshold. To add the Threshold filter, choose Filter>Adjustments>Threshold, but you will not get an Adjustment layer.

Remove Color

From the Menu bar choose Enhance>Adjust Color>Remove Color or use the shortcut Shift>Ctrl>U (Mac: Shift>Cmd>U).

Adjust Saturation (Desaturate)

From the Menu bar choose Enhance> Adjust Color>Adjust Hue/Saturation. The shortcut is Ctrl>U (Mac: Cmd>U). Slide the Saturation slider all the way to the left, or change the amount in the Saturation box to -100. Click OK.

Black and White with the Smart Brush or Detail Smart Brush Tool
Use either the Smart Brush or Detail Smart Brush tools in these examples. My example will show the Smart Brush tool. The difference between these tools is that the Smart Brush tool makes a selection where you click.

As shown circled on the Toolbar below, select the Smart Brush tool. On the Options bar increase the brush size to 2500 px or tap the right Bracket key until the brush won't get any bigger. On the Options bar, click the Preset drop down list and choose Show All.

Choose Pewter from the drop down list. Position your cursor so that the brush covers the entire photo and click. If there are any areas of color left, click on them again so that the entire photo is selected. There should be a selection border (marching ants) surrounding the outside edge of the photo. The photo will change from color to black and white. Notice in the Layers panel that an Adjustment layer has been added above the Background layer.

Click the Preset drop down list and choose other options to try out to produce a wide range of black and white photos. My examples show: Pewter, Cold Tone BW, Infrared, Neutral Tone BW, Tin Type, Yellowed Photo, and High Contrast Red Filter (appears to be the same option found in Quick Edit). The Rubber Stamp option is the same as adding a Threshold Adjustment Layer.

Other options you may want to try are: Antique Contrast, Blue Filter, Green Filter, Red Filter, Silver Sparkle, and Yellow Filter. With all these options there should be at least one of then that you like!

Black and White with a Gradient Map Adjustment Layer or Filter
Set the Foreground and Background color chips located at the bottom of the Tool bar to the default colors of black and white. From the Menu bar, choose Filter>Adjustments>Gradient Map to add a Gradient Map filter. Once the Gradient Map dialog box opens, you can click inside the gradient box to choose another gradient or, as shown at the bottom of the page, adjust the existing one. Once you click OK, the filter is applied.

A good reason to use the Adjustment layer instead of the filter method would be because the Gradient Map filter does not allow you to make changes after it's applied, whereas a Gradient Map Adjustment layer does. To add a Gradient Map Adjustment layer click on the Adjustment Layer icon (half black, half white circle) at the bottom of the Layers panel. Choose Gradient Map from the list.

 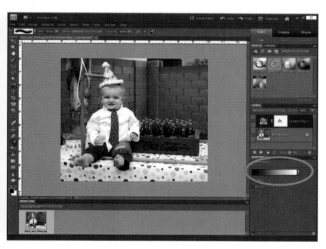

To adjust the gradient for either method, click inside the gradient, as shown circled in both examples above. Click and drag the black and white color stops and the opacity stops, as shown circled on the right to adjust the photo to your liking.

Convert to Black and White

From the Menu bar, choose Enhance>Convert to Black and White, or use the shortcut Alt>Ctrl>B
(Mac: Opt>Cmd>B). A convert to Black and White dialog box will be displayed with a preview showing the
Before (color) and After (black and white) view. If you're happy with the After view, click OK.

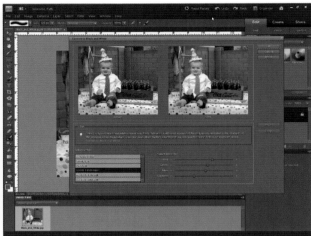

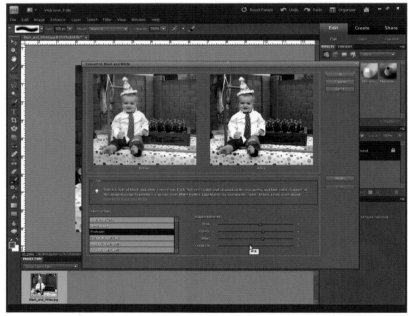

If you want to make changes, you can
start by selecting a different style for
the photo. Photoshop Elements has
defaulted to the Scenic Landscape
style for this photo. Click on another
style and the After preview will
change.

Adjust intensity by sliding the Red,
Green, Blue, and Contrast sliders.
You're thinking to yourself…this is a
black and white photo, why would I
adjust the red, green, or blue part of
it? The mode for this photo
(Image>Mode) is RGB. Even though
we have converted it to black and
white, the mode remains RGB. The
first method I showed you changed
the mode to Grayscale but this one doesn't.

If you make changes you are not happy with, click the Reset
button. Otherwise, if you tap the Cancel button you will have
to choose Enhance>Convert to Black and White again. Once
you are happy with the results, click the OK button.

In the next tutorials you will learn how to add some color to
your black and white photos.

How to Create Black and White Photos with Some Color

This technique is the number one technique that people want to learn. Whenever I teach a beginning photo editing class, I include this technique because it's so easy, and my students get really excited about learning how to do this. One word of warning: Don't tell anyone how easy this is to do or you'll have all kinds of new friends popping up asking you to do this for them.

When I hired a photographer for my daughter's wedding, she made a point to tell the photographer that she wanted a specific photo for her wedding album. She wanted a black and white photo of her and her husband, but she wanted her red roses to still be red. His response to her was…(I'll never forget it) "Well..that's a very intricate and time consuming technique to do. However, if you sign up today I'll throw in one photo like that for free".

We happened to be sitting right next to a bookcase at her house that had my book in it. I couldn't resist, I pulled out the book, put it on the table and said: "I guess I didn't tell you that I teach photo editing". He looked a little embarrassed and said he'd do as many as she wanted. I'd like to say there was a happy ending to the story, but there wasn't. It turns out he was a con man and ended up bilking hundreds of brides out of thousands of dollars. As an extra bonus for my readers, I'm throwing in a little bit of mother of the bride advice: Always use a credit card when pre-paying for services for a wedding. We were one of the few people who got our money back thanks to VISA and a little bit of work on my part.

As usual there are several methods in Photoshop Elements to do this technique. I'll cover a few of them here. As in the preceding color to black and white photo tutorials I'll list the techniques in the order that I use them with the most used listed last.

Black and White Photo Colorful Center
This Effect is really fast to do, but you don't get any control over what part of the photo is in color and what part is black and white.

Open a photo and from the Effects panel and choose the Faded Photo option. Double click on the Colorful Center thumbnail. Photoshop Elements adds an additional layer and completes several automated steps. When it's finished, the center of the photo will remain in color and will fade outward to black and white.

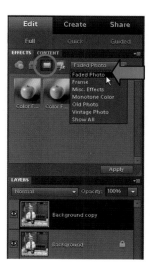

This is a fast and easy fix, but it's not the right technique for some photos. If it's not want you want simply click Undo.

Black and White with Color with the Smart Brush or Detail Smart Brush Tools
Use either the Smart Brush or Detail Smart Brush tools in these examples. My example will show the Detail Smart Brush tool. The difference between these tools is that the Smart Brush tool makes a selection where you click, and the Detail Smart Brush tool allows you to use a regular brush to paint in the areas to remain in color. If you are comfortable working with selections, use the Smart Brush tool. If you are just starting out, use the Detail Smart Brush tool.

Select the Detail Smart Brush tool shown circled on the tool bar. On the Options bar, increase the brush size to about 70 px or tap the right Bracket key until the brush is about as wide as the baby's tie. On the Options bar, click the Preset drop down list and choose Reverse Effects.

Choose Reverse black – white from the drop down list. Position your cursor so that the brush covers the red tie and click and drag over the tie area only. Continue dragging/ painting over the tie adjusting the brush size so that the entire tie is red. The rest of the photo will be black and white.

If you are using the Smart Brush tool, keep the brush size at the default setting of 30 px. When you click once on the tie, the photo will turn black and white and most of the tie will turn red.

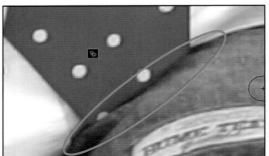

Notice in the Layers panel that an Adjustment layer has been added above the Background layer (when using either tool).

Zoom in so that you can see if you are missing any areas, or, as I have done on his pants if you have painted away too much of the black and white layer.

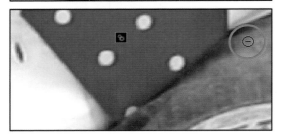

To paint away the blue area, click on the brush with the – (minus sign) next to it on the image, or on the Options bar. Notice that the brush now has a – (minus sign) inside it shown circled below. Reduce the size of the brush and paint over the blue pants to change them back to black and white.

To expose more of the color areas, click on the brush with the + (plus) and continue dragging/painting on those areas.

To remove the selection border (marching ants) from the Menu bar, choose Select>Deselect (Ctrl>D, Mac: Cmd>D), or tap the Esc key which will work for most people if you are using the Smart Brush tool.

Black and White with Color with a Mask

If you've been in one of my hands on classes, or purchased my first book, I showed you how to use this technique using the Eraser tool because it was easier than setting up a mask in earlier versions of Photoshop Elements. The most exciting new feature of Photoshop Elements 9 is the ability to add masks. As I explain in class, it's always better to use a mask than erase, because you can go back and fix your mistakes. Because this is so easy, you'll never use the Eraser again!

Open a photo and duplicate the layer. From the Menu bar, choose Layer>New>Layer via Copy or type the shortcut Ctrl>J (Mac: Cmd>J).

Change the top photo layer to black and white using your favorite method. There are several to choose from several pages back. If you chose the Gradient Map Adjustment layer or one of the Smart Brush or Detail Smart Brush Tool techniques, you already have a mask to work on shown circled on the right.

If you chose the Convert to Black and White method, you need to add a mask yourself. Click on the Layer Mask icon at the bottom of the Layers panel and a mask will be added to the Black and White photo layer.

I changed the name on the Black and White photo layer for demonstration purposes. If you would like to change your layer name, double click on the Layer name and type the new name.

Type the letter D to set your Foreground and Background colors located at the bottom of the Toolbar to the default settings. Your Foreground color should be black, and your Background color should be white.

Type the letter B or click on the Brush tool icon on the Toolbar. Click inside the Layer mask thumbnail and paint over the areas of the photo that you want to be in color.

Continue dragging/ painting over the tie, adjusting the brush size until the entire tie is red. The rest of the photo will remain black and white.

Zoom in so that you can see if you are missing any areas, or if you have painted away too much of the black and white layer. If you have painted away too much of the black and white layer, switch the Foreground color to white by typing the letter X to paint it back in.

To expose more of the color areas, continue dragging/painting on those areas with black.

If you see black or white painted on your photo, you did not click in the Layer mask thumbnail before painting.

How to Turn a Photo into a Vignette

Vignettes evoke a feeling of years gone by, but in reality they're used all the time. For some strange reason, I see a lot of rectangular vignette photos in the "All About our Hotel" books that I find in my room while I'm traveling. As usual, there are several techniques for making a vignette, I'll show you two here.

Normally you want to add a vignette to a photo that you will use on a scrapbook page or card so, in my example I'm showing you how to do this technique on a simple card. Instructions for making a simple card can be found in the *How to Use* chapter. Just to help me center things I have also added Guide lines to my card. To add Guides, click and drag them from the Rulers (View>Rulers). The beige, crumpled linen paper on the card is available from *www.TheDigitalScrapbookTeacher.com* in the Funtime Paper kit.

Open a photo and make the card file. In my example I made the card 8.5" x 11", but you can make your card any size you want. From the Toolbar, choose the Elliptical Marquee tool (M). Click, hold, and drag out an oval selection over the main area of the photo. Do not get too close to the edge of the photo.

From the Menu bar, choose Select>Feather, or use the shortcut Alt>Ctrl>D (Mac: Opt>Cmd>F). Enter 100 in the Feather Radius box and click OK. Don't choose Feather from the Marquee tool Options bar because it does not automatically clear. If you do this, you'll forget you did it and it will drive you crazy…I know this from experience!

From the Toolbar choose the Move tool (V). Click, hold, and drag the **center** part of the photo down into the Project bin until you **touch** the card file (Window users will see a + appear on their cursor).

Because you clicked in the center of the photo the photo will drop in the center of the card.

Resize and reposition the photo on the card by using the Move tool (V). With the Move tool active click on a corner sizing handle and drag to resize/transform the photo.

Add some text, hide the Guides if you added them (View>Guides), and print your card!

Another way to turn a photo into a vignette is to use a mask. Open a photo and make a new blank card as we did in the preceding example. This is a photo of one of the hotels we stayed at while teaching on the road.

From the Toolbar, select the Move tool (V). Click, hold, and drag the center part of the photo down into the Project bin until you **touch** the card file (Window users will see a + appear on their cursor).

The photo will drop in the center of the card. Click and drag a corner sizing handle to resize/transform the photo. Hint: Hold the Alt (Opt) key to size the photo from the center. To confirm the transformation (resizing), check the green checkmark ✓. Click and drag the photo to where you want it with the Move tool (V).

From the Toolbar, select the Rectangular Marquee tool (M). Click and drag a selection (marching ants) around the main part of the photo. In my example above, I have drawn my selection right at the top of the chimney.

From the Menu bar, choose Select>Feather or use the shortcut Alt>Ctrl>D (Mac: Opt>Cmd>F). Enter 50 in the Feather Radius box and click OK. You will notice that the rectangle selection now has rounded corners.

In the Layers panel, check to make sure the photo layer is selected. Click on the Layer Mask icon at the bottom of the layers panel. A Layer Mask (circled below) has been added to the photo layer and has concealed the outer hard edges of the photo.

If you're not happy with the photo, you can Undo and try it again, or you can select the Brush tool and adjust the mask. Select a soft brush and use black to conceal more areas of the photo, or use white to reveal.

Add some text, hide the Guides if you added them (View>Guides), and print your card!

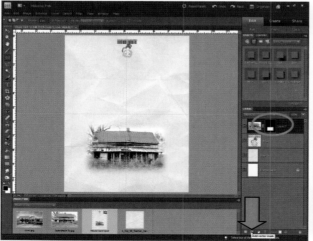 

How to Add a Dark Vignette around the Edge of a Photo or Scrapbook Page

Adding a soft dark vignette around the edge of an image is a great way to bring more focus to the center of the image. This can also help hide distracting things in the background of some photos.

Open a photo. From the Toolbar, choose the Elliptical Marquee tool (M). Click, hold, and drag out an oval selection over the main area of the photo.

From the Menu bar, choose Select>Feather or use the shortcut Alt>Ctrl>D (Mac: Opt>Cmd>F). Enter 250 in the Feather Radius box and click OK.

Click on the New Layer icon at the bottom of the Layers panel to create a new transparent layer, or type the shortcut Shift>Alt>Ctrl>N (Mac: Shift>Opt>Cmd>N)

From the Menu bar, choose Select>Inverse, or use the shortcut Shift>Ctrl>I (Mac: Shift>Cmd>I) to inverse the selection. The selection border will remain in the center, but will also be added to the outside edge of the image.

Type the letter D to set your Foreground and Background colors located at the bottom of the Toolbar to the default settings. Your Foreground color should be black, and your Background color should be white. To add a vignette of a different color, choose a different Foreground color and follow all of the same steps.

Choose Edit>Fill Selection. Choose to fill with the Foreground color and make sure that the Preserve Transparency box is not checked, or use the shortcut Alt>Backspace (Mac: Opt>Delete).

To remove the selection border (marching ants), from the Menu bar, choose Select>Deselect (Ctrl>D, Mac: Cmd>D), or tap the Esc key which will work for most people.

Because the black vignette is on its own layer, if the effect is too intense, you can adjust the opacity of that layer. To adjust the Opacity, slide the Opacity slider located at the top of the Layers panel shown circle above.

I wonder if those cows, at a farm somewhere in the middle of Pennsylvania realized they would become celebrities when that crazy lady in a red shirt took their photo late one Sunday afternoon.

A future tutorial in this chapter: *How to Add a Lomo Effect to Photos* shows you how you can also add a preset dark vignette. However, you will not be able to change the color or opacity of this vignette as you can in the tutorial above.

Adding a Blue Sky to a Photo

While I love the Smart Brush and Detail Smart Brush tools, they come up short when trying to add a blue sky to a photo like this one. I was pretty disappointed when I looked at my photos after a trip to Pennsylvania. As someone who was born and raised in Southern California, I don't have an occasion to photograph many cows, so I dragged my husband and girlfriend through some beautiful farms. The sun was setting faster than I wanted it, to so my photos came out pretty dark.

Here's how I fixed this photo... Of course, I'm working on copies of my originals. Open the Cows_Original and Blue Skies photo which can be found on the *Photoshop Elements - Basics & Beyond* DVD. Take photos of beautiful skies when you see them. Add them to your own photos, and be sure to tag them in the Organizer so you can find them when you need them.

Select the Cows_Original image and duplicate the layer (Ctrl>J, Mac: Cmd>J). I renamed my layers so that it would be easier for you to see the changes. With the Move tool (V), drag the Blue Skies photo onto the cows photo. Drag the Blue Skies layer down so that it's sandwiched in between both cow layers.

Add a Layer mask by clicking on the Layer Mask icon at the bottom of the Layers panel. From the Toolbar, choose the Brush tool (B), choose a soft round brush. Type the letter D to set your Foreground and Background colors located at the bottom of the Toolbar to the default settings. Your Foreground color should be black and your Background color should be white.

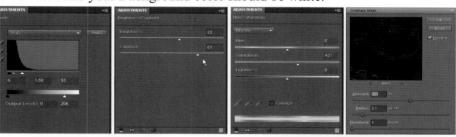

Click in the mask (circled above) and paint out the gray sky so that the blue sky will show from the layer below. The photo looks better, but the bottom portion is still very dark.

Add a Levels Adjustment layer by clicking on the half black/half white icon at the bottom of the Layers panel. The numbers under my histogram are 6-black, 1.58 gray, 53 white. Output levels are 0 and 206. I used the Brush tool to paint out the sky and part of the bottom edge with a dark gray color (Hex #535252).

Add a Brightness/Contrast Adjustment layer. I adjusted the Brightness to 23 and the Contrast to 51. I used the Brush tool to paint out the sky and part of the bottom edge with a dark gray color (Hex #535252).

Add a Hue Saturation Adjustment layer. Adjust the Saturation to +21. I did not paint on this mask.
Select the top cow layer, Cows 2 in my example. From the Menu bar choose Enhance>Unsharp Mask. Adjust the sharpness as desired. My settings are Amount 121%, Radius 2.1, Threshold 1. If you over sharpen, you may get red spots on the cows. If the rest of the image is OK, mask out the red spots on the Cows 2 and Blue Skies layers so the bottom cow layer shows through.

Blurring Out Distracting Backgrounds

If adding a dark vignette around the edge of your photo doesn't hide distractions, there is another technique you can use to simply blur them out making it look like the camera took a great shot!

Open a photo; I'm using Blur_Distracting_Background copy.**jpg** which can be found on the *Photoshop Elements- Basics & Beyond* DVD. This is a nice photo of my husband experiencing his first formal tea at Butchart Gardens, but the waiter in the background is very distracting.

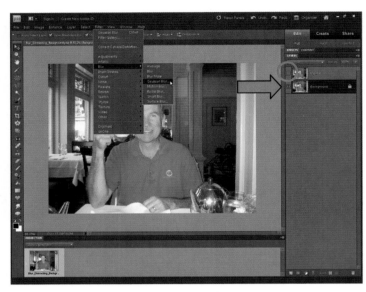

First, we're going to duplicate the layer. From the Menu bar, choose Layer>New>Layer via Copy or type the shortcut Ctrl>J (Mac: Cmd>J). Hide the top layer by clicking on the eyeball icon to the left of the Layer thumbnail.

Click on the Background layer, and from the Menu bar, choose Filter>Blur>Gaussian Blur.

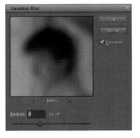

Click and drag inside the preview box until you find the waiter. Slide the radius slider until he is sufficiently blurred out. I'm using 8 pixels in my example. Click OK.

Once you click OK, the entire image appears to be blurry. Click on the eyeball icon to reveal the top layer that does not have the blur filter applied to it.

Make a selection around the part of the photo you want to keep. You can use the Marquee tool or any other selection tool. Because the waiter appears to be coming out of the tea cup, I used the Selection Brush tool (A) because I wanted a more irregular area than the Marquee tool would have given me. I used a 45 px soft round brush. Don't worry about making the selection perfect but be sure to get the area under the tea cup.

From the Menu bar, Choose Select>Feather (Alt>Ctrl>D, Mac: Opt>Cmd>F) and choose 25 pixels.

As shown below click on the top layer to make it the active layer so that it's highlighted. Click on the Add a Layer Mask icon at the bottom of the Layers panel shown circled below. As soon as the mask is applied, the waiter and surrounding background is blurred out.

If you're not happy with the image, choose the Brush tool (B), and choose a soft round brush.

Type the letter D to set your Foreground and Background colors located at the bottom of the Toolbar to the default settings. Your Foreground color should be black, and your Background color should be white.

Click inside the Mask and paint away the areas that you wish to conceal. Switch to white to paint back in the areas that were removed in error.

If you're really not happy with your selection, understand that making good selections takes practice. Open the file Blur_Distracting_Background.**psd** which can be found on the *Photoshop Elements - Basics & Beyond* DVD. Repeat all the steps taken before we made the selection.

From the Menu bar, choose Select>Load Selection.

When the Load Selection dialog box appears, click OK to load the "Mike at tea" Selection.

Select the top layer and tap the Add a Layer Mask icon at the bottom of the Layers panel, and you're done.

Blur Out Distracting Backgrounds and Add Motion

With some photos, when you blur out a background and add
motion so it appears that there's movement in the photo it adds to
the interest of the photo. In the photo I'm using for this example
there was movement, but because I had my camera set on the
sports setting it froze all of the movement.

Even after I've cropped most of it away this photo has a very
distracting background. I also used the straighten tool to straighten
the photo.

We are going to essentially follow the same exact steps in the preceding tutorial, with one change. Open a
photo; I'm using Motion Blur copy.**jpg** which can be found on the *Photoshop Elements - Basics & Beyond*
DVD.

First, duplicate the layer. From the Menu bar, choose Layer>New>Layer via Copy or type the shortcut Ctrl>J
(Mac: Cmd>J). Hide the top layer by clicking on the eyeball icon to the left of the Layer thumbnail.

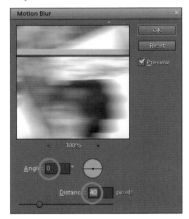

Click on the Background layer, and from the Menu bar choose
Filter>Blur>Motion Blur. I kept the Angle at 0 and changed the Distance to 40
pixels, but you can experiment.

Once you click OK, the entire image appears to be blurry. Click on the eyeball
icon to reveal the top layer that does not have the blur filter applied to it.

Make a selection around the part of the photo you want to keep; this will take
you a few minutes. I used the Magnetic Lasso tool (L) and the Selection Brush
tool (A) to make my selection.

From the Menu bar, choose Select>Feather (Alt>Ctrl>D, Mac: Opt>Cmd>F)
and choose 3 pixels.

If you're "Selection Challenged" you can open the Motion Blur copy.**psd** file where I have saved 3 selections for
you. Choose Select>Load Selection to use them.

As shown below, click on the top layer to make it the active layer so that it's highlighted. Click on the Add a
Layer Mask icon at the bottom of the Layers panel, shown circled below. As soon as the mask is applied, only
the riders remain in focus.

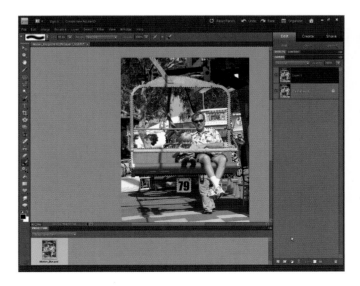 

How to Add a Lomo Effect to Photos

Lomo cameras are a type of 35mm film camera that was intended to be a fun camera used for candid photo snapshots. In the 1960's, you could purchase the "Diana" camera, which was manufactured in China. While some people liked the unpredictable effects these cameras produced, others did not, and the camera disappeared in the 1970's. Lomo cameras have made a comeback and are once again available for purchase. As for their original price of one dollar…don't count on it!

Adding a Lomo Camera Effect to a regular digital photo is a multi step process involving adding a vignette, and adjusting color, lighting, and sharpness.

Lomo Camera Effect has been added as a new feature of Photoshop Elements 9 in the Guided Edit, Fun Edits portion of the program. You can choose to add the full Lomo Camera Effect to your photo, or you can choose to just add a dark dreamy vignette around the edges of your photo.

To add the Lomo Camera Effect to one of your photos, open the photo in Guided Edit as shown circled below. Click on Lomo Camera Effect under the Fun Edits section. You may have to scroll down to see these.

To apply the full Lomo Camera Effect, click on the Cross Process Image button and then on the Apply Vignette button. To intensify either/both effects, you can click more than once.

If you're not happy with the change, tap the Reset button and start over. Once you're happy with the changes, click the Done button and you will return to Guided Edit. If you don't like the effect on this photo, click the Cancel button.

Example photos shown below:
Original Photo, Cross Process Image & Vignette, Cross Process Image only, Vignette only.

How to Use Photomerge Style Match

Also, another new feature that's been added to Photoshop Elements 9 is something that you need to check out, because it can make your photos look really impressive with just a couple of clicks!

It's probably easiest to access Photomerge Style Match from Guided Edit, but it can also be found in the Editor or Organizer by choosing File>New>Photomerge Style.

Select the image and choose Photomerge Style Match as shown by the red arrow on the example on the right.

Double click on the style thumbnail in the Style Bin, or click and drag it up where it says: Drag Style Image Here and the style will be applied. To see a Before and After view of your photo, click the View drop down list above the Style Bin. Click Done to exit the Photomerge Style Match dialog box. When you return to Full Edit, you will see that a new layer has been added to the Layers panel named Style Layer with all of the changes on it. The Background layer is the original photo.

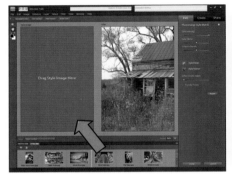
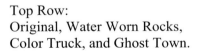
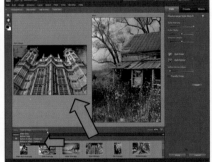

I applied each of the default Photomerge Style Match Styles available in the Photomerge Style Match dialog box individually to this photo without making any other adjustments to: Style Intensity, Style Clarity, Enhance Details, or Transfer Tones.

Top Row:
Original, Water Worn Rocks, Color Truck, and Ghost Town.

Bottom Row:
Silver Hotel, Pier Rope, Bristlecone, and Sunset

To match the style to a photo on your hard drive or in your Organizer, click on the green + button under the Style Bin shown circled below on the left.

Select the photo(s) and click done. Drag the new style thumbnail to the box and Photoshop Elements will match the style. In my example below, I used a photo of the same abandoned house that I had previously edited.

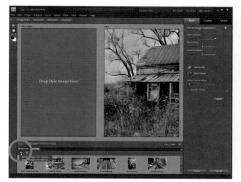
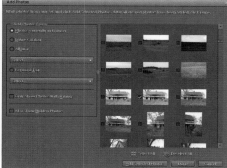
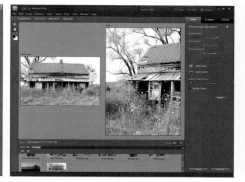

In the two examples below, I added my own photos as new styles by following the steps above. The photo I used for the style match is shown on the left (black, white and color baby and edited old house), and the resulting photos are shown on the right. The far right examples on each row show the results after I clicked in the Transfer Tones box on the Photomerge Style Match dialog box.

How to Turn a Color Photo into a Sketch

There are several ways to turn a photo into a sketch with Photoshop Elements, and each one results in a little bit different effect. I'll show you three ways that I use the most. The results you experience will depend on the photo and the method you use to apply the sketch. For this reason, I usually try all three methods to see which one I like best.

Photo Effects –Pencil Sketch

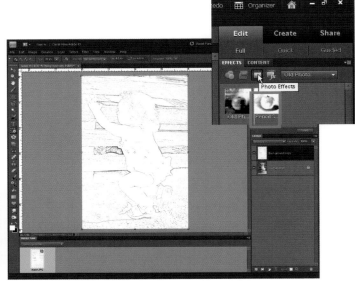

This Photo Effect duplicates the Background layer and changes the new layer to a black and white sketch. You do not have any ability to edit the sketch.

In the Edit panel, click on the Photo Effects icon. Click on the dropdown list and choose Old Photo. Double click on the Pencil sketch thumbnail (circled on the right).

You may adjust the Opacity slider (circled) on the sketch layer to reveal the color layer below. With the photo I'm using, I wasn't crazy about the effect.

Guided Edit-Pencil Sketch

Open the photo in Guided Edit by clicking on the Guided tab at the top right corner of your screen shown circled on the right.

Click on Line Drawing in the Photographic Effects section marked by the arrow on the right.

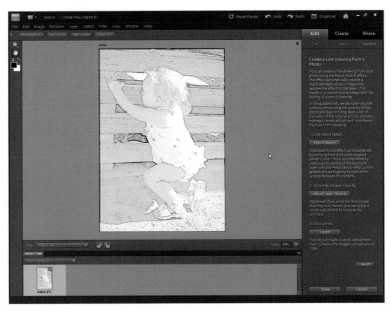

To apply the sketch filter, click on the box marked Pencil Sketch. The layer is duplicated and a sketch is added to the top layer (you can't see this right now)

To adjust the opacity of the sketch layer and let some of the color photo through, click on the Adjust Layer Opacity box. Photoshop Elements will automatically adjust the opacity for you.

To darken the lines in the sketch, click on the Levels box. Click Done to return to Guided Edit.

Using a Filter to Create a Sketch

Open a photo in Full Edit.

Type the letter D to set your Foreground and Background colors located at the bottom of the Toolbar to the default settings. Your Foreground color should be black, and your Background color should be white.

From the Menu bar, choose Layer>New>Layer via Copy, or type the shortcut Ctrl>J (Mac: Cmd>J) to create a duplicate layer of the photo.

From the Menu bar, choose Filter>Sketch>Photocopy.

If you only see part of your photo, click the dropdown arrow on the bottom left corner of the screen and choose Fit on Screen (red arrow).

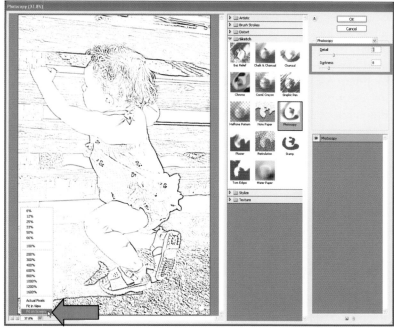

Adjust the Detail and Darkness settings to your liking. My settings in the example on the right are Detail 6, Darkness 8, but that doesn't mean they are the right settings for you. Experiment and use whatever you like.

For fun, click on some of the other thumbnails to try out other filters (this is the part where you pretend you're a four year old).

Click OK.

The example on the left shows the photo with the filter applied at the settings listed above.

The center example shows the filter applied with the same settings, but I changed the layer opacity to 90% on the top filter layer.

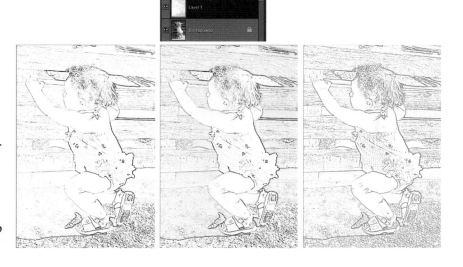

The right example shows what happens if the Foreground color is set to red (I did change the Detail and Darkness settings on this example). While I wouldn't use this technique for this particular photo, it could look really good on a football photo.

For even more special effects, change the blending mode on the filter layer to Hard Light, Overlay, or any other one you like.

Blending Photos with Other Images

You can blend two or more photos together, or you can blend a photo with another image like a piece of digital scrapbook paper to create a work of art. Blended photos are often used on scrapbook pages shown in magazines, but they usually don't show you how they created the effect.

Open two photos; I'm using Blend_1 and Blend_2 which can be found on the *Photoshop Elements - Basics & Beyond* DVD. Blend_1 is a piece of digital scrapbooking paper that I cropped for you from our Funtime paper and embellishment kit available at *www.TheDigitalScrapbookTeacher.com*.

Duplicate the images (File>Duplicate) so you are not working with the original images. Activate the Move tool on the Toolbar. Drag the Blend_2 photo on top of the Blend_1 photo. The Project bin will appear to have two of the same photos in it, but if you look at the Layers panel you will see that the picture of the children is stacked on top of the paper.

Change the blending mode of the top layer by clicking on the drop down list that says Normal under the Layers panel tab. Try different blending modes and opacities. In my example on the right I chose Pin Light at 100% Opacity.

The pillows (all white areas) in the original paper have now been replaced with the pattern from the paper. The lines from the paper run through the entire photo. I had a student in class ask: "How do I get rid of those ugly blue lines?" The answer is, choose another paper.

Recompose a Photo

Ever try to get a four year old and a two year old to sit close together, especially when they're more interested in their Halloween candy than what you're telling them to do?

In the original photo on the left (Recompose.jpg which can be found on the *Photoshop Elements - Basics & Beyond* DVD) there's too much grass in between the children. While it's nice grass for a background, I want to fill my photo with the children.

From the Toolbar, choose the Recompose tool which is nested with the Crop tool (C). From the Options bar, choose the first green brush icon (Mark for Protection) and paint over the parts of the photo you want to keep (children). Choose the third brush icon (red with x) and like the middle example, paint over the grass. Click and drag on the side sizing handles to push the photo in from either side. To confirm the transformation (resizing), check the green checkmark ✓. If you are going to print this photo, crop it so that it is a standard photo size. If you are using it on a digital project, you don't have to crop it. If there is a little disruption in the grass, you can fine tune it with the Clone Stamp tool (S) or Healing Brush tool (J), or you can tell people you just had the sprinklers redone.

Straightening a Photo

One surefire way improve a photo is to just straighten it!

Open the photo, and from the Toolbar, select the Straighten tool (P). Choose part of the photo Click, hold, and drag your cursor along a line that should be level across the screen. In the photo below, it would be best to drag across the line on the building, but if I did that, you couldn't see my line at all.

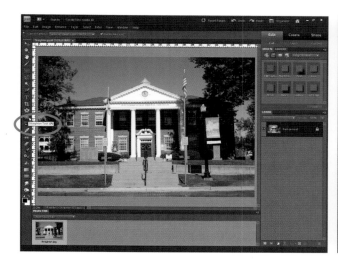

Release the mouse and with one small problem the photo is straightened. The problem is that, as shown in the example on the bottom left, you now have white edges that were added when the photo was straightened. Remember, I keep telling you, if you don't like something Undo it and try something else, so Undo.

On the Straighten tool's Options bar, click on the Canvas Options drop down list and choose the option that says Crop to Remove Background and try it again. This time the photo will be straightened and the white edges will be automatically cropped off.

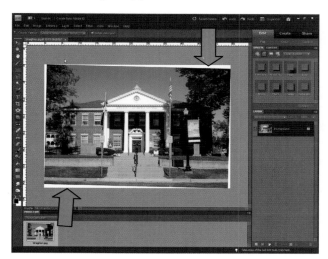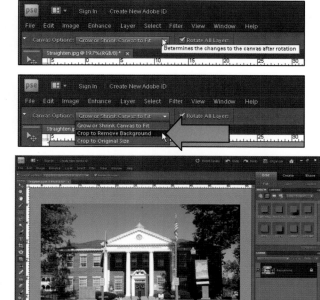

If you have trouble with this tool, try dragging a shorter or longer line until you find one that does a good job straightening the photo for you.

Cropping Photos

One of the hardest things to get across in my photo editing classes is, what you see on your screen may not be what you pick up from your photo processor. Most digital cameras take photos in a 4 x 5.3 aspect ratio. Most photo processors print 4" x 6" photos although some are now starting to print 4" x 5.3". What does this mean to you? It means that if you don't crop the photo before you print it, you may not end up with the photo you wanted because pieces of it get left out.

If you are adding your photos to a scrapbook page or other digital project you don't have to worry about cropping to a specific size first, unless it's part of your page design (i.e. a row of 3 inch photos). However, you **must** enter 300 in the Resolution box or your photo won't be that size when you drag it onto a new 300 px file.

Cropping a photo is easy, all you need to do is open the photo, select the Crop tool (C), select the Aspect Ratio, from the Options bar and crop.

The lighter area is your selected area, the darker area is called the shield and will be cropped off.

If you drag out a landscape (wide) selection (for example 6" wide and 4" high), and decide you want it to crop the photo with a portrait (tall) orientation (for example 4" wide and 6" high,) tap the button with the two arrows on it (shown circled between the height and width boxes on the Options bar) instead of typing in the numbers manually. This time saving button will swap the height and width numbers for you.

Click and drag in the selected area to move the selection. Click and drag the corner sizing handles to resize the selection in proportion. If you have a preset Aspect Ratio chosen, dragging the side sizing handles will also resize the selection in proportion. To confirm the crop, check the green checkmark ✓.

The examples below show how changing the aspect ratio will change the photo. Notice that I began my crop just to the left of the barn and included the cow on the right. The 4" x 6" photo on the left has much less sky than the 5" x 7" photo in the middle, or the 8" x 10" photo on the right.

Notice the difference cropping makes in a photo as shown below. All of the photos are cropped in a 4" x 6" size. The original photo is the one on the far left. To bring focus to the children, crop out as much of the distracting areas of the photos as possible. Now, if they happen to be standing on their Dad's fire truck (they're not), you'll need to keep more of the truck in the photo and be sure to include the engine number.

One mistake that I often see in hands-on classes is shown on the right.

Students drag out a crop selection and then decide they want to fine tune their crop, not realizing that their crop outline is beyond the photo. Once they release their mouse, part of the photo is filled with the Background color.

You can actually make this mistake on purpose so it works in your favor. This "mistake" will produce a mat around your photo in your Background color. It does have some limitations, because unlike other methods included in this book the mat becomes part of the photo layer and is not placed on its own layer.

First, click inside your **Background** color swatch to set the color of the mat. I prefer to use black for mats of this type, because with this method I can't add a drop shadow to the photo to make it look realistic. Both black and white mats are shown at the end of this tutorial.

From the Crop tool Options bar, choose a preset size from the Aspect Ratio dropdown list. Crop your photo. To confirm the crop, check the green checkmark ✓.

Click and drag to crop your photo in the same exact size as before and release the mouse. Once you release the mouse, you will see sizing handles surrounding the photo. Hold the Alt key (Mac: Opt key) to drag the outline from the center as shown on the right. To confirm the crop, check the green checkmark ✓.

 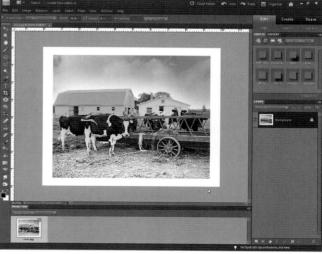

Using a Photo as a Background Paper on a Project

As usual…there are several techniques on how to use a photo as a background for a scrapbook page or other project. Open a photo and create a new blank file, as demonstrated in the *How to Use* Chapter.

In my example, I want to use a photo to cover the background of a template that I'm building. I can use the Crop tool to crop the photo to a 12" x 12" inch size before I drag it onto the page, or I can drag it onto the page and resize it. If you're using a photo of a sunset, it's pretty easy to crop the photo first. But in my example, if I crop the photo first I'm afraid I won't crop it correctly. I'll show you both methods.

To crop the photo, choose the Crop tool (C). From the Crop tool Options bar, choose No Restriction from the Aspect Ratio dropdown list. Type 12 inches for the width and height (or the size of your project) and enter 300 in the resolution box. Click and drag the mouse to select the portion of the photo you want. To confirm the crop, check the green checkmark ✓.

Photo credit Madeline Arenas Cubrix Photography

From the Toolbar, select the Move tool (V). Click, hold, and drag the photo down into the Project bin until you **touch** your new file (Window users will see a + appear on their cursor). In this example, I'm adding the photo to a template. I will select the layer of the template (blue paper) that I would like the photo to be placed above in the Layers panel to save me a little bit of time.

The photo will drop right in the middle of the template page, and unfortunately, the template pieces are covering my grandson's face. I used the Move tool to drag the photo to the right, but since I already cropped the photo, it leaves a gap which is showing in bright green (I added a green layer to illustrate this problem).

My other option is not to crop the photo before I drag it onto my page following the same steps above. The photo will drop in the center of the page. Click and drag a corner sizing handle to resize/transform the photo. Hint: Hold the Alt (Opt) key to size the photo from the center. To confirm the transformation (resizing), check the green checkmark ✓.

Click and drag the photo to reposition it with the Move tool (V) as shown on the next page.

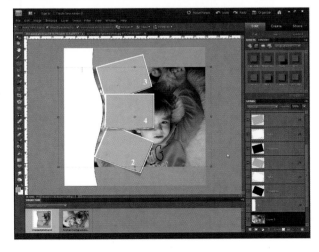

To get the portion of my grandson's face to show on the template, I've had to stretch it a little bit and move it over. As you can see by the example on the right, the photo is overhanging the template. This is OK.

If you want to you can leave the photo larger than the template, or you can crop the image with the Crop tool in a 12" x 12" size (300 Resolution). Cropping the scrapbook page will reduce the file size which would be a good idea. Personally, I would wait until I'm completely done with the page and then maybe I'd crop it. I have made too many projects in the past that I want to change later and I can't because I have done things like cropping this photo, so now I tend to work on the cautious side and….I've got a 1.5 TB external hard drive!

After I finish assembling the template (instructions can be found in the *How to Use* chapter), I decide that, while I like the photo as a background, I'd like it to be a little more subtle so that the other photos are a little bit more visible. Right now, when I look at the page, all I see is the large background photo.

I had originally added a piece of blue linen paper as the background for the template (see the previous page), and wasn't crazy about it.

I can easily blend the photo and the paper together to make it appear like the photo has a linen texture and a blue tint. To do this, click on the Blending Mode drop down list at the top of the Layers panel. Try different blend modes. Normally, to blend a photo and a scrapbook paper together, I choose Overlay, but in this example I chose Screen. You can also adjust the photo layer opacity.

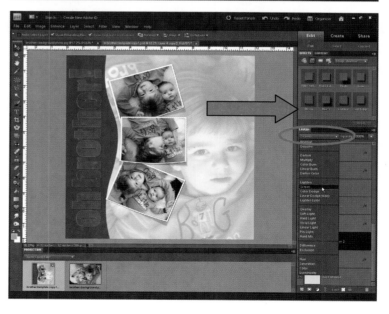

Save!

All products shown in this example are available from: *www.TheDigitalScrapbookTeacher.com.* They are not included on the *Photoshop Elements-Basics & Beyond* DVD. The papers and alphas are from the Funtime and Springtime kits. The template is from the 12 x 12 #F Template set.

Pop Art

Looking for something a little bit different? You just found it!

Open the Pop_Art photo which can be found on the *Photoshop Elements - Basics & Beyond* DVD. This action works best on images with simple backgrounds, so I have cropped the original image, which is shown on the right. It also does not work well with blonde hair. When I tried this on photos of my grandson with dry hair, they didn't look good. Since his hair was wet, it made it darker and the final image is better.

Adjust the lighting. I chose to use Levels (Ctrl>L Mac: Cmd:L). Use the Clone tool to clone out the base of the faucet so there are fewer distractions. To do this, select the Clone Stamp tool (S) and Alt click (Mac: Opt Click) on the sink and then click on the faucet area to paste the white porcelain over the faucet.

Go to Guided Edit, and choose Pop Art under Fun Edits at the bottom of the column. Follow the numbered steps provided by Adobe.

1. Choose a style, I chose the default (left preview circled).
2. Click on the Convert Image Mode button and the image turns black & white (yet another way to make a black and white photo).
3. Click the Add Color button to add a blue color fill Adjustment layer (we can change this later). If you only want one image, click the Done button.
4. Click on Duplicate Image to have three more images duplicated with different background colors and placed on their own layer in the final image.
5. Return to Full Edit. Notice that each different colored image has been placed on its own layer in the Layers panel.

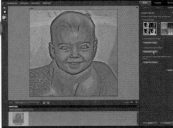  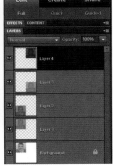

The photos on the bottom row above are the result of using the style preview shown circled above in the example on the left. I like the effect the first step (Posterize Image) does on the photo, but I'm not crazy about the end result. Try it with other photos and see how you like it.

Out of Bounds

Another new addition to Photoshop Elements 9 is the Out of Bounds effect, known also by the abbreviation OOB. Maybe you didn't know the technical term for this type of photo, but you have seen them before. This type of photo really gets noticed on a scrapbook page and is very easy to do since Photoshop Elements now does most of the work now. You can print the final photo, or you can add them to a project.

Open the Out of Bounds photo which can be found on the *Photoshop Elements - Basics & Beyond* DVD. Choose Guided Edit and choose Out of Bounds from the Fun Edits Category at the bottom of the column. Basically, all you need to do is follow the steps that Adobe has numbered for you.

1a. Click the add a frame button and a frame selection will be added to your photo.
1b. Drag the frame smaller so that the top of it is right across the top of his eyebrows, and the bottom of it is right under his lower hand. Pull the frame in so that it does not go off the edges of the high chair.
1c. Hold the Ctrl & Alt button (Mac Cmd & Opt) as you drag the corner sizing handle to add perspective (slant) to the frame. To confirm the transformation (resizing), check the green checkmark ✓.

2a. Click and drag to make the actual frame wider, hold the Alt key (Mac: Opt key) to size it proportionately.
2b. To confirm the transformation (resizing), check the green checkmark ✓.

3. Click on the Quick Selection Tool icon and select the birthday hat and his head. Drag over the frame as shown in the example on the right.

Zoom in to make sure you're making a good selection. Hold the Spacebar to move around the screen.

Click on the Refine Edge button on the Quick Selection tool Options bar. Experiment with the settings.

4. Click on Create Out of Bounds Button.

5. Stylize: Click on Small to add a small shadow.

6. Click add a gradient if you will not be adding this photo to a scrapbook page.

Click Done. Return to Full edit.

To drag this onto a scrapbook page or other project you will need to first select or link the top three layers in the Layers Panel. Then choose the Move tool (V) to drag it onto the other file.

The drop shadow can be adjusted by double clicking on the *fx* symbol.

Stitching Photos Together with Photoshop Elements

Have you ever wanted to stitch several photos together to make one large photo? If you have, you are not alone; I have students ask me how to do this all the time.

To get the best results, use a tripod to take your photos. If you don't have a traditional tripod or don't want to carry it around, there are some great inexpensive, flexible tripods available that are small and can even be used to wrap around trees and poles. Sometimes a well placed rock will do, or if all else fails, as you take the photo try to stand very still and just rotate your body. Be aware that as you rotate to take the photos, the lighting angles are also changing, which may affect the final panorama photo. I also wait until after I stitch the photos together to edit them.

Open only the photos you want to stitch together. The photos I'm using were taken at Niagara Falls and can be found on the *Photoshop Elements- Basics & Beyond* DVD in the Photo Editing Examples folder.

From the Menu bar, choose File>New>Photomerge Panorama. Click on the Add Open Files button and the open files will appear in a list. Click on the first file name in the list and Shift click on the last file name in the list to select them all. Click OK.

 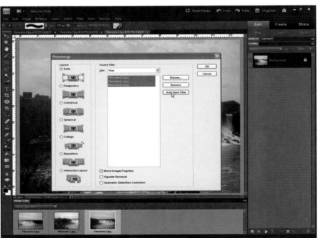

As soon as you click OK, Photoshop Elements takes over and begins to stich the photos together. A Clean Edges dialog box will appear that asks: Would you like to automatically fill in the edges of your panorama? Choose Yes, but don't check the box that says Always perform this action because you may not want to do it in the future.

After filling the edges, there are now four layers. The top layer is a copy of the three lower layers merged together. Check the photo to make sure the edges filled well. While the photo looks good in the view below, when I zoom in I see that I have half of a boat along the bottom edge of the photo. The reason I have half of a boat is because there was only half a boat in the original photo. Photoshop Elements is good, but it's not good enough to reproduce the other half of the boat.

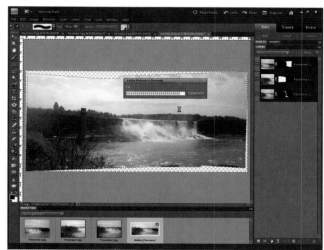 

There are a couple of things you can do to fix a problem like this:

Crop the photos before you stitch them together. You will need to save the cropped photos first before you stitch them together.

When asked if you want to fill in the edges, choose No. Crop the photo yourself with the Crop tool (C) as shown below on the left. You will end up with a smaller photo doing it this way.

When cropping the photo file yourself, notice that because we didn't fill the edges, there are three separate layers. To edit the photo, it would be nice if there was only one layer. To merge the layers together into one layer **and** still keep the individual layers, type this shortcut: Shift>Ctrl>Alt>E (Mac: Shift>Cmd>Opt>E).

In my final example below I have added a Levels, Hue/Saturation, and Brightness/Contrast Adjustment layers and as shown in earlier examples in this chapter, painted out some areas on the Mask.

Cleaning Up Photos with Photomerge Scene Cleaner

Ever try to take photos in a public place where people you don't know end up in your photos? We all have! What would you say if I told you that there's a way that you can quickly edit them out? Obviously you won't do this for all of your photos, but if you have a special photo, or have to do a tutorial in a book, I'll show you the way to do it.

For the best results, use a tripod to take the photos so that you are getting good clean shots that will line up correctly. With that said, I did not take these photos with a tripod. The photos below were taken at Butchart Gardens which is a National Historic Site in Canada. If you have never been there, try to go when it's in full bloom.

I was trying to take a photo of this beautiful fountain, but every time I took a shot someone new walked into the photo. Short of screaming at everyone not to move, and knowing I had to write this tutorial, as shown circled in red, I took several photos with the intruders in them.

The key is to take several photos so that as people move through the photos you will have all the parts for the final photo. When I looked at the photos at home, I realized that I only needed to use two of the photos.

Photomerge Scene Cleaner can be accessed from the Full or Guided Edit in the Editor, or from the Organizer. My example will show starting in Full Edit mode.

To help avoid confusion, open just the photos that will be used to complete this task into the Editor. From the Menu bar, choose File>New>Photomerge Scene Cleaner. A dialog box will open that tells you to select the photos, and then choose Photomerge Scene Cleaner or select Open All. Since you only have the photos open, choose Open All.

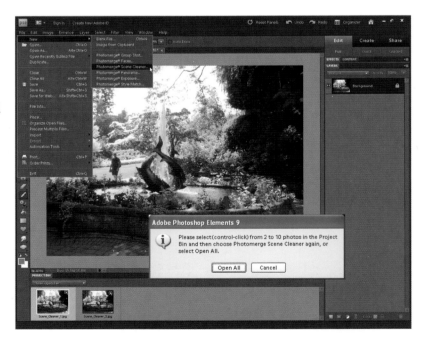

The photos I am using in this tutorial are available for your use on the *Photoshop Elements - Basics & Beyond* DVD. (When you're using this technique on your own photos you can use up to ten photos if you need that many to display clean areas).

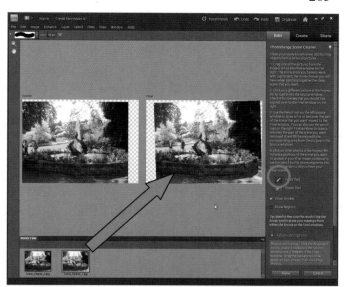

From the Project bin, drag the best photo (Scene_Cleaner_1.jpg) to the Final preview box on the right.

If the Scene_Cleaner_2.jpg photo is not showing in the Source preview box on the left, click on it in the Project bin and it should be placed there.

Because I didn't use a tripod, the photos are different shapes. Don't worry about this; we will crop it when we're done.

There are a couple of different ways you can move the good parts of the Source photo to cover the bad parts of the Final photo. I prefer to click on the Pencil tool on the right of the screen (circled above) and draw over the areas I want to remove on the Final image.

You can also draw over the areas on the Source image that you want to place on the Final document if that makes more sense to you, but that's harder for me.

Zoom or scroll in so that you can see what you are doing. Click and drag over the intruders in the Final photo, they will turn blue (or the color of the outline of the image you're using in the Project bin). Notice on the Source image the area that is being copied also turns blue. If you don't like that, uncheck the Show Strokes box below the Pencil tool.

If you are using more than one photo, click on it to become the new source document and repeat the steps.

Preferably before you click the Done button, zoom in close and check the image in the areas where you made the corrections. My photo shows the fence doesn't line up in the new image, so I had to go back and redo my work.

When you're finished cleaning the image, make any lighting, color, etc. changes. Crop the photo if you are printing it because it won't be a standard photo size.

Photomerge Group Shot

If you can get the knack of using the other Photomerge options, this one is a snap. Trying to take a group shot especially with small children is difficult. In this example I'm going to take the best part of three photos to make a good family photo. As usual, if you use a tripod you will have better luck with this technique.

| Group Shot 1 | Group Shot 2 | Group Shot 3 |

It's helpful to decide in advance which photos you'll use for different people. I actually went through about ten photos taken at the same time and wrote down the names of the people in the photo and the photo that had the best shot of them. I started with ten photos and whittled it down to three. Open the photos. It was helpful for me to arrange the photos in the bin in numerical order and my instructions will make more sense to you if you do this. To do this, click and drag them sideways in the bin.

Photomerge Group Shot can be accessed from the Full or Guided Edit in the Editor or from the Organizer. My example will show starting in Full Edit mode. To help avoid confusion, open just the photos that will be used to complete this task into the Editor. From the Menu bar, choose File>New>Photomerge Group Shot. A dialog box will open that tells you to select the photos and then choose Photomerge Scene Cleaner or select Open All. Click on the Open All button.

When the Photomerge Group Shot Panel opens, drag the Group Shot 2 photo to the Final window. I chose this photo for the final image because it has three out of five smiling faces that I want to keep.

Double click on the Group Shot 1 photo and it will appear in the Source window.

Because the photos are so similar it's difficult to tell which photo is which. If you notice, there is a tiny colored outline around the Source window (blue in my example). Look in the Project bin and the images in the bin are also surrounded by color. My Group Shot 1 outline is blue in the Project bin, but yours may be a different color.

Click on the Pencil tool on the right panel and paint over the face in the Source window that you want to move to the final window. In this example, it's the mom.

Because I'm working with the blue outlined photo, the Pencil tool paints blue. As soon as I let go of the mouse, the new face is painted into the final Window.

Double click on Group Shot 3. The mom's face will show covered in blue, that's OK. Click on the pencil tool and drag/paint over the baby's face. Because the image is outlined in green, the pencil tool will paint in green.

Click the Done button when you are happy with the results.

The new merged image will appear in the Project bin, it will probably need to be cropped.

If a new image does not appear in the Project bin, restart Photoshop Elements and try it again…don't ask me how I know this works!

Fixing Blurry Photos

There's a common misconception that if you take a blurry photo you can just pop it into Photoshop Elements and sharpen it into a great photo. You can do a lot to improve them, but if they're really blurry you'll never end up with a perfect photo.

After you're done adjusting the lighting, color, contrast, etc. it's time to sharpen the photo. Several things you can try from the Enhance menu are Auto Sharpen, Unsharp Mask, and Adjust Sharpness. If they don't work to your satisfaction, try this trick.

Open the Blurry image from the *Photoshop Elements - Basics & Beyond* DVD. From the Menu bar, choose Layer>New>Layer via Copy or type the shortcut Ctrl>J (Mac: Cmd>J) to duplicate the layer. From the Menu bar, choose Filter>Other>High Pass. In the High Pass dialog box, click in the preview window until you see an important detail, it will turn to color when you click on it. Slide the Radius slider until you are happy with the sharpening.

In my example I used 15 pixels but this is a pretty blurry photo. Click OK; the new layer will be gray. Cycle through the blending modes until you find an effect you like. In my example I chose Hard Light (circled above). If the effect is too intense, adjust the opacity too.

Creating a Montage

One of the effects my students want to create the most is a Montage. You can apply this technique to a scrapbook page or to just a single photo. Basically, you will blend two or more images (photos or digital scrapbooking papers) together to create this effect.

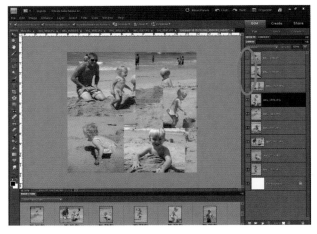

Open the photos to be used in the project. It's helpful if they have similar backgrounds like sand, water, or grass. If you're a big fan of this technique, you will find yourself taking pictures of sand or water to help fill in areas on your projects.

Create a New Blank File in the size of your choice as illustrated in the *How to Use* chapter. Select the Move tool (V) and drag the images onto the new page. As shown in the example, arrange them on the page so that they are overlapping.

I have added several extra photos to my page that I may not use, so I hide them by clicking on the eyeball icon next to the Layer thumbnail (circled).

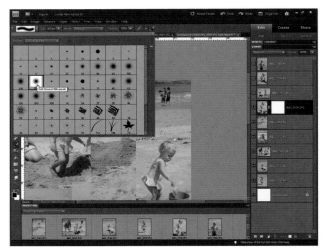

Start with the top visible layer and add a Mask to the layer by clicking on the Add a Layer Mask icon at the bottom of the Layers Panel.

Type the letter D to set your Foreground and Background colors located at the bottom of the Toolbar to the default settings. Your Foreground color should be black, and your Background color should be white.

Select the Brush tool (B) from the Toolbar. From the brush drop down list on the Options bar, choose a soft round brush. In my example I am using the 300 px Soft Round Brush.

Click inside the Layer Mask, and then click on the photo to begin painting/masking away the areas you don't want to show. If you paint away too much of an image, type X to switch the Foreground color to white and paint back in the area.

Follow the same steps for each layer. Lowering the Opacity temporarily to see the layers below may be helpful. As you reveal pieces of the white Background layer, add more photos, or in my example I can add a photo of sand on the bottom layer to fill in the white areas.

While the page is busy, it relays the feeling of a young uncle trying to keep track of two very active toddlers at the beach.

Save the page as it is, or add grunge overlays or digital papers to complete the page. In my example below, I have used several grunge edges from the Essentials #1 kit and three papers from the Funtime paper kit available at *www.TheDigitalScrapbookTeacher.com*. I have adjusted the blending modes and opacities of each layer.

To see how to add the titles behind the people, be sure to read the *Cool Stuff with Type* chapter.

Changing the Color of a Shirt

Do the people in your photos wear the right color clothes to coordinate with the other photos in your projects? If not, it's fairly easy to change the color of a shirt or some other article of clothing. If you have a picture of someone in a red shirt standing against a white wall, it's easy to change the shirt color. If you have a photo of a person in a red shirt standing against a red wall, it's not so easy.

To try this out, open the Teeth_Whitening image from the *Photoshop Elements - Basics & Beyond* DVD.

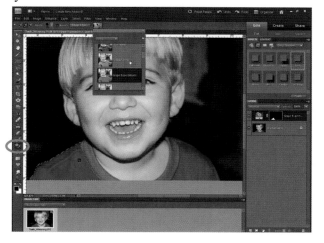

Select the Smart Brush tool (F) from the Toolbar (circled). From the Options bar, choose Color and choose a color. I chose Grape Expectations (where do they come up with these names).

Click on the red area of the shirt and it will change to purple. In my example, the purple did not fill all of the red areas. To fix this you can try clicking again or you can click on the Refine Edge button on the Options bar.

Chose to Smooth, Feather, or Contract/Expand (we don't want to Contract) the selection and click OK.

To clean up the edges I will usually use the Smart Brush tool first, and then switch to the Detail Smart Brush tool.

In the past I have used the Color Replacement tool (B), but have found that the Smart Brush & Detail Smart Brush tools work better. If you want to try the Color Replacement tool, I would suggest making a selection of the area you want to change first. Choose the replacement color as the Foreground color. Make your brush very large and without releasing the mouse paint over the area until the color change is done.

Removing/Adding Someone from/to a Photo

A question often asked in classes is how to remove an ex from a photo. If you haven't read the *Cool Stuff with Photo-Cosmetic Surgery* chapter, you may just want to skip ahead to find the perfect fix there. I show you how to use the Liquify filter to turn them into the real monster they were. If that's not socially acceptable in your circle, there are several other things you can try.

I love this photo of my son, but there are a lot of things wrong with it, including the pole growing out of his neck and the unknown people milling around. I can remove some of the pole and people by simply cropping the photo.

If I had taken more photos at the time, I could use the Photomerge Scene Cleaner feature that we used in an earlier tutorial to remove people around the fountain.

Cloning a person out using a wall is much easier than if the person is in the middle of a large group of people. In the family photo situation what are you going to cover them up with?

Open the Remove_Someone image from the *Photoshop Elements - Basics & Beyond* DVD. Select the Clone Stamp tool (S) from the Toolbar and Alt click (Mac: Opt click) on an area of the brick wall near the man in the yellow hat to sample/copy the wall. Click, or click and drag on the man to paste the copied brick wall and cover him up. Continue by sampling the grass and then the concrete to completly remove the man and the pieces of the other people. You can see that this is a very time consuming process.

Sometimes it's easier to cover one person up with another. Open the photo Brotherly_Love from the *Photoshop Elements - Basics & Beyond* DVD. Use the Move tool (V) to drag it on top of the Remove_Someone photo.

Lower the Opacity of the Brotherly_Love photo to help you position and resize the photo correctly (circled below). Change the Opacity back to 100%. Add a Layer Mask by clicking on the icon at the bottom of the Layers panel.

Type the letter D to set your Foreground and Background colors located at the bottom of the Toolbar to the default settings. Your Foreground color should be black, and your Background color should be white.

Select the Brush tool (B) from the Toolbar. From the brush drop down list on the Options bar choose a soft round brush. In my example I am using the 300 px Soft Round Brush in the beginning but change to smaller brush at times.

Click in the Mask thumbnail and begin painting away areas of the top photo. To paint areas back that were removed in error (like his foot), switch the Foreground color to white. Use your artistic talents to help paint back in the grass and concrete areas. Add drop shadows as required.

Cool Stuff with Photos – Cosmetic Surgery

Who doesn't have a photo where they wished they looked younger, thinner, etc., etc.? Let's face it, how many photos of yourself have you ever been 100% happy with. When I first proposed teaching a class with cosmetic fixes at a scrapbook convention I was turned down because they didn't think there would be much interest in it. After finally convincing them to try it, it became one of the most popular classes of the show.

With a little bit of editing we can look great in our photos, and if you don't have time to fix the other people in the photo…oh well!

Remember to always work on a duplicate copy of your photos, I can't stress this enough! I also suggest working on a duplicate layer on cosmetic edits for a couple of reasons: First, if you don't like the changes, you can easily delete the layer instead of Undoing all of your steps. Second, sometimes I make the top layer perfect, (no wrinkles, etc.) but in reality no one's face is perfect. By lowering the opacity on the perfect layer, it will show through to the original layer and provide a more realistic photo.

To duplicate a layer, from the Menu bar, choose Layer>New>Layer via Copy or type the shortcut Ctrl>J (Mac: Cmd>J). Make all of the edits on the top layer. To see your original unedited photo, click on the eyeball icon (circled) to temporarily hide the top copy layer (Layer 1). Click on the empty box to display the top layer and eyeball icon again.

Removing Pimples, Moles, Scars, and Owies

The Spot Healing Brush tool works great for removing small imperfections like the owie on my granddaughter's nose. Open the Owie photo which can be found on the *Photoshop Elements - Basics & Beyond* DVD. I have reset the tool to show the default settings. To reset your tool if you've already used it, click on the ▼ at the beginning of the Spot Healing Brush's Option bar and choose Reset tool.

Zoom into the owie on her nose using the Scroll wheel on your mouse or the Move tool (V).

Activate the Spot Healing Brush tool (J) by clicking on the band-aid icon on the Toolbar.

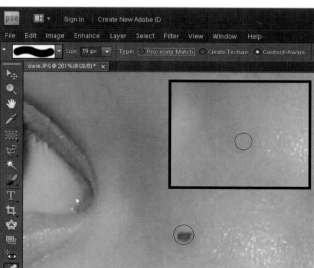

Click on the red spot with your mouse and the spot disappears.

Undo if you're not happy, and this time click in the Create Texture option on the Options bar.

Adjusting the size of the brush can also be helpful. The easiest way to make a brush larger is to tap your Right Bracket key], to make it smaller, use the Left Bracket key [. The brush should be about 10% larger than the size of the blemish to do a good job.

There is another way to fix this that I will show you in the Wrinkles section.

Red Eye

Photoshop Elements has a built in red eye remover, but it doesn't always do a very good job as you can see by my examples. My baby grandson (two photos I put together to save space) looks like he's already been in a brawl, while the effect on my granddaughter's ear looks more like she played with a black marker.

When my daughter emailed the photos of my grandson to me to use in class, my husband happened to glance over to see what I was doing. He came over and started asking me questions, amazed at my Photoshop Elements skills. I was confused because I hadn't done anything; I was just flipping back and forth between the two photos. It seems he thought that I started with the photo of the baby in the green shirt and undressed him digitally. I laugh every time I think of this, as do my students when I tell them about it in class! If you know any one that teaches this type of skill let me know and I'll sign up immediately!

The black marks appear because my daughter had the Automatically Fix Red eye "feature" turned on in her Organizer (Edit>Preferences>Camera or Card Reader>Automatically Fix Red Eyes). I suggest you turn it off.

 Open the Red Eye photo which can be found on the *Photoshop Elements - Basics & Beyond* DVD. Duplicate the layer (Ctrl>J, Mac: Cmd>J). Activate the Red Eye (Y) tool by clicking on the icon on the Toolbar.

On the Red Eye tool Option bar is a button for Auto red eye fix, click it, or you can choose Enhance>Auto Red Eye Fix (Ctrl>R, Mac: Cmd>R). Do the red eyes disappear on both people? I've used this photo in classes for the past year and I know from experience that different people get different results.

If all of the red eyes did not fix, try these two things: Use your mouse to click directly on each red eye. If clicking doesn't work, clicking and dragging a box around the eye will sometimes work.

If your results are not what you want, and there is still red showing, or the eye is too dark, as shown below adjust the Pupil Size and Darken amount on the Options bar. If you make changes to the Options bar remember to reset the tool, because the next time you use it, the Red Eye tool won't work the way you will expect it to.

Toggle the top layer off to see your original photo below to make sure you are happy with your results.

The Red Eye tool will not correct pet eye, but it will sometimes remove a red date marker that some people have on their photos because they don't know how to turn off that camera option.

When is Red Eye not really Red Eye? In some instances, the presence of a golden/white glow reflected by a camera flash, in a child's eye indicates Coats' disease or Retinoblastoma (an eye cancer). My niece was diagnosed with Retinoblastoma when she was just six months old. For more information see *www.KnowTheGlow.com.*

Whiten Teeth

There are several ways to whiten teeth with Photoshop Elements. Open the Teeth_Whitening photo which can be found on the *Photoshop Elements - Basics & Beyond* DVD.

Open Quick Edit (Quick Fix). Click on the Whiten Teeth icon which looks like a toothbrush. The same option can be found on the Smart Brush tool or Detail Smart Brush tool in Full Edit.

Click on the teeth, a selection border should surround the teeth. The problem I have with this tool is that most of his tongue ends up being selected and I don't want to lighten his tongue too. I don't have much luck with this tool, so I don't use it. Undo if you have done this, because this tool automatically adds an Adjustment layer that we don't need.

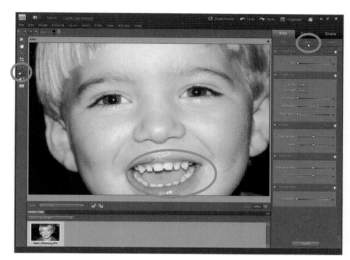

If I only want to lighten the teeth, I will normally choose the Dodge tool (O).

The Dodge tool is nested with the Sponge and Burn tools, so it may not be displayed on your Toolbar. To activate the Dodge tool, click on the black triangle on the lower right corner of the tool to display all three tools. Click on the Dodge tool.

Duplicate the layer (Ctrl>J, Mac: Cmd>J). I decreased the size of my brush to about 20 pixels from the default setting of 65 pixels. The brush should be slightly smaller than a tooth.

On the top layer, click and scrub over the teeth and you will see them whiten. Any area you scrub over will also lighten, so you need to pay attention to what you're doing.

A more precise way to whiten his teeth would be to make a selection around his teeth using the Magic Wand tool (W). To do this, select the Magic Wand tool on the Toolbar. I am using the default tool settings on the Magic Wand Option bar which are: Tolerance 32, Anti Alias-checked, Contiguous-checked.

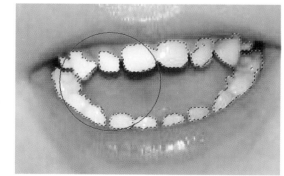

Click on each tooth and only the white area should be selected, however you can only select one tooth at a time with the current default settings. Click on the Add to Selection button on the Options bar shown circled below to enable you to select all of the teeth. If you select part of his mouth, Undo or click on the next button, which is Subtract from Selection. Be sure to click on the white area of the teeth only.

Select the Dodge tool again and scrub over the teeth. Because you are working on a selection, only the selected areas will be whitened. As shown in my example you can use a larger brush to work faster. In my example, I have over whitened the teeth on the left so that it's easier for you to see. Make your teeth look realistic. You can also use the Dodge tool to whiten the white areas in eyes.

To remove the selection border (marching ants), from the Menu bar, choose Select>Deselect (Ctrl>D, Mac: Cmd>D), or tap the Esc key which will work for most people.

Lose Weight with a Click of Your Mouse

Photoshop Elements makes it easy to instantly lose weight. Open the The_Works photo which can be found on the *Photoshop Elements - Basics & Beyond* DVD. This photo was taken for an article about my husband for a local magazine. I was in a hurry, crabby, and didn't really want my photo taken that day. There are a lot of problems with the photo, including the lack of an earring in one of my ears (you'll fix that later) and the nice tree branch behind us. One photography tip I've since learned is that when taking a photo of a couple, their hair should touch, which would have made this photo a lot better to begin with.

Select Guided Edit.

To compare the changes you will make on the photo click on the View drop down list above the Project bin and choose Before & After-Horizontal.

Click on Action Player and follow the numbered steps.

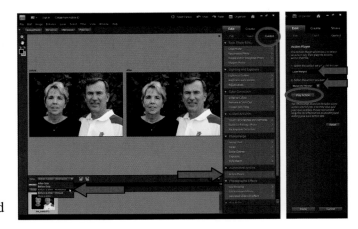

1. From the Action Player drop down list, choose Lose Weight.

2. There are two choices here: 2% thinner or 4% thinner…can you believe it? Further proof that the Adobe staff must be young and male. Have you ever said to yourself: "Oh, gee, I need to lose 2% of my weight"? Of course not!

Click Play Action and we'll lose 4% of our weight (I knew you wouldn't choose the 2% option!). Once you click the Play Action button, you will not notice that the sides of the photo moved in. Basically, you are making the photo taller which makes us look thinner.

From the left: Original, 2% thinner, 4% thinner, 4% thinner ten times (do you think anyone will notice?)

If you were going to add this photo to a scrapbook page or other project, don't follow the instructions above. To make this change manually, drag the photo onto your project (a plain white background is shown in the example on the right). Choose the Move tool (V), and click on a side sizing handle to activate the Transform command (Ctrl>T, Mac:Cmd>T). Uncheck the Constrain Proportions box on the Options bar, and click and drag inward to become thinner. Note: reducing the width (circled) of the photo more than 5% (95% or lower), is going to produce obvious results but as more than one student has said "If I look thinner, who cares?".

The Lose Weight action resizes the image. To resize the image yourself from the Menu Bar, choose Image>Resize>Image Size. Check the Resample Image box and uncheck Constrain Proportions.

In the width box, change inches to percent.

Change the Width number to 96 and we will be 4% (100 -4 percent thinner = 96%) thinner. Do not change the Height box.

After you are done trying this technique, put the checkmark back in the Constrain Proportions box.

At about this point in class someone raises their hand and asks "What if you only want one of the people in the photo to lose weight?" It's bad enough that I put my own photo out there for these types of fixes, but when I get that kind of question, it really makes me question my sanity!

The short answer is that you could make a selection around my husband using a tool like the Magnetic Lasso tool (L). Choose Ctrl>J (Mac: Cmd>J) to put the selection on its own layer. Apply the Lose Weight fixes to the Background layer. Move my husband closer to me and add a little bit more greenery to fill in areas behind us.

If you'll be printing a photo with any method you use to lose weight, be sure to crop the photo when you're done into a standard photo size. If you drag the edited photo onto a project, the final size of the skinny photo won't matter.

Liposuction

Better than just plain old losing weight, you can spot reduce with Photoshop Elements. Not only can you reduce areas, you can also enlarge areas….like biceps…what were you thinking? Why have plastic surgery when you can fix all of your flaws digitally?

Before you practice on a photo of me, I'll have you practice on a walrus. Open the Walrus photo which can be found on the *Photoshop Elements - Basics & Beyond* DVD.

From the Menu bar, choose Filter>Distort>Liquify. Once the Liquify dialog box opens, choose Pucker from the Toolbar on the left.

Enlarge the view of the walrus by choosing 100% from the drop down list on the bottom left corner (arrow).

To move around and see different areas of the photo, hold your Spacebar instead of choosing the Hand tool from the Toolbar to save time.

Also, as you are making changes, use the Reconstruct tool on the Toolbar to fix spot areas instead of using the Reset button.

In this example, my Brush Size is 64 and the Brush Pressure is 50 (circled).

To begin the procedure on the walrus, click your brush on the top portion of his back, away from the blue door. Click, hold, and drag inward to instantly slim the walrus. Work on your stroke to soften the effect so there aren't any telltale bulges.

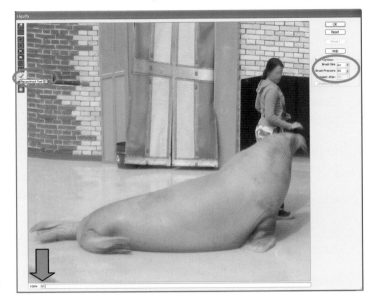

Continue working towards his tail. As you work in his stomach area, drag your cursor up to tuck in his belly. Watching the trainer's foot work around the walrus' chest. When wowrking around his head, also watch for changes you may be making to the trainer. The toughest area to suction is on the back area of his neck where the wall and door may get distorted. To work in areas like these, reducing the brush size may help.

After you've mastered smoothing out the walrus, slim down the seal in the same photo. Next, open the photo Chin which can be found on the *Photoshop Elements - Basics & Beyond* DVD.

Follow the same steps used for the walrus photo. Sucking in my chin near the black shirt is no problem, but be careful when you get near the baby's face, because you will end up distorting her face too.

Pump It Up!

Instead of suctioning out fat with the Pucker tool, you can pump up areas with the Liquify Filter's Bloat tool. From the Menu bar, choose Filter>Distort>Liquify. Click on the Bloat tool icon and click and drag over any areas you wish to enlarge like the male, seal trainer's biceps. Suddenly our male seal trainer, who also appears in the photo with the female walrus trainer turns into Mr. Weight Lifter.

More Fun With the Liquify Filters

It happened quite innocently in class one day…honestly. We were working on the teeth whitening example and a student asked a question about how to fix a broken tooth. Explaining that there are several ways to fix a broken tooth, I proceeded to show her how to use the Warp tool. After that, the class had the time of their lives at the expense of my grandson…and then my daughter walked into class to bring me lunch…oops! After the weekend was over she said to me "Mom is that the stuff you do in class with pictures of my kids?" Well…no, not normally, but sometimes stuff just happens.

Imagine that your kids were not the angels that they normally are 364 days a year. The idea of creating a page that says something like:"Little Johnny was a real monster today" appeals to you. This would be a great photo to add to the page.

Another thought always comes to mind when I'm constantly asked how to remove someone from a photo. While you can remove someone from a photo, remember that you need to fill that area with something else. Instead of spending the time removing an ex from a photo, why not Warp them instead?

Open the Teeth_Whitening photo which can be found on the *Photoshop Elements - Basics & Beyond* DVD.

From the Menu bar, choose Filter>Distort>Liquify. Click on the Warp tool icon and click and drag over the areas to warp. Resize the brush with the Bracket keys to the width of a tooth and click and drag the tooth to create fangs.

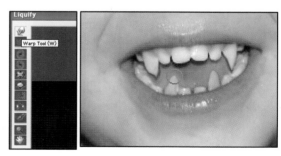

Enlarge the brush and pull up eyebrows or drag on the ears.

Remember to use the Reconstruct tool (red arrow) to paint/drag over areas to undo your changes instead of tapping the Cancel or Revert buttons to Undo all of your changes.

Change your view to 100% (circled) or more so that you can see what you're doing.

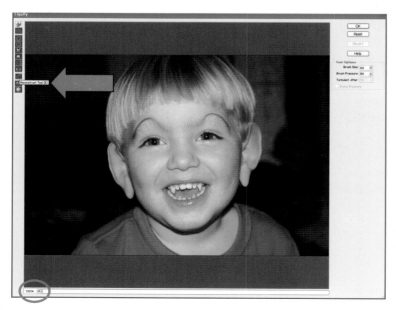

Wrinkles

Got wrinkles? I do! We'll use The_Works photo that we worked on in the Lose Weight tutorial to remove my wrinkles.

Zoom or scroll in close to see my wrinkles in all their glory. We used the Spot Healing Brush tool (J) to remove an owie earlier, but if we try to use it now, we quickly find out that all it does is paste new wrinkles on top of my existing wrinkles, which doesn't look too good!

Choose the Healing Brush tool instead of the Spot Healing Brush tool from the Toolbar.

From the Menu bar, choose Layer>New>Layer via Copy or type the shortcut Ctrl>J (Mac: Cmd>J) to duplicate the layer. We'll make all of the changes on the top layer for two reasons: first, if we don't like the changes, we can easily delete the layer, second, we'll make the top layer "perfect" and then adjust the opacity so that the "perfect" layer blends to the "real me" layer below, creating a more realistic effect.

The difference with the Healing Brush tool is that you tell Photoshop Elements the area you want to copy from. To do this you must Alt click (Mac: Opt click) on a good (unwrinkled) area of skin and then click on a bad (wrinkled) area to cover it up. If you forget and just click, you'll receive this warning.

Sample an area of unwrinkled skin (look hard) by Alt clicking (Mac: Opt clicking) on it and then click on an area with wrinkles. The wrinkles will be covered with the sampled skin. You may click, or click and drag, depending on whichever method gives you better results.

In the example on the right, the + indicates the sampled area, and the ◯ is the brush that is pasting the sampled area onto the layer.

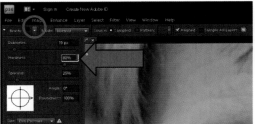

To soften the brush, click on the brush drop down list (circled) on the Healing Brush Options bar and lower the hardness of the brush. In my example above, the hardness of my brush is 80% and I am using a 19 px brush.

Once the top layer is "perfect" and free of wrinkles, lower the Opacity slider to allow some of the original layer to show through.

"Real Me" Top Layer Opacity 0%   "Perfect" Me Top Layer Opacity 100%   "Perfect" Me Top Layer Opacity 70%

Adding Something to a Photo

In The_Works photo I am missing an earring because I took it out while talking on the phone and forgot to put it back on for the photo. It's easy to add the missing earring with the Healing Brush tool that we used in the preceding example to fix my wrinkles.

Reset the Healing Brush tool.

For the best results, create a new transparent layer by clicking on the New Layer icon at the bottom of the Layers panel. I renamed this layer "New Earring Layer" by double clicking on the layer name and typing in the new name.

Select the Background layer.

Hover the brush over the earring and adjust the size so that the brush just covers the earring. I chose a 28 px brush and adjusted the brush hardness to 70% (see wrinkles example).

Alt click (Mac: Opt click) on the earring to copy it. Select the New Earring Layer. Click to paste the earring on the layer all by itself. To make sure the earring is on the right layer, click on the eyeball icon on the New Earring Layer and it should disappear. If you pasted the earring on the wrong layer, Undo, and repeat the steps. To fine tune the earring, add a mask and paint away any unwanted areas with the Brush tool.

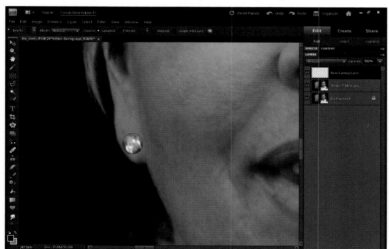

Using the same technique, make a new transparent layer and name it leaves. Sample some of the leaves and paste them onto this layer to cover up the bare tree branches.

Pet Eye

Unfortunately, there is no Pet Eye tool in Photoshop Elements. I have tried various techniques on different photos without a whole lot of luck. Sometimes I revert to copying a good eye from another photo of the animal and paste it over the bad eye with the Healing Brush tool like we did with my earring in the preceding lesson.

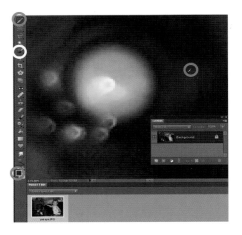

If the Healing Brush method won't work, I've found that sometimes adding color to the eye will work, providing that the eye isn't totally blown out. Open the Pet_Eye photo which can be found on the *Photoshop Elements - Basics & Beyond* DVD.

Zoom or scroll in close to the eye. Activate the Eyedropper tool (I) to copy the color the eye should be; this may be from another photo of the animal. In this example I don't have another photo of this dog, so I chose some of the dark brown color near his eye. Click in the brown area with your cursor, which now looks like an eyedropper, and your Foreground color chip at the bottom of the Toolbar will change to dark brown.

Activate the Selection Brush tool (A) on the Toolbar (shown circled in white above). Change the brush size to 53, the Mode to Selection, and the Hardness to 70%. The brush size I've chosen is the size of the eye. The hardness is the softness around the edges. I tried several settings until I found one that worked.

Click on the eye and you will have a round selection (marching ants). If you have the selection in the wrong place, Select>Deselect (Ctrl>D, Mac: Cmd>D). It's important that the selection cover the bad part of the eye.

From the Menu bar, choose Layer>New>Layer via Copy or type the shortcut Ctrl>J (Mac: Cmd>J). From the Menu bar, choose Enhance>Adjust Color>Remove color (Shift>Ctrl>U, Mac: Shift>Cmd>U). The eye on its own layer will now be black and white. Type the shortcut Ctrl>J (Mac: Cmd>J) to duplicate the eye layer.

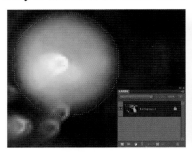
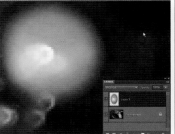

Shift>Alt>Backspace (Mac: Shift>Opt>Delete) to fill the top layer with the brown Foreground color. If your entire image filled with dark brown, you forgot to add the Shift key when typing the shortcut. On the top brown fill layer, change the blending mode to Overlay. On the brown fill eye, adjust the Opacity by sliding the slider to about 30%. Change the blending mode to Screen. If it makes it easier to see what you're doing, turn off the Background layer so that only the eyeball is visible.

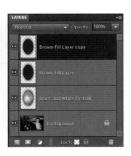
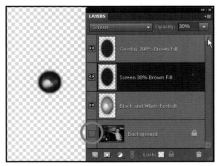

Cool Stuff with Text

Adding text to photos, scrapbook pages, and other projects tells a story and can add documentation or humor to your projects. The text can be the focal point of the page, or it can be artistically added so that it becomes part of the design.

If you are creating a scrapbook page think about who will be looking at the page. Will they understand what's happening on the page, or will you need to explain it? If you are creating your pages to preserve memories, you better write the stories on the pages, because I can tell you from experience you'll forget what was happening! If you are creating a brochure, are you answering questions about the product or service you are advertising?

The Type tool (T) makes it easy to add text to your pages. To learn about Type tool specifics, be sure to read all about it in the *Tools* chapter.

What the Font?

Ever see a scrapbook page online and like the font but have no idea what it is? It drives me crazy when online galleries require that you list the source of your digital supplies, but not the names of the fonts that were used on the page.

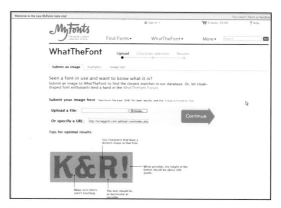

To search for the font, you will need a copy of the image. If you're not sure how to copy the image, see the *Techie Stuff* chapter. Go to *www.WhatTheFont.com*.

Instead of uploading the entire image, I cropped off the rest of the page and chose to only upload the portion on the right.

Once you click the continue button, you will need to tell the program which character each letter is. As shown below, type the character in the box below the preview. Sometimes it will list several characters together and sometimes it will divide the characters in half. If the characters are divided in half, follow the instructions on the side panel. Once you have entered the characters, click the Continue button and a list of possible matches will be displayed. Click on the match to find out where you can conveniently purchase or download the font.

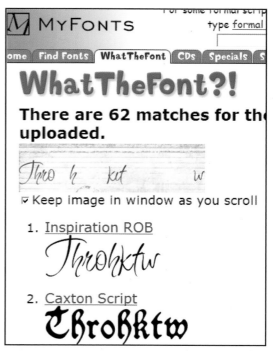

In my example, the Inspiration ROB font can be purchased at *www.MyFonts.com*.

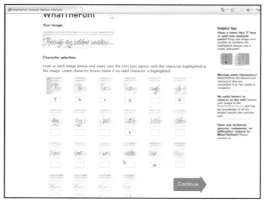

Personalized Fonts

Traditional scrapbookers will sometimes tell me that digital scrapbooking isn't "real" because the journaling on the pages is done on the computer. I personally don't agree with this statement. My children have many pages in their traditional scrapbooks that have no journaling on them because I was going to do the journaling later, when my handwriting was neater and my hand wasn't tired.

With Photoshop Elements, I can add journaling in different fonts to add to the theme of my page. If I want my pages to have my handwriting on them, I can have my handwriting made into a font. To have a font made for you, type "personalized font" into your favorite search program like Google.com and choose a service. Download and fill in a template sheet provided by the service. Take your time completing the template, if you write your letters on the template sloppy, your font will be sloppy. Scan the completed template sheet, and upload it to the font provider through their website. Preview the completed font and if you like it pay for it. Once you pay for the font download it and install it in your computer.

Realistic Looking Text

The example below is text I added to the template in the *How to Use a Layered Template* tutorial. The ribbon is from the Kelly Jo Scraps Snips N Snails kit.

On the top example, I clicked on the page and added the text normally. In the lower example, I added the text the same exact way, but I changed the Blending Mode to Overlay after I committed the text. The text now appears that it is actually part of the ribbon instead of floating above it, and the text color is lighter. Try different Blending Modes on your text to see which ones you like better. The Blending Modes I use most often for type are Multiply and Overlay.

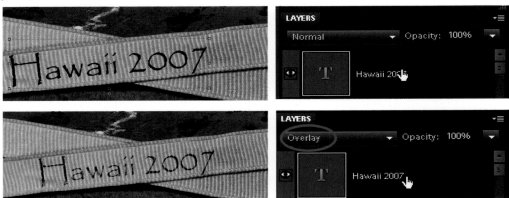

Letter, Number, or Punctuation Templates

Use a number template and include photos of your subject at that age. Fill a letter template like the letter Z with photos of a recent visit to the zoo. Fill punctuation templates like question marks or exclamation points with photos that display those emotions.

Use the included text path to add journaling around the template piece.

The number template shown in the example is available for purchase at: *www.TheDigitalScrapbookTeacher.com* and includes 40 different templates and text paths. Photos by Madeline Arenas, Cubrix Photography.

To complete a letter or number template, follow the *How to Use a Layered Template* and *How to Use a Text Path* in the *How to Use* chapter.

Font Doesn't Look Right?

I really like the Scriptina font, but a lot of times the words it types are not spaced out well with the swirly letters. As shown in my example on the right, there is a large space in between the two t's in Patty. To fix this problem I have typed Pat on one layer and ty on another layer. As shown in my example, after I committed the text I moved them together with the Move tool (V). It would probably look even better if I typed the letter y on its own layer using the same steps above.

Adding Perspective to Text

Type the text onto the image. From the Toolbar, choose the Move tool (V) and move the text close to where you want it.

Hover over a corner sizing handle until a two headed rounded arrow cursor appears and click (or type Ctrl>T, Mac: Cmd>T). Drag to rotate the type as shown in the example below on the left.

Hold the Ctrl key (Mac: Cmd key) and drag the sizing boxes to distort the type until you're happy with the results.

To confirm the transformation (resizing), check the green checkmark ✓.

Adding a Custom Drop Shadow to Text

As shown in my example, this technique works better with thick fonts like Impact.

Type the text. From the Menu bar, choose Layer>New>Layer via Copy or type the shortcut Ctrl>J (Mac: Cmd>J). Change the color of the text on the bottom layer to black.

From the Toolbar, choose the Move tool (V). Hover over a corner sizing handle until a two headed rounded arrow cursor appears and click (or type Ctrl>T, Mac: Cmd>T). Hold the Ctrl key (Mac: Cmd key) and drag the sizing boxes to distort the type until you're happy with the results.

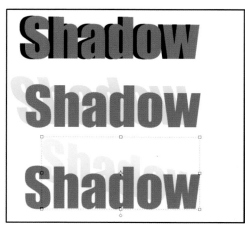

If desired, lower the opacity of the bottom shadow layer. To soften the edges of the shadow, choose Filter>Blur>Gaussian Blur. A dialog box will appear that says the layer must be simplified and will no longer be editable, click OK. Increase the Gaussian Blur Radius amount for a softer edge.

Cutting a Photo or Scrapbook Paper Out of a Word

Because we take so many photos, we want to use as many as possible in our projects. One cool way to use a photo is to cut it in the shape of words or the title you will use on the page. As usual, there are several techniques that can be used to accomplish this task; I'll show you three of them. As shown in my examples, this technique works better with thick fonts like Impact. I have listed my favorite method last.

Make a new blank file in the correct size for your project, as shown in the *How to Use* chapter. Open the photo you wish to use to cut out the title. I am using the Filter_Waikiki photo which can be found on the *Photoshop Elements - Basics & Beyond* DVD.

Horizontal Type Mask Tool (T) Method
I don't ever use this method, but some people love it, which is the reason I'm including the tutorial in my book. Select the Horizontal Type Mask tool from the Toolbar. Click on the photo. The cursor will turn into a flashing I beam (normal when starting to type something), and the entire photo will turn red. Type the text. As you type, the letters will reveal the photo; the surrounding area will remain red.

To reposition the text, move away from the text and the cursor will change to the Move tool cursor. Click and drag the text to a new location on the photo. As soon as you let go of the mouse, the red will be removed from the photo and the letters will be surrounded by a selection border (marching ants).

If you don't need to reposition the text, click on the green checkmark ✓ on the Options bar. The letters will now be surrounded by a selection border (marching ants).

Select the Move tool (V) from the Toolbar. Click inside the selection border surrounding the text. Click, hold, and drag the letters down to the new blank file in the Project bin. The photo title will be added to the page on its own layer. Now, change the Horizontal Type Mask tool back to the Horizontal Type tool so that you don't freak out when you're trying to add regular text in the future.

Selected Text Method
Make a new blank file. Type the text (text color does not matter) and reposition it as desired (left example below). Drag the photo onto the page with the Move tool (V) (second from the left example below). Reposition the photo so that it covers up the text (second from the right example below).

Select the Text layer in the Layers panel. Ctrl click (Mac: Cmd click) in the Layer thumbnail (circled below), a selection border will be added around the shape of the text (second from right example below). From the Menu bar, choose Select>Inverse (right example below).

Tap the Delete key. To remove the selection border (marching ants), from the Menu bar choose Select>Deselect (Ctrl>D, Mac: Cmd>D), or tap the Esc key which will work for most people. The photo will be cut into the shape of the text, as shown in the example on the right. Hide or delete the Text layer.

Clipping Mask Method
I think that this is the best method for two reasons: first, you can edit the text if required. In my examples I've used the Impact font in all caps. If I change my mind and want to use a different font, or change to lower case letters, I won't need to start over. Second, I can easily adjust the part of the photo that shows in the text.

This example will exactly follow the same three steps as in the preceding tutorial. See those screenshots if necessary. Make a new blank file. Type the text and reposition it as desired. Drag the photo onto the page with the Move tool (V). Reposition the photo so that it covers up the text.

Select the photo layer in the Layers panel as shown below. From the Menu bar, choose Layer>Create Clipping Mask (Ctrl>G, Mac: Cmd>G). The photo has been cut into the shape of the text.

To reposition the areas of the photo that show, select the Move tool (V) from the Toolbar, and click and drag the layer. To edit the text, double click on the Text layer thumbnail to select the text and make your changes, as shown in the example below on the right.

In this example, I used a piece of scrapbook paper instead of a photo. The paper can be found on the *Photoshop Elements - Basics & Beyond* DVD in The Digital Scrapbook Teacher's folder. I also added a stroke around the edge of the letters, as shown in the *Cool Stuff with Strokes* chapter.

Embossing Words
If you would like a more subtle effect, you can emboss words in your photo or scrapbook paper. To do this, open a photo, type the text (text color does not matter), and reposition it as desired (left example below).

Select the photo layer in the Layers panel. From the Menu bar, choose Layer>New>Layer via Copy or type the shortcut Ctrl>J (Mac: Cmd>J). Drag the photo layer up above the text layer; you will no longer see the text layer.

From the Menu bar, choose Layer>Create Clipping Mask (Ctrl>G Mac: Cmd>G). You won't notice any obvious changes, other than that the layer in the Layers panel has stepped in and there is a small bent arrow pointing down to the photo layer.

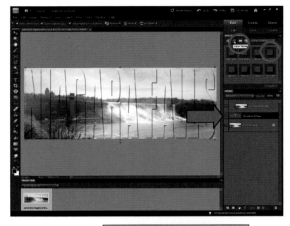

Click on the text layer and add a Low Drop Shadow Layer Style from the Effects panel. The text is softly displayed within the photo.

Try out different Layer styles to create different effects. In the example below, I removed the Low Drop Shadow. From the Layer Styles Options on the Effects panel I added: High Inner Shadow, Simple Inner Glow, and Simple Outer Glow.

I added a Simple Outer Bevel, but the effect was more than what I wanted. To adjust it, I double clicked on the *fx* symbol on the layer. I changed the Bevel Size to 1 px and changed the direction from Up to Down, as shown circled on the right.

Talk Bubble

Adding a talk bubble allows you to add some journaling or documentation and sometimes some humor to a photo or project.

Select the Custom Shape tool (U) from the Toolbar. On the Custom Shape tool Options bar, click the drop down list and choose a talk bubble. If your shapes do not look like mine in the example below, read the *First Things First* chapter.

Double click on one of the talk bubbles to select the shape and close the drop down list at the same time.

Click the color drop down list and a swatch of colors will be displayed. Click in a color to select it, I selected white.

Click and drag out a talk bubble. Once you let go of your mouse, the filled in shape will appear as will a new Shape layer in the Layers panel. If the shape is not in the correct position, use the Move tool (V) to move it.

In my example, I would like to move the talk bubble in front of her and flip it. To do this, choose Image>Rotate>Flip **Layer** Horizontal.

Use the Move tool to move the talk bubble in place. Don't tilt or rotate it yet.

From the Toolbar, select the Type tool. Choose left align text, a font, font size and color from the Type tool Options bar. The type color must be a different color than your talk bubble. Click, hold and drag out a text box inside the talk bubble. Type the text.

A new Text layer has been added to the Layers panel. Adjust the size of the font and leading to fill the text box. If you overfill the text box, a + will appear in the bottom right corner sizing box. To confirm the text, check the green checkmark ✓on the Type tool Options bar (circled).

If required use the Move tool to move the text. When the Move tool is active, you will have a bounding box around your type, which is OK.

If you need to move or tilt your text and talk bubble, it will be easier to move them together. To move them both together, select both layers or link them. To link layers, select both layers in the Layers panel and click on the link symbol at the bottom of the Layers panel.

Multi-Colored Text

While I don't do it often, occasionally I will make each letter of a word a different color. Normally I will type the word all in one color (top example), and then go back and highlight the letter and then change the color as shown in the middle example. You can change the color as you type each letter, if that's easier for you. The Impact Font is shown.

To adjust the placement of the letters or overlap them, you must type each letter on its own layer as shown in the bottom example.

In the example on the right, I typed the word Run on the photo and duplicated the Text layer three times (Ctrl>J, Mac: Cmd>J). I used the Move tool (V) to reposition each Text layer.

I changed the color of each Text layer by double clicking on the Text layer thumbnail. I matched the color of the text to colors in the photo. I also reduced the opacity of each Text layer.

To see how I added the vellum layer and added the stroke, see the *Cool Stuff with Strokes* chapter.

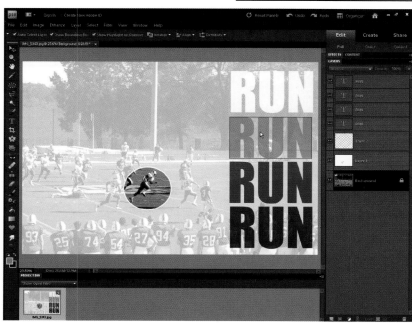

Multi-Colored Text #2

While we can easily change the colors of each character we type as shown in the Multi-Colored text example on the preceding page, what happens if you want a single character to be two different colors? There are several ways you can do this, but I'll show the way my students think is the easiest.

Select the Type tool (T) and type the text as you normally would. From the Menu bar, choose Layer>New Layer>Via Copy, or use the shortcut Ctrl>J (Mac: Cmd>J) to duplicate the text layer.

Double click on the text layer thumbnail to select the text. Click in the color box on the Type tool Options bar and choose the second color. To confirm the color change, check the green checkmark ✓ on the Type tool Options bar.

Right click on the top Text layer and choose Simplify Layer. Select the Rectangular Marquee tool (M) and click and drag a selection around the area of text you want to remove. Make sure the top text layer is still selected and tap the Delete key.

To remove the selection border (marching ants), from the Menu bar, choose Select>Deselect (Ctrl>D, Mac: Cmd>D).

Word Art

Word Art is nothing more than dressed up text. Type your own journaling or quotes, or use Word Art that's included in many digi kits. To make your own Word Art, vary the size of the text and the font. One trick to use when adding a new text layer close to existing text is to hold the Shift key when you click, otherwise you may end up selecting or editing the existing text layer. Use Alphas from your digi-kits to make Word Art. Some of the Word Art included on the *Photoshop Elements - Basics & Beyond* DVD is shown here reduced in size. Be aware that sometimes when you look at Word Art on your computer you may miss some of the details, as I first did when I previewed Ali Edward's Winter Word Art. I've added a light blue background so that you can see it actually has a white outline around the word that is easily missed.

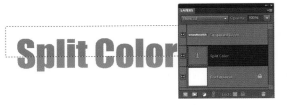

Renew, Refresh, Recharge and In summer… by Nancie Rowe Janitz; Winter and Winter Joy by Ali Edwards; Computer Geek and Decorated With Love…by Miss Mint-Peppermint Creative; Drama Queen by Meredith Cardall; Fairy Tale Princess by Danielle Young; From the Heart by SuzyQ Scraps; Bloom by Angel Hartline; Autumn Leaves swirl by Linda Walton-Bonscrapatit Designs; Every moment…by Royanna Fritschmann.

Adding Text Behind Something

If you completed the Montage tutorial in the *Cool Stuff with Photos* chapter you noticed that the title of the page appeared to be behind several of the photos, but in reality, the text is above the photos.

To do this, open an image and select the Type tool from the Toolbar. Click and add text with a thick font like Impact. To confirm the text, check the green checkmark ✓ on the Type tool Options bar. As shown circled on the right, click on the Mask icon at the bottom of the Layers panel to add a mask to the text layer.

Type the letter D to set your Foreground and Background colors located at the bottom of the Toolbar to the default settings. Your Foreground color should be black, and your Background color should be white.

Choose the Brush tool (B) from the Toolbar and select a soft round brush. Click inside the mask in the Layers panel and paint over the areas you wish to remove. Switch to a hard edged brush if necessary. If you paint away too much, switch the Foreground color to white and paint over it again. If you have a Wacom tablet, now is the time to use it!

Notice that black has been added to the layer mask in the Layers panel. To make it look realistic continue painting away areas until you cover all areas. As shown in the example on the right, if you add a drop shadow from the Effects panel, it won't look realistic.

To create a custom drop shadow, from the Menu bar, choose Layer>New>Layer via Copy or type the shortcut Ctrl>J (Mac: Cmd>J) which duplicates the text and the mask. Change the color of the text on the bottom layer to black by double clicking on the text layer thumbnail and choosing black on the Type tool Options bar. To confirm the text, check the green checkmark ✓ on the Type tool Options bar.

Right click on the bottom black text layer in the Layers panel and choose Simplify. The text will be simplified and is not uneditable, but the layer mask remains. If desired, lower the opacity of the bottom shadow layer. To soften the edges of the shadow, choose Filter>Blur>Gaussian Blur. Increase the Gaussian Blur Radius amount for a softer edge.

Using the Polar Coordinates Filter to Write Words in a Circle

Open a new 12" x 12" file on a transparent background. Select the Type tool (T) from the Toolbar and choose a font. In the example shown, I used the Bookman Old Style Font, Regular Style, 23 pts. Start typing your text at the very edge of the left side and continue all the way to the right side. To confirm the text, check the green checkmark ✓ on the Type tool Options bar. If your text does not extend all the way to the edge of the page stretch it slightly with the Move tool (it will be slightly distorted, but not noticeably).

From the Menu bar, choose Layer>New>Layer via Copy or type the shortcut Ctrl>J (Mac: Cmd>J) to duplicate the text layer for a back up copy. Click on the eyeball icon in the layers panel to turn off the bottom text layer. From the Menu bar, choose Filter>Distort>Polar Coordinates and you will get a message that the text needs to be simplified; click OK. After simplifying your text you will be unable to change the type, font, or font size but that's OK because you have your back up copy.

The default setting for this filter is Rectangular to Polar which is what you want, so click OK. You will now have a circle of your text exactly in the middle of your page. To move or transform the circle, use the Move tool (V). Save this file by itself for later use or make it directly on a scrapbook page.

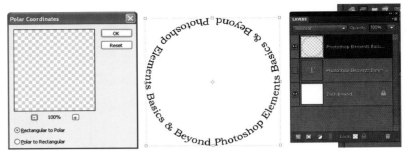

I prefer to use a Text Path to write my text in a circle because it is editable and faster. How to use a Text Path is covered in the *How to Use…*chapter.

www.Wordle.net

Wordle is a pretty cool free internet site that you may want to try out when you have an extra half hour or so. Basically you type in words and Wordle rearranges them for you. As shown on the right I entered in several Photoshop Elements terms and matched the colors to my book cover using the Eyedropper tool (I). There are many options to choose from when it comes to displaying the text.

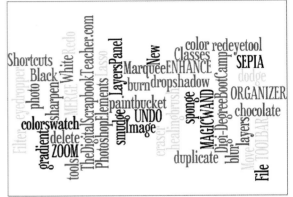

The only glitch is that at the time this book was written the only way you could get your finished word puzzle was to print it to a PDF file and many people don't have this capability. Don't worry; Wordle lists a free PDF printing program on their website.

Photoshop Elements will open a PDF file just fine so you can open your puzzle there and add it to your other projects or save it as a JPEG file.

How to Use Dingbats

Dingbats are fonts that have images instead of letters; sometimes they have letters and images combined. One of the popular dingbats that is installed on most computers is Wingdings, but there are many available that you can install. The hardest part about using a dingbat is that you don't know which key to press to get the image you want. Many times you'll just end up typing all the different keys to find the one you want.

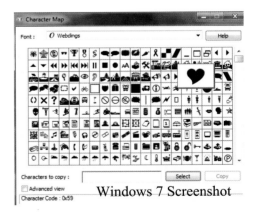

Windows 7 Screenshot

If you are using a Windows computer press your Start button, click on Run and type charmap. If you are using a Mac choose Applications>Utilities > Key Caps which will display the characters.

The character map for fonts like Arial and Times New Roman are huge because they have all different kinds of symbols and characters, but for Dingbats, they are usually pretty small. The example shows Webdings which came installed on my computer.

Click on the Character you want to use and then click on the Select Key. Go to your scrapbook page and type Ctrl>V (Mac: Cmd>V) to paste the dingbat on your page. It may take a few seconds to paste the dingbat. Notice in the Layers panel that the layer name is sort of a mess and shows the corresponding keyboard letters instead of the symbols that are displayed. If you are having trouble and letters are displaying on your file, check the font drop down list to see if it switched back to the default font. If it did, switch it to the ding bat font name. You can also make dingbats into brushes.

Magazine Cover

Over the years I've had a lot of fun making faux magazine covers. If you ever meet my famous Aunt Carol, please don't ask her about the personalized cover I made for the cookbook I gave her!

My friend Nami Aoyagi had a great idea when she made magazine covers for a high school football banquet and saved a lot of money on the centerpiece budget. She made a basic design with the team name and logo and then added a photo of each senior with some personalized text. She printed them and slid them into an inexpensive stand up acrylic frame and everyone loved them. If you need a good idea for a school banquet, try Nami's idea.

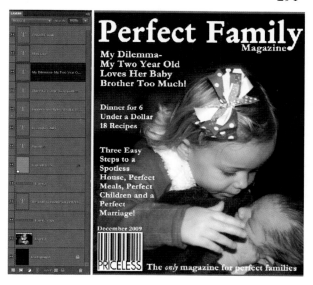

To make a magazine cover, start with a blank new file. (File>New>Blank File). I made my file 8 ½" x 11". Next, with the Move tool (V) selected, I dragged on the photo. In this example I was lucky because it fit perfect. I really didn't have a cover design in mind when I started so I just started adding the different text layers. The Priceless barcode is made with the 2PeasPriceCheck font available at *www.twopeasinabucket.com*. Underneath it is a white shape layer made with the Rectangle tool (U). I started with a white background layer but filled it with black by selecting black as my Foreground color and using the shortcut Alt>Backspace (Mac: Opt>Delete). The two red strips at the top and bottom can be made with the Rectangle tool or by creating a new blank layer and creating a selection with the Rectangular Marquee tool (M) and filling it with red by using the shortcut Alt>Backspace (Mac: Opt>Delete).

Journaling Fun

I recently saw this idea on a Mexican fast food billboard. The billboard was filled with type but they bolded just the key words. Open a photo and select the Type tool from the Toolbar. If you are going to print this photo on its own, crop it to a standard photo size first. Click and drag out a text box the size of the photo. Fill the text box with text, varying the size of the text. Add some key points in bold or italics. Text can be any color and you may want to lower the Opacity (I did in the example on the far right) or change the blending mode on the text layer.

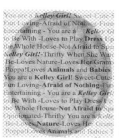 

In my example, I also added a vignette to cover up the distracting patio. Instructions for making a vignette can be found in the *Cool Stuff with Photos* chapter. After adding the text, I added a layer mask by clicking on the Layer Mask icon at the bottom of the Layers panel. I selected the Brush tool from the Toolbar and just like I did in the *Adding Text behind Someone* tutorial in this section painted away the area on the mask with black.

In the example above I used the same text to cover a tag from the Vintage Days kit by K Designs which can be found on the *Photoshop Elements - Basics & Beyond* DVD. The right example shows the tag after I clipped the text to it with a clipping mask (Layer>Create Clipping Mask). I also added a Simple Outer Glow from the Effects panel to make the text pop.

Gradient Text

It's easy to add a gradient to text, but did you know you can match the gradient to colors in your photos or digital papers? In this example I am going to match a gradient to Meredith Cardall's Cherry Limeade which can be found on the *Photoshop Elements - Basics & Beyond* DVD. Add some text to a file with the Type tool (T). Use a wide font so that the gradient shows. In my example I'm using the Clarendon Extended font. Click on the New Layer icon at the bottom of the Layers panel and then Ctrl click on the text layer thumbnail. You will have a selection border around the text.

Select the Gradient tool (G) from the Toolbar. Click the Edit button on the Options bar. Select a gradient by clicking on the thumbnail. Click in a color stop (circled) at the bottom of the gradient bar and then click on the paper or photo. Repeat for each color you wish to include in the gradient. Drag the color stops to adjust the amount of each color in the gradient. Adjust the opacity stops by clicking on the opacity stops above the gradient bar. Click the OK button.

With the empty transparent layer selected, click and drag across the selection and the gradient will be added to the transparent layer. If you don't like how it looks, try dragging in a different direction or adjusting the gradient. To remove the selection border (marching ants), from the Menu bar, choose Select>Deselect (Ctrl>D, Mac: Cmd>D), or tap the Esc key. More about gradients can be found in the Gradient tool section in the *Tools and Tips* chapter.

To add a plastic look to the text, duplicate the gradient layer and fill it with white by changing the Foreground color to white using the shortcut Shift>Alt>Backspace (Mac: Shift>Opt>Delete). Add a Wow-White Plastic layer style to the white layer. Double click on the *fx* symbol on the layer and remove the drop shadow. Change the blending mode to Luminosity.

Columns of Text

You can trick Photoshop Elements into making columns of text similar to a newspaper. In my example I added some guide lines (View>New Guide) to help me space the columns in even thirds. Select the Type tool and click and drag out a text box. If you are using guides, don't go all way to the ends.

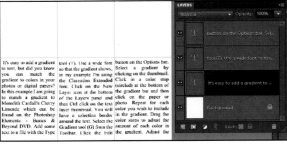

For me it's easier to type all of my journaling in a word processing program first and then copy and paste it into the text box. To select all the text, type the shortcut Ctrl>A (Mac: Cmd>A) then copy it using the shortcut Ctrl>C (Mac: Cmd>C). Click inside the text box in Photoshop Elements and type the shortcut Ctrl>V (Mac: Cmd>V) to paste it into the box. It will overfill the box as evidenced by the + in the right bottom corner of the text box. To confirm the text, check the green checkmark ✓ on the Type tool Options bar.

From the Menu bar, choose Layer>New>Layer via Copy or type the shortcut Ctrl>J (Mac: Cmd>J) to copy the text box onto another layer. Select the Move tool from the Tool bar and move it into position.

Double click on the second text layer thumbnail and delete the text that appeared in the first text box. Repeat the steps for the third text box. To justify the type like a newspaper column, select the text and type the shortcut Shift>Ctrl>J (Mac: Shift>Cmd>J). To remove the guides from the Menu bar, choose View>Clear Guides.

If the text doesn't fit right, it's easy to fix. Select all three layers in the Layers panel and adjust the font size and leading and they will all change together.

Cool Stuff with Brushes

How to Use a Brush like a Rubber Stamp - Multiple Colors

Visions of trying to use markers to color in different areas of a rubber stamp are enough to drive me crazy! I tried this once with a real rubber stamp and quickly decided it was just way too much work! There are several ways to stamp with different colors, but I think this way is the easiest.

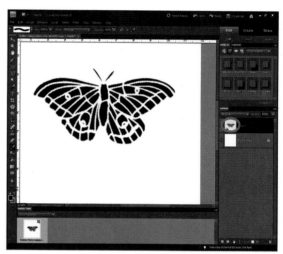

Follow the instructions to load the brush set, make a new blank file, and new transparent layer as explained in the preceding *How to Use a Brush like a Rubber Stamp - Single Color* tutorial.

Select the butterfly brush (256 pixels). Enlarge the brush to 2500 pixels using the right Bracket key so that we have a large area to practice with. Making the brush this large has caused it to get a little bit pixilated, but that will be OK for this example. The maximum size for any brush is 2500 pixels.

Make a new transparent layer (Shift>Alt>Ctrl>N, Mac: Shift>Opt>Cmd>N), choose black for the Foreground color, and stamp the butterfly.

Hold the Ctrl key (Mac: Cmd key) and click on the Layer thumbnail (shown circled above). The butterfly should be surrounded with marching ants.

Click on the brush drop down list on the Brush tool Options bar and choose Default brushes. Switching to the Default brushes will cause the brush set that you previously loaded to no longer appear in the brush drop down list. To reload it, simply follow the earlier steps.

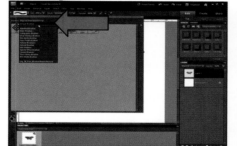
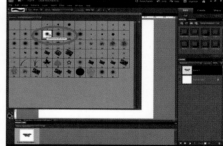

Choose the 65 px Soft Round brush. Make a new transparent layer. Change the Foreground color. Click and drag in an area of the butterfly that you want to recolor. Because the butterfly is selected, you do not have to worry about coloring in the areas that are supposed to be transparent.

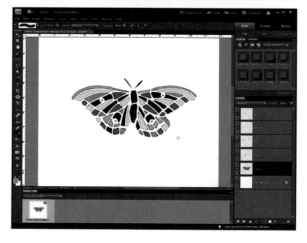

Change colors and adjust the brush size as needed. I selected a soft brush to allow the colors to softly blend, but you can choose a hard round brush if it works better for you. I would suggest making a new transparent layer for each different color you use.

To remove the selection border (marching ants) when you're done, choose Select>Deselect (Ctrl>D, Mac: Cmd>D) from the Menu bar, or tap the Esc key which will work for most people.

How to Use a Brush like a Rubber Stamp – Outline

Follow the instructions to load the brush set, make a new blank file, and new transparent layer as explained in the preceding *How to Use a Brush like a Rubber Stamp - Single Color* tutorial. You may also add a stroke to a shape from the Custom Shape tool (U) in the same manner.

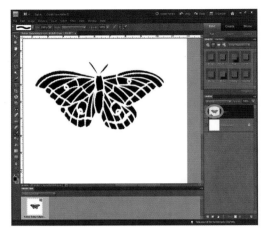

Select the butterfly brush (256 pixels). Enlarge the brush to 2500 pixels using the right Bracket key so that you have a large area to practice with. Making the brush this large has caused it to get a little bit pixilated, but that will be OK for this example. The maximum size for any brush is 2500 pixels.

Make a new transparent layer (Shift>Alt>Ctrl>N, Mac: Shift>Opt>Cmd>N), choose black for the Foreground color, and stamp the butterfly.

Hold the Ctrl key (Mac: Cmd key) and click on the Layer thumbnail (shown circled above). The butterfly should be surrounded with marching ants.

Make another new transparent layer. From the Menu bar, choose Edit>Stroke (Outline) Selection. Choose 10 px for the Width. Click inside the color box to choose a color. Choose Inside for Location. Click OK.

To remove the selection border (marching ants), from the Menu bar, choose Select>Deselect (Ctrl>D, Mac: Cmd>D) or tap the Esc key which will work for most people.

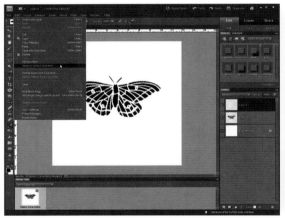

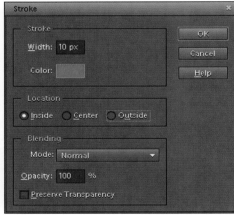

The black butterfly will now be surrounded by a thin red line. Hide the black layer by clicking on the eyeball icon (shown circled in the example below on the left) to the left of the Layer thumbnail to display only the outline. Practice making outlines in different sizes and colors.

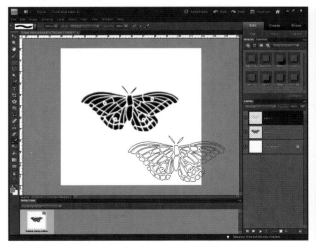

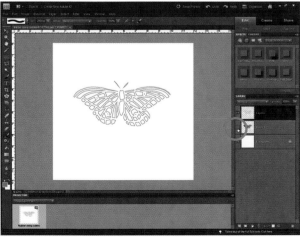

How to Use a Brush like a Die Cut Machine

Follow the instructions to load the brush set, make a new blank file, and new transparent layer as explained in the preceding *How to Use a Brush like a Rubber Stamp - Single Color* tutorial.

Select the flower-diamond brush (669 pixels). Enlarge the brush to 2500 pixels using the right Bracket key so that you have a large area to practice with. Making the brush this large has caused it to get a little bit pixilated, but that will be OK for this example. The maximum size for any brush is 2500 pixels.

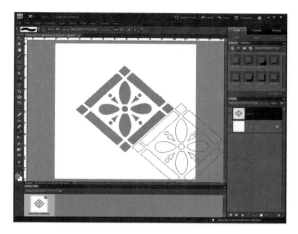

Make a new transparent layer (Shift>Alt>Ctrl>N, Mac: Shift>Opt>Cmd>N), choose any color (the color won't show) for the Foreground color, and stamp the flower diamond brush.

Open a paper. I am using a paper from the Bon Scrapatit Designs Falling Again kit, which can be found on the *Photoshop Elements - Basics & Beyond* DVD.

Select the Move tool and drag and drop the paper onto the page. It will cover the brush work completely.

From the Menu bar, choose Layer>Create Clipping Mask (Ctrl>G Mac: Cmd>G). Note: If you are using Photoshop Elements 7 or lower, choose Layer>Group with Previous (same command, new name).

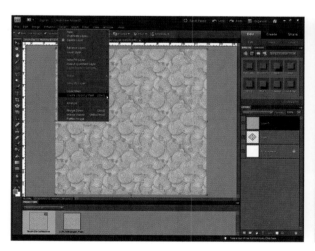

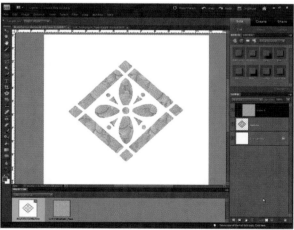

Add a stroke by following the previous tutorial; be sure to add the stroke outline on the layer above the paper layer or you won't be able to see it.

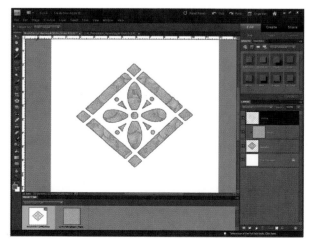

How to Use a Brush like a Rubber Stamp - Embossing

I can easily emboss without a heat gun and messy embossing powders. No mess to clean up or put away! No more worrying if I have the right color embossing powder or enough of it to finish my project!

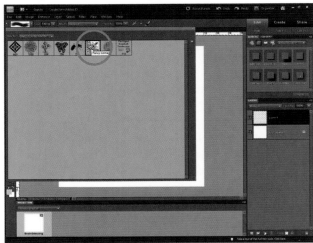

Follow the instructions to load the brush set, make a new blank file, and new transparent layer as explained in the preceding *How to Use a Brush like a Rubber Stamp - Single Color* tutorial.

Select the fancy corner brush (1301 pixels).

Make a new transparent layer (Shift>Alt>Ctrl>N, Mac: Shift>Opt>Cmd>N), choose a color you like for the Foreground color, and stamp the fancy corner brush.

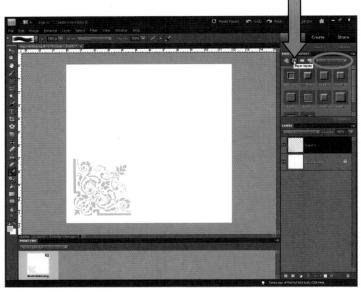

At the top of the Effects panel, click on the Layer Styles icon (red arrow) as shown on the example to the left.

Choose Bevels from the drop down list (circled).

Double click on the Simple Inner bevel. If the names do not appear under the bevels, read how to turn them on in the *First Things First* chapter.

Experiment trying different bevels.

To adjust the bevel, double click on the *fx* symbol on the layer (circled) to display the Style Settings box shown below.

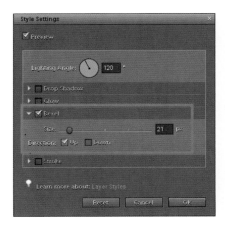

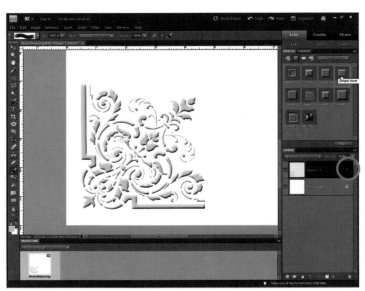

How to Use a Brush like a Rubber Stamp – in a Selected Area

Follow the instructions to load the brush set, make a new blank file, and new transparent layer as explained in the preceding *How to Use a Brush like a Rubber Stamp - Single Color* tutorial.

Select the crocus brush (334 pixels). Enlarge the brush to 2500 pixels using the right Bracket key so that you have a large brush to practice with. Making the brush this large has caused it to get a little bit pixilated, but that will be OK for this example. The maximum size for any brush is 2500 pixels.

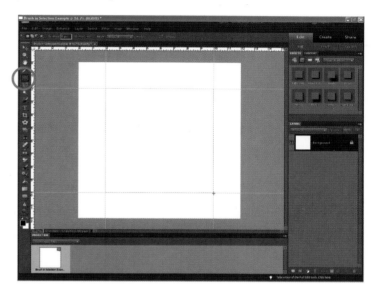

From the Menu bar choose View>Rulers (Shift>Ctrl>R, Mac: Shift>Cmd>R) to turn on the rulers. Click and drag on one of the rulers to drag out a Guide. Position the Guides so that there is a two inch border around the page. The Guides will not print. You can skip this step if you prefer to just eyeball the selection we make in the next step.

Choose the Rectangular Marquee tool (M) from the Toolbar. Click, hold, and drag out a selection the size of the inner square. You should have an 8" x 8" square selection (marching ants) in the center of the page.

Make a new transparent layer (Shift>Alt>Ctrl>N, Mac: Shift>Opt>Cmd>N), and choose a color you like for the Foreground color.

Select the Brush tool (B) from the Toolbar. Click to stamp the brush on the page. The brush will only stamp in the area surrounded by the selection border (marching ants).

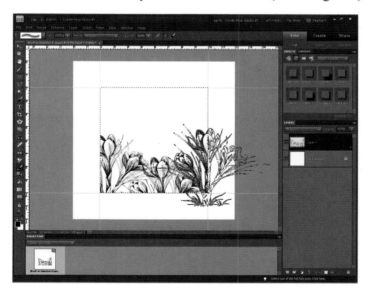

Make a new transparent layer and choose Edit>Stroke (Outline) Selection from the Menu bar to put a thin border around the selection border.

Choose any width or color, but be sure to choose Inside for the Location or the corners will not be completely square.

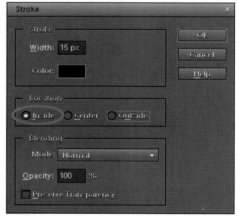

To remove the selection border (marching ants), from the Menu bar, choose Select>Deselect (Ctrl>D, Mac: Cmd>D), or tap the Esc key which will work for most people.

To hide the guides, from the Menu bar, choose View>Guides (Ctrl>; Mac: Cmd>; apostrophe). To clear the Guides, choose View>Clear Guides.

Following the same steps, experiment by filling circles and ovals with brushwork using the Elliptical Marquee tool (M), which is nested with the Rectangular Marquee tool.

Time saving tip: To drag out a circle in the middle of the page, position your cursor at the center point of the page. Hold the Shift and Alt (Mac: Opt) keys as you drag out toward the corner of the page. This will draw the selection from the center and constrain the shape to a circle instead of an oval.

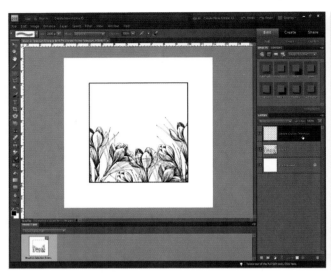 

If you would like the brushwork to fill the outside edges of the selection, instead of the center example shown above, it's easy to do.

Follow the same steps above: Make a new blank white file, add the Guides, select a Foreground color, select the brush, and make a selection.

Add the border by making a new transparent layer, choose Edit>Stroke (Outline) Selection from the Menu bar to put a thin border around the selection border.

Choose any width or color, but be sure to choose Inside for the Location or the corners will not be completely square.

Make another new transparent layer for the brushwork.

From the Menu bar, choose Select>Inverse (Shift>Ctrl>I, Mac: Shift>Cmd>I). The selection border (marching ants) will now be around the outside edge of the page, and around the original selected area. Click and stamp the brush.

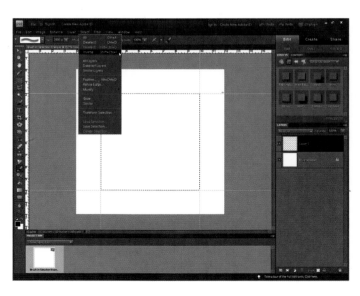

The brushwork will appear only inside the selection border, which is the outer edge of the page. This is a great technique to use for a scrapbook page, card, or other project.

You can continue using the brush at this angle, or you can rotate either the page or the brush as shown on the next page.

To rotate the brush, click on the Brush Options icon (white circle in the example on the right) on the Brush tool Options bar.

There are two ways to change the brush angle:

Click and drag the arrow (red circle in the example on the right). If you're not sure if you moved the arrow to the right position, let go of it and you will be able to see the brush again.

Click inside the Angle box (yellow circle in the example on the right) and change the number. You can also use your Arrow keys or scroll wheel to increase or decrease this number. Enter numbers ranging from -180° to 180°; let's see how well you remember your angles from Algebra 101!

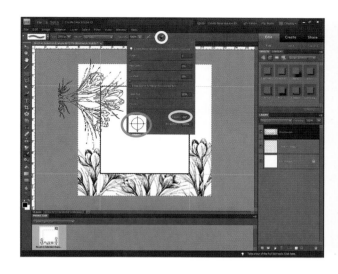

To return to the original angle, enter 0 in the Angle box, or choose another brush in this set, and then switch back to the Crocus brush.

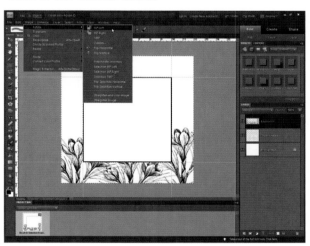

Because we want to rotate the brush just 90° each time, it may be just as easy to rotate the whole page, but the problem is that your selection border may disappear.

From the Menu bar, choose Select>Save Selection. In the Name box, type a name for your selection. Under Operation, New Selection is the default setting and should be selected. Click OK.

Choose Image>Rotate 90° left. If your selection border (marching ants) disappears, choose Select>Load Selection. Click OK. Add your brushwork and repeat for each side.

To remove the selection border (marching ants), from the Menu bar, choose Select>Deselect (Ctrl>D, Mac: Cmd>D), or tap the Esc key which will work for most people.

To hide the guides, from the Menu bar, choose View>Guides (Ctrl>; Mac: Cmd>; apostrophe). To clear the Guides, choose View>Clear Guides.

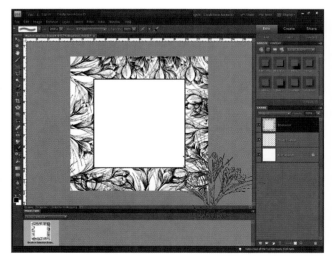

How to Use a Brush like a Rubber Stamp - Grunged Paper Edges

Follow the instructions to load the brush set, make a new blank file, and new transparent layer as explained in the preceding *How to Use a Brush like a Rubber Stamp - Single Color* tutorial.

Use the Paint Bucket tool (K) to fill the Background layer with any color (shortcut: Alt>Backspace, Mac>Opt>Delete). In my example, I am using a medium blue color (Hex # 4187bb).

Make a new transparent layer (Shift>Alt>Ctrl>N, Mac: Shift>Opt>Cmd>N).

Select the Brush tool (B) from the Toolbar. Select the grunge brush (2390 pixels).

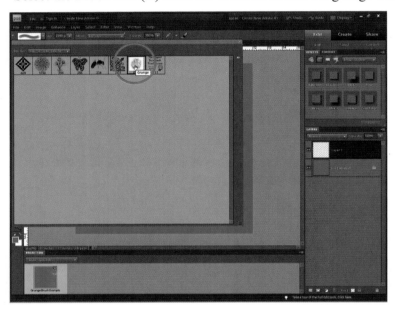

Choose a color a little bit darker or lighter for the Foreground color. To do this, click inside the Foreground color box at the bottom of the Toolbar and click above or below the current color indicator. In the example below, the red circle indicates the current Foreground color. The yellow circle is my cursor. Once I click, my new Foreground color will be the darker blue color.

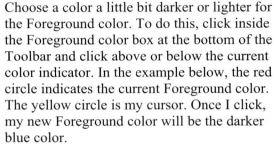

Click and stamp the edge of the grunge brush along the outer edge of the paper, keeping most of the brush off of the paper. Change the color, size, and angle of the brush.

Alternate using different grunge brushes to make the edge look interesting. You may want to stamp on separate transparent layers when using different brushes and colors. Check out *www.TheDigitalScrapbookTeacher.com* for a wide selection of brushes.

If you like the final grunged edge and may want to use it in another project, save that layer by itself as a PNG file. If there are several layers that comprise the grunged edge, select those layers in the Layers panel and choose Layer>Merge Layers (Ctrl>E, Mac: Cmd>E).

Instructions for saving as a PNG file, can be found in *The Basics* chapter.

How to Use a Brush like a Paper Punch/Laser Cut

Rubber stamps drove me crazy, but as a traditional scrapper I enjoyed using punches. The biggest problem with punches is that they're so heavy, and take up a lot of room. And of course, then there's the problem that they stick and don't punch when you want them to. Did I mention that they're also expensive?

Even now in my office/scrapbook room I have several drawers devoted to storing my paper punches that I never use. I just can't make myself get rid of them. Recently my grandchildren discovered them and were pretty excited about them. Maybe my punches will soon find a new home at their house! My four year old grandson was surprised that I had an entire set of letter punches. I hate to admit that I've just used a few letters only a couple of times.

Brushes can be used just like punches, but with so many more options. After you see how easy they are to use you may forget all about your paper punches just like I have! In this example, we're going to use the Eraser tool (E) to cut a hole in a digital paper and let the layer below show through.

This technique gets lots of ooh's & aah's from my students, because it looks like we used a traditional paper laser cut-out on the page.

Follow the instructions to load the brush set, make a new blank file, and new transparent layer as explained in the preceding *How to Use a Brush like a Rubber Stamp - Single Color* tutorial.

Use the Paint Bucket tool (K) to fill the Background layer with any color (shortcut: Alt>Backspace, Mac>Opt>Delete). In my example I am using a medium aqua color (Hex # 79c9c6).

Make a new transparent layer (Shift>Alt>Ctrl>N, Mac: Shift>Opt>Cmd>N). Fill this layer with white. Your Layers panel should look exactly like the example on the right.

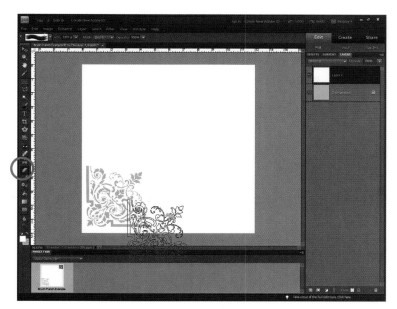

Select the **Eraser tool (E)** (circled in the example on the left) from the Toolbar. Don't choose the Brush tool because it won't work!

Select the fancy corner brush (1301 pixels).

Select the top white layer in the Layers panel and click on the page to cut out the fancy corner shape.

Right now, it looks like you stamped the brush in the aqua color. However, if you look closely at the Layers panel you can see that the white layer is cut out.

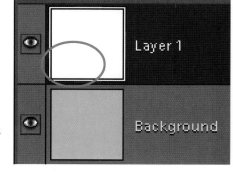

If you think about this from a paper scrapper's point of view…You have two pieces of 12" x 12" paper. You punch the top white paper, so the colored paper shows through from the bottom. This is exactly what we've done in this example, only we don't have to clean up the mess.

If we were using a real punch and paper our page would have more dimension, because a shadow would fall onto the colored paper automatically.

To add dimension to your page, add a drop shadow to the top (white) layer. To add a drop shadow, choose the Layer Styles icon from the Effects panel. Choose Drop Shadows from the drop down list. Double click on the Low icon to add the drop shadow. If the names do not appear under the drop shadows as mine do, read the *First Things First* Chapter.

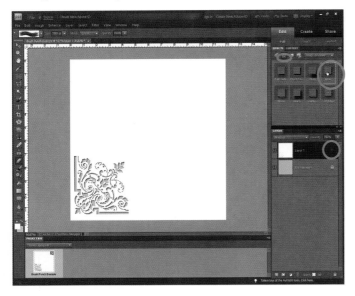

Once a drop shadow is added to a layer, a tiny *fx* symbol will be added to the right of the layer name, which is very dark and hard to see.

If you would like to adjust the drop shadow, double click on the *fx* symbol to display the Style Settings dialog box.

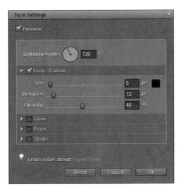

The Eraser tool (E) does not have the option to rotate brushes like the Brush tool (B) has. If you wanted to punch all four corners of the page, you would have to rotate the entire page. From the Menu bar, choose Image>Rotate>90° to rotate the page.

All brush sets sold at *www.TheDigitalScrapbookTeacher.com* that include corners like these, will automatically include all four corners so you won't have to rotate the page.

I had one student who thought that you could achieve the same look by simply stamping the brush on a transparent layer and adding a drop shadow. To see the difference, select the Brush tool (B) and make a new transparent layer (Shift>Alt>Ctrl>N, Mac: Shift>Opt>Cmd>N).

Select the color that you used for the Background layer and stamp the brush on the transparent layer. Add a drop shadow and compare.

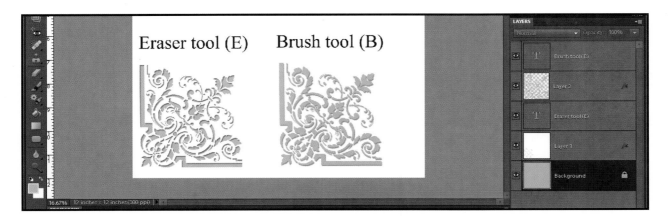

Distressing a Brush

If you have a new looking brush and you want to make it look distressed there are several ways to do it. This example is my favorite method. You will need an image with a lot of texture in it, so I am using a grunge overlay from the *Essentials #1* kit and a brush from the *Hearts & Royalty #1* set which are both available at *www.TheDigitalScrapbookTeacher.com*.

Follow the instructions to load the brush set. Make a new blank file and new transparent layer as explained in the preceding *How to Use a Brush like a Rubber Stamp - Single Color* tutorial.

 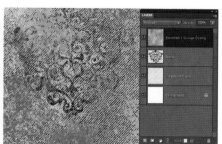

Stamp the brush on the transparent layer. In my example I am using black so that you can see it better. From the Toolbar, select the Move tool (V). Click, hold, and drag the grunge overlay down into the Project bin until you **touch** the file (Windows users will see a + appear on their cursor).

Choose the Magic Wand tool (W) and lower the Tolerance on the Options bar. I lowered my Tolerance setting to four, but you may want to experiment depending on the image and brush you are using. With the grunge overlay layer selected in the Layers panel, click on the page.

Hide the grunge overlay layer by clicking on the eyeball in the Layers panel. Click on the brush stroke layer and tap the Delete key on your keyboard.

To remove the selection border (marching ants), from the Menu bar, choose Select>Deselect (Ctrl>D, Mac: Cmd>D) or tap the Esc key.

If you are not happy with the result, you can try these options: increase or decrease the Tolerance setting on the Magic Wand Options bar, choose a different grungy image, rotate the grungy layer and repeat the steps to delete more of the brush work.

Realistic Stamped Effect

To make the brush appear like it was really stamped on top of multiple layers, position the brush so that it covers the end of at least two different layers (photos or papers).

Ctrl click (Mac: Cmd click) on the Layer thumbnail for the layer underneath the brush layer. In my example it is the beige scrapbook paper. A selection border will surround the edges of the paper.

Click on the brush layer in the Layers panel. From the Menu bar, choose Layer>New>Layer via Cut or type the shortcut Shift> Ctrl>J (Mac: Shift>Cmd>J). This cut the brush layer and placed part of it on its own layer.

Select the Move tool (V) from the Toolbar. Select the layer with the bottom half of the brush on it. Tap the Down Arrow key a couple of times to move it down slightly. Click on the layer below the brush in the Layers panel (in my example the beige paper) and add a drop shadow to it from the Effects panel.

Custom Brush Ideas

The Make Your Own Chapter has step by step instructions for making your own brush from a sketch and a photo. Shirley Lewerenz made a great brush for this cute page from the Fontdinerdotcom Sparkly font available free at *www.Dafont.com*.

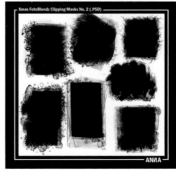

To make the brush, close Photoshop Elements and download and install the font according to directions that can be found at *www.Dafont.com*. Choose the Type tool from the Toolbar, increase the font size so that you create a decent size brush and type some text that includes the sparkle. To confirm the text, check the green checkmark ✓on the Type tool Options bar. From the Toolbar select the Rectangular Marquee tool (M) and drag a selection around one of the sparkles. From the Menu bar, choose Edit>Define Brush from Selection and you have created a brush.

Make a new blank file and new transparent layer as explained in the preceding *How to Use a Brush like a Rubber Stamp - Single Color* tutorial. Choose the Brush tool (B) from the Toolbar, select the new brush from the Brush drop down list and stamp away.

As explained in the Brush tool section of the *Tools and Tips* chapter, to scatter the brush indiscriminately, change the Scatter and Spacing setting on the brush options drop down located at the end of the Brush tool Options bar.

As shown on the highlighted layers on the left, Shirley also made two masks with different brushes to clip her photos to.

Shown on the top example on the right is the original photo, below it is the photo mask Shirley created with brushes.

The bottom example shows what happens when I clip the photo to the mask with a clipping mask. To do this, position the photo above the mask, both on the page and in the Layers panel.

From the Menu bar, choose Layer>Create Clipping Mask (Ctrl>G Mac: Cmd>G). Note: If you are using Photoshop Elements 7 or lower, choose Layer>Group with Previous (same command, new name). Once clipped, the top photo layer will step to the right a little bit and a bent arrow will point down to the clipping mask which will have its name underlined in the Layers panel (outlined on the left).

Masks can also be purchased as brushes and/or masks at many digital scrapbooking websites including *www.TheDigitalScrapbookTeacher.com*. Included on the *Photoshop Elements - Basics & Beyond* DVD is a great set of masks from Anna Aspnes.

The digital kit used on this page is the April Morning kit by Miss Mint at *wwwPeppermintCreative.com* which is also included on the *Photoshop Elements - Basics & Beyond* DVD. Photo credit Madeline Arenas Cubrix Photography.

Cool Stuff with Strokes

A stroke is a simple outline that you can add around photos, text, embellishments, shapes, and anything else you can think of. Strokes can also be added to a project as a design element on their own. Adding a white border to a photo makes it appear that it's part of the photo. A colored border makes it look like it has a cardstock mat.

Stroke around Text

As shown in the example on the right, adding a stroke around text is a great way to accent titles. The top example shows text that has a paper clipped to it with a stroke added above the paper layer. The technique of clipping the paper to the text is shown in the *Cool Stuff with Text* chapter.

The middle example shows regular text with a different color stroke added above the text layer.

The bottom example shows a stroke that was added around regular text for an outline type effect. In this example, the regular text layer is discarded.

To add a stroke around text, first, type the text with the Type tool (T). In the Layers panel Ctrl click (Mac: Cmd click) on the Text layer thumbnail. The text will be surrounded by a selection border (marching ants).

Click on the New Layer icon at the bottom of the Layers panel, or type the shortcut Shift>Alt>Ctrl>N (Mac: Shift>Opt>Cmd>N).

From the Menu bar, choose Edit>Stroke (Outline) Selection.

Enter a Width in pixels or inches. Choose a color.

Choose Inside for Location if you want to keep the edges of the outline square, otherwise you can choose Center or Outside. Click OK.

To remove the selection border (marching ants), from the Menu bar choose Select>Deselect (Ctrl>D, Mac: Cmd>D).

To display only the outline as shown in the top example, hide the Text layer by clicking on the eyeball icon to the left of the Layer thumbnail. You may also delete the Text layer by dragging it to the trashcan icon at the bottom of the Layers panel.

Another way to add a stroke is to add a Stroke Layer Style from the Effects panel. Unlike my method above where we add it to a transparent layer, the stroke will be added directly to the layer. The stroke choices are limited, but you can modify the stroke by double clicking on the *fx* symbol on the layer after it's been added.

I prefer to add my stroke on its own layer so that it can be used either as an outline alone, or I can change the blending mode or I can use it as a clipping mask.

How to Use a Stroke to Outline a Brush Stroke or Shape

If you want to jazz up brush strokes or shapes, add a
Stroke Outline around them.

In my example on the right, the seahorse is from the
Tropical Paradise Brush kit available at:
www.TheDigitalScrapbookTeacher.com. The umbrella is .
a shape drawn with the Custom Shape tool (U).

The first example shows the brush or shape without an
outline. The middle example shows it with a stroke added.
The final example shows the stroke alone.

For complete instructions, read the *How to Use a Brush
like a Rubber Stamp – Outline* in the *Cool Stuff with
Brushes* chapter.

Seahorses-Made with a Custom Brush Set (details below)
Umbrellas-Made with Custom Shape tool (U)

Seahorse Tropical Paradise Brush available at www.TheDigitalScrapbookTeacher.com

How to Add a Stroke around a Photo

Strokes can be added around photos to mimic matting. You can add a stroke to photos on a scrapbook page or
other project, or you can add them directly to the photo and print them.

If you add the stroke to photos you will print, you **must** crop the photo to the print size with the Crop tool (C)
prior to placing the stroke around the edge of a photo. Experiment with your photo processor to see how the
photos print out before spending all day adding a mat (stroke) around your photos.

If you are using the photo on a project, use the Move tool (V) to drag a photo onto a new blank document. Ctrl
click (Mac: Cmd click) on the photo Layer thumbnail. A selection border (marching ants) will surround the
photo. If you are adding the stroke directly to the photo from the Menu bar, choose Select>All (Ctrl>A, Mac:
Cmd>A).

Click on the
New Layer
icon at the
bottom of the
Layers panel,
or type the
shortcut
Shift>Alt>Ctrl
>N (Mac:
Shift>Opt>Cm
d>N).

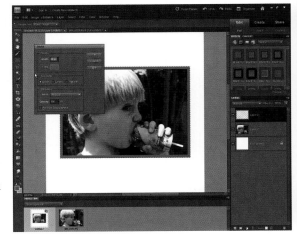
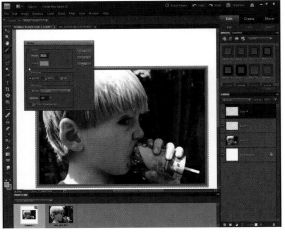

From the Menu bar, choose Edit>Stroke (Outline) Selection. In the Width box enter an amount in pixels or
inches (like .25 in) and choose a color. In my example, I used the blue from the ice cream wrapper. Click OK.
The stroke is placed on its own layer.

To make a multi-colored mat, make a new layer and add a smaller stroke to it following the same steps above.
To remove the selection border (marching ants), from the Menu bar, choose Select>Deselect (Ctrl>D, Mac:
Cmd>D).

Outline What's Important on Your Photos with a Stroke Outline

How many times have you taken a photo and had a hard time finding the part you wanted to see? As a mother of two quarterbacks, I can tell you that it's very difficult to take a photo of just my sons, because they're usually surrounded by their own teammates in the same uniforms and the opposing team.

One way I've found to spotlight them is to add a stroke around them. That way when you first look at the photo there's no question where you're supposed to look first. In this example I'll also show you how to add a layer of digital vellum to further spotlight the important parts of your photos.

Open a photo. Make a blank transparent layer above the photo layer, by clicking on the New Layer icon at the bottom of the Layers panel, or type the shortcut Shift>Alt>Ctrl>N (Mac: Shift>Opt>Cmd>N).

Type the letter D to set your Foreground and Background colors located at the bottom of the Toolbar to the default settings. Your Foreground color should be black, and your Background color should be white. Type the letter X to swap your Foreground and Background colors. Your Foreground color should now be white.

From the Menu bar, choose Edit>Fill Layer. In the Contents Use box, choose Foreground Color or use the shortcut Alt>Backspace (Mac: Opt>Delete) to fill the layer with white. Adjust the Opacity of the white layer by clicking and dragging the Opacity slider at the top of the Layers panel (circled below).

From the Toolbar, choose the Elliptical Marquee tool (M). Click and drag a selection over the area you would like to cut out of the vellum. To create a circular selection, hold the Shift key as you drag your mouse. Tap the Delete key to cut a hole in the vellum layer.

Click on the New Layer icon at the bottom of the Layers panel, or type the shortcut Shift>Alt>Ctrl>N (Mac: Shift>Opt>Cmd>N) to add a new layer to put a stroke on.

From the Menu bar, choose Edit>Stroke (Outline) Selection. In the Width box enter an amount in pixels or inches (like .25 in) and choose a color. In my example I used white. Click OK. The stroke is placed on its own layer.

Now, when you look at the photo, there is no question which player I am interested in.

If you have something in a photo that's very difficult to see, like the grasshopper in this example, you can add a stroke around it to make it more visible. Without the stroke on this photo, I would completely miss what the children are looking at.

Adding a Stroke as an Accent

Strokes can be added to a photo or other project just for fun.

Open the photo and decide what parts you want to feature. In the example on the right, I wanted to feature the children's faces, which I will also do in my step by step directions. You can feature any areas of your own photos.

Choose the Rectangle tool (U) from the Toolbar. Click and drag a rectangle (the color doesn't matter) over the first face. If you want to use the Move tool (V) or the Transform Command (Ctrl>T, Mac: Cmd>T) to rotate the shape by clicking and dragging a corner. Rotating the shape can be done now or in the future.

Ctrl click (Mac: Cmd>click) on the Shape layer thumbnail. A selection border (marching ants) will surround the rectangle.

Make a blank transparent layer above the photo layer by clicking on the New Layer icon at the bottom of the Layers panel, or type the shortcut Shift>Alt>Ctrl>N (Mac: Shift>Opt>Cmd>N).

From the Menu bar, choose Edit>Stroke (Outline) Selection. In my examples I have used a 25 px white Stroke, use whatever color and size you wish. Location must be Inside to retain sharp corners. Blending Mode is Normal, Opacity 100%, and the Preserve Transparency box is not checked.

From the Menu bar, choose Select>Deselect (Ctrl>D, Mac: Cmd>D) to remove the selection border (marching ants).

Link the Shape and Stroke Outline layers by selecting them both in the Layers panel and clicking on the link symbol at the bottom of the Layers panel.

Click on the photo layer in the Layers panel and duplicate it (Ctrl>J, Mac: Cmd>J). Note: you should be duplicating the entire photo layer. If you only duplicated part of the photo, you forgot to remove the selection border.

In the Layers panel, drag the photo layer above the Shape layer and under the stroke layer. From the Menu bar, choose Layer>Create Clipping Mask (Ctrl>G Mac: Cmd>G). To verify that the technique worked, hide the bottom photo layer. To hide the bottom layer, click on the eyeball icon to the left of the Layer thumbnail shown circled on the right. You should only see the rectangle shaped photo surrounded by the stroke.

Complete the sequence of steps for each rectangle shape to be added. Turning off the Background photo layer each time you finish a section will help you check your work. Link each stroke with the corresponding shape so that you can resize and rotate them together. So that you know which layers go together renaming your layers may be helpful.

You may need to change the layer order for some of the rectangles. In my example below on the left, I would prefer that the baby's photo be on top of his brother and sister. I need to move the photo, stroke and shape layer above his sister's layers. For me, it's easier to drag layers down in the Layers panel than to drag them up.

Add more rectangles as desired. In my example, I have added one large rectangle below the children's faces.

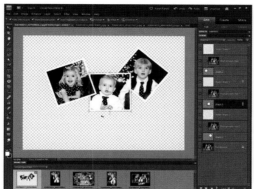 

If you are working on a scrapbook page, the paper behind your photo will show around the rectangles as shown below in the example on the right. Add drop shadows to the template pieces if desired.

If you are working on a photo, you may want to fill in the background as shown by the two examples on the left.

To fill the background with black, create a new layer (Shift>Alt>Ctrl>N (Mac: Shift>Opt>Cmd>N) above the Background photo layer. Type the letter D to set your Foreground color to black. Type the shortcut Alt>Backspace (Mac: Opt>Delete) to fill the transparent layer with black.

Photo credit: Jill Phillips, Font: Inspiration, Digital Supplies: Paper Funtime, Essentials #1 Grunge Edge Overlay available at *www.TheDigitalScrapbookTeacher.com*.

Creating a Gallery Print

My friend Nami Aoyagi's students love it when she teaches this technique in class. Next time you visit an art gallery, notice how many artists showcase their photos or other artwork with this simple, classic technique.

In this example I am going to make this photo for a frame, but you can use this technique on a scrapbook page or other project.

From the Menu bar, choose File>New and make a new 10" x 8" file.

Open a photo and drag it onto the new file with the Move tool (V). My photo is centered, but I have moved it up a little bit.

Type the letter D to set the Foreground color to black. Type the shortcut Alt>Backspace (Mac: Opt>Delete) to fill the Background layer with black.

I have turned on my Rulers (View>Rulers) and Grids (View>Grid). My gridlines are set at 50% with one subdivision, as demonstrated in *The Basics* chapter. I have also added four Guides by clicking on the rulers and dragging them out. The top and side guides are ¾ " from the edge and the bottom guide is 1" from the edge.

Ctrl click (Mac: Cmd>click) on the photo layer thumbnail. A selection border (marching ants) will surround the photo.

Type the letter X to change the Foreground color to white. Make a blank transparent layer above the photo layer by clicking on the New Layer icon at the bottom of the Layers panel, or type the shortcut Shift>Alt>Ctrl>N (Mac: Shift>Opt>Cmd>N). Rename the layer Inside Stroke.

From the Menu bar, choose Edit>Stroke (Outline) Selection. In my example I have used a 15 px white Stroke, use whatever color and size you wish. Location must be Inside to retain sharp corners. Blending Mode is Normal, Opacity 100%, the Preserve Transparency box is not checked.

Make another blank transparent layer, and rename it Outside Stroke.

From the Toolbar, select the Rectangular Marquee tool (M). Using the Guides as a pattern, drag out a new selection. From the Menu bar, choose Edit>Stroke (Outline) Selection and click OK to keep the same settings as the first stroke.

From the Toolbar, select the Type tool (T). Add text along the bottom of the Outside Stroke using the Grid to center it. Your text will cover the stroke.

Select the Rectangular Marquee tool (M) again. Drag a box around the text. Select the Outside Stroke layer in the Layers panel and tap the Delete key.

To remove the selection border (marching ants), from the Menu bar choose Select>Deselect (Ctrl>D, Mac: Cmd>D), or tap the Esc key which will work for most people. From the Menu bar, choose View>Grid and View>Guides to remove the Grid and Guides.

Photo Credit Lance Aoyagi

Slice and Stroke a Photo

Photoshop Elements does not have a slice tool like its big brother Photoshop does, but with a little inconvenience, we can work around that.

Open a photo and turn on the Grids (View>Grid). My gridlines are set at 33.33% with one subdivision as demonstrated in *The Basics* chapter. If your photo includes people, and the grids cut through them in unattractive ways, you can try cropping the photo first with the Crop tool (C) as I did in my example.

From the Toolbar, select the Rectangular Marquee tool (M). Using the Grid as a pattern, drag out a new selection starting from the top left corner and dragging to the bottom right corner of the first section, as shown in the example.

Type the shortcut Ctrl>J (Mac: Cmd>J) to put the selection on its own layer. Nothing will look any different at this point, unless you hide the Background layer so that you can see the new layer.

Repeat for the center section. After you create the selection border, click on the Background layer and type the shortcut Ctrl>J (Mac: Cmd>J) to put the selection on its own layer. Repeat the same steps for the final section.

Link the three cut sections together by selecting all three layers in the Layers panel and clicking on the Link symbol at the bottom of the Layers panel.

From the Menu bar, choose File>New (Ctrl>N, Mac: Cmd>N) to create a new blank file. Type the letter D to set the Foreground color to black. Type the shortcut Alt>Backspace (Mac: Opt>Delete) to fill the Background layer with black.

From the Toolbar, select the Move tool (V). Click and drag the photo down to the new file. All of the photo layers will be highlighted in the Layers panel. Unlink the photo layers by clicking on the Link symbol at the bottom of the Layers panel.

Click on the left photo piece and tap the Left Arrow key ten times (or any amount you choose). Click on the right photo piece and tap the Right Arrow key ten times.

Ctrl click (Mac: Cmd>click) on the left photo layer thumbnail. A selection border (marching ants) will surround the photo.

Type the letter X to change the Foreground color to white. Make a blank transparent layer above the left photo layer by clicking on the New Layer icon at the bottom of the Layers panel, or type the shortcut Shift>Alt>Ctrl>N (Mac: Shift>Opt>Cmd>N). Rename the layer Left Photo Stroke.

From the Menu bar, choose Edit>Stroke (Outline) Selection. In my example I have used a 15 px white Stroke but use whatever color and size you wish. Location must be Inside to retain sharp corners. Blending Mode is Normal, Opacity 100%, and the Preserve Transparency box is not checked.

Repeat for each photo piece.
Photo credit: Jill Phillips, Font: Garamond Italic

Stray Pixel Cleanup

If you've ever used the Eraser tool (E) to cut something out of an image (extract) you know that sometimes you don't get the results you would like, especially if you're a Photoshop Elements novice.

In this example I want to extract the statue from the background to use on another project. I used several selection tools including the Lasso and Magic Wand tools. I thought I did a pretty good job until I added the statue onto my page.

Some of the ways to search for stray pixels are: Place the extraction on a black or white background, add a Noisy or Heavy Drop Shadow, and finally add a brightly colored Stroke to the extracted image.

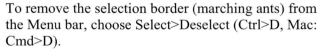

Original Image

To add the Stroke, Ctrl click (Mac: Cmd: click) on the Layer thumbnail. Click on the New Layer icon at the bottom of the Layers panel, or type the shortcut Shift>Alt>Ctrl>N (Mac: Shift>Opt>Cmd>N).

From the Menu bar, choose Edit>Stroke (Outline) Selection. Enter 10 pixels for the width. Choose a bright color that isn't in the image. In my example I chose red so that it really stands out.

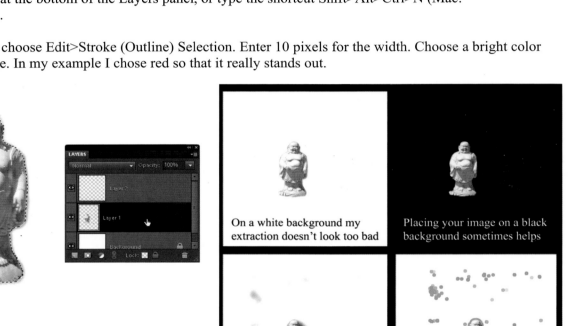

On a white background my extraction doesn't look too bad

Placing your image on a black background sometimes helps

Stray pixels exposed by adding a Noisy Drop Shadow

All stray pixels exposed by applying a Stroke Outline

To remove the selection border (marching ants) from the Menu bar, choose Select>Deselect (Ctrl>D, Mac: Cmd>D).

From the Toolbar, choose the Eraser tool (E). Select image layer and erase the stray pixels. Delete the Stroke layer when you're done erasing. Repeat the same steps again to make sure that you cleaned up all of the stray pixels.

Cool Stuff with Actions

I'm often asked by my students what an action is. My best definition is that it's a set of steps recorded in Photoshop and saved so that you can do really cool stuff with the push of a button. Instructions for installing actions can be found on the last page of this chapter. Once installed, actions are easy to use and addicting. To play/run an action, double click the action thumbnail. You may see a message box that pops up and tells you to do something or Photoshop Elements may just take over on its own. As the action runs, things are happening very quickly on the screen without you doing a thing, which is the beauty of it all!

Some actions may tell you to select the layer before it will work. Depending on the designer, this may mean that you need to just click on the layer in the Layers panel or actually add a selection border (marching ants) around the layer.

So it knows what color to use when working its magic, actions such as the Inked or Chalked Edges actions require you to set the Foreground color. If you want to intensify the effect, try running the action again and see what happens. As shown below on the Old Paint action example, I started with new red text and ended up with old distressed red text. However, with the Weathered Steel action example I also started with red text that was changed into old steel. Each action will work a little differently so be prepared to play around with them a little bit.

An action may require that your type, shape or image be at least 300 pixels high/ On a 300 resolution page, this is only one inch (72 pts for the Type tool setting). You may not be warned that you have to Simplify Text and Shape layers before running some actions, so if you're having trouble, try that. Be aware that if you have a layer style like Sepia applied to an image, it may be removed during the course of the action, as I found out when running the Burnt Edges action below. If this happens to you, Simplify the layer before running the action.

AtomicCupcake.com Actions

The Atomic Cupcake Inked Edges Action is included on the *Photoshop Elements - Basics & Beyond* DVD for you to play with. I am a terrible traditional scrapbook inker, I admit it! By the time I'm done inking something, it looks like I've basically taken a bath in the ink. Using this action you don't get dirty at all! You can apply this action to photos that you will print and use on traditional pages.

In this example, I created the light gray text with the Type tool. I changed the Foreground color to black. I selected the text by Ctrl clicking on the text layer thumbnail in the layers panel. I double clicked on the action thumbnail once to produce the effect shown on the middle example. To intensify the effect, I ran the action two more times to produce the top example.

Atomic Cupcake Weathered Steel

Atomic Cupcake Burnt Edges

Atomic Cupcake Tight Stitching

Atomic Cupcake Chalked Edges

Atomic Cupcake Old Painted Metal

PanosFx.com Actions

Puzzle Effects

Included on the *Photoshop Elements - Basics & Beyond* DVD is a great set of puzzle templates from PanosFx.com. Photoshop Elements has a puzzle texture that you can apply through the Texturizer filter, but the pattern is small and then you have to cut the pieces out yourself. I've actually dragged several of my hands-on classes through that tortuous technique. With these actions, with the click of a button, your image is cut into six or twenty pieces with a thin, thick or normal edge. Not only that, each piece is on its own numbered layer so you know which one is which. The layers are linked together so you don't accidentally move one. In my example I dragged the finished image onto a larger new document. I unlinked a couple of pieces so I could move them around with the Move tool (V) to make it look like an unfinished puzzle. Panos also has puzzle actions available for purchase with 30, 56, and 100 pieces.

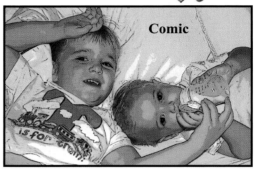

Comic

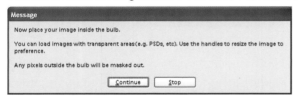

You will be guided along the way by a series of message boxes.

Magnifying Glass

Postage Stamp

If your photos need to be lightened, darkened, etc. I suggest editing them before you use the action. If you are using an action that uses several photos like the film strip, decide in advance which photos you will use. I have found it's easier if I put them in a separate folder because then I don't' have to search for them again.

Analysis

Analysis

Film Machine

Graffi's Graffishop-Graficalicus.com

Included on the *Photoshop Elements - Basics & Beyond* DVD is a sampler action set from Graficalicus.com. This action set is self installing by just double clicking on it. To find the action, click on the All option on the Effects panel or in the Action Player section of Guided Edit. A full set of ATN, PNG, and HML files are included. If you want to install the action, follow the directions at the end of this chapter. He has also included a coupon, so don't miss that!

Old Romance

Weaver

Soft Black & White

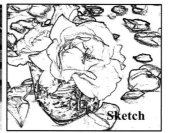

Sketch

Installing Actions

The three previous pages have shown you that actions are very cool! So what's the problem? Why don't more Photoshop Elements users use them? The reason people don't use them is that they either don't know about them or they're afraid of them. Some actions are made for Photoshop and will not work on Photoshop Elements, so be sure to read the fine print carefully when you purchase actions. Some actions are created for Windows only and will not work on a Mac.

The process of installing an action has become more complicated in the last few years. Some actions come with several files and that's where it gets confusing. All you have to do to run an action is copy the ATN file into a folder and delete the two specified files as detailed on the next page. If this is all you do, the action will show in your Effects panel under the All heading (circled) with a blank black thumbnail, which is fine. The action names will appear when you hover over the thumbnail and under the thumbnail (if yours don't, go back and read the *First Things First* chapter).

Using the Add-O-Matic program available from *www.graficalicus.com* will also install the ATN file and save your sanity at the same time. Drag the ATN file to the gray box and click on Go. The action will show up in the Photo Effects section of the Effects Panel under Add-O-Matic Heading, which was automatically added for you. As shown on the right, all of the thumbnails will look identical, but the action name will show under the thumbnail. They will also be added to the Guided Edit Action Player. Not all actions will work correctly in Guided Edit, especially the ones where you have to perform a task while the action is running.

If you are manually installing actions and want to display an image on the action thumbnail instead of the black box shown above, you must also copy a PNG file along with the ATN file into the folder detailed on the next page. If the designer included the PNG file, that's a great timesaver for you. Just copy it in the folder with the ATN file following all the steps on the next page.

There may be a PSD file image included in the action folder because earlier versions of Photoshop Elements required a PSD file for the thumbnail. If there's no image file included with the action, you may be able to copy a preview from the designer's website and modify it. Open any image you have in Photoshop Elements.

Panos FX Light Bulb

Select the Crop tool (C) and enter a crop size of 64 x 64 px, resolution 72 ppi on the Options bar and crop the image. From the Menu bar choose File>Save As and save it as a PNG file with the same **exact** name as the ATN file or it won't work. Copy the PNG file with the ATN file following the directions below.

The last file you may have included with your actions is an XML file. The purpose of an XML file is to make its own category in the Photo Effects section of the Effects panel. As shown in the example above, all of the puzzle actions from Panos FX are listed in their own Panos FX FREEBIE category. If your action doesn't include a XML file, make one using the instructions on the *What's New* tab at *www.TheDigitalScrapbookTeacher.com*.

If you are unable to find the appropriate folder or file listed below, go to the *What's New* tab at *www.TheDigitalScrapbookTeacher.com* to see how to show hidden files and folders. Follow these instructions **exactly** to install your actions and styles. Don't worry; it's not as difficult as it looks. Panos FX and Graffi have supplied all three files needed to install actions per the instructions below. These instructions are for Photoshop Elements 9. If you have a different version, be sure to put them in the correct folders for your version number. Installing actions and styles is the same except for step 2, be sure you note the underlined word for step 2.

*1. **Download and Unzip action folder. To save time, install several actions or styles at one time.***

2. <u>Actions</u> Copy the ATN, XML, and PNG files (Ctrl>C, Mac: Cmd>C). Paste (Ctrl>V, Mac: Cmd>V) the files into the appropriate folder listed below:

Windows XP C:>Documents and Settings>All Users> Application Data>Adobe>Photoshop Elements> 9.0> Photo Creations>photo effects

Windows 7 & Vista C:>ProgramData>Adobe>Photoshop Elements>9.0>Photo Creations> photo effects

Mac Library>Application support>Adobe >Photoshop Elements>9.0>Photo Creations>photo effects>

2. <u>Styles</u> Copy the ASL file (Ctrl>C, Mac: Cmd>C). Paste (Ctrl>V, Mac: Cmd>V) the file into the appropriate folder:

Windows XP C:>Documents and Settings>All Users> Application Data>Adobe>Photoshop Elements> 9.0> Photo Creations>layer styles

Windows 7 & Vista C:>ProgramData>Adobe>Photoshop Elements>9.0>Photo Creations> layer styles

Mac Library>Application support>Adobe >Photoshop Elements>9.0>Photo Creations>layer styles

*3. **Delete MediaDatabase.db3 file. You will find it in the folder here:***

Windows XP C:>Documents and Settings>All Users>Application Data>Adobe>Photoshop Elements> 9.0>Locale>en_US

Windows 7 & Vista C:>ProgramData>Adobe>Photoshop Elements>9.0>Locale>en_US

Mac Library>Application support> Adobe >Photoshop Elements>9.0> Locale>en_Us

*4. **Delete ThumbDatabase.db3 file. You will find it in the folder here:***

Windows XP C:>Documents and Settings>All Users>Application Data>Adobe>Photoshop Elements> 9.0

Windows 7 & Vista C:>ProgramData>Adobe>Photoshop Elements>9.0

Mac Library>Application support> Adobe >Photoshop Elements>9.0

5. Start Photoshop Elements, it will take longer than normal to start because it is rebuilding and updating. When it opens, check the Effects panel for your newly added actions and styles.

You can also copy an ATN file in the following folders to have the action show up in Guided Edit only:

Windows XP C:>Documents and Settings>All Users>Application Data>Adobe>Photoshop Elements> 9.0>Locale>en_US>Workflow Panels>Actions

Windows 7 & Vista C:>ProgramData>Adobe>Photoshop Elements>9.0>Locale>en_US>Workflow Panels>Actions

Mac Library>Application support> Adobe >Photoshop Elements>9.0> Locale>en_Us>Workflow Panels>Actions

Make Your Own

If you've ever been frustrated because you couldn't purchase a digital item that meet your needs, or if you have a lot of time on your hands and want to create your own digital art, this chapter is for you.

How to Make Your Own Drop Shadow

Drop shadows can be easily added from the Layer Styles menu on the Effects Panel. You can easily adjust the Lighting Angle, Size, Distance, Opacity, and Color of the Photoshop Elements drop shadows. To do this, double click on the *fx* symbol to display the Style Settings dialog box. The settings shown in the example on the right are for the Low Drop Shadow.

If you want more control over your drop shadows, it's easy to make your own. To begin, drag your photo onto a scrapbook page which is covered in the *Hot to Use* chapter.

From the Menu bar, choose Layer>New>Layer via Copy or use the shortcut Ctrl>J (Mac: Cmd>J).

Select the bottom photo layer in the Layers panel. Set the Foreground color chip at the bottom of the Toolbar to Black (or another color of your choice). Choose Edit>Fill Layer (Contents Use: Foreground Color, Blending Mode: Normal, Opacity 100%, ✓ Preserve Transparency), or use the shortcut Shift>Alt>Backspace (Mac: Shift>Opt>Delete). Check the Layers panel to make sure that the bottom photo layer is filled with black.

With the solid black layer selected, from the Menu bar, choose Filter>Blur>Gaussian Blur. Slide the slider to adjust the amount of blur. In my example, the Radius is 10 pixels, but you can experiment to see what looks best with your photo. Clicking and dragging in the preview box to see the edge of the layer can be helpful to see how much the layer is blurred.

The blurred black layer will surround the photo. To make it look like the light is coming from the top left corner you need to move the solid black down and to the right a little bit. Use the Arrow keys while the Move tool (V) or Transform command is active (Ctrl>T, Mac: Cmd>T) to nudge the layer.

Adjust the blending mode and the opacity setting on the solid black layer shown on the right. I normally choose the Multiply blending mode. I lowered the Opacity to 73% but that will vary depending on what kind of project I'm working on.

How to Make Your Own Drop Shadow with Lifted Corners

Follow the preceding tutorial. Select the black drop shadow layer. From the Menu bar, choose Filter>Distort>Liquify. The Liquify dialog box will display the black layer, if something else is showing, tap the Cancel button and select the correct layer in the Layers panel.

Make the brush big enough to cover the entire layer as shown. The easiest way to do this is to tap the right Bracket key]. Gently click and drag up so that the center of the black rectangle arcs slightly. Adjust the brush size as needed. If you make a mistake, click on the Revert button and start over. Click OK when you're finished and both of the bottom corners will appear to be lifted as shown below.

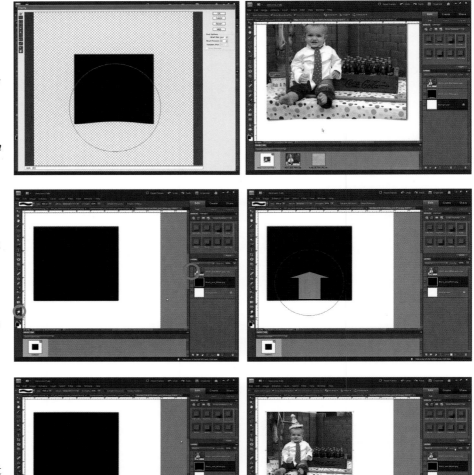

As always, there's more than one way to do something with Photoshop Elements. If you're having a hard time with the Liquify filter method; try the next technique.

Follow the *How to Make Your Own Drop Shadow* tutorial at the beginning of this chapter.

After making a drop shadow on its own layer, hide the photo layer by clicking on the eyeball icon, shown circled below. Select the black drop shadow layer in the Layers panel.

Choose the Smudge tool (R) on the Toolbar. The Smudge tool is nested with the Blur and Sharpen tool. To display the nested tools, right click on the tool icon or click and hold on the ◢ located at the bottom right corner of the tool icon.

Enlarge the brush so that it's almost as wide as the drop shadow layer. Click, hold, and drag upward slightly. It may take a little bit of time for Photoshop Elements to complete this operation.

Show the photo layer again by clicking on the eyeball icon. Select the drop shadow layer in the Layers panel. Tap the Arrow keys while the Move tool (V) or Transform command is active (Ctrl>T, Mac: Cmd>T) to nudge the drop shadow layer where you want it.

Believe it or not, it may be easier to lift two corners than just one. Check out the next page to see how to lift just one corner.

Follow the *How to Make Your Own Drop Shadow* tutorial in the beginning of this chapter. Select the photo layer in the Layers panel, and then from the Menu bar, choose Filter>Distort>Liquify. To lift the bottom right corner, click and drag the corner up and in just slightly as shown below. Reducing the Brush Pressure on the Liquify Filter dialog box may make it easier to warp the photo. Click OK.

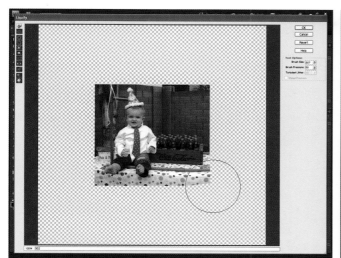 

To make the lifted corner look a little more realistic, select the black drop shadow layer in the Layers panel and from the Menu bar, choose Filter>Distort>Liquify. To lift the bottom right corner, click and drag the corner down and out just slightly as shown below. Click OK.

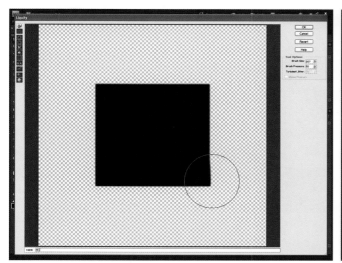 

If you are going to add a mat to your photo, you will need to follow the same steps for the mat.

Some designers sell actions that will simulate lifted corners. You can also use templates that have lifted corners like the 12 x 12 #F Template set available at *www.TheDigitalScrapbookTeacher.com*. Instead of using the entire template, you can choose one of the sets of template shapes from the template to use on your scrapbook page. Unlink the pieces from the template, and then link the pieces you want to use together and drag it onto your page.

Make Your Own Custom Drop Shadow for an Embellishment

While the Drop Shadows in Photoshop Elements work well most of the time, sometimes you get a more realistic effect if you make your own.

Open the pink ribbon from the Ribbons folder inside the Digital Scrapbook Teacher's Examples folder on the *Photoshop Elements - Basics & Beyond* DVD. This ribbon is from the Summertime Paper & Embellishment kit available at *www.TheDigitalScrapbookTeacher.com*.

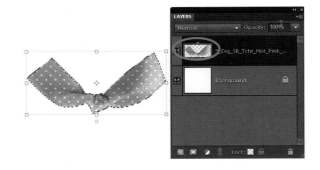

Use the Move tool (V) to drag the ribbon onto a plain white piece of paper (Instructions can be found in the *How to Use* chapter).

Ctrl click (Mac: Cmd click) on the ribbon layer thumbnail shown circled. A selection border (marching ants) will surround the ribbon.

Hold the Ctrl key (Mac: Cmd key), and click on the New Layer icon at the bottom of the Toolbar to create a new transparent layer **below** the ribbon layer.

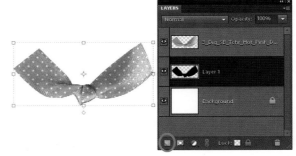

Type the letter D to set your Foreground and Background colors located at the bottom of the Toolbar to the default settings. Your Foreground color should be black, and your Background color should be white. Type the shortcut Alt>Backspace (Mac: Opt>Delete) to fill the selection with black.

Type Ctrl>D (Mac>Cmd>D) to remove the selection border.

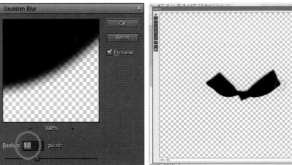

With the black fill layer selected, choose Filter>Blur>Gaussian Blur from the Menu bar. Set the Radius about 8.0 px and click OK.

With the Move tool (V) selected, tap the Down Arrow key one or two times to move the shadow layer down so that it can be seen.

From the Menu bar, choose Filter, Distort, Liquify. Adjust the size of the brush to about 25 px. Click and drag the two bottom ends of the ribbon shadow down and out. Click OK.

Lower the Opacity of the shadow layer until you like the effect, my example shows the Opacity at 42%.

How to Make Your Own Brush

Brushes are similar to rubber stamps and punches. You can make a brush out of shapes, text, ding bats, photos, clip art, and by combining other brushes. The one rule to remember when making a brush is that the image must be less than 2500 pixels in height and width.

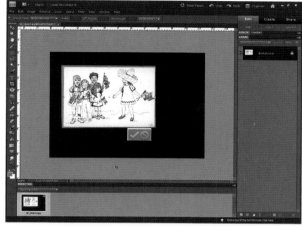

If you're a doodler, you can convert your doodles into brushes. The best way to doodle is with a Wacom tablet, because your doodles instantly become digital images. If you doodle with a pen and paper, you will need to scan the doodles first. I'm not a doodler or an artist, but in this example I'm going to turn a sketch by my mother, Gayle Kelley, into a brush. She drew this sketch when she worked on my sister's school's newsletter in the 1970's. I really liked the sketch so she framed it and gave it to me. I've had it for more than 20 years, and when I tried to remove it from the frame it wouldn't budge, so I scanned it with the mat on it.

First, I'll crop the mat from the sketch with the Crop tool (C). Next, I'll check the size of the image to make sure it's not too big. To do this, from the Menu bar, choose Image>Resize>Image Size.

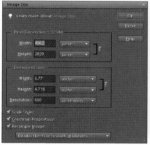
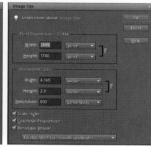

Even after I cropped the image, it's too big. Because the brush must be smaller than 2500 px, I entered 2499 pixels in the Width box. Note that the Scale Styles, Constrain Proportions and Resample Image boxes are checked.

To help clean up the image and adjust the lighting, choose Enhance>Adjust Lighting>Levels (Ctrl>L, Mac: Cmd>L). This works well except for the lower right corner near her initials. I could remove the initials, but it's important to me to keep them.

The Dodge tool (O) helps me lighten up the edges of the sketch.

From the Menu bar, choose Edit>Define Brush.

From the toolbar, select the Brush tool (B). Select a Foreground color by clicking in the color chips at the bottom of the Toolbar. Make a new transparent layer and stamp the brush on your project. For more information about how to use a brush, read the *How to Use* chapter.

Photos can make interesting brushes. The example on the right shows the different brushes you can make with the same photo.

The top row of images is the photo after editing. The bottom row of images is the brush that was created by the photo above it.

You can try these out with the Pop Art photo which can be found on the *Photoshop Elements - Basics & Beyond* DVD.

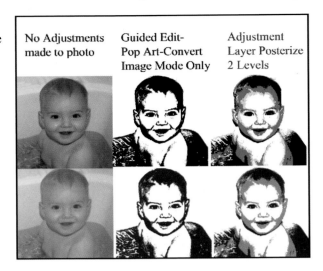

How to Save a Brush

If you've spent the time making a brush, you should take the time to save it so that you have it for future use. I also recommend backing up your brush files, so that should you need to reinstall Photoshop Elements, you will still have a copy of your brush files.

To save a brush, click on the brush drop down list and choose Preset Manager. Once the Preset Manager opens, check to make sure that the Preset Type is Brushes (circled below).

The procedure is also the same to save Patterns, Gradients, and Swatches. The Preset Manager can also be accessed by choosing Edit>Preset Manager from the Menu bar.

Select the brushes to be saved in the set by Ctrl (Mac: Cmd) clicking on each one to select it. Click on the Save Set button.

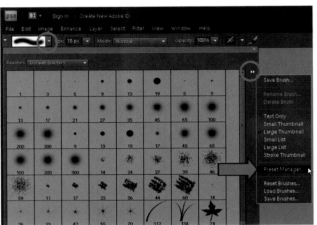

Type a name for the Brush set and click the Save button. You will be returned to the Preset Manager, click the Done button. If you have saved the brush set in the Photoshop Elements Program Files Preset Brushes folder, the next time you start Photoshop Elements the new brush set will show in the Brushes drop down list. For more information about this read the *Where to Install the Extras* chapter.

Saving too many brushes in the Preset Brushes folder can cause Photoshop Elements to slow down. If you saved the brush set in another folder you will need to load it whenever you want to use it.

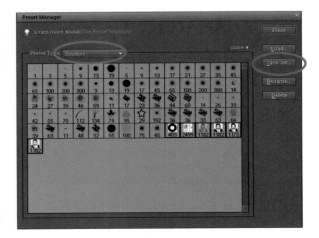

How to Make Your Own Edge Template

An edge template will turn a plain straight edge into a fancy scalloped edge. Don't like scallops? Use a different shaped brush to make a custom edge. Don't want to make your own? Edge templates can be purchased at many digital scrapbooking websites, including *www.TheDigitalScrapbookTeacher.com.*

Make a new, white 12" x 12" document as illustrated in the *How to Use* chapter. To create a new transparent layer, click on the New Layer icon at the bottom of the Layers panel or use the shortcut Shift>Ctrl>Alt>N, Mac: Shift>Cmd>Opt>N).

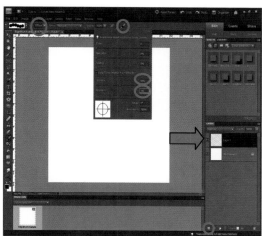

Select the Brush tool (B) from the Toolbar. Type the letter D to set your Foreground and Background colors located at the bottom of the Toolbar to the default settings. Your Foreground color should be black, and your Background color should be white.

Set the size of the brush to 175 px. Click on the Brush Options icon on the Options bar and change the Spacing to 90% and the Hardness to 100%.

To make a larger scalloped edge, increase the brush size and maybe the spacing. You will need to experiment to find the perfect settings so that your edge doesn't end up with half of a scallop. An example using a larger brush is shown below.

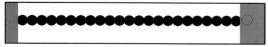

Beginning at the edge of the page, click and drag while holding the Shift key from one side to the other. Holding the Shift key while you drag insures that your line will be straight.

Select the Marquee tool (M) from the Toolbar and drag a selection. My selection starts at the left edge of the page in the center of the brush stroke, down to the bottom right side of the page. Type the shortcut Alt>Backspace, Mac: Opt>Delete to fill the selection with black.

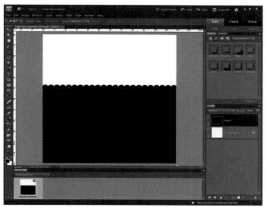

To remove the selection border (marching ants) from the Menu bar, choose Select>Deselect (Ctrl>D, Mac: Cmd>D), or tap the Esc key which will work for most people.

Hide the Background layer by clicking on the eyeball icon to the left of the Layer thumbnail and save the file as a PNG file (see *The Basics* chapter) for future use.

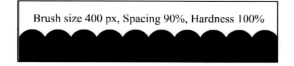

Brush size 400 px, Spacing 90%, Hardness 100%

Create your own brush as shown in the preceding tutorial to customize your edge templates.

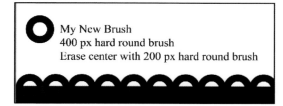

My New Brush
400 px hard round brush
Erase center with 200 px hard round brush

In the bottom example I created a new brush using a 400 px hard round brush. I stamped the brush once, and then used the Eraser tool (E) to erase the center with a 200 px hard round brush. From the Menu bar I chose Edit>Define Brush to make a new brush.

I stamped my new brush as we did in earlier examples. The brush size was 400 px and the spacing was 90% .

How to Make a Layered Template

If you are going to be making a card, scrapbook page, brochure, or other project using the same design several times, to save time it would probably be a good idea to make a template. If you like to draw you may want to make a preliminary sketch of your template or you can do all your creating on the computer. Templates can be easily changed as shown in the *Change It* chapter.

To begin, make a new, blank, white file the dimensions of your template (Ctrl>N, Mac: Cmd>N). Be sure that the template name is something that you'll be able to easily recognize in the future.

If you are making a square template, I would suggest that you make the template 12" x 12" even if you want the finished page in a smaller size. There are two reasons for this: Scrapbook paper is 12" x 12" inches and if you make your template 8" x 8" you will spend a lot of time resizing the paper to include the edges of the paper which often have a grungy, distressed edge. The second reason is that if you decide later that you want to print the template 12" x 12", the print quality won't be great because you enlarged it.

If you have a lot of traditional supplies that you would like to use on pages or don't have access to a wide format printer, consider making some 8.5" x 11" templates. You can print the finished pages on a standard color printer, adhere them to "real" scrapbook paper, and add "real" embellishments; thus relieving some of the guilt you feel over purchasing and storing traditional supplies.

From the Toolbar, choose one of the Shape tools (U). In my example I'm going to use the Rectangle tool.

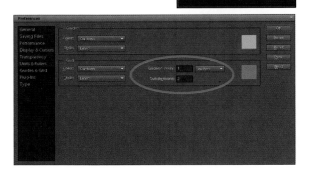

To help align the template pieces, you may want to turn on the Grid (View>Grid) and also choose the Snap To function (View>Snap To>Grid). To make adjustments to the Grid, choose Edit>Preferences>Guides & Grid (Mac: Photoshop Elements>Preferences>Guides & Grid). I have changed my Grid specifications to: Gridline Every 1 inch, and Subdivisions 2.

Unless you tell it otherwise the Shape tool allows you to drag out shapes in any size or proportion.

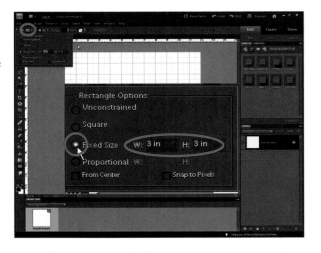

In my example, I am going to make my template pieces 3 inch squares. Instead of eyeballing it, with the grid I can instruct Photoshop Elements to draw a 3 inch perfect square every time I click. To do this, click on the Rectangle Options drop down arrow on the Options bar (shown circled).

Click to select the Fixed Size option on the Rectangle Options dialog box, shown enlarged on the right. Enter the size of the rectangle you wish to make.

Double click on an empty area of the Options bar to close the box.

Using the grid as a guide, click on the template where you would like to place the first template piece. In my example, I clicked at the intersection of the one inch grid lines (shown circled). Once I click, a square template piece in my Foreground color is added on a new layer. Save the File (File>Save) as a PSD file now, and as you add more template pieces. For more information about saving as a PSD file, see *The Basics* chapter.

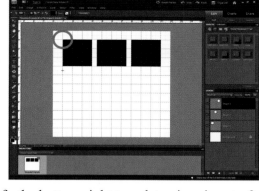

Continue clicking to add more pieces. Try to keep the pieces in line, but if they get out of line, we can easily fix it.

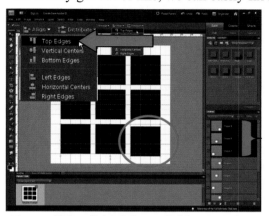

In my example on the left, the bottom right template piece is out of alignment. Instead of Undoing and adding the piece again, I can easily align it by selecting the Move tool (V) from the Toolbar.

Select the three layers in the Layers panel by clicking on the top one (Shape 9 in my example) and Shift clicking on the third one (Shape 7). All three layers should be selected as shown in my example.

From the Move tool Options bar, click on the Align drop down arrow (shown enlarged on the left) and choose Top Edges. The three pieces will be aligned to the highest selected layer.

Turn off the Grid (View>Grid) to see how your template looks. If some of the layers are out of alignment, continue aligning them as required by following the same steps.

From the Menu bar, choose File>Save (Ctrl>S, Mac: Cmd>S) to save the template for the final time as a PSD file. Make sure that you are saving the template in a folder where you can find it in the future, like Patty's Scrapbook Templates inside my Scrapbook Supplies folder. Importing the template into your Scrapbooking Supplies Organizer Catalog and tagging it will also help you find it in the future. All templates sold at *www.TheDigitalScrapbookTeacher.com* are pre-tagged for you.

The template can be used now or in the future. When you use the template in the future, be sure to duplicate (File>Duplicate) the file or choose File>Save As (Shift>Ctrl>S, Mac: Shift>Cmd>S) as soon as you open it so that you don't save over the original template.

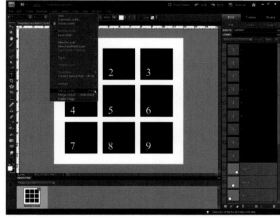

If you would like to number your template pieces as we do at *www.TheDigitalScrapbookTeacher.com,* there are at least two different ways you can do it. If you are going to save your template as a single layer PNG file per the instructions on the next page, save it before adding the numbers.

Select the Type tool (T) from the Toolbar. On the Options bar, choose white or another light color. As shown above, type a number over each template piece on its own layer which will add nine new layers. Select all of the type layers. From the Menu bar, choose Layer>Merge Layers (Ctrl>E, Mac: Cmd>E) and merge them together.

Double click on the merged type layer name and rename the layer *Layer Numbers*. Rename all of the template pieces with the corresponding template number. The advantage of doing it this way is that you can turn off the number layer when you don't want to see the numbers, or when you want to save the file as a JPEG or PNG file.

Do not use this method until after you have saved your template as a JPEG or PNG file. Click on the first template layer in the Layers panel to select it.

Select the Type tool (T) from the Toolbar. On the Options bar, choose white or another light color. Type the number one above the template piece. A new type layer will be added and the layer name will be *1*. Select the type layer and the template layer in the Layers panel. From the Menu bar, choose Layer>Merge Layers (Ctrl>E, Mac: Cmd>E) and merge them together. The layer number is permanently embedded into the template piece, and the template layer is renamed automatically.

To save the file as a JPEG, choose File>Save as and choose the JPEG format. Saving as a JPEG is for preview purposes for Windows users only. A PSD file on a PC displays the icon, not a thumbnail image as the Mac does.

You can decide if you want to save your templates in a JPEG format with or without the numbers. At *www.TheDigitalScrapbookTeacher.com* we save our JPEG template files without the numbers because the numbers may be distracting to some.

Microsoft Windows 7 Screenshot

More information about saving as a JPEG can be found in *The Basics* chapter.

Saving a file as a single layer PNG file will only work well if none of the pieces overlap, like our example. To save the file as a single layer PNG file, duplicate the file (File>Duplicate). By default, the word copy will be added to the file name, which is fine. Close (File>Close or Ctrl>W, Mac: Cmd>W) the original template.

Select all of the layers and merge them together (Layer>Merge Layers or Ctrl>E, Mac: Cmd>E).

It will be easier to preview and use the template in the future if it's black. To change the white areas to black and the black areas to white choose Filter>Adjustments>Invert or type the shortcut Ctrl>I (Mac: Cmd>I).

From the Toolbar, select the Magic Wand tool (W). Uncheck Contiguous on the Options bar and click on a white area of the template. All white areas of the template should be selected. Tap the Delete key, the white areas will be removed and a checkerboard pattern indicating transparency will be displayed.

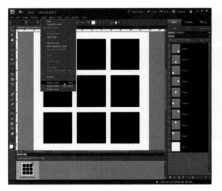
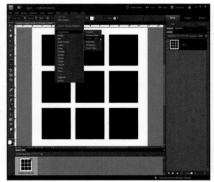
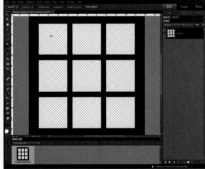

From the Menu bar, choose File>Save As (Shift>Ctrl>S, Mac: Shift>Cmd>S). Choose PNG as the format. For Interlace PNG Options, choose None. For more information about saving files, see *The Basics* chapter.

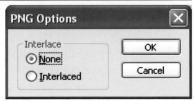

Read the *How to Use* chapter to see how to use a PNG template.

How to Make Your Own Paper Patterns

Want to make your own custom paper? Use Photoshop Elements to make patterns with shapes, text, ding bats, brushes, photos, clip art, and anything else you can think of.

Patterns can be made in any size, but there are two important things to remember: First, if you make a 3" x 3" pattern and use it on an 8.5" x 11" scrapbook page, part of the pattern will be missing which may or may not look OK. Second, if you make the pattern too small, it may look pixilated when you make it larger.

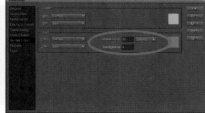

In this example, we will assume that we're making a pattern for a 12" x 12" scrapbook page. From the Menu bar, choose File>New>Blank File (Ctrl>N, Mac: Cmd>N). Make the file 2" x 2" inches, Resolution 300 ppi, Color Mode RGB Color, and Background Contents Transparent.

Turn on the Grid (View>Grid). I have set my grid so that it divides the file in half. To do this, from the Menu bar, choose Edit>Preferences>Guides & Grid (Mac: Photoshop Elements>Preferences>Guides & Grid). Make the following changes: Gridline every 50 **percent**, Subdivisions 2.

Type the letter D to set your Foreground and Background colors located at the bottom of the Toolbar to the default settings. Your Foreground color should be black, and your Background color should be white.

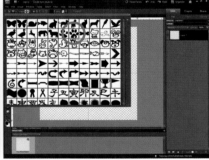

From the Toolbar, choose the Custom Shape tool (U). On the Options bar, click on the Custom Shape Picker drop down list. If your Shape Library does not look like mine, go back and read the *First Things First* chapter.

Choose the Paw Print 2 shape. Click, hold, and drag out a paw print on your transparent document. Rotate the shape if desired. Add more paw prints or other shapes as desired, being careful not to extend the shape past the edges of the document.

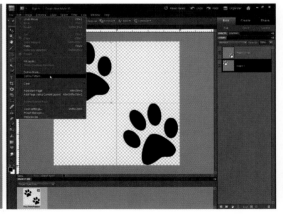

From the Menu bar, choose Edit>Define Pattern. If the option is grayed out, select both layers in the Layers panel and try again. If desired type a new name for your pattern, and click the OK button.

From the Menu bar, choose File>New>Blank File to make a new white blank document for our paper. Click on the New Layer icon at the bottom of the Layers panel to create a new transparent layer, or use the shortcut Shift>Ctrl>Alt>N, Mac: Shift>Cmd>Opt>N).

There are several methods to fill a layer with a pattern. I'll show you two of the methods first, and then I'll show you the best method last.

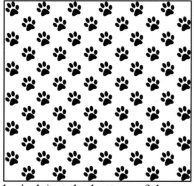

 Paint Bucket tool (K)

From the Toolbar, select the Paint Bucket tool. On the Options bar check the empty box next to the word Pattern (circled). Click on the Pattern drop down list (arrow) and choose a pattern. Click on the page and the transparent layer will be filled with the pattern.

Fill Layer Command

From the Menu bar choose Edit>Fill Layer. When the dialog box appears, click on the Contents drop down list and Use: Pattern. Choose the pattern from the Custom Pattern drop down list. Click OK and the transparent layer you created fills with the pattern.

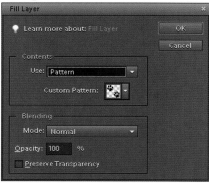

Add a Fill Layer Method (Best!)

Click on the Adjustment layer icon (half white/half black circle) at the bottom of the Layers panel. When the list of options appears, click on Pattern.

The Pattern Fill dialog box will appear as shown on the right. The scale percentage will default to 100% if you don't choose another setting. Choose the pattern **and** the Scale percentage.

This is the best method because it allows you to choose the size of the pattern. Because the pattern is on a Fill layer, you can resize it as you're working on your project. To adjust the pattern, double click on the Fill layer thumbnail (circled on the right).

The original pattern (shown below on the left) is shown at 100%, 25%, and 200% Scale on a 12" x 12" page.

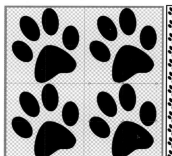

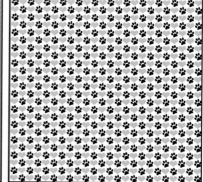

Experiment with different shapes to make all kinds of patterns. To make colorful patterns, you can start with colored shapes or you can recolor your paper patterns using the steps outlined in the *How to Use a Paper Pattern Overlay* tutorial in the *How to Use* Chapter. Grunge them up, add texture, and vary opacity to further customize your patterns.

To save the layer as a paper pattern overlay for future use, first hide the white Background layer and then save it as a PNG file. More information about saving as a PNG file, can be found in *The Basics* chapter.

Paper or Pattern with Text
You can make a pattern with text the same way you did with the shapes in the preceding tutorial. You can also make a 12" x 12" paper with text by filling the document with text and shapes. The one thing to remember about using words for a pattern is that you should fill the file with the text or you will have blank areas on your page.

To start, make a new file. Make the file 2" x 2" inches, Resolution 300 ppi, Color Mode RGB Color, and Background Contents White. To help see the text better, I am using a white background.

From the Toolbar, select the Type tool (T). Fill the file with text using different colors and fonts as shown in my example. I also added two shape layers with the custom shape tool. Save the pattern as a PSD file so you can make changes in the future if you're not happy with the result.

Hide the Background layer by clicking on the eyeball icon on the Layer thumbnail. From the Menu bar choose Edit>Define Pattern.

Make a new 12" x 12" file. Click on the New Layer icon at the bottom of the Layers panel to create a new transparent layer, or use the shortcut Shift>Ctrl>Alt>N, Mac: Shift>Cmd>Opt>N).

Click on the Adjustment layer icon (half white/half black circle) at the bottom of the Layers Panel. When the list of options appears, click on Pattern to fill the layer.

If you're not happy with your first result, try making changes to the pattern until you're happy with it. In my example I have changed only the Big Apple and Taxi Cab text to make the resulting papers look quite a bit different. To further customize the paper, I added some grunge edges and overlays from the Essentials 1 kit, and a beige piece of crumpled cardstock from the Funtime paper kit available at *www.TheDigitalScrapbookTeacher.com.*

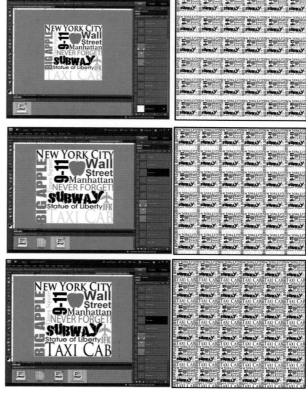

To save the pattern, see the preceding *How to Make your Own Brush* tutorial.

Where to Install the Extras

For the most part, adding extras to Photoshop Elements is easy. Inside the Photoshop Elements program file is a Presets folder that is automatically added to your computer when you install Photoshop Elements. Inside the Presets folder are individual folders for brushes, patterns, etc. For example, if you want to install a Custom Shape Set, you will close Photoshop Elements and copy and paste the brush CSH file into the Presets Custom Shapes folder. The next time you open Photoshop Elements, the new shape set will appear in the Custom Shape and Cookie Cutter drop down list on the Options bar. In the Presets folder you can install these types of files into the appropriate folder:

·Brushes-ABR File	·Custom Shapes-CSH File	·Patterns-PAT File
·Color Swatches-ACO & ACT File	·Gradients-GRD File	·Textures-PSD File

To install actions and styles see the last page of the *Cool Stuff with Actions* chapter.

The Presets folder can be found here:
Windows-C:>Program Files>Adobe>Photoshop Elements 9>Presets
Mac-Applications>Photoshop Elements 9>Presets, or hold the Cmd key and click on the Photoshop Elements icon on your dock and you will be taken to the Photoshop Elements applications folder, double click on the Presets folder to open it.

If you are unable to find the appropriate folder or file, you may need to show hidden files and folders. For a tutorial how to do this, go to the *What's New* tab at our website *www.TheDigitalScrapbookTeacher.com.*

Installing a lot of "extra" files can bog down your computer so be selective. I recommend temporarily loading brushes that you don't use all the time. Instructions for loading a brush temporarily can be found in the *How to Use a Brush like a Rubber Stamp - Single Color* tutorial in the *How to Use* chapter.

It's important that you also keep an extra copy of the files that you add to the Presets folder as a back-up. In the event that you need to reinstall Photoshop Elements because of a problem your "extra" files will be deleted from the Presets folders. If you upgrade to a newer version of Photoshop Elements, you will need to add your "extra" files to the new version as they unfortunately don't automatically migrate.

Included on the *Photoshop Elements - Basics & Beyond* DVD is a coupon for the Graffi's Add-O-Matic Automatic Add-On Installer and other products. Purchase, download, and unzip this program (only available to Windows users at press time) and simply drag your "extra" files to it, and they're automatically installed for you.

Things get a little more confusing when it comes to installing actions and styles. Some actions and styles are made for Photoshop and will not work on Photoshop Elements, so be sure to read the fine print carefully when you purchase actions.

Some actions and styles are created for Windows only and will not work on a Mac. Some designers will provide only an ATN file with their action and others will provide a PNG and XML file. What's the difference? Read the last page of the *Cool Stuff with Actions* chapter and I'll explain it all.

With the Add-O-Matic, all you need to do is drag the ATN or ASL file to the gray box. The action will show up in the Photo Effects section of Effects Panel under the Add-O-Matic Heading. As shown above, all of the thumbnails will display the same button and Add-O-Matic text but the names will appear under the thumbnail (if yours don't, go back and read the *First Things First* chapter). They will also be added to the Guided Edit Action Player. However, if you have to do something yourself like change a setting, they will not work correctly. For other methods to install actions, see the *Cool Stuff with Actions* chapter.

Speed it Up!

I admit it…my scrapbooks are not complete and up to date! There it is, all out in the open for the whole world to know! Sorry…I'm sure you're very disillusioned now. You probably purchased this book expecting the author would, of course, have all of her scrapbooks complete and up to date. You also probably expected that same author would have perfect, exquisite works of art for each of her scrapbook page layouts. Well…if you've been in one of my classes, you already know this isn't the case.

I have another secret to tell…99% of the people I meet aren't caught up either, so you're not alone! How do I know this? I ask my students in class and they tell me they can't possibly live long enough to ever get caught up. Every once in awhile, one of my students will quietly mention that all of their scrapbooks are completely up to date. This seemingly innocent statement causes havoc in my classroom, prompting the other students to sneer and throw sharp objects (like scissors) at them. After I administer first aid and confiscate the scissors and other weapons, I share some of my time saving tips with them.

1. **Use the Organizer!** Yes, I know it takes time to tag your photos and scrapbook supplies, but I can promise you that every minute you spend tagging will save you at least ten minutes in the long run. After you get the hang of tagging, do it while you're watching TV or waiting for soccer practice to finish up.

Be sure to tag your favorite photos using the star tags. I can't count how many times my children would come home from school and need a photo for something. This was before digital cameras were around so I would dig through my boxes of photos, or, if I was lucky, pull one off of a completed scrapbook page and make a color copy.

Even if you think your digital photos are well organized in folders, read through the Organization chapter and see what you can do by tagging your photos. I teach a hands-on class about the Organizer. Many people are reluctant to sign up because they don't think they really need the class. When I see these students months after the event the one class they talk about is the Organizer class. Does that mean the other classes weren't any good? No, they're just extra excited about how much easier it is to find what they're looking for.

Using your tagged scrapbook supplies is like shopping in a well organized scrapbook store. If you are/were a paper scrapper, what kind of organizational system did you use for your traditional supplies? Did you have your papers and embellishments organized by color, type, and theme? Or, maybe you used the method that I did for awhile…bags of stuff piled up waiting for someone…anyone…to organize it for me.

One really good reason for tagging your scrapbook supplies in the Organizer is saving money. You can't believe how many people actually buy the same kits more than once, because they didn't remember that they'd already purchased it.

How are you ever going to get all of your photos and scrapbook supplies imported into the Organizer and tagged right away? Plain and simple, you're not! It takes time to do, but I have faith in you and know you can do it! Begin today. Import all of your new pictures to the Organizer and tag them as you take them. Do the same thing with your scrapbook supplies. As you add new kits to your stash, make a rule not to use them unless you tag them first. Don't try to take a weekend and tag everything you've got because you'll only end up frustrated. Let's face it, there are times when we're better at organizing than we are at creating and vice versa, so take advantage of those times. Set a goal to tag for a couple of hours a week and break that time up over the course of two or three days. You'll be surprised how much you can get done by setting up a schedule like this.

Wouldn't it be nice if someone tagged your scrapbook supplies for you? If you have purchased templates, texture overlays, or paper kits from *www.TheDigitalScrapbookTeacher.com* they already have tags applied to the PSD and JPEG files. Unfortunately at this time (December 2010), we are unable to attach tags to PNG files (which are the files that contain transparency, like the buttons, bows, ribbons, etc). We're currently working on this challenge and hope to come up with an answer in the future. I don't know of any other digital scrapbooking designer that adds tags to their files, but it might be worth asking for at your favorite online store.

Perhaps when you purchased this book, you also purchased the Organizer Back-up Catalog. This item, available at: *www.TheDigitalScrapbookTeacher.com* has already tagged all of the images on the *Digital Scrapbooking Basics & Beyond* DVD that comes with this book. This DVD will save you at least ten hours of time, and give you a solid organizational foundation to start with.

Using my Scrapbook Supplies Organizer Catalog I can find a piece of red, white, and blue, paper with stars and stripes on it in less than a minute searching through more than 50,000 scrapbook elements. I purchased this particular piece of paper more than five years ago. Do you think that if I needed to use it on a 4th of July page I could ever find it if I didn't use the Organizer?

2. Use Templates! Why spend time making sketches and designing your own pages? You're trying to get some pages done, right? I have a student named Laurie who attended one of our Boot Camps in April of 2010. She returned for one of our Intermediate/Advanced Digital Scrapbooking Workshops in November 2010 (less than seven months later) with more than 400 pages completed. She said that before she started using templates she didn't think she'd ever get caught up. When I asked Laurie how she did it, she told me that she made simple pages with templates. Her pages are beautiful…they're done…and her family can look at them in a book…what a concept!

It will take you longer to pick out your pictures and scrapbook supplies than it will to actually assemble a template after you get the hang of it. I'm not going to lie to you and tell you that you will immediately have the knack for assembling a template, but with a little practice you can knock one out in less than a minute. In the *How to Use* chapter is a tutorial for a template. The template is included on the *Photoshop Elements Basics & Beyond* DVD. Put the template together one time, and then do the same template three or four times until you get the hang of it. The key is to pop open Photoshop Elements more than once a month or you'll forget everything you learned.

If you are using templates with mats for several photos, instead of filling each mat separately, merge all of the mat layers together and fill just one layer.

Sure, *www.TheDigitalScrapbookTeacher.com* sells great template sets at great prices, but that's not the reason I'm telling you to use them. Templates can be purchased at every digital scrapbooking website I've ever visited while surfing the web in the middle of the night, so try them.

3. Stop Surfing the Web for Freebies! I call this the Freebie Frenzy. I admit it, I've done it. Stop and figure out how much time you've spent clogging up your computer with supplies that you will probably never use. You will probably never use them because you won't remember what you've got or where you put it. I did the same thing when I first started out, because, after all, the stuff 1s free. The really big problem was that I was collecting it but I didn't know how to use any of it yet.

Start spending the time you normally spend surfing the web trying out new techniques in this book and making some simple pages. You'll soon see that you can accomplish something, instead of jumping from website to website.

4. Use the Scroll Wheel! With Photoshop Elements 9, Adobe has brought back some of the capabilities of the Scroll Wheel that were removed beginning with Photoshop Elements 6. I use the Scroll Wheel to zoom in and out, change the size of my fonts, select different fonts, change blending modes (PC only), and change opacity and other settings. If your Scroll Wheel isn't working, choose Edit>Preferences>General and check the box that says Zoom with Scroll Wheel (Mac: Photoshop Elements>Preferences>General.

5. Save Often! Saving only takes a second, and with Photoshop Elements 9 it's easy to see if you have unsaved changes. Check the top right corner of the document you're working on in the Project bin. If the icon circled on the right appears, that means that you have unsaved changes. From the Menu bar choose File>Save or use the shortcut Ctrl>S, Mac: Cmd>S. Mac users have a nifty floppy disc icon at the top of their screen that they can just tap to save.

If you don't save often, you run the risk of losing all of your work if your computer crashes. This will usually only happen to your finest work, on your most important projects, that you don't have time to do over. How do I know this? I've learned everything the hard way!

5. Follow This Simple Rule-Always make a new transparent layer for brushwork and Stroke Outlines. If you add brushwork or a stroke directly to a photo or other image, and you don't like it later on, you're pretty much stuck with it unless you Undo everything. By adding the brushwork or stroke to its own layer, you can modify the layer or simply delete it. In the long run, this simple rule will save you a lot of time.

6. Get Educated! You've already taken the first step by purchasing this book (hopefully you purchased it and didn't steal it from your best friend!). Take a hands-on Photoshop Elements class. If you don't have classes for digital scrapbooking in your area, you can always travel to one that The Digital Scrapbook Teacher offers. Check the Classes page on our website at *www.TheDigitalScrapbookTeacher.com* for updates and sign up for our free newsletter to find out when new classes are offered.

If you can't find a hands-on Photoshop Elements class for digital scrapbooking, take one for photo editing. You'll gain confidence in your computer skills, which will help you with digital scrapbooking.

7. Practice, Practice, Practice! I can't say this enough. If you don't practice you won't get better, and you'll forget everything you learned the last time you used Photoshop Elements. Turn off your cell phone, text messaging, emails, etc. and focus on what you're doing. In my household this is much easier to do at 2 a.m. than it is at 6 p.m.

8. Set Goals and Write Them Down. I'd like to make a scrapbook for my granddaughter's birthday in May. It is a great idea. But just because I say I want to make the scrapbook, doesn't mean it's going to happen. I want to do a lot of things: lose weight, clean my closet, take an Alaskan cruise, etc. All of the things on my To Do List take planning. If I set a deadline and make a plan for the scrapbook now and work towards my goal I have a much better chance of finishing the book for her party. I've heard it said that "If you fail to plan, you plan to fail".

To get your project started, make two lists and hang them where you can see them daily. On the first list write down the pages that must be in the book, such as birthday parties, holidays, special events, etc. On the second list, write down the extra pages you would like to put in the book. Check off the pages as they're completed.

One great way I've found to include a lot of photos on a scrapbook page is to use a calendar template showing what we did during the month. These calendar templates are available at *www.TheDigitalScrapbookteacher.com*.

9. Use Quick Pages! I had a student who told me once that if you use a Quick Page it's not really scrapbooking. I disagree! Scrapbooking is getting photos and/or memories on a page so that others can view them. My older son once asked me if I ever thought about printing my photos and sticking them in photo albums that held 4 x 6 photos so that he could look at them…what a concept! If you had any visions of grandeur about me, they're completely shattered now!

Quick Pages have a come a long way from when digital scrapbooking was in its infancy. Many designers make Quick Pages to match their kits in many different styles. Why not use a Quick Page, and then make your own page with the kit to match it? By doing this, you'll finish great looking pages with lightening speed and no one needs to know you used the Quick Page; and if they do, no big deal!

These are several of the Quick Pages that are included on the *Digital Scrapbooking Basics & Beyond* DVD that came with this book.

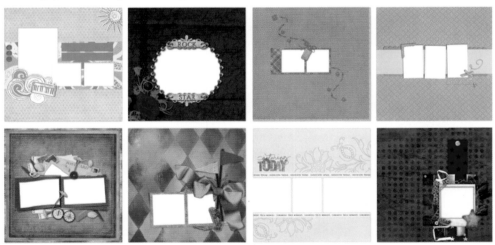

Top row Left to Right Amy Teets, Kelly Jos Scraps, Bon Scrapatit Designs, Danielle Young
Bottom row Left to Right KellyJos Scraps, Dusty Bear Designs, Ali Edwards, Farrah's Creations

10. Plan Your Pages In Advance As a traditional scrapbooker, I had a system that worked quite well. I would take the pictures, papers, embellishments, memorabilia, and any notes and tuck them into a 12 x 12 plastic envelope made just for scrapbookers. I'm sure that the company that made those envelopes flourished because of all the envelopes I purchased. This system was great; because when I finally had some free time I could pull out an envelope and finish the pages.

It's easy to do something similar as a digital scrapbooker without
purchasing any special envelopes. First, open all of the images for
the page. If you are using a template (which I recommend)
choose File>Save As and save the template with a different name.
If you are starting from scratch choose File>New>Blank File and
save it. Drag all the papers up onto the page from the Project bin
(this will name the layer with the file name to hopefully help you
track the products used on the page). Follow with all of the
embellishments and photos. Each item will drop in the center of
the page and they will cover the layer below. As seen in the
example, it won't be pretty, but it will be similar to my plastic
envelope technique. Add notes to the page with the Type tool (T)
to help you remember what was going on at the time.

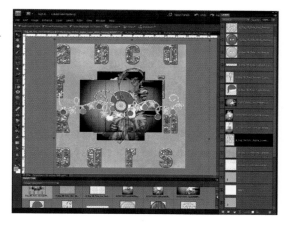

Save the file and open it when you have time to construct the page. If so many layers distract you, click on the
eyeball icon to hide the layer until you want to use it.

Be sure to read how to save the Project bin as an Album in the Organizer in the *Organization* chapter. Scanning
Multiple Images at one time in the *Techie Stuff* chapter will also help you save time scanning lots of photos and
memorabilia.

11. Use Shortcuts! So…you're just starting out and you've got enough on your plate to begin with. Now I'm
telling you to learn shortcuts, and you don't even know the long cuts. Relax, don't panic! As I look back, I wish I
would have made it a point to learn shortcuts early on. In my hands-on classes, I show my students how to
accomplish our tasks the regular way, but also mention the shortcuts. I've found that after one two hour class,
many of my students remember three or four shortcuts, which is great. The shortcut card included with your
book will also help you learn shortcuts quickly.

Make it a point to learn at least one new shortcut a week when you're first learning, and you'll be surprised how
much faster you can work. I've listed below some of my favorites so you can decide which ones to learn first. I'll
be honest, I originally was going to list my top ten shortcuts, but after I started writing them all down, the list
more than doubled!

Using shortcuts to switch between tools is a real timesaver. Just be smarter than me and when you're using the
Type tool (T), don't get ahead of yourself and type the letter B to switch to the Brush tool (B). You must commit
your type before typing a single letter shortcut, or you'll just end up typing that letter along with your text.

Did you know that if you want to cycle through a group of nested tools you can tap the tool shortcut? For
example: I selected the Rectangular Marquee tool (M) and I want to use the Elliptical Marquee tool which also
shares the same M shortcut. Instead of clicking and holding the black triangle symbol (◢) on the bottom right
corner of the tool icon (circled below) to pop out a list of the nested tools, just type the letter M, and it will select
the Elliptical Marquee tool automatically. To select the Rectangular Marquee tool again, type the letter M again.

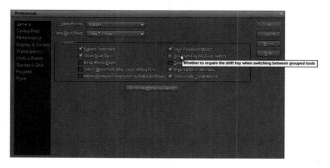

If you don't like this feature, you can easily change it.
Choose Edit>Preferences>General (Mac: Photoshop
Elements>Preferences>General. Check the Use Shift Key
for Tool Switch box. Now instead of typing just the letter
M to cycle through nested Marquee tools, you will need
to tap the Shift key and the letter M key at the same time.

Patty's Favorite Top 20+ Photoshop Elements Shortcuts

These are all Editor Shortcuts unless the Organizer is specified. They are not listed in any order of preference.

PC (Mac)	What it Does
Ctrl>Z (Cmd>Z)	Undo. Much faster than tapping the Undo button or choosing Edit>Undo
Ctrl>G (Cmd>G)	Create Clipping Mask, faster than Layer>Create Clipping Mask
Ctrl>A (Cmd>A)	Select all, faster than Select>All
Esc or Ctrl>D (Cmd>D)	Removes Selection Border (Marching Ants) Faster than Select>Deselect, the Esc key. Doesn't work for some Windows 7 users
Shift>Ctrl>I (Shift>Cmd>I)	Inverse selection. Much faster than choosing Select>Inverse.
Ctrl>O (Cmd>O)	Open a file. Much faster than File>Open
Ctrl>0 (Cmd>0)	Displays your document in full screen view. Much faster than View>Fit on Screen.
Ctrl>S (Cmd>S)	Save. Do it often or you'll have to redo your page when you crash. You WILL crash someday; it will be the day that you don't have time to redo your page.
Ctrl>J (Cmd>J)	Duplicates active layer. Much faster than Layer>New>Layer Via Copy
Alt key (Opt key)	When resizing/transforming, click on corner sizing handle and hold this key to size from the center and you won't have to reposition the layer.
Alt key (Opt key)	Tap to change Cancel buttons to Reset buttons where there is no Reset button like Adjust Hue/Saturation
Alt key (Opt key)	With Move tool selected, click on image and hold this key to duplicate image
Ctrl key (Cmd key)	Hold this key to temporarily switch to the Move tool except when Hand or Shape tools are selected.
Ctrl key (Cmd key)	Hold this key when using the Move tool to temporarily switch off/on Auto Select Layer on the Options bar; This is great when working with small transparent images like brads.
Bracket keys	Tap the left Bracket key to make brushes smaller, right Bracket key to make brushes larger. This is much faster than using the size box on the Options bar, because you can actually watch the brush resize using the Bracket keys.
Shift key	Hold this key to constrain a rectangle to a square, an oval to a circle or other shapes in proportion
Shift key	Hold this key to paint brush strokes in a straight line or to move layers like brads in a straight line
Ctrl>E (Cmd>E)	This will merge all layers that are selected in the Layers panel together into one layer.
Shift>Alt>Ctrl>E (Shift>Opt>Cmd>E)	Merge all visible layers into one new layer; the best part of this is that it keeps all of the original layers intact. Hidden layers are not affected.
Alt>Ctrl>N (Opt>Cmd>N)	Makes a new blank file with the exact same specifications as the last one you made. If you are on a roll, and making 12 x 12 pages all day this will speed things up. If you want to make a page with different dimensions, the dialog box is displayed and it's easy to make changes.
Shift>Alt>Ctrl>N (Shift>Opt>Cmd>N)	Makes a new transparent layer. If you're following my simple rule (and you better be) to always make a new transparent layer for brushwork and stroke outlines, this tip is a life saver.
D	Resets Foreground color to black, Background color to white
X	Swaps existing Foreground color and Background color. Does not change colors
Shift >Alt>Backspace (Shift>Opt>Delete)	Fills a layer with transparency with the Foreground color. It also fills solid. Easier than using the Paint Bucket tool or Edit>Fill.
Shift>Ctrl>Backspace (Shift>Cmd>Delete)	Fills a layer with transparency with the Background color. It also fills solid layers. Easier than using the Paint Bucket tool or Edit>Fill.
Copy & Paste Layer Styles	Instead of applying a Layer Style to each individual layer, I apply it to one layer, right click on the layer name (not the *fx* symbol) to copy it, and then select the other layers, right click and paste it.
Ctrl>I (Cmd>I) Organizer	Opens selected images into Full Edit Mode
Ctrl>Shift>G (Cmd>Shift>G) Organizer	Gets images from files and folders and imports them into the Organizer. This is much faster than choosing File>Get Photos and Videos>from Files and Folders

Editor Tool Shortcuts

Tool (listed in order on the Toolbar)	Shortcut	Description
Move tool	V	Moves layers from one file to another or within a file
Zoom tool	Z	Zooms in and out so you can see your image
Hand tool	H	Moves your view of an image
Eyedropper tool	I	Samples color from an image
Rectangular Marquee tool	M	Makes a rectangular or square selection
Elliptical Marquee tool	M	Makes an oval or round selection
Lasso tool	L	Makes a selection by clicking and dragging
Magnetic Lasso tool	L	Makes a selection by clinging to edges where colors change
Polygonal Lasso tool	L	Makes a selection with straight lines
Magic Wand tool	W	Makes a selection based on color
Quick Selection tool	A	Makes a selection of similar colors
Selection Brush tool	A	Makes a selection wherever you paint
Horizontal Type tool	T	Types text horizontally
Vertical Type tool	T	Types text vertically
Horizontal Type Mask tool	T	Types a mask horizontally(make text from photos, etc)
Vertical Type Mask tool	T	Types a mask vertically (make text from photos, etc)
Crop tool	C	Crops images into standard or freehand sizes
Recompose tool	C	Resizes images without losing important content
Cookie Cutter tool	Q	Crops images into shapes
Straighten tool	P	Straightens photos
Red Eye tool	Y	Removes Red Eye
Spot Healing Brush tool	J	Removes image imperfections by clicking or dragging
Healing Brush tool	J	Fixes imperfections, you choose the good area to paste over the bad area
Clone Stamp tool	S	Copies area of an image to another area or image
Pattern Stamp tool	S	Copies a pattern to an image
Eraser tool	E	Erases an image
Background Eraser tool	E	Erases the background area, turns Background layer into regular layer
Magic Eraser tool	E	Erases an image based on color, turns Background layer into regular layer
Pencil tool	N	Draws a thin line
Brush tool	B	Paints/stamps brush strokes by clicking or dragging
Impressionist Brush tool	B	Changes color & details to look like a painting
Color Replacement Brush tool	B	Replaces color in your image with Foreground color
Smart Brush tool	F	Makes color and tonal adjustments to areas of a photo with selection, also adds adjustment layer
Detail Smart Brush tool	F	Makes color and tonal adjustments to areas of a photo, adds adjustment layer
Paint Bucket tool	K	Fills an area or selection with color or a pattern
Gradient tool	G	Fills a layer or selection with a gradient
Rectangle tool	U	Makes rectangle or square shapes
Rounded Rectangle tool	U	Makes rectangles or squares with rounded edges
Ellipse tool	U	Makes oval or round shapes
Polygon tool	U	Makes multi-sided shapes
Line tool	U	Makes lines and arrows
Custom Shape tool	U	Makes many different shapes
Shape Selection tool	U	Moves shapes that have not been simplified
Blur tool	R	Blurs area you drag over
Sharpen tool	R	Sharpens area you drag over
Smudge tool	R	Smudges area you drag over like finger painting
Sponge Tool	O	Removes/adds color in area you click or drag over
Burn tool	O	Darkens area you click or drag over
Dodge tool	O	Lightens area you click or drag over
Default Foreground/ Background colors	D	Restores Foreground (Black)-Background (White) colors
Switch Foreground/ Background colors	X	Swaps the Foreground and Background colors

Editor Commands and Shortcuts

Command - Editor	Shortcut PC (Mac)	Description
File	Alt>F	Opens File drop down menu.
File>New>Blank File	Ctrl>N (Cmd>N)	Create a New Blank Document (File).
None	Alt>Ctrl>N (Opt>Cmd>N)	Creates a New Blank Document with the same specifications as the last one you made.
File>New>Image from Clipboard	None	Copy an image, choose this command and the new image is copied onto its own file. Great for making screenshots.
File>New>Photomerge Group Shot	None	Creates a great group photo by choosing the best parts of several photos.
File>New>Photomerge Faces	None	Combine facial features to create funny faces.
File>New>Photomerge Scene Cleaner	None	Clean the scene in your photo by removing parts of several photos.
File>New>Photomerge Panorama	None	Combine several photos to create one panorama photo.
File>New>Photomerge Exposure	None	Create one well exposed photo from several photos of the same shot taken with different exposure.
File>New>Photomerge Style Match	None	Matches the style of one image and applies it to another image.
File>Open	Ctrl>O (Cmd>O)	Opens a file like a photo, element, or scrapbook page.
File>Open As	Alt>Ctrl>O	Opens a file in a specific format. You can open and edit a JPEG file in the Camera RAW dialog box.
File>Open Recently Edited Photo	None	Choose this option if you want to quickly open one of the last ten files that you edited.
File>Duplicate	None	Duplicates a file so you don't have to worry about ruining your original. Be sure to specify new file name, & close original file.
File>Close	Ctrl>W (Cmd>W)	Closes your active (displayed) file only.
File>Close All	Alt>Ctrl>W (Opt>Cmd>W)	Closes all open files. You will be asked if you want to accept changes on each file individually.
File>Save	Ctrl>S (Cmd>S)	Saves File to the same place that it was originally saved.
File>Save As	Shift>Ctrl>S Shift>Cmd>S	Saves File with a name and you are asked to specify a folder you want to save it to.
File>Save for Web	Alt>Shift>Ctrl>S (Opt>Shift>Cmd>S)	Saves images in formats to be used on the web.
File>Info	(Opt>Shift>Cmd>I)	Allows you to store copyright and other info for some files.
File>Place	None	Opens a file as a smart object and places it on the active image.
File>Organize Open Files	None	Adds open images to the current Organizer Catalog.
File>Process Multiple Files	None	Applies changes to files in a folder, you can choose where to save the processed files. Choose Image Size, Rename Files, Automatic Quick Fix Adjustment, Captions or Labels (like a copyright notice) and change file type.
File>Import Frame from Video	None	Allows you to import a video clip that is on your computer and save a frame as a still image.
File>Import WIA Support	None	WIA (Windows Image Acquisition) is used with some digital cameras and scanners to import photos into Photoshop Elements.
File>Export	None	This item will be grayed out unless you have installed a plug-in that uses this option.
File>Automation Tools	None	This item will be grayed out unless you have installed a plug-in that uses this option.
File>Print	Ctrl>P (Cmd>P)	Opens Print dialog box. Also available in the Organizer.

Command - Editor	Shortcut PC (Mac)	Description
File>Order Prints	None	Launches the Organizer and Shutterfly or Kodak websites to order prints.
File>Contact Sheet	(Opt>Cmd>P)	Create Contact Sheet Mac Only
File>Exit	Ctrl>Q (Cmd>Q)	Closes all open files. You will be asked if you want to accept changes on each file individually AND closes the program. Remember Q for QUIT.
Edit	Alt>E	Opens Edit drop down menu.
Edit>Undo	Ctrl>Z (Cmd>Z)	Undoes the last thing you did.
Edit>Redo	Ctrl>Y (Cmd>Y)	If you Undo and decided you actually liked it you can Redo.
Edit>Revert	Shift>Ctrl>A (Shift>Cmd>A)	Undoes all changes that were made since the last save.
Edit>Cut	Ctrl>X (Cmd>X)	Copies and removes selection so you can paste somewhere else. This is easier than Copy and Pasting and then going back and deleting what you copied.
Edit>Copy	Ctrl>C (Cmd>C)	Copies selection.
Edit>Copy Merged	Shift>Ctrl>C (Shift>Cmd>C)	Copies all layers in a selection.
Edit>Paste	Ctrl>V (Cmd>V)	Pastes your copied selection (to remember, think Velcro).
Edit>Paste Into Selection	Shift>Ctrl>V (Shift>Cmd>V)	Pastes into a selection. This is very helpful when using single layered templates.
Edit>Delete	Delete key	Deletes image inside selection. Backspace key also works for PC users.
Edit>Fill Layer	Shift>Backspace (Shift>Delete)	Opens Fill dialogue box.
Edit>Fill Layer	Alt>Backspace (Opt>Delete)	Fills layer or selection with Foreground color.
Edit>Fill Layer add ✓	Shift>Alt>Backspace (Shift>Opt>Delete)	Fill with Foreground color and preserves transparency.
Edit>Fill Layer	Ctrl>Backspace (Cmd>Delete)	Fills layer or selection with Background color.
Edit>Fill Layer add ✓	Shift>Ctrl>Backspace (Shift>Cmd>Delete)	Fill with Background color and preserves transparency.
Edit>Stroke Outline Selection	None	Adds a stroke/outline around a layer or selection. Always add the stroke to a new transparent layer.
Edit>Define Brush	None	Choose this to make your own brush and it will turn the active image into a brush as long as the image is 2500 pixels or less in size.
None	Right click	To delete brush from brush drop down list, right click and confirm.
None	Alt (Opt) click	To delete brush from brush drop down list, Alt (Opt) click and the brush will be automatically removed without asking you to confirm deletion.
Edit>Define Pattern	None	Choose this to turn an image into a pattern that can be used by the Paint Bucket tool or Edit>Fill Layer.
Edit>Clear	None	This will allow you to clear your Undo History and Clipboard which may help speed up your computer.
Edit>Add Blank Page	Alt>Ctrl>G (Opt>Cmd>G)	Adds a blank page for a Photo Creation Project (PSE file).
Edit>Add Page Using Current Layout	Alt>Shift>Ctrl>G (Opt>Shift>Cmd>G)	Adds a duplicate of the current page for a Photo Creation Project (PSE file).
Edit>Delete a Current Page	None	Deletes the current page for a Photo Creation Project (PSE)
Edit>Color Settings	Shift>Ctrl>K	Allows you to choose to manage color in images, choose optimize for computer screens or printing.

Command - Editor	Shortcut PC (Mac)	Description
Edit>Preset Manager	None	Displays Presets for Brushes, Gradients, Swatches, and Patterns. You can Load, Name, Reset, and Delete sets here.
Edit>Preferences (Photoshop Elements>Preferences)	General Preferences Ctrl>K (Cmd>K)	Opens General Preferences dialog box and allows you to Change default settings. Read the *First Things First* Chapter to learn about changing many of these settings.
Edit>Preferences (Photoshop Elements>Preferences)	Last Preferences Changed Alt>Ctrl>K (Opt>Cmd>K)	Opens the last Preferences dialog box that was opened. Read the *First Things First* Chapter to learn about changing many of these settings.
Image	Alt>I	Opens the Image drop down menu.
Image>Rotate	None	Rotates or flips the entire image or just a layer, also includes an option to straighten and straighten and crop. You can also rotate by choosing the Move tool and right clicking on a corner sizing handle
Image>Transform>Free Transform	Ctrl>T (Cmd>T)	Another way to access this command is to select the Move tool and click on a sizing handle. Dragging on a corner sizing handle will re-size/transform the layer in proportion. Dragging a side sizing handle will re-size/transform out of proportion.
Image>Transform> Skew	Choose Move tool and then Ctrl>Shift (Cmd>Shift) click and drag sizing handle	Choose layer, click on a sizing handle while holding Ctrl key (Cmd key), cursor turns into gray arrow. Click and drag to distort image.
Image>Transform> Distort	Choose Move tool and then Ctrl (Cmd) click and drag sizing handle	Choose layer, click on a sizing handle while holding Ctrl key (Cmd key), cursor turns into gray arrow. Click and drag to skew image.
Image>Transform> Perspective	Choose Move tool and then Ctrl>Alt>Shift (Cmd>Opt>Shift) click and drag sizing handle	Choose layer, click on a sizing handle while holding Ctrl key (Cmd key), cursor turns into gray arrow. Click and drag to adjust the perspective.
Image>Crop	None	Crops all layers of an image, similar to the Crop tool, but with less choices.
Image>Recompose	Alt>Ctrl>R (Opt>Cmd>R)	Launches Recompose tool dialog box which can be disabled. You can also choose the Recompose tool directly from the Toolbar where it's nested with the Crop tool.
Image>Divide Scanned Photos	None	Scan multiple pieces of memorabilia, photos, etc. and choose this command to automatically split them up. This is much faster than scanning photos individually. Read the *Techie Stuff* chapter for more information.
Image>Resize	None	Options available to resize Image Size, Canvas Size, Reveal All, and Scale.
Image>Resize>Image Size	Alt>Ctrl>I (Opt>Cmd>I)	Displays Image Size dialog box.
Image>Resize>Canvas Size	Alt>Ctrl>C (Opt>Cmd>C)	Displays Canvas Size dialog box.
Image>Mode	None	Choose to change Image Mode to: Bitmap, Grayscale, RGB, or Indexed Color. This will also allow you to view a color table for Indexed Color images.
Image>Convert Color Profile	None	Choose to convert to sRGB Profile, Adobe RGB Profile, or remove Profile.
Image>Magic Extractor	Alt>Shift>Ctrl>V (Opt>Shift>Cmd>V)	Opens the Magic Extractor dialog box.
Enhance	Alt>N	Opens Enhance drop down menu.

Command - Editor	Shortcut PC (Mac)	Description
Enhance>Auto Smart Fix	Alt>Ctrl>M (Opt>Cmd>M)	Automatically corrects layer, you may or may not like it! Fixes applied will be the same as if you used Auto Smart Fix in Quick Edit. Shortcut is the same in the Organizer.
Enhance>Auto Levels	Shift>Ctrl>L (Shift>Cmd>L)	Automatically applies Levels adjustment to layer. If you don't like it, try Ctrl>L (Cmd>L) to adjust Levels yourself. Also available in Quick Edit.
Enhance>Auto Contrast	Alt>Shift>Ctrl>L (Opt>Shift>Cmd>L)	Automatically applies Lighting Contrast Adjustment to layer. If you don't like it, try Enhance>Adjust Lighting>Brightness Contrast to adjust it yourself. Also available in Quick Edit.
Enhance>Auto>Color Correction	Shift>Ctrl>B (Shift>Cmd>B)	Automatically applies Color Adjustment to layer. If you don't like it, try Enhance>Adjust Color>Adjust Hue/Saturation (the shortcut is Ctrl>U (Cmd>U)) to adjust it yourself. Also available in Quick Edit.
Enhance>Auto Sharpen	None	Automatically sharpens layer. Also available in Quick Edit.
Enhance>Auto Red Eye Fix	Ctrl>R (Cmd>R)	Automatically fixes red eye. Will not work on pet eye problems. Also available on the Full and Quick Edit Toolbars.
Enhance>Adjust Smart Fix	Shift>Ctrl>M (Shift>Cmd>M)	Opens Adjust Smart Fix dialog box and allows you to adjust Smart Fix amount from 0 to 100%.
Enhance>Adjust Lighting>Shadows/ Highlights	None	Opens Shadow/Highlights dialog box and allows you to lighten shadows, darken highlights, and adjust midtone contrast.
Enhance>Adjust Lighting>Brightness/ Contrast	None	Opens Brightness/Contrast dialog box and allows you to adjust brightness and contrast of the layer.
Enhance>Adjust Lighting>Levels	Ctrl>L (Cmd>L)	Opens Levels dialog box to allow you to adjust the contrast of the image.
None	Ctrl>Alt>L (Cmd>Opt>L)	Applies the same Levels change from the last settings and opens the Levels dialog box.
Enhance>Adjust Color>Remove Color Cast	None	Corrects color cast.
Enhance>Adjust Color>Adjust Hue/Saturation	Ctrl>U (Cmd>U)	Opens Hue/Saturation dialog box, to adjust Hue, Saturation, and Lightness.
None	Ctrl>Alt>U (Cmd>Opt>U)	Applies the same Hue/Saturation change from the last settings and opens the Hue/Saturation dialog box.
Enhance>Adjust Color>Remove Color	Shift>Ctrl>U (Shift>Cmd>U)	Removes/desaturates color from a layer.
Enhance>Adjust Color>Replace Color	None	Opens Replace Color dialog box and allows you to change or match another color.
Enhance>Adjust Color>Adjust Color Curves	None	Opens Adjust Color Curves dialog box and allows you to improve the colors by making several adjustments by choosing presets or sliding four different sliders.
Enhance>Adjust Color>Adjust Color for Skin Tones	None	Opens Adjust Color for Skin Tone dialog box and allows you to click on a person's skin and Photoshop Elements will correct the color of the entire photo.
Enhance>Adjust Color>Defringe Layer	None	Opens Defringe dialog box and allows you to choose a pixel width to remove fringe or a halo from around a selection.
Enhance>Adjust Color>Color Variations	None	Allows you to add/remove and/or lighten/darken red, green, or blue on a layer.

Command - Editor	Shortcut PC (Mac)	Description
Enhance>Convert to Black and White	Alt>Ctrl>B (Opt>Cmd>B)	Opens Convert to Black and White dialog box and converts layer to black and white. There are several presets to choose, or you can adjust four sliders.
Enhance>Unsharp Mask	None	Opens Unsharp Mask dialog box and allows you to sharpen the layer. Use this as the last step of photo editing and don't apply too much, especially watch the dark colors in your photos.
Enhance>Adjust Sharpness	None	Opens Adjust Sharpness dialog box and allows you to sharpen image by sliding sliders. Try Unsharp Mask first.
None	Ctrl>I (Cmd>I)	Inverts colors on a layer. Black becomes white, white becomes black, etc.
Layer	Alt>L	Opens the Layer drop down menu.
Layer>New>Layer	Shift>Ctrl>N (Shift>Cmd>N)	Creates new transparent layer directly above selected layer with a New Layer dialog box. Clicking on the New Layer icon at the bottom of the Layers panel while holding the Alt (Mac: Opt key) will also do the same thing.
Click on New Layer icon	Alt>Ctrl>Shift>N	Creates new transparent layer directly above selected layer without a New Layer dialog box. Clicking on New Layer icon at the bottom of the Layers panel will also do the same thing.
Click on New Layer icon	Ctrl key (Cmd key)	Hold Ctrl key (Mac: Cmd key) while clicking on the New Layer icon at the bottom of the Layers panel will create a new transparent layer below the selected layer without a dialog box.
Layer>New Layer>From Background	None	Displays dialog box to change the Background layer to a regular layer, also allows you to make blending mode, clipping mask, and opacity changes. Double clicking on a Background layer will also produce the same dialog box.
Layer>New>Layer Via Copy	Ctrl>J (Cmd>J)	Creates a duplicate layer of a selection or layer. You can also drag layer in the Layers to the New Layer icon, or right click (Mac: Ctrl click) and choose Duplicate Layer.
None	Alt>Ctrl>J (Opt>Cmd>J)	Creates a duplicate layer of a selection or layer with a New Layer dialogue box.
Layer>New>Layer Via Cut	Shift>Ctrl>J (Shift>Cmd>J)	Copies **selection** onto its own layer and removes it from the original layer. This leaves a hole or if it's a Background layer the selection filled with the Background color.
None	Alt>Ctrl>Shift>J (Opt>Cmd>Shift>J)	Same as above, but a New Layer dialog box is displayed.
Layer>Duplicate Layer	None	Duplicates layer and displays a dialog box that allows you to send the duplicate layer to another file. You could also use the Move tool to do this.
Layer>Delete Layer	None	Deletes layer and asks to confirm before proceeding. You can also delete a layer other ways. With the layer selected, right click (Mac: Ctrl click) and choose delete, tap the trashcan icon, or, with the Move tool selected, tap the Delete key on the keyboard.
None	Trashcan icon	Deletes layer without a dialog box. With the layer selected: drag it to the trashcan, or tap the Alt key and the trashcan icon.
Layer>Rename Layer	None	Displays Layer Properties dialog box, layer name is highlighted, type to rename layer. A faster way to do this is to double click on the layer name and type the new name. Double click on the Layer thumbnail to display the Layer Properties dialog box.
Layer>Layer Style>Style Settings	Double click on *fx* symbol	Displays Style Settings dialog box to allow you to change Drop Shadow, Glow, Bevel, and Stroke Layer Styles. Double clicking on the *fx* symbol for the specific layer in the Layers panel will also display this dialog box.

Command - Editor	Shortcut PC (Mac)	Description
Layer>Layer Style>Copy Layer Style	Right click on Layer name	Allows you to copy Layer Styles so that you can paste them onto other layers which saves a lot of time, especially if you have modified them. To work faster, right click on Layer name and choose Copy Layer Style. The Layer Style will generally be saved until you copy another one or turn off Photoshop Elements.
Layer>Layer Style>Paste Layer Style	Right click on Layer name	Allows you to paste Layer Styles from other layers, which saves a lot of time, especially if you have modified them. To work faster, right click on Layer name and choose Paste Layer Style.
Layer>Layer Style>Clear Layer Style	Drag *fx* symbol to Trashcan icon	Removes all Layer Styles.
Layer>Layer Style>Hide all Effects	None	Temporarily hides all effects.
Layer>Layer Style>Scale Effects	None	Displays Scale Layer Effects dialog box, which allows you to scale effects from 0 to 1000% on a selected layer.
Layer>New Fill Layer>Solid Color	None	Creates a new Solid Color Fill layer (with Mask) and allows you to choose the fill color. The Foreground color is the default fill color. You can also choose this by clicking on the Adjustment Layers button at the bottom of the Layers panel.
Layer>New Fill Layer>Gradient	None	Creates a new Gradient Fill layer (with Mask) and allows you to choose the gradient. The Foreground color to Transparent gradient is the default fill. You can also choose this by clicking on the Adjustment Layers button at the bottom of the Layers panel.
Layer>New Fill Layer>Pattern	None	Creates a new Pattern layer (with Mask) and allows you to choose the pattern. You can also choose this by clicking on the Adjustment Layers button at the bottom of the Layers panel.
Layer>New Adjustment Layer>Levels	None	Creates a new Levels Adjustment layer (with Mask) and allows you to easily adjust settings now, and at any time in the future. You can also choose this by clicking on the Adjustment Layers button at the bottom of the Layers panel.
Layer>New Adjustment Layer>Brightness/Contrast	None	Creates a new Brightness/Contrast Adjustment layer (with Mask) and allows you to easily adjust settings now, and at any time in the future. You can also choose this by clicking on the Adjustment Layers button at the bottom of the Layers panel.
Layer>New Adjustment Layer>Hue/Saturation	None	Creates a new Hue/Saturation Adjustment layer (with Mask) and allows you to easily adjust settings now, and at any time in the future. You can also choose this by clicking on the Adjustment Layers button at the bottom of the Layers panel.
Layer>New Adjustment Layer>Gradient Map	None	Creates a new Gradient Map Adjustment layer (with Mask) and allows you to easily choose different gradients and adjust settings now, and at any time in the future. You can also choose this by clicking on the Adjustment Layers button at the bottom of the Layers panel.
Layer>New Adjustment Layer>Photo Filter	None	Creates a new Photo Filter Adjustment layer (with Mask) and allows you to easily adjust settings or choose different filters or colors now, and at any time in the future. You can also choose this by clicking on the Adjustment Layers button at the bottom of the Layers panel.
Layer>New Adjustment Layer>Invert	None	Creates a new Invert Adjustment layer (with Mask). There are no options for this adjustment layer that can be changed. You can also choose this by clicking on the Adjustment Layers button at the bottom of the Layers panel.

Command - Editor	Shortcut PC (Mac)	Description
Layer>New Adjustment Layer>Threshold	None	Creates a new Threshold Adjustment layer (with Mask) and allows you to easily adjust settings now, and at any time in the future. You can also choose this by clicking on the Adjustment Layers button at the bottom of the Layers panel.
Layer>New Adjustment Layer>Posterize	None	Creates a new Posterize Adjustment layer (with Mask) and allows you to easily adjust the levels of posterization now, and at any time in the future. You can also choose this by clicking on the Adjustment Layers button at the bottom of the Layers panel.
Layer>Layer Content Options	None	Choose this option to make changes to an Adjustment Layer. To do this faster, double click the Adjustment Layer thumbnail.
Layer>Type>Horizontal	None	Changes the selected Type layer to horizontal type. You can also click the icon on the Type tool Options bar.
Layer>Type>Vertical	None	Changes the selected Type layer to vertical type. This can also be done by clicking on the icon on the Type tool Options bar.
Layer>Type>Anti Alias On	None	Turns on Anti Alias on the selected type layer. This can also be done by clicking on the icon on the Type tool Options bar.
Layer>Type>Anti Alias Off	None	Turns off Anti Alias on the selected type layer. This can also be done by clicking on the icon on the Type tool Options bar.
Layer>Type>Warp Text	None	Displays the Warp Text dialog box. This can also be done by clicking on the icon on the Type tool Options bar.
Layer>Type>Update All Text Layers	None	This often must be done when files with text are transferred between computers (especially PC & Mac).
Layer>Type>Replace All Missing Fonts	None	Photoshop Elements will replace any missing fonts with a font on your computer that it considers to be the closest match.
Layer>Simplify Layer	None	Changes a shape or type layer to a regular layer. Also known as rasterize the vector layer.
Layer>Layer Mask>Reveal All	None	Adds a new Layer Mask to the selected layer. This Mask is completely white, so it reveals everything.
Layer>Layer Mask>Hide All	None	Adds a new Layer Mask to the selected layer. This Mask is completely black, so it hides everything on the layers below.
Layer>Layer Mask>Reveal Selection	None	Adds a Layer Mask to a layer that has an active selection. The selected area is filled with white on the Layer Mask to reveal, while the rest of the area is filled with black to conceal.
None	\ (back slash)	Toggles Layer Mask as a rubylith (red highlighted area).
Layer>Layer Mask>Hide Selection	None	Adds a Layer Mask to a layer that has an active selection. The selected area is filled with black on the Layer Mask to hide, while the rest of the area is filled with white to reveal.
Layer>Layer Mask>Delete	None	Deletes Layer Mask from the selected layer.
Layer>Layer Mask>Apply	None	Applies the Layer Mask to the regular layer, almost like merging them together. The black part of the mask will delete the layer, while the white areas will remain unchanged.
Layer>Layer Mask>Enable or Disable	None	This option temporarily turns the Layer Mask off. Once the Layer Mask is disabled, there is a red X that covers the Layer Mask in the Layers panel.
Layer>Layer Mask>Link or Unlink	None	By default, Layer Masks are linked to their layers. Choose this option to unlink the Layer Masks so that you can move it with the Move tool (V).
Layer>Create Clipping Mask	Ctrl>G (Cmd>G)	Clips two layers together temporarily. Similar to cutting out a layer into the shape below it and pasting them together. Note: in Photoshop Elements 7 and lower this was called Layer>Group w/Previous
Layer>Create Clipping Mask	Alt (Opt) click on line between two layers	This is the fastest way to create a Clipping Mask.

Command - Editor	Shortcut PC (Mac)	Description
Layer>Release Clipping Mask	Ctrl>G (Cmd>G)	Unclips layers. This command will be visible only if you have a clipped layer selected. Note: In Photoshop Elements 7 this was called Ungroup Layers and the shortcut was Shift>Ctrl>G.
Layer>Arrange>Bring to Front	Shift>Ctrl>] (Shift>Cmd>])	Brings selected layer (except for a Background Layer) to the top (front) of the Layers panel.
Layer>Arrange>Bring Forward	Ctrl>] (Cmd>])	Moves selected layer (except for a Background Layer) up one layer in the Layers panel.
Layer>Arrange>Send Backward	Ctrl>[(Cmd>[)	Moves selected layer (except for a Background Layer) down one layer in the Layers panel.
Layer>Arrange>Send to Back	Shift>Ctrl>[(Shift>Cmd>[)	Moves selected layer to the back (bottom) of the Layers panel but above Background layer.
Layer>Arrange>Reverse	None	Choosing this will reverse layer order for all selected layers.
None	Alt (Opt)>, (comma)	Selects bottom layer.
None	Alt (Opt)>. (period)	Selects top layer.
None	Alt (Opt)>]	Selects next layer above, if you are at the top, it will cycle to the bottom layer in the Layers panel.
None	Alt (Opt)>[	Selects next layer below, if you are at the bottom, it will cycle to the top layer in the Layers panel.
Layer>Merge Down	Ctrl>E (Cmd>E)	Merges selected layer with the layer directly below it.
Layer>Merge Layers	Ctrl>E (Cmd>E)	Merges two or more selected layers.
Layer>Merge Visible	Shift>Ctrl>E (Shift>Cmd>E)	Merges all visible layers, will not merge hidden layers.
None	Ctrl>Alt>E (Cmd>Opt>E)	Merges layer with the layer below it, but keeps original layer intact.
None	Shift>Alt>Ctrl>E (Shift>Opt>Cmd>E)	Merges all visible layers into one new layer. The best part of this is that it keeps all of the original layers intact. Hidden layers are not affected.
Layer>Flatten Layer	None	Merges all layers together.
Select	Alt>S (Opt>S)	Opens Select drop down menu.
Select>All	Ctrl>A (Cmd>A)	Selects All
None	Ctrl (Cmd) click on Layer Thumbnail	Add selection around layer (not Background layer).
None	Ctrl (Cmd)>Shift click on Layer Thumbnail	Make a selection and then Ctrl >Shift click (Cmd>Shift click) on another Layer Thumbnail to add to the selection (not Background layer).
None	Ctrl (Cmd)>Alt (Opt) click on Layer Thumbnail	Make a selection and then Ctrl>Alt click (Cmd>Opt click) on another Layer Thumbnail to subtract from the selection (not Background layer).
None	Ctrl (Cmd)>Shift>Alt (Opt) click on Layer Thumbnail	Make a selection and then Ctrl>Shift>Alt click (Cmd>Shift>Opt click) on another Layer Thumbnail to intersect with the selection (not Background layer).
None	Hold Shift key while dragging selection	Constrains rectangle selection or shape to a square, oval selection or shape to a circle.
None	Hold Alt (Opt) key while dragging selection	Drags selection or shape from the center.
None	Shift>Alt (Opt) keys while dragging selection	Constrains shape or selection and draws from the center
None	V or select Move tool	Click and drag to move contents of a selection.
None	Ctrl>Arrow keys (↑) (Cmd>Arrow keys (↑))	To move a selection by one pixel, hold the Ctrl (Cmd) key and tap one of the four arrow keys to move in the direction of the arrow. Does not put the selection on a new layer.
None	Shift>Ctrl>Arrow keys (↑) (Shift>Cmd>Arrow key (↑))	To move a selection by ten pixels, hold the Shift and Ctrl (Cmd) key and tap one of the four arrow keys to move in the direction of the arrow. Does not put the selection on new layer.

Command - Editor	Shortcut PC (Mac)	Description
None	Click and drag inside selection	Moves Selection Border (Marching Ants). Will not move the contents of a selection.
None	Arrow keys (↑)	To nudge a selection border one pixel, tap one of the four arrow keys to move in the direction of the arrow.
None	Shift> Arrow keys (↑)	To nudge a selection border ten pixels, hold the Shift key and tap one of the four arrow keys to move in the direction of the arrow.
None	Spacebar	Hold Spacebar and drag mouse to move a selection made by one the Marquee tools **before** you let go of mouse.
None	Ctrl>Alt> Arrow keys (↑) Cmd>Alt> Arrow keys (↑)	To move a duplicate of selection one pixel, hold the Ctrl (Cmd) and Alt (Opt) key and tap one of the four arrow keys to move in the direction of the arrow. This does not put the selection on a new layer.
None	Shift>Ctrl>Alt> Arrow keys (↑) (Shift>Cmd>Alt> Arrow keys (↑))	To move a duplicate of selection one pixel, hold the Ctrl (Cmd) and Alt (Opt) key and tap one of the four arrow keys to move in the direction of the arrow. This does not put the selection on a new layer.
None	Shift key	Make first selection; hold Shift key and drag to make next selection and it will add to the first selection.
None	Alt key (Opt) key	Make first selection, hold Alt (Opt) key and drag and it will subtract from the first selection.
None	Shift>Ctrl>V (Shift>Cmd>V)	Paste into a selection, you must select and copy what you want to paste into it first.
Select>Deselect	Ctrl>D (Cmd>D) Or Esc key	Removes Selection Border (Marching Ants). The Esc key doesn't work for some Windows 7 users
Select>Reselect	Shift>Ctrl>D (Shift>Cmd>D)	Reselects the last selection made. This is helpful if you've removed your selection and need it later.
Select>Inverse	Shift>Ctrl>I (Shift>Cmd>I)	Inverses a selection.
Select>All Layers	None	Adds a selection border around the edge of all layers.
Select>Deselect Layers	None	Deselects all selected layers.
Select>Similar Layers	None	Will select all layers of the same type - Shape layers, Text layers, and regular layers. Helpful if changing a color or font.
None	Alt>Shift>, (Opt>Shift>,)	Select a layer, type the shortcut, and all layers down to the bottom (back) layer in the Layers panel will be selected.
None	Alt>Shift>. (period) (Opt>Shift>.)	Select a layer, type the shortcut, and all layers up to the top (front) layer in the Layers panel will be selected.
Select>Feather	Alt>Ctrl>D (Opt>Cmd>F)	Displays Feather dialog box. Feathering is used to soften the edge of a selection.
Select>Refine Edge	None	Displays Refine Edge dialog box. Used to smooth, feather, and contract/expand a selection.
Select>Modify>Border	None	Creates a selection that you can fill with color to create a soft edged border. If you want a border with a hard edge choose Edit>Stroke Outline Selection
Select>Modify>Smooth	None	Rounds the edges of selections.
Select>Modify>Expand	None	Displays Expand Selection dialog box, enter pixel amount to expand selection.
Select>Modify>Contract	None	Displays Contract Selection dialog box, enter pixel amount to contract selection.
Select>Grow	None	Adds contiguous colors to the selection.
Select>Similar	None	Adds all pixels of the same color to the selection.

Command - Editor	Shortcut PC (Mac)	Description
Select>Transform from Selection	None	Activates the Transform command and adds sizing handles to the selection to allow you to resize/transform the selection.
None	Ctrl>H (Cmd>H)	Hide/Show Selection.
Select>Load Selection	None	Loads a selection that was previously saved.
Select>Save Selection	None	Save a selection that you may need in the future. If you save the file as a PSD file, you will be able to load it at any time.
Select>Delete Selection	None	Deletes a saved selection.
Filter	Alt>T	Opens Filter drop down menu.
Filter>Last Filter	Ctrl>F (Cmd>F)	Applies the last filter with the same specifications.
None	Alt>Ctrl>F	Opens the last filter's dialog box.
Filter>Filter Gallery	None	Displays dialog box to add Artistic, Brush Strokes, Distort, Sketch, Stylize, and Texture filters.
Filter>Correct Camera Distortion	None	Allows you to fix vertical and horizontal perspective, and add a vignette around the edge of the image.
Filter>Adjustments	None	Equalize, Gradient Map, Invert (Ctrl>I), Posterize, Threshold, Photo filters can be added from this drop down list.
Filter>Artistic	None	Colored Pencil, Cutout, Dry Brush, Film Grain, Fresco, Neon Glow, Paint Daubs, Palette Knife, Plastic Wrap, Poster Edges, Rough Pastels, Smudge Stick, Sponge, Underpainting, and Watercolor filters can be added from this drop down list. Most of these filters can also be added from the Filters section on the Effects panel.
Filter>Blur	None	Blur your images using the Average, Blur, Blur More, Gaussian Blur, Motion Blur, Radial Blur, Smart Blur, and Surface Blur from this drop down list. These filters can also be added from the Filters section on the Effects panel.
Filter>Brush Strokes	None	Add Accented Edges, Angled Strokes, Crosshatch, Dark Strokes, Ink Outlines, Spatter, Sprayed Strokes, or Sumi-e filters from this drop down list. These filters can also be added from the Filters section on the Effects panel.
Filter>Distort	None	Some of the more interesting filters can be found in this drop down menu such as: Diffuse Glow, Displace, Glass, Liquify, Ocean Ripple, Pinch, Polar Coordinates, Ripple, Shear, Spherize, Twirl, Wave, and Zig Zag. These filters can also be added from the Filters section on the Effects panel.
Filter>Noise	None	Add Noise, Despeckle, Dust & Scratches, Median, and Reduce Noise can be added from this drop down list. These filters can also be added from the Filters section on the Effects panel.
Filter>Pixelate	None	Choose Color Halftone, Crystallize, Facet, Fragment, Mezzotint, Mosaic, and Pointillize from this drop down list. These filters can also be added from the Filters section on the Effects panel.
Filter>Render	None	Clouds, Difference Clouds, Fibers, Lens Flare, Lighting Effects, Texture Fill filters can be added from this drop down list. Most of these filters can also be added from the Filters section on the Effects panel.
Filter>Sketch	None	Add Bas Relief, Chalk & Charcoal, Charcoal, Chrome, Conte Crayon, Graphic Pen, Halftone Pattern, Note Paper, Photocopy, Plaster, Reticulation, Stamp, Torn Edges, Water Paper filters from this drop down list. These filters can also be added from the Filters section on the Effects panel.

Command - Editor	Shortcut PC (Mac)	Description
Filter>Stylize	None	Diffuse, Emboss, Extrude, Find Edges, Glowing Edges, Solarize, Tiles, Trace Contour, and Wind filters can be found on this drop down list. These filters can also be added from the Filters section on the Effects panel.
Filter>Texture	None	Add textures to your layers with a Craquelure, Grain, Mosaic Tiles, Patchwork, Stained Glass, Texturizer filter. These filters can also be added from the Filters section on the Effects panel. If you are going to use your own textures for the Texturizer filter, you will need to use this drop down list.
Filter>Video	None	The DeInterlace & NTSC Colors Filters can be found on this drop down list and from the Filters section on the Effects panel.
Filter>Other	None	High Pass, Maximum, Minimum, and Offset can be found on this drop down list, and from the Filters section on the Effects panel. The Custom Filter can be found only on the Effects panel.
Filter>Digimarc	None	Use this filter to search for a Digimarc watermark which supplies copyright information.
View	Alt>V	Opens View drop down menu.
View>Zoom Out	Ctrl>= (Cmd>=) (equal)	Zooms In. The + and = share the same key, it's easier to think of + zooming in.
View>Zoom Out	Ctrl>- (Cmd>-) (minus)	Zooms Out.
View>Fit On Screen	Ctrl>0 (Cmd>0) Or Double click Hand tool	Show image at full screen view.
None	Home key	View top left corner of file.
None	End key	View bottom right corner of file.
None	Page Up key	Scroll view up one screen.
None	Page Down key	Scroll view down one screen.
None	Shift>Page Up or Down Button	Scroll up or down 10 units.
None	Ctrl >Page Up or Down Button	Scroll right or left 10 units.
None	Ctrl>Alt>0 (Cmd>Opt>0)	Magnify View 100%.
View>Actual Pixels	Ctrl>1(Cmd>1)	View image at actual size.
View>Print Size	None	View image at print size.
View>Selection	Ctrl>H (Cmd>H)	Show/hides a selection.
View>Rulers	Shift>Ctrl>R (Shift>Cmd>R)	Toggles Rulers on and off.
View>Grid	Ctrl>' (Cmd>') (apostrophe)	Toggles Grids on and off.
View>Guides	Ctrl>; (Cmd>;) (semicolon)	Toggles Guides on and off.
View>Notes	None	Allows you to view notes that were added using the Note tool in Photoshop (not Elements).
View>Snap to Guides or Grids	None	Choose to have Snap to Grids or Guides active or inactive. Sometimes I turn this feature off if my layers snap to places I don't want them to.
View>Lock Guides	Alt>Ctrl>; (Opt>Cmd>;) (semicolon)	By locking your Guides you are making sure that you won't move them in error. A ✓ will appear when the guides are locked on the View Menu drop down list.
View>Clear Guides	None	To clear all Guides, choose this command. You may also clear Guides by dragging them back to the Ruler.

Command - Editor	Shortcut PC (Mac)	Description
View>New Guide	None	This displays the New Guide dialog box which will place a Guide for you at exact locations.
None	Tab key	Displays/hides all panels including the Tool panel (Toolbar).
None	Shift>Tab	Displays/hides all panels except the Tool panel (Toolbar).
Window	Alt>W	Opens Window drop down menu.
Window>Images>Tile	None	Tiles all open files and displays them like tile on a wall. If this option is gray, add a ✓ to Allow Floating Documents in Full Edit Mode in the General Preferences Dialog box.
Window>Images>Cascade	None	If this option is gray add a ✓ to Allow Floating Documents in Full Edit Mode in the General Preferences Dialog box. You will also need to remove the images from the tab. Images can be placed side by side or arranged however you want to. Many people prefer to work in Cascade mode, but it drives me crazy!
Window>Images>Float in Window	None	Allows active image to float in active image window. To float other images click and drag other images by the tab. If this option is gray, add a ✓ to Allow Floating Documents in Full Edit Mode in the General Preferences Dialog box.
Window>Images>Float All in Windows	None	Floats all images like the Cascade setting used to do. If this option is gray, add a ✓ to Allow Floating Documents in Full Edit Mode in the General Preferences Dialog box.
Window>Images> Consolidate All to Tabs	None	All images are tabbed but you can pull them into the active image window by clicking and dragging the tab. If this option is gray, add a ✓ to Allow Floating Documents in Full Edit Mode in the General Preferences Dialog box.
Window>Images>New Window	None	This option displays your image in a duplicate window. This is a great way to zoon in on one window and see the other one at full screen. Changes are made to both images.
Window Images>Match Zoom	None	All open images will be displayed at the same zoom level, which would be helpful if you are editing photos from the same camera.
Window Images>Match Location	None	Zoom into the bottom left corner of one image and choose this option. All of your images will be zoomed into the bottom left corner.
Window>Tools	None	Displays/hides Toolbar (Tool panel). On by default.
Window>Adjustments	None	Displays/hides the Adjustment Layer panel.
Window>Color Swatches	None	Displays/hides the Color Swatches panel.
Window>Content	F7	Displays/hides the Content panel.
Window>Effects	None	Displays/hides the Effects panel. On by default.
Window>Favorites	None	Displays/hides the Favorites panel.
Window>Histogram	F9	Displays/hides the Histogram panel.
Window>Info	F8	Displays/hides the Info panel.
Window>Layers	F11	Displays/hides the Layers panel. On by default.
Window>Navigator	F12	Displays/hides the Navigator panel.
Window>Undo History	F10	Displays/hides the Undo History panel.
Window>Panel Bin	None	Displays/hides the Panel Bin. On by default.
Window>Reset Panels	None	Resets all panels to the default setting.
Window>Welcome	None	Displays the Welcome Screen.
Window>Project Bin	None	Displays/hides the Project Bin. On by default.
Help	Alt>H	Opens the Help drop down menu
Help>Photoshop Elements Help	F1	Launches Adobe Help Website
Help>Getting Started	None	Launches Adobe Help Website and displays video and PDF tutorials to help you learn the basics of Photoshop Elements.

Command - Editor	Shortcut PC (Mac)	Description
Help>Key Concepts	None	Launches Adobe Help Website and displays a list of basic Photoshop Elements terms. Each page explains the basic terms and how to use different parts of Photoshop Elements.
Help>Support	None	Launches Adobe Help Website with links for help downloading, installing, and setting up. Also includes link for Getting Started and Tutorials, along with Editor and Organizer help.
Help>Video Tutorials	None	Launches Adobe Help Website with links for several video tutorials.
Help>Forum	None	Launches the Photoshop Elements Forum where you can post questions or help other users. If you are going to ask a question, it's always wise to search for your problem first, because it may have already been answered.
Help>About Photoshop Elements	None	Displays the version of Photoshop Elements you are using along with the names of the team that developed the product.
Help>About Plug In>Many	None	Displays a large list of plug ins. Click on a specific plug in and it will tell you the version number, the developer, and other information.
Help>Legal Notices	None	Copyright information for Adobe and other companies involved with Photoshop Elements.
Help>System Info	None	Displays Photoshop Elements version number and information about your computer that you may need when talking with technical support.
Help>Complete/Update Adobe ID Profile	None	Launches Adobe sign in screen to enable you to create an Adobe account or make changes to your existing account.
Help>Deactivate	None	Choose to suspend activation or deactivate permanently so that you can install Photoshop Elements on another computer per their Software License Agreement. You must be connected to the internet to deactivate.
Help>Updates	None	Launches Adobe Updates website.
Help>Elements Inspiration Browser	None	Sign in to see tutorials. You will have to upgrade your membership to a Plus membership for a fee to view all of the tutorials.
Help>Product Improvement Program	None	Choose to participate in the Adobe Product Improvement Program and Adobe will receive anonymous information about how you use Adobe products on your computer.
None	Alt click eyeball icon (Opt click eyeball icon)	When several layers in the Layers panel, Alt click the eyeball icon on one and all of the other visible layers are hidden.
None	Alt click (Opt click)	Alt (Opt) click on Cancel buttons in dialog boxes to change to Reset buttons.
Image>Transform	Ctrl>T (Cmd>T)	Activates the Transform tool to allow you to resize/transform layers. This can also be activated by dragging on a sizing handle when the Move tool (V) is selected.
None	Ctrl>Alt>T (Cmd>Alt>T)	Activates the Transform tool, makes a copy and allows you to resize/transform the copy layer. This can also be activated by dragging on a sizing handle when the Move tool (V) is selected.
None	Ctrl>Spacebar (Cmd>Spacebar)	Temporarily activates the Zoom tool, except when editing text.
None	Spacebar	Temporarily activates Hand tool, except when editing text.
None	Ctrl key (Cmd key)	Temporarily activates the Move tool (V), except when Hand or Shape tools are active.
None	Alt key (Opt key)	Temporarily activates the Eyedropper tool when Brush, Pencil, Color Replacement Brush, Paint Bucket, Gradient, & Shape tools are selected.

Command - Editor	Shortcut PC (Mac)	Description
None	Alt key (Opt key) Eyedropper tool active	Click to select Background color instead of Foreground color.
None	Esc key	To cancel an operation, instead of tapping the ⊘, tap the Esc key.
None	Enter key	To accept an operation, while using Crop, Move, or Transform instead of tapping the ✓, tap the enter key.
None	Ctrl Enter (Cmd Enter)	When using the Type tool, to accept an operation, tap the Ctrl (Cmd) and Enter key instead of tapping the ✓.
None	/ (forward slash)	Remove crop shield on Crop tool (C) (toggle).
None	Y or Enter (S or Enter)	Rather than tapping the Yes button when prompted to Save a file, tap these shortcuts to Save.
None	N (D)	Rather than tapping the No button when prompted to Save a file, tap these shortcuts to Don't Save.
None	Esc key (C or Esc)	Rather than tapping the Cancel button when prompted to Save a file, tap these shortcuts to Cancel.
Edit>Preferences>Units & Rulers	Double click on Ruler	To change the Units & Rulers Preferences, double click on the Ruler. For Mac choose (Photoshop Elements > Preferences > Units & Rulers)
None	/ (forward slash)	Locks transparent pixels on the selected layer (toggle). You can also do this by clicking on the Lock Transparent Pixels icon at the bottom of the Layers panel.
None	Caps Lock key	Changes regular cursor to crosshair. This can also be changed on the Display & Cursors Preferences dialog box.
None	Bracket keys [&]	Right bracket] Key Increases brush size, Left bracket [Key decreases brush size. Tap to increase slowly, or hold down key to quickly size brush.
None	Shift & Bracket keys [&]	Right bracket key]Hardens brush tip Left bracket key [Softens brush tip
None	Right click on file	Displays brush drop down list when most tools using brushes are active.
None	Shift , (comma)	Selects the first brush in the set.
None	Shift . (period)	Selects the last brush in the set.
None	, (comma)	Selects the previous brush.
None	. (period)	Selects the next brush.
None	1 to 100	Quickly type number to change the opacity of a layer or brush.
None	Hold Shift key & Drag	Draws a straight or 45° line. Also, when dragging with the Marquee or Shape tools, draws a shape in the correct proportions or a perfect square, circle.
None	Alt (Opt) Drag	Draws selection or shape from the center point outward
None	Alt (Opt) Drag	Click on resizing handles along with the Alt (Opt) key to resize/transform Resize from center.
None	Ctrl>Tab (Ctrl>Tab)	Cycles through open files in the Project bin.
None	Ctrl>Shift>Tab	Cycles back to the previous open file in the Project bin.
None	↑ and Move tool (V)	Nudges layer one pixel.
None	Shift key ↑ and Move tool (V)	Nudges layer ten pixels.
None	Alt key (Opt key) ↑ and Move tool (V)	Duplicates layer and nudges the duplicate one pixel.
None	Shift >Alt (Opt key) ↑ and Move tool (V)	Duplicates layer and nudges the duplicate ten pixels.
None	Alt (Opt) drag in Layers Panel	Click on layer Alt (Opt) key and drag up or down in layers panel to duplicate layer.
None	Ctrl >Spacebar Alt>Spacebar	Hold Ctrl and the Spacebar and drag to zoom into a selected area. Hold Alt and the Spacebar to zoom out.

Type Tool (T) Shortcuts-Select Type tool first

Shortcut	Description
Double click on Type layer thumbnail	Selects text and temporarily activates the Type tool.
Ctrl (Cmd) Enter key/Esc key	Accept Changes/Cancel Changes
Ctrl (Cmd) Drag	Move type on image when Type layer is selected. When type is selected, if you hover a small distance away from the type, the cursor will turn into an arrow and you can move it.
Ctrl>Shift>C (Cmd>Shift>C)	Align – Center (Horizontal & Vertical Type tool)
Ctrl>Shift>L (Cmd>Shift>L)	Align – Left (Horizontal Type tool) Top (Vertical Type tool)
Ctrl>Shift>R (Cmd>Shift>R)	Align – Right (Horizontal Type tool) Bottom (Vertical Type tool)
Ctrl>Shift>F (Cmd>Shift>F)	Align – Justify (force last line)
Ctrl>Shift>J (Cmd>Shift>J)	Align – Justify (left align last line)
Ctrl>Shift>B (Cmd>Shift>B)	Bolds selected type (Faux Bold if Bold is not available) (toggle)
Ctrl>Shift>I (Cmd>Shift>I)	Italicize selected type (Faux Italic if Italic is not available) (toggle)
Ctrl>Shift>/ (Cmd>Shift>/)	Strikethrough selected type (toggle)
Ctrl>Shift>U (Cmd>Shift>U)	Underline selected type (toggle)
Ctrl>Shift>Y (Cmd>Shift>Y)	Regular type selected type (no bold, etc)
Ctrl>Shift> < or > (Cmd>Shift> <or>	Increase/decrease font size of selected type by 2 pts
Alt>Ctrl>Shift> < or > (Opt>Cmd>Shift> <or>	Increase/decrease font size of selected type by 10 pts
Double click on word	Selects word, you must click quickly
Triple click on word	Selects line, you must click quickly
Quadruple click on word	Selects paragraph, you must click quickly
Left/Right Arrow keys →	Move cursor one character to the left or right
Ctrl (Cmd)>Left/Right Arrow keys →	Move cursor one word to the left or right
Up/Down Arrow keys ↑	Move cursor one line up or down
Home	Move cursor to the beginning of the line
Ctrl (Cmd)>Home	Move cursor to the beginning of the story
End	Move cursor to the end of the line
Ctrl (Cmd)>End	Move cursor to the end of the story
Ctrl (Cmd)>Up/Down Arrow keys ↑	Move cursor to next paragraph
Click and then Shift Click	Select type from first click point to second click point
Shift>Left/Right Arrow keys →	Select one character to the left or right
Shift>Up/Down Arrow keys ↑	Select one line up or down
Ctrl (Cmd) Shift>Left/Right Arrow keys →	Select one word to the left or right
Ctrl (Cmd)>Shift> Up/Down Arrow keys ↑	Select one line to the end.
Shift>Home	Select text to the beginning of the line
Ctrl (Cmd)>Shift>Home	Select text to the beginning of story
Shift>End	Select text to the end of the line
Ctrl (Cmd)>Shift>End	Select text to the end of story
Hold Ctrl (Cmd) key while dragging text box sizing handles	Scales text as you drag
Alt click on file with Type tool active	Displays Paragraph Text Size dialog box which allows you to make a text box in an exact size.
Double click on Font Name, Size, or Leading	First select type and then double click on Font Name, Size, or Leading use Up/Down Arrow keys ↑ to change the values. Windows users can also use the Scroll Wheel on their mouse to do this.

Blending Mode Shortcuts

The blending modes drop down list is located at the top of the Layers panel, next to the Opacity setting. Blending modes control how a layer blends with the layer below it.

The easiest way to learn about blending modes is to just try them out. The best way to try them is to cycle through the list of blending modes, to see which one you like best.

Mac users can use the shortcut Shift>+ (plus) and Shift>-(minus) instead of opening the drop down list each time you want to switch blending modes. Windows users can choose a blending mode and the use the Up and Down Arrow keys on their keyboard to cycle through the list. Photoshop Elements 9 Window users can also select a new blending mode, and then use the Scroll Wheel to scroll through the list. To change a blend mode on an adjustment layer, use the shortcut Alt>Shift>=(equals) or Alt>Shift>-(minus). Mac Opt>Shift>+(plus), Opt>Shift>-(minus).

As you learn to use blending modes, you will quickly see that you will like some more than others. I have made a note next to some of my favorite blending modes below. If you also have favorite blending modes, make it a point to learn the shortcut so you can quickly apply them. Notice that some of the shortcuts are pretty easy to figure out on the fly, because the letter in the shortcut corresponds to either the first letter of the blending mode or is included in the blending mode name.

Normal Blending Modes	PC Shortcut	Mac Shortcut
Normal (default setting)	Shift>Alt>N	Shift>Opt>N
Dissolve (must be set at 99% opacity or less to have any effect)	Shift>Alt>I	Shift> Opt >I
Darken Blending Modes		
Darken	Shift>Alt>K	Shift> Opt >K
Multiply (my favorite to darken washed out photos)	Shift>Alt>M	Shift> Opt >M
Color Burn	Shift>Alt>B	Shift> Opt >B
Linear Burn	Shift>Alt>A	Shift> Opt >A
Darker Color	None	None
Lighten Blending Modes		
Lighten	Shift>Alt>G	Shift> Opt >G
Screen (my favorite to lighten photos that are too dark)	Shift>Alt>S	Shift> Opt >S
Color Dodge	Shift>Alt>D	Shift> Opt >D
Linear Dodge (additive blending mode if used at 100% Opacity)	Shift>Alt>W	Shift> Opt >W
Lighter Color	None	None
Light Blending Modes		
Overlay (my favorite to blend photos and pictures together)	Shift>Alt>O	Shift> Opt >O
Soft Light (my favorite for a drab photo, may have to lower layer Opacity)	Shift>Alt>F	Shift> Opt >F
Hard Light	Shift>Alt>H	Shift> Opt >H
Vivid Light	Shift>Alt>V	Shift> Opt >V
Linear Light	Shift>Alt>J	Shift> Opt >J
Pin Light	Shift>Alt>Z	Shift> Opt >Z
Hard Mix	Shift>Alt>L	Shift> Opt >L
Invert/Difference Blending Modes		
Difference	Shift>Alt>E	Shift> Opt >E
Exclusion	Shift>Alt>X	Shift> Opt >X
Color/Chromatic Blending Modes		
Hue	Shift>Alt>U	Shift> Opt >U
Saturation	Shift>Alt>T	Shift> Opt >T
Color	Shift>Alt>C	Shift> Opt >C
Luminosity	Shift>Alt>Y	Shift> Opt >Y

Organizer Commands and Shortcuts

Command - Organizer	Shortcut PC (Mac)	Description
File	Alt>F	Displays File Menu
File>Get Photos and Videos>From Camera or Card Reader	Ctrl>G (Cmd>G)	Imports images from your Camera or Card Reader onto your computer and into the Organizer.
File>Get Photos and Videos>From Scanner	Ctrl>U	Imports images from your Scanner onto your computer and into the Organizer.
File>Get Photos and Videos>From Files and Folders	Ctrl>Shift>G (Shift>Cmd>G)	Imports images from the folders you specify on your computer into the Organizer.
File>Get Photos and Videos>By Searching	None	Imports images into the Organizer by searching your computer and hard drives for images.
File>New>Photoshop Elements Image File	None	Opens New File dialog box in the Editor.
File>New>Photoshop Elements Video Project	None	You must have Adobe Premiere Elements installed on your computer to make a video project. If you don't have Premiere, you can download a 30 day trial version here.
File>New>Image from Clipboard	None	After you have copied an image, choose this command, the Editor is opened, and the new image is copied onto its own file. Great for making screenshots.
File>New>Photomerge Group Shot	None	Opens the Editor to create a great group photo by choosing the best parts of several photos.
File>New>Photomerge Faces	None	Opens the Editor to combine facial features to create funny faces.
File>New>Photomerge Scene Cleaner	None	Opens the Editor to clean the scene in your photo by removing parts of several photos.
File>New>Photomerge Panorama	None	Opens the Editor to combine several photos to create one panorama photo.
File>New>Photomerge Exposure	None	Opens the Editor to create one well exposed photo from several photos of the same shot taken with different exposures.
File>New>Photomerge Style Match	None	Opens the Editor to match the style of one image and apply it to another image.
File>Open Recently Edited File in Editor	None	Copy an image, choose this command and the new image is copied onto its own file. Great for making screenshots. This command opens in the Editor.
File>Catalog	Ctrl>Shift>C (Shift>Cmd >C)	Opens Catalog Manager dialog box which allows you to convert, rename, move, remove, optimize, repair, make a new catalog, or switch catalogs.
File>Copy/Move to Removable Drive	Ctrl>Shift>O (Shift>Cmd >O)	This command deletes the file from its original location, but leaves the preview thumbnail in the Organizer.
File>Back up Catalog to CD, DVD, or Hard Drive	Ctrl>B (Cmd>B)	Backs up the Catalog to protect against hard drive failure or disaster. Choose incremental or full back up. I normally choose full back up and store the external hard drive at another location for safe keeping.
File>Restore Catalog from CD, DVD, or Hard Drive	None	Restores the Catalog in the event of a computer issue, or if you want to move it to another computer.
File>Duplicate	Ctrl>Shift>D (Shift>Cmd >D)	Duplicates the image and adds the word "copy" to the end of the file name.

Command - Organizer	Shortcut PC (Mac)	Description
File>Reconnect>Missing File	None	Reconnects the selected file that has been moved since it was imported into the Organizer. You can let Elements search for it, or you can browse yourself.
File>Reconnect>All Missing Files	None	Reconnects all files that have been moved since they were imported into the Organizer. Let Elements search for them or browse yourself. If there are many disconnected files, let the computer search after you go to bed.
File>Watch Folders	None	Specify folders that you want Elements to watch to see if there are files that you have not yet imported into the Organizer. You can choose to be notified when new files have been added or it will automatically add the files to the Organizer.
File>Rename	Ctrl>Shift>N (Shift>Cmd >N	Displays Rename dialog box, type new name.
File>Write Keyword Tag and Properties Info to Photos	None	Writes tag information to some file types. It will not write tag information to PNG files.
File>Move	Ctrl>Shift>V (Shift>Cmd >V)	Moves selected images to another location on your computer. Using this command will save you from having disconnected files.
File>Export as New File(s)	Ctrl>E	Exports selected files; you may choose location, file type, name, and size and quality.
File>Print	Ctrl>P (Cmd>P)	Opens Print dialog box, also available in the Editor or by right clicking on the thumbnail. You can also mark images for printing in the Quick Edit panel in Full Screen View (F11) and Photo Compare (F12), tap the Esc key to return to the Media Browser window.
File>Order Prints>Order Shutterfly Prints	None	Connects to Shutterfly website to order prints. Also available by right clicking on the thumbnail.
File>Order Prints>Order Kodak Prints	None	Connects to Kodak website to order prints. Also available by right clicking on the thumbnail.
File>Exit	Ctrl>Q (Cmd>Q)	Closes the program. Quit.
Edit	Alt>E	Opens Edit drop down menu.
Edit>Undo	Ctrl>Z (Cmd>Z)	Undoes last operation. You can also Undo in the Quick Edit panel in Full Screen View (F11) and Photo Compare (F12), tap the Esc key to return to the Media Browser window.
Edit>Redo	Ctrl>Y (Cmd>Y)	Redoes what you just undid. You can also Redo in the Quick Edit panel in Full Screen View (F11) and Photo Compare (F12), tap the Esc key to return to the Media Browser window.
Edit>Copy	Ctrl>C (Cmd>C)	Copies, also available by right clicking on thumbnails.
Edit>Select All	Ctrl>A (Cmd>A)	Selects all thumbnails displayed.
Edit>Deselect	Ctrl>Shift>A (Shift>Cmd >A)	Deselects selected thumbnails
Edit>Delete from Catalog	Delete key	Deletes images from current catalog. You also have the opportunity to delete them from your computer too. Also available by right clicking on thumbnail. You can also Delete in the Quick Edit panel in Full Screen View (F11) and Photo Compare (F12), tap the Esc key to return to the Media Browser window.

Command - Organizer	Shortcut PC (Mac)	Description
Edit>Rotate 90° Left	Ctrl (Cmd) Left Arrow ←	Rotates selected image(s) 90° Left. To rotate, tap the icon at the top of the Media Browser window. You can also rotate in the Quick Edit panel in Full Screen View (F11) and Photo Compare (F12); tap the Esc key to return to the Media Browser window.
Edit>Rotate 90° Right	Ctrl (Cmd) Right Arrow →	Rotates selected image(s) 90° Right To rotate, tap the icon at the top of the Media Browser window. You can also rotate in the Quick Edit panel in Full Screen View (F11) and Photo Compare (F12); tap the Esc key to return to the Media Browser window.
Edit>Auto Smart Fix	Ctrl>Alt>M Opt>Cmd>M)	Automatically corrects layer, you may or may not like it! Fixes applied will be the same as if you used Auto Smart Fix in Quick Edit or Auto Smart Fix from the Enhance Menu in Full Edit. You can apply Auto Smart Fix in the Quick Edit panel in Full Screen View (F11) and Photo Compare (F12); tap the Esc key to return to the Media Browser window. A duplicate file is created and saved in a Version Set when you do this in the Organizer.
None	Tap Auto Color button in Quick Edit Panel found in Full Screen View (F11) and Photo Compare (F12).	Improves color balance and contrast. Tap the Esc key to return to the Media Browser window when you're finished editing photo. A duplicate file is created and saved in a Version Set when you do this in the Organizer.
None	Tap Levels button in Quick Edit Panel found in Full Screen View (F11) and Photo Compare (F12).	Improves tonal range. Tap the Esc key to return to the Media Browser window when you're finished editing photo. A duplicate file is created and saved in a Version Set when you do this in the Organizer.
None	Tap Auto Contrast button in Quick Edit Panel found in Full Screen View (F11) and Photo Compare (F12).	Improves contrast without affecting colors. Tap the Esc key to return to the Media Browser window when you're finished editing photo. A duplicate file is created and saved in a Version Set when you do this in the Organizer.
None	Tap Auto Sharpen button in Quick Edit Panel found in Full Screen View (F11) and Photo Compare (F12).	Enhance Details. Tap the Esc key to return to the Media Browser window when you're finished editing photo. A duplicate file is created and saved in a Version Set when you do this in the Organizer.
Edit>Auto Red Eye Fix	Ctrl>R (Cmd>R)	Also available in the Editor. You can also fix red eye in the Quick Edit panel in Full Screen View (F11) and Photo Compare (F12); tap the Esc key to return to the Media Browser window. A duplicate file is created and saved in a Version Set when you make this change in the Organizer.
Edit>Edit with Photoshop Elements	Ctrl>I (Cmd>I)	Opens selected image(s) in Full Edit. You can also launch Photoshop Elements in the Quick Edit panel in Full Screen View (F11) and Photo Compare (F12); tap the Esc key to return to the Media Browser window

Command - Organizer	Shortcut PC (Mac)	Description
Edit>Edit with Premiere Elements	Ctrl>M (Ctrl>M)	Opens selected image(s) in Premiere Elements which is a video editing program. You can also launch Premiere Elements in the Quick Edit panel in Full Screen View (F11) and Photo Compare (F12); tap the Esc key to return to the Media Browser window. You must have this program installed to choose this option.
Edit>Edit with Photoshop	Ctrl>H	Opens selected image(s) in Photoshop. You must have this program installed to choose this option.
Edit>Adjust Date & Time	Ctrl>J (Cmd>J)	Opens Adjust Date &Time dialog box with choices to make for changing the date or time.
Edit>Add Caption	Ctrl>Shift>T (Shift>Cmd >T)	Opens Caption dialog box so you can type caption which is displayed under the image in full screen view or in the Properties panel.
Edit>Update Thumbnail	Ctrl>Shift>U (Shift>Cmd >U)	Updates changes made to selected files using another application if the changes were saved to the original file. You add the other application on the Editing Preferences dialog box. Also available by right clicking on the thumbnail and choosing this option.
Edit>Set as Desktop Wallpaper	Ctrl>Shift>W (Shift>Cmd >W)	Sets selected image as your desktop wallpaper. You will need to remove it through your operating system.
Edit>Ratings No Rating to 5 Star Rating	Click on stars under thumbnail (small view) bottom left (full screen view)	Add stars to rate your images. This is very helpful when you want to find your best photos. You can also add star ratings in the Quick Edit panel in Full Screen View (F11) and Photo Compare (F12); tap the Esc key to return to the Media Browser window.
Edit>Visibility>Mark as Hidden	Alt>F2	Hides selected images that you do not want to appear in the browser. Once hidden, a hidden file icon will appear on the thumbnail. If no images are selected this option will not appear. Also available by right clicking on the thumbnail and choosing this option. You can also choose to hide images in the Quick Edit panel in Full Screen View (F11) and Photo Compare (F12); tap the Esc key to return to the Media Browser window.
Edit>Visibility>Mark as Visible	None	This command will only appear if you have a hidden image selected. Choose this option to unhide the image. Also available by right clicking on the thumbnail and choosing this option.
Edit>Visibility>Hide Hidden Files	None	Choose this option to hide images that are marked as hidden files. Also available by right clicking on the thumbnail and choosing this option.
Edit>Visibility>Show All Files	None	Choose this option to show all images, whether they are marked as hidden or not. Also available by right clicking on the thumbnail and choosing this option.
Edit>Visibility>Show only Hidden Files	None	Choose this option to show only hidden images. Also available by right clicking on the thumbnail and choosing this option.
Edit>Place on Map	None	Places your selected image(s) on a map after you type in the address. You can also drag the photo to the map or, right click and choose Place on Map.

Command - Organizer	Shortcut PC (Mac)	Description
Edit>Remove from Map	None	Removes an image(s) you placed on the map. You can also right click on the thumbnail or on the map and choose Remove from Map.
Edit>Show on Map	None	Shows image(s) on map. You can also right click on the thumbnail and choose Show on Map.
Edit>Stack >Automatically Suggest Photo Stacks	Ctrl>Alt>K (Opt>Cmd>K)	Select a group of photos and Elements will suggest stacks for them so that they take up less space in the Browser. Also available by right clicking and choosing this option.
Edit>Stack >Stack Selected Photos	Ctrl>Alt>S (Opt>Cmd>S)	Select several photos and choose this command to stack photos. A stacked photos icon will be added to the top right corner of the top image, a black arrow will be added to the right side and the words "Photo Stack" will appear at the bottom of the thumbnail when the images are stacked. Also available by right clicking and choosing this option.
Edit>Stack>Unstack Photos	None	Unstacks a previously created photo stack. Also available by right clicking and choosing this option.
Edit>Stack>Expand Photos in Stack	Ctrl>Alt>R (Opt>Cmd>R)	Displays all images in a photo stack. Also available by right clicking and choosing this option.
Edit>Stack>Collapse Photos in Stack	Ctrl>Alt>Shift>R (Opt>Shift>Cmd>R)	Collapses images that were previously expanded back into a stack. Also available by right clicking and choosing this option.
Edit>Stack>Flatten Stack	None	Deletes all images except for the top image in the stack. You can also choose to delete those images from your computer's hard drive. Also available by right clicking and choosing this option.
Edit>Stack>Remove Photo from Stack	None	You must expand a photo stack and select an image for this command to be available. Choose this option and the image(s) will be deleted from the stack, but will remain in the Browser. Also available by right clicking and choosing this option.
Edit>Stack >Set as Top Photo	None	You must expand a photo stack and select an image (other than the current top image) for this command to be available. Choose this option and the image will be moved to the top of the stack. Also available by right clicking and choosing this option.
Edit>Version Set>Expand Items in Version Set	Ctrl>Alt>E (Opt>Cmd>E)	Displays all images that you have saved in a version. Also available by right clicking and choosing this option.
Edit>Version Set>Collapse Items in Version Set	Ctrl>Alt>Shift>E (Opt>Shift>Cmd>E)	Collapses all images that were previously expanded back into a set. Also available by right clicking and choosing this option.
Edit>Version Set>Flatten Version Set	None	Deletes all images, except for the top image in the set. You can also choose to delete those images from your computer's hard drive. Also available by right clicking and choosing this option.
Edit>Version Set>Convert Version Set to Individual Items	None	Select a version set; choose this command to remove all of the images from the set. Also available by right clicking and choosing this option.

Command - Organizer	Shortcut PC (Mac)	Description
Edit>Version Set>Revert to Original	None	Select a version set; choose this command to delete all images other than the original image. You can also choose to delete those images from your computer's hard drive. Also available by right clicking and choosing this option.
Edit>Version Set>Remove Item(s) from Version Set	None	You must expand a version set and select an image for this command to be available. Choose this option and the image(s) will be deleted from the set but will remain in the Browser. Also available by right clicking and choosing this option.
Edit>Version Set>Set As Top Item	None	You must expand a version set and select an image (other than the current top image) for this command to be available. Choose this option and the image will be moved to the top of the set. Also available by right clicking and choosing this option.
Edit>Video Scene>Expand Items in Scene Group	None	Expands Video Scene Group so you can view, tag, or delete an item. If this option is grayed out, you must first choose Edit>Auto Analyzer on the video file. Also available by right clicking on thumbnail or clicking the expand button.
Edit>Video Scene>Collapse Items in Scene Group		Collapses scene group. Also available by clicking on the Collapse button or right clicking.
Edit>Run Auto Analyzer	None	Adds smart tags that you don't really need. I turned mine off in the Preferences.
Edit>Color Settings	Ctrl>Alt>G (Opt>Cmd>G)	Allows you to choose to manage color in images, choose optimize for computer screens, or printing.
Edit>Contact Book	None	Opens Contact Book dialog box to allow you to add contacts.
Edit>Preferences>General (Photoshop Elements>Preferences > General)	General Preferences Ctrl>K (Cmd>K)	Allows you to change options for: Print size units of measure, Date Format, Date (Newest First Options), Closely Matching Sets, Resize Photos, System Font, Adjust Date, Fade Transitions
Edit>Preferences>Files (Photoshop Elements>Preferences>Files)	None	Allows you to change options for: Import EXIF Caption, Auto Search for Missing Files, Enable Multi Session Burning to CD/DVD, Rotate JPEG & TIFFs, Folders for Saved Files.
Edit>Preferences>Editing (Photoshop Elements>Preferences>)	None	Allows you to change options for: Supplementary Editing Application, Show Photoshop Elements Options, Show Premiere Elements Options.
Edit>Preferences>Camera or Card Reader (Photoshop Elements> Preferences> Camera or Card Reader)	None	Allows you to change options for: Saving Files, Auto Fix Red Eye, Auto Suggest Photo Stacks, Make Group Custom Name a Keyword Tag, and Download Options.
Edit>Preferences>Scanner (Photoshop Elements>Preferences>Scanner)	None	Allows you to specify Scanner, File Type and Quality, Auto Fix Red Eyes. Choose a destination file to save files in.
Edit>Preferences>Date View (Photoshop Elements>Preferences>Date View)	None	Allows you to Use Monday as first day of the week, choose holidays, and mark new events.
Edit>Preferences>Keyword Tags and Albums (Photoshop Elements>Preferences>Keyword Tags and Albums)	None	Allows you to set options to change sorting from either Manual to Alpha for Categories, Sub-Categories, Keyword Tags, Album Categories, and Albums. You are able to choose two different Keyword Tag Display Options.

Command – Organizer	Shortcut PC (Mac)	Description
Edit>Preferences>Sharing (Photoshop Elements>Preferences>Sharing)	None	Add your E-mail address and choose between E-mail Clients. Also includes option to write E-mail captions to catalog.
Edit>Preferences>Adobe Partner Services (Photoshop Elements>Preferences > Adobe Partner Services)	None	Choose to Check for Services including Service Updates, Adobe Promotions, Product Support Notification and Third Party Services.
Edit>Preferences>Media Analysis (Photoshop Elements>Preferences> Media Analysis)	None	Choose to run Analyze Photos for People Automatically and to Auto Analyze Media for Smart Tags Automatically and for 3 smart filters.
Edit>Preferences>Back up Synchronization	None	Allows you to share and back up your catalog through Photoshop.com. Mac: Photoshop Elements>Preferences> Back up Synchronization
Find	Alt>I	Opens Find drop down menu.
Find>Set Date Range	Ctrl>Alt>F (Opt>Cmd>F)	Enter a specific date range to search for an image.
Find>Clear Date Range	Ctrl>Shift>F (Shift>Cmd >F)	Clears the date range previously entered and displays all images.
Find>By Caption or Note	Ctrl>Shift>J (Shift>Cmd >J)	To search by a caption or note that you have added to an image, choose this command.
Find>By File Name	Ctrl>Shift>K (Shift>Cmd >K)	Choose this command to search by file name.
Find>All Version Sets	Ctrl>Alt>V (Opt>Cmd>V)	Choose this command to display all version sets.
Find>All Stacks	Ctrl>Alt>Shift >S (Opt>Shift>Cmd>S)	Choose this command to display all stacks.
Find>By History>Imported On	None	Displays dialog box to allow you to search by date imported.
Find>By History>Emailed to	None	Displays dialog box to allow you to search by person you emailed it to.
Find>By History>Printed on	None	Displays dialog box to allow you to search by date printed.
Find>By History>Exported on	None	Displays dialog box to allow you to search by the date you exported it on.
Find>By History>Ordered Online	None	Displays dialog box to allow you to search by date you ordered it online.
Find>By History>Shared Online	None	Displays dialog box to allow you to search by date you shared it online.
Find>By History>Used in Projects	None	Displays dialog box to allow you to search by project you used it in.
Find>By Media Type>Photos	Alt> 1 (Opt>1)	Searches all photo files.
Find>By Media Type>Video	Alt> 2 (Opt>2)	Searches all video files.
Find>By Media Type>Audio	Alt> 3 (Opt> 3)	Searches all audio files.
Find>By Media Type>Projects	Alt> 4 (Opt> 4)	Searches all projects files.
Find>By Media Type>PDFs	Alt>5 (Opt> 5)	Searches all PDF files.
Find>By Media Type>Items with Audio Captions	Alt> 6 (Opt>6)	Searches all files with audio captions.
Find>by Details (Metadata)	None	Searches for files by options that you specify including, tags, file name, rating, albums and more.
Find>Items with Unknown Date or Time	Ctrl>Shift>X (Shift>Cmd >X)	Searches for files with unknown date or time.
Find>By Visual Similarity with Selected Photo(s) and Video(s)	None	Select an image and choose this command to display images that are visually similar to the selected image. You can also do this by dragging the image to the Find bar.

Command - Organizer	Shortcut PC (Mac)	Description
Find>Untagged Items	Ctrl>Shift>Q (Shift>Cmd >Q)	To search for untagged files choose this command. This is a great way to find images you missed tagging, but it will only find files with no tags. If you didn't finish tagging files with all of the tags you wanted to add, it isn't able to read your mind, so you're out of luck.
Find>Unanalyzed Content	Ctrl>Shift>Y (Shift>Cmd >Y)	Finds images that have not been analyzed.
Find>Items Not In Any Album	None	Finds images that are not in any albums.
Find>Find People for Tagging	Ctrl>Shift>P (Shift>Cmd >P)	Finds what it thinks are people for tagging, but it will not find all images with people in them.
View	Alt>V	Opens View drop down menu.
View>Refresh	F5	Refreshes the thumbnails after they have been edited in another program.
View>Media Types>Photos	Ctrl>1 (Cmd>1)	To display photo files, check this option.
View>Media Types>Video	Ctrl>2 (Cmd>2)	To display video files, check this option.
View>Media Types>Audio	Ctrl>3 (Cmd>3)	To display audio files, check this option.
View>Media Types>Projects	Ctrl>4 (Cmd>4)	To display project files, check this option.
View>Media Types>PDF	Ctrl>5 (Cmd>5)	To display PDF files, check this option.
View>Hidden Files>Hide Hidden Files	None	Hides all files marked as hidden. To mark a file as hidden, choose Edit>Visibility>Mark as Hidden, or right click and choose the same option.
View>Hidden Files>Show all Files	None	Shows all files whether they are hidden or not. You can also choose Edit>Visibility> Show all Files, or right click and choose the same option.
View>Hidden Files>Show Only Hidden Files	None	Shows only files you have hidden. You can also choose Edit>Visibility> Show only Hidden Files, or right click and choose the same option.
View>Details	Ctrl>D (Cmd>D)	Displays the date the file was created under the thumbnail. I keep this option turned on.
View>Show File Names	None	Displays the file name under the thumbnail.
View>Show People Recognition	None	Displays "Who's This" box over some faces when this option is turned on to help you with tagging people.
View>Expand All Stacks	None	Displays all images in a photo stack. Also available by right clicking and choosing this option.
View>Collapse All Stacks	None	Collapses images that were previously expanded back into a stack. Also available by right clicking and choosing this option.
Window	Alt>W	Opens Window drop down menu.
Window>Hide Task Pane	None	Displays/hides Task Pane Panel (list of tags, etc.)
Window>Show Map	None	Displays/hides Map panel.
Window>Timeline	Ctrl>L (Cmd>L	Displays/hides Timeline Panel.
Window>Properties	Alt>Enter (Opt>Enter)	Displays/hides Properties Panel.
Help	Alt>H	Opens the Help drop down menu
Help>Elements Organizer Help	F1	Launches Adobe Help Website
Help>Key Concepts	None	Launches Adobe Help Website and displays a list of basic Photoshop Elements terms. Each page explains the basic terms and how to use different parts of Photoshop Elements.
Help>Support	None	Launches Adobe Help Website with links for help downloading, installing, and setting up. Also includes link for Getting Started and Tutorials, along with Editor and Organizer help.

Command - Organizer	Shortcut PC (Mac)	Description
Help>Video Tutorials	None	Launches Adobe Help Website with links for several video tutorials.
Help>Forum	None	Launches the Photoshop Elements Forum where you can post questions or help other users. If you are going to ask a question, it's always wise to search for your problem first, because it may have already been answered.
Help> Elements Organizer	None	Displays the version of Photoshop Elements you are using, along with the names of the team that developed the product.
Help>Legal Notices	None	Copyright information for Adobe and other companies involved with Photoshop Elements.
Help>System Info	None	Displays Photoshop Elements version number and information about your computer that you may need when talking with technical support.
Help>Updates	None	Launches Adobe Updates website.
Help>Elements Inspiration Browser	None	Sign in to see tutorials. You will have to upgrade your membership to a Plus membership for a fee to view all of the tutorials.
None	F11	Full Screen View. View, Edit, and Organize in Full Screen. Use the shortcut or press the icon at the top of the Media Browser window. Press Esc to return to the regular Organizer screen.
None	F12	Photo Compare. View Photos Side by side in full screen. Press Esc to return to Organizer.
None	Ctrl>= (equal) Cmd>=	Make Thumbnails larger
None	Ctrl>- (minus) Cmd>-	Make Thumbnails smaller
None	Double click on thumbnail	Toggles to largest Thumbnail view
None	Enter	Show full size Thumbnail of selected image.
None	Arrow keys	Move to another Thumbnail.
None	Click>Shift >Arrow keys	Select row of Thumbnails
None	Click>Ctrl (Cmd) key click	Select non continuous Thumbnails.
None	Click>Shift key click	Select continuous Thumbnails
None	Ctrl>0 (Cmd>0)	Fit in Window – Works only for Full Screen View (F11) and Photo Compare View (F12). Tap the Esc key to return to the Media Browser window.
None	Ctrl>Alt>0 (Cmd>Opt>0)	Actual Size – Works only for Full Screen View (F11) and Photo Compare View (F12). Tap the Esc key to return to the Media Browser window.
None	Ctrl>= (equal) Cmd>=	Zooms in.
None	Ctrl>-(minus) Cmd>-	Zooms out.
None	Home/ End	Selects first/last thumbnail, this will vary depending on if you are using Thumbnail View (Date Newest First or Oldest First), Folder View, etc.
None	Page Up/Page Down	Scrolls up or down but keeps selected thumbnails selected.
None	Esc	Exit Full Screen View (F11) and Photo Compare View (F12).
None	Enter/Esc	OK/Cancel

Index

*For updates to this book, or to sign up for our
free Photoshop Elements Tips Newsletter, go to
www.TheDigitalScrapbookTeacher.com*

About the Book DVD

Included in the Photo Editing Examples folder on the DVD are the photos that were used in the *Cool Stuff with Photos* chapter so that you can practice with them. **Please note that the photo file name is the book page number where it was first used in a tutorial.**

This DVD includes more than 4.3GB of digital scrapbooking supplies which includes more than 3200 elements that can be used for all sorts of projects. To help you quickly find one when you need it, I recommend using the Photoshop Elements Organizer to tag your digital supplies. Instructions for tagging images can be found in the Organizing Chapter.

Tagging more than 3200 elements is going to take you quite a bit of time. If you don't want to spend the time tagging the items yourself, and would rather it was all done for you, please check out our Organizer Back-Up Catalog available at *www.TheDigitalScrapbookTeacher.com*. Installing our Organizer Back-Up Catalog applies the tags to each item for you automatically, and will save you more than 15 hours of your valuable time.

Please read, and respect each designer's terms of use (TOU). Help stop Digital Piracy!
For more information about Copyright and Digital Piracy please see page 24.

Name	Website or Blog
Ali Edwards	www.AliEdwards.com
Amanda Rockwell*	www.AmandaRockwell.com
Amy Teets*	www.AmyTeetsDesigns.blogspot.com
Anna Aspnes	www.AnnaAspnes.typepad.com
Angel Hartline Designs*	www.AngelHartline.com
Atomic Cupcake	www.AtomicCupcake.com
Danielle Young Designs*	www.DanielleYoungDesigns.com
DeDe Smith	www.DesignzbyDeDe.blogspot.com
Design by Anita-Anita Richards	www.AnitaRichards.typepad.com
The Digital Scrapbook Teacher*	www.TheDigitalScrapbookTeacher.com
Dusty Bear Designs*	www.DustyBearDesigns.blogspot.com
Farrah's Creations*	www.FarrahsCreations.blogspot.com
Graffi's Graficalicus Workshop*	www.Graficalicus.com
K Designs New name: MandogScraps	www.KDesignsCreations.blogspot.com www.ManDogScraps.blogspot.com
Kelly Jo's Scraps*	www.K-JosScraps.blogspot.com
Linda Walton	www.BonScrapatitDesigns.blogspot.com
Meredith Cardall*	www.MeredithCardall.com
Miss Mint - Peppermint Creative*	www.PeppermintCreative.com
Nancie Rowe Janitz*	www.NancieRoweJanitz.com
Panos Efstathiadis	www.PanosFX.com
ProjectB – designs by Bianca*	www.ProjectBDesigns.com
Royanna Fritschmann *	www.DivineDigital.com
SuzyQ Scraps - Suzy Iverson*	www.SuzyQScraps.com/blog
Vera Lim*	www.VeraLimDesigns.com

*Designers marked with an asterisk have contributed coupons that can be found in the Coupon folder on the DVD. Coupons also included for: Persnickety Prints & Scrapbook Dimensions Magazine

Photographer contact information:
Ray Lopez - *www.RaysPhotography.net*
Madeline Arenas Cubrix Photography-please contact *www.TheDigitalScrapbookTeacher.com*
Jill Phillips- please contact *www.TheDigitalScrapbookTeacher.com*
Tutus provided by *www.KirrasBoutique.com*